MEMORIALS OF
ST. PAUL'S CATHEDRAL

BROOKLYN
PUBLIC LIBRARY

BROOKLYN
PUBLIC LIBRARY

BROOKLYN
PUBLIC LIBRARY

MEMORIALS OF ST. PAUL'S CATHEDRAL

BY

WILLIAM MACDONALD SINCLAIR, D.D.

ARCHDEACON OF LONDON, CANON OF ST. PAUL'S
AND HON. CHAPLAIN TO THE KING

WITH ILLUSTRATIONS BY LOUIS WEIRTER, R.B.A.

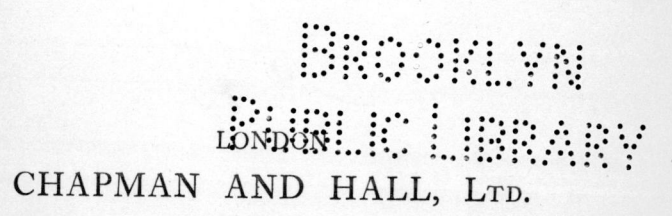

LONDON
CHAPMAN AND HALL, LTD.
1909

283
S616

RICHARD CLAY & SONS, LIMITED,
BREAD STREET HILL, E.C., AND
BUNGAY, SUFFOLK

TO

THE VERY REVEREND ROBERT GREGORY, D.D.

THE VETERAN DEAN OF ST. PAUL'S

WHOSE STRENUOUS WORK AND FAITHFUL COURAGE

DURING OVER FORTY YEARS

HAVE MAINLY CONTRIBUTED TO THE

REVIVED LIFE OF THE GREAT CATHEDRAL

THESE MEMORIALS

ARE DEDICATED WITH RESPECT AND GRATITUDE

ERRATA

P. 76, l. 8. Some say John of Gaunt's tomb, but it was really Sir John de Beauchamp's that was taken for Duke Humphrey's.

P. 91, l. 20. *For* "the King-maker" *read* "in the time of Edward II." (The King-maker was Richard Neville, Earl of Warwick and Salisbury, 1428-71.)

P. 114, l. 20. *After* "Durham" *read* "*John Stokesley*, Ambassador to Rome about the Divorce."

P. 141, l. 29. *For* "Jean Bocher" *read* "Joan Bocher."

P. 183. Note to third line from top, attached to "after."—"On October 21, 1610, an interesting scene took place in the Chapel of London House; three Scotsmen, in Presbyterian Orders, were consecrated Bishops by the Bishop of London (Abbot) and the Bishops of Ely, Rochester and Worcester: Spotswood to the Archbishopric of Glasgow, Lamb to Brechin, and Hamilton to Galloway.

P. 233, l. 18. *For* "Abber" *read* "Cibber."

P. 362, 1899, May 10. *Delete* "Centenary."

GROUND PLAN OF ST. PAUL'S COMPARED WITH ST. PETER'S, ROME (SHADED)

PREFACE

WHEN I was asked to write a book about St. Paul's which might bring its history and life before the people, I naturally hesitated; partly from the greatness of the subject and the importance of the enterprise, and partly because the ground had been so thoroughly traversed by Dean Milman in his *Annals*. At St. Paul's, whenever we think of its long and wonderful career, our minds naturally turn to the luminous writings of our own historian. But Milman's work was published in 1868, and the whole development of the modern popular life of St. Paul's has been since that date. The book is also out of print, and the copyright has expired. Feeling that it would be impossible to give the story of the earlier centuries of St. Paul's without taking advantage of the abundant stores set out in stately style and with masterly treatment by the historian of *Latin Christianity* and of *the Jews*, I wrote to Mr. John Murray, and asked his permission to quote from the *Annals*, which he very kindly granted. Those who are familiar with that admirable work will see that, to compare small things with great, Milman has been to me as Virgil to Dante. It would be absurd to suppose that my performance could by any be regarded as a rival to the accomplished historian's; so I have nothing to do but to express sincerely and gratefully my unbounded obligations. I am also indebted to Longman's *Three Cathedrals dedicated to St. Paul;* to my late friend Dr. Sparrow Simpson's three very interesting antiquarian volumes on St. Paul's; to Lena Milman's *Sir Christopher Wren;* to my friend Mr. John S. Bumpus's exhaustive work, *Organists and Composers of St. Paul's Cathedral;* to Mr. John B. Marsh's *St. Paul's Cross;* to my friend the Rev. Lewis Gilbertson's very clear and concise *Official Guide;* and to the *Index and Epitome* volume of the *Dictionary of National Biography.* I am fortunate also in having had placed in my hands the extremely valuable and interesting diaries of the late Mr. Robert Green, Dean's Verger, who served St. Paul's with the utmost loyalty and great ability for forty-eight years (1852–1900), and who all that time was a keen and perspicuous observer. He had a delightful character, humorous and friendly, but keen and autocratic; he used to speak of "my choir," "my procession," "my service," and was very concise in his orders: "Fetch 'em out" was quite a usual direction with regard to even the most august procession. He noted with great assiduity the numerous visits of members of our own Royal Family, and of foreign potentates; these are so frequent that in making my selection from his notes I have, after transcribing those of a few years, left them out. I think that the records of the last fifty years will show how strongly, and with what increasing power, the Cathedral of the capital of the empire has attracted to itself the affections of the people; but at the same time probably few who are not familiar with the facts will be prepared to realize how large a part it has played in the national life of the past. I have been favoured in having the co-operation of a very enthusiastic, skilful and sympathetic artist in Mr. Weirter, a genuine admirer of the incomparable genius of Wren. Conscious of the imperfections of my own contribution to the work, and wishing that I were more worthy of so noble and sacred an enterprise, I yet hope that through these pages St. Paul's and its eventful past and present may become better known to the English-speaking race.

CONTENTS

CHAPTER I

ANCIENT LONDON 1–11

PAGE

Uncertainty of origin—Tacitus—British names—Thames restrained by Roman banks—Image of Diana—Roman road (Watling Street)—Suetonius and Boadicea—Allectus defeated by Asclepiodotus—Roman wall—A.D. 369-412, London the capital—Introduction of Christianity in second century, or earlier—Fable of King Lucius—Evidence of Tertullian and others to British Church—Restitutus—Destruction of records by Anglo-Saxons—Pope Gregory and Augustine — Mellitus, Ethelbert, Tillingham — Sebert—Failure of Mellitus prevents London from being an Archbishopric—Sigebert, St. Aidan, St. Finan and Cedd, first Anglo-Saxon Bishop of London—Jaruman—St. Erkonwald, St. Dunstan, St. Alphege.

CHAPTER II

THE DAYS OF THE NORMANS 12–25

Edward the Confessor and Norman appointments—Bishop William of London—Privileges granted by the Conqueror: his gift of the castle of Bishop's Stortford—Lanfranc's Council in St. Paul's—Precedence: canons—Bishop Hugh de Orivalle: a leper — Bishop Maurice: the Norman Cathedral—Grant by the Conqueror of the Palatine Tower for the building—Bishop Maurice crowns Henry I.—Bishop Richard de Belmeis: his enthusiasm for the Cathedral: his attempt to recover the lost dignity of an Archbishopric to London: founds the monastery of St. Osyth—Bishop Gilbert the Universal: accused of avarice: defended by St. Bernard of Clairvaux—The days of Matilda and Stephen. Dispute as to succession: Abbot Anselm of St. Edmunds and Robert de Sigillo of Reading: diocese placed by Pope in charge of Henry of Blois, Bishop of Winchester—Robert de Sigillo appointed—Great Fire of 1136—Geoffrey de

Mandeville, Earl of Essex, holding the Tower of London for Stephen, carries off Bishop Robert from Fulham—Poisoned Bishop Robert de Belmeis—Bishop Gilbert Foliot, the opponent of Becket: Pope Alexander sanctions his translation from Hereford: entrusted by the Pope with the reconciliation of Henry II. and Becket—Becket's deputy excommunicates Foliot in St. Paul's—Foliot appeals to the Pope, and revives the archiepiscopal claims of London—Foliot at length submits—Receives absolution after the assassination of Becket—Foliot on the reforming opinions of the weavers of Worcester.

CHAPTER III

THE PAPAL LEGATES 26-37

Bishop Richard de Ely, or Fitz Neal, author of *Dialogus de Scaccario* and *Tricolumnus*—Dean Radulph de Diceto, author of *Imagines Historiæ* and *Abbreviatio Chronicorum*—Dean Radulph's deplorable account of the clergy—Arraignment of Bishop William de Longchamp of Ely, Chancellor, in St. Paul's, during the absence of Richard I.—The popular movement of William Fitz Osbert—Dean Radulph builds the Deanery—Peter of Blois Archdeacon of London—Bishop William de Santa Maria: reads the Pope's interdict in St. Paul's—Persecution of the clergy by King John—Archbishop Langton and Bishop de Santa Maria procure at Rome sentence of deposition against King John—Submission of the King—Prelude at St. Paul's to Runnymede—The Legate, Cardinal Nicolas, receives the kingdom as a fief of the Papacy—Louis the Dauphin received at St. Paul's—Henry III.: the great charter published at St. Paul's in a new form—Resignation of Bishop de Santa Maria by brief of Pope Honorius III.—Bishop Eustace de Fauconberge: the Pope permits the Province to grant the King a subsidy in a Council at St. Paul's—Bishop Roger Niger—The Usurers—The Legate, Cardinal Otho the White, asserts his authority over the whole clergy at a Council in St. Paul's—Honours to the Legate—His sermon—The new canons—Protests by Bishop Walter de Cantilupe of Worcester, the Earl of Lincoln and others—Misadventure of the Legate at Oxford—Archbishop Rich retires abroad—Influence of Bishop Roger: he promotes the building of the Cathedral by the sale of Indulgences.

CONTENTS

CHAPTER IV

THE PAPAL LEGATES (*continued*) 38–49

Popular canonization of Bishop Roger—Disputed succession: Fulk Basset appointed Bishop: he tries to enforce Pope Innocent IV.'s demand for one-third of ecclesiastical income: a Council at St. Paul's remonstrates—The Queen's uncle, Boniface of Savoy, made Archbishop of Canterbury: obtains from Pope grant of first-fruits from whole Province: his rapacity opposed by Bishop Fulk Basset, who, with the Dean and Chapter, is excommunicated by the Primate—The Legate, Rustand, demands a tenth on England, Scotland and Ireland—Refusal of Bishop Fulk and Bishop Walter de Cantilupe—Fulk espouses the cause of the Barons, and signs the Provisions of Oxford—Bishop Henry de Wingham: during vacancy on his death, a Papal Bull is read at Paul's Cross absolving Henry III. from the Provisions of Oxford—Bishop Henry de Sandwich: joins Simon de Montfort—The Legate, Ugo Falcodi, forbidden to cross the Channel: becomes Pope Clement IV., and excommunicates Bishop Henry with three other prelates—Henry, after six years of exile, pardoned by Pope Gregory V.—The Legate, Cardinal Ottobuoni, promulgates new Constitutions founded on those of Cardinal Otho: the ecclesiastical law of England to the Reformation—Bishop John de Chishull—Bishop Richard de Gravesend: protests, with Archbishop Winchelsey, against the exactions of Edward I., on the authority of the Lateran Council and a Bull of Pope Boniface VIII.—Catalogue of Bishop Richard's property—Bishops Ralph de Baldock, Gilbert de Segrave, Richard de Newport, Stephen de Gravesend—Murder of Bishop Walter de Stapleton of Exeter, of Edward II.'s party, by partisans of Queen Isabella—Bishop Stephen and others convicted of high treason—Bishop Simon of Sudbury: an enemy to superstition: beheaded, when Primate, in Wat Tyler's rebellion.

CHAPTER V

THE COMPLETION OF OLD ST. PAUL'S 50–57

Nearly two hundred years from Bishop Maurice's foundation to completion under Edward I.—Choir lengthened about 1255—Spire repaired about 1315: height from 460 to 500 feet—Subscriptions gathered throughout England, Scotland and Ireland, chiefly by Indulgences—The wall—The

Bishop's Palace—The Chapter House—The Burial (or Charnel) Chapel—Folk-motes at the east and parade of armed bands at the west—Pardon Churchyard—Sherrington Chapel—Chapel of the Holy Ghost—Jesus Chapel—Church of St. Faith—The Belfry of Jesus Chapel—Church of St. Gregory—Architectural description—Ferrey's measurements.

CHAPTER VI

THE DAYS OF WYCLIFFE 58–68

Bishop Courtenay: his protest against Edward III.'s exactions: Edward III. makes him withdraw Pope Gregory XI.'s edict against the Florentine bankers—Milman's description of Wycliffe appearing before Courtenay in St. Paul's—Wat Tyler's rebellion—Bishop Robert de Braybrooke appointed by Pope Urban VI.—Richard II. at St. Paul's—The Bishop makes peace between King and citizens—Action against the Lollards—Henry of Bolingbroke at St. Paul's—Richard II.'s lying-in-state—Reforms of De Braybrooke—The Residentiaryship—Merchandise and games in the Cathedral—Honours to the Bishop—Bishop de Walden—Archbishop Arundel's Convocations—The writ *De hæretico comburendo*—Bishop Nicholas Bubwith—Bishop Robert Clifford: present at Council of Constance—*Te Deum* for Agincourt—Trials for heresy—Bishop John Kemp appointed by Pope Martin V.—Bishop William Gray appointed by the Pope—Bishop Robert FitzHugh—Bishop Robert Gilbert.

CHAPTER VII

BISHOP PECOCK AT ST. PAUL'S 69–74

Bishop Pecock preaches at Paul's Cross in defence of the Bishops against the Lollards—The episcopate unpopular through grave scandals: censured by Bishop Hallam and Thomas Gascoigne—Pecock's *Repressor of Overmuch Blaming of the Clergy*: his *Treatise on Faith* (1456) for converting the Lollards: he was now too liberal: his work severely attacked by a Council at Westminster: he is forced to recant at Paul's Cross: cajoled into resigning his Bishopric: imprisoned for life in Thorney Abbey: "by far the most eminent and learned Bishop in England of that day."

CONTENTS

CHAPTER VIII

THE WARS OF THE ROSES 75–82

Bishop Thomas Kempe: appointed through provisor of Pope Nicholas V.—Penance of Roger Bolingbroke, and of Eleanor Cobham—Oath of fealty by Richard Duke of York at St. Paul's, 1452—Reconciliation between Henry VI. and Duke of York at St. Paul's, 1458—Duke of York's succession ratified by Henry VI. in St. Paul's, 1460—Homage to Edward IV. in St. Paul's, 1461—Bodies of Salisbury and Warwick in St. Paul's, 1471—Lying-in-state of Henry VI.—Prayers of Richard, Duke of Gloucester, at St. Paul's—The infamous sermon of Dr. Shaw at Paul's Cross on the succession—Events of Richard III.'s reign—Bishop Kempe rebuilds Paul's Cross—Archbishop Morton's Convocation.

CHAPTER IX

THE DAWN OF THE REFORMATION 83–89

Bishop FitzJames—Dean Colet: his lectures at Oxford: his views on Genesis—Friendship with Erasmus, Charnock, Grocyn, Linacre and Thomas More—Dean of St. Paul's: his sermon before Convocation—St. Paul's School—King Henry VIII. and Colet—Colet's statutes: his early death.

CHAPTER X

THE INTERIOR OF OLD ST. PAUL'S 90–99

Dr. Sparrow Simpson's proposed walk in 1510—Court of Convocation—Font—Chantry of Bishop Kempe—Opening in the roof for the Whit-Sunday pigeon, and the swinging censer—The Twelve Scribes—Monument of Sir John de Beauchamp: mistaken for that of Humphrey, Duke of Gloucester—Cloisters—Chapter House—Image of the Virgin—Chapel of St. Paul—Chapels of St. Catherine and the Holy Trinity—Altar of the Apostles—Chapel of St. John the Evangelist—The great North Rood—Chapels of James, St. Thomas, the Holy Ghost, St. John Baptist and St. Margaret—Brasses in Choir: Bishop FitzHugh, Dean Evere, Canon Newcourt, Archdeacon Lichfield—Image of St. Wilgefort—Monuments of Bishops de Fauconberge and De Wingham—St. Dunstan's Chapel—Tomb of Henry de Lacy, Earl of Lincoln—Tombs of King Sebba and

King Ethelred — Tombs of Bishops de Chishull and Roger — Tombs of Burley, counsellor of Richard II., John of Gaunt, Blanche, Duchess of Lancaster, and Constance of Castile ; and Chief Justice de Hengham — Chapel of St. George — Choir — High Altar, dedicated to St. Paul — Altars of St. Ethelbert and St. Mellitus — The great Rose Window — Shrine of St. Erkonwald — Guild of the Minstrels — Tomb of Richard de Braybrooke — The Crypt, divided into Church of St. Faith and Jesus chapel — Chapels of St. John Baptist, St. Anne, St. Sebastian and St. Radegund — Picture of Christ — Tomb of Margaret, Countess of Shrewsbury — Guilds of Jesus, St. Catherine, the Annunciation and All Saints — Tombs of Dean Donne, Dean Colet, William Hewit, Lord Mayor Sir William Cokayne, Sir Nicholas Bacon, Bishop King, Lord Chancellor Sir Christopher Hatton, Sir Philip Sidney, Sir Francis Walsingham, William Earl of Pembroke, Sir John Mason, William Aubrey, Sir John Wolly, Sir Thomas Heneage, Dean Nowell, Dr. Thomas Linacre and Sir Anthony Vandyke.

CHAPTER XI

SOURCES OF REVENUE BEFORE THE REFORMATION . 100–106

Estates and manors — Royal and public funerals — Masses for the dead — Obits — A multitude of chantries — The Mass Priests — Complaints of the Corporation — Oblations — Relics — Indulgences.

CHAPTER XII

PERSONAL STAFF OF THE CATHEDRAL IN THE MIDDLE AGES 107–113

Cathedrals of the Old Foundation and of the New — The Bishop — The Archdeacon in days before the Conquest — The Dean after the Conquest — The Archdeacons — The Treasurer and Sacrist — The Precentor and Master of the Singing School — The Chancellor — The thirty Canons or Prebendaries — Rise of Residentiaries — Duties of the Canons and their Vicars — The Common Hall — The twelve Minor Canons The Cardinals — The Chantry Priests — The Sub-dean — The Brewer — The Baker.

CHAPTER XIII

HENRY VIII. AND THE APPROACH OF THE REFORMATION 114–136

Growing influence of sermons at Paul's Cross — Bishops Fitz-James, Tunstall, Stokesley, Bonner, Ridley, Grindal —

CONTENTS

Marriage of Catherine of Aragon and Prince Arthur—Marriage of Princess Margaret and James IV. of Scotland—Death of Henry VII.—The Pope's sword and cap for Henry VIII.—Thanksgiving of Henry VIII. and Wolsey for the Peace of 1515—Proclamation of the Emperor Charles V.—Promulgation of the Pope's sentence against Martin Luther in the Cathedral—Visit of Charles V.—Wolsey removes Convocation to Westminster—Rejoicings for the Battle of Pavia—Thanksgiving for the sack of Rome—Dean Pace: Shakespeare on Pace: his mental disturbance and death—The solemn destruction of Tyndale's Bible—Riotous meeting against Bishop Stokesley at the Chapter House—Procession of Anne Boleyn—Exposure of the Nun of Kent—Official sermons at Paul's Cross against Papal supremacy—Gardiner, Stokesley and Bonner support the Royal supremacy—Burnings—James Bainham—Latimer's Convocation sermon—Exposure of the Rood of Boxley—The debate in Parliament on the Sacraments under Thomas Crumwell—Death of Stokesley—Bishop Bonner—Contest between Barnes and Bishop Gardiner—Cranmer and Bonner and the *First Book of Homilies*—Thanksgiving for the Peace of 1546—Burning of Anne Askew and others.

CHAPTER XIV

EDWARD VI. AND THE REFORMATION 137-145

English service in the Chapel Royal—Reformation sermons at Paul's Cross—Old and new ideas—Procession of Edward VI. to Westminster—Order to remove images—English Litany—Bonner and Gardiner—Obits and chantries abolished—Four Commissions appointed to remove the treasures of the unreformed faith—Frontals from St. Paul's at Valencia—Petition of the Dean and Chapter to retain necessary articles—Ridley rebukes wranglers about the Lord's Supper—Easter: English Communion Office begun—Bishop Ferrar's sermon at Paul's Cross—Violence of Protector Somerset in removing buildings—Discontinuance of the Skinners' Whitsuntide Office, *Corpus Christi*, the Reservation of the Eucharist, the Mass of the Apostles and of the Virgin—Burning of Joan Bocher, Anabaptist—The revolt of Devonshire, Cornwall and Norfolk—Imprisonment of Bonner after his sermon on the Corporal Presence—Bishop Ridley—High Altar replaced by Holy Table—

General demolition of altars and chapels in St. Paul's—The Prayer Book of 1552 inaugurated by Bishop Ridley—Bridewell and Christ's Hospital owed to Bishop Ridley.

CHAPTER XV

REACTION: QUEEN MARY 146-155

Upheaval of the Reformation arrangements—Bonner, the Mass and Latin service restored—Ridley, after vainly supporting Lady Jane, submits to Mary at Cambridge, and is sent to the Tower—Thanksgiving for the proclamation of Mary—Mary's procession to Westminster—Tumult at Dr. Bourne's Romish sermon at Paul's Cross—Rapid changes: important sermons: imprisonment of Reformers—Processions to St. Paul's—Convocation of 1553: denunciation of Catechism and Book of Common Prayer: debate on Real Presence—Re-erection of the Great Rood—Thanksgiving for suppression of Wyatt's rebellion—Gardiner preaches for King Philip at Paul's Cross—Cardinal Pole received at St. Paul's—Ceremonial anticipations of Mary's maternity—Multiplied burnings: Bishop Ridley and Canon Rogers—Bonner's inquisitions—Ceremonials, processions, interspersed with burnings—Procession of the Fat Buck—Procession for Philip's victory at St. Quentin—Share of Pole in the burnings—Mary's last order—Death of Mary and Pole.

CHAPTER XVI

ST. PAUL'S, QUEEN ELIZABETH AND THE REVIVED REFORMATION 156-177

Silence prudently enjoined on Paul's Cross—Sermons resumed after five months—Moderate policy recommended by Elizabeth's Council—London House assigned to the French Ambassadors for the Coronation—The Apostles' Mass discontinued, and soon after the Mass generally—Sermons by Grindal, Sandys, Jewel—Election of five Bishops (Parker, Grindal and others)—Queen's Commissioners hold Visitation of St. Paul's—Rood and images disappear: Holy Table restored: amices and copes forbidden—Obsequies of Henry II. of France—The new service restored—Bishop Jewel's challenge at Paul's Cross—Consecration of Archbishop Parker—Bonner returned to prison for safety: his comforts—The great debate on religion in Westminster Abbey—Bishop Grindal—Difficulties of Elizabeth's Bishops—Questions of Church lands : the Paddington estate given to the See of London— Alexander Nowell dean—The Great Fire of 1561 : spire and roofs destroyed—Sermon on the fire by Bishop Pilkington of Durham—Contributions for repairs—The roofs finished in 1566—Procession of Lord Mayor and Guilds—Remonstrances against the profanation of St. Paul's : those of medieval Bishops renewed by Philip and Mary, Bishop Pilkington and Queen Elizabeth— Illustrations from Shakespeare, Dekker's *Gull's Handbook*, Ben Jonson and Bishop Earle's *Microcosmography*— Elizabeth's first reformed Convocation : Dean Nowell prolocutor : innovation of adjourning to Westminster continued—Grindal succeeded by Sandys—Pius V.'s Bull of excommunication and deposition against Elizabeth nailed to the gate of London House—Rise of Puritanism—Puritan preachers at St. Paul's : Crick, Wake, Dering—Bishop Aylmer : parsimony—Bishop Fletcher : errors of taste and judgment—Bishop Bancroft—Dean Nowell's encounters with Elizabeth—Thanksgiving for the defeat of the Armada.

CHAPTER XVII

JAMES I. 178–186

Bishop Bancroft at the Hampton Court Conference—Four Gunpowder Plot conspirators hanged before West Front of St. Paul's—Bishop Vaughan—Bishop Ravis—Questions about the repairs of the Cathedral—Perseverance of Henry Farley at length persuades James I. to come in state to St. Paul's to promote restoration—Royal Commission appointed—Inigo Jones—Hostility of some of the Commissioners to Bishop and clergy : interposition of Southampton and other zealous Churchmen—Subscriptions and estimate—Bishop Abbot—Bishop King—The last burning : Bartholomew Leggatt for Arianism—Bishop Montaigne— Deans Overall, Carey, Donne—Donne's sermons.

CHAPTER XVIII

CHARLES I. 187–193

Bishop Laud—Activity in restoration : the Court of High Commission—Clearing away of intruding houses and the Church of St. Gregory—Horace Walpole's criticism of Inigo Jones's work at St. Paul's—Munificence of Sir Paul

b

CONTENTS

Pindar—Accounts of receipts in Dugdale and Stow—Dwindling of annual contributions through the Civil War—Paul's Cross destroyed by Parliament in 1642—The property and revenues of the Chapter seized the same year—Bishop Juxon: appointed Lord High Treasurer—Execution of Laud—Juxon at Fulham—Vow of Charles I.

CHAPTER XIX

St. Paul's under the Commonwealth 194–200

Seizure of the remainder of the repair fund (£17,000)—Scaffolding of the tower granted for pay of a regiment: fall of part of south transept—Seizure of all that could be found in St. Paul's: copes, silver vessels, etc.—Appointment of Dr. Cornelius Burgess as Lecturer, with £400 a year: accounts of him by Neal and Wood: his lead of the militiamen and apprentices: his sermons: his unhappy end—Bishop Juxon removed from Fulham in 1647—Fulham temporarily the property of Richard Harvey, decayed silk-mercer—Degradation of the Cathedral: Nave made a cavalry barrack and stable—Details of the end of Paul's Cross.

CHAPTER XX

The Restoration of Monarchy 201–208

Restoration of Bishop Juxon—Bishop Sheldon: the Bartholomew Act, the Act of Uniformity: Puritanism made a perpetual schism—Bishop Henchman—Dean Barwick: his strange adventures in support of monarchy: revives the choir at St. Paul's—Commission of Charles II. to consider what could be done for the Cathedral—The Subscription-book—John Evelyn—Wren a Commissioner: his report on the fabric: proposal for a dome in place of the tower, in the centre of the old Latin cross: Choir, Nave and Transepts.

CHAPTER XXI

The Great Fire of 1666 209–219

Plans and estimates ordered for Monday, August 27, 1666: the Great Fire breaks out on Sunday, September 2—Account by Pepys—Origin: the King's bakehouse in Pudding Lane—Rapid spread westwards—Helplessness of the Lord Mayor—Confusion—The King approaches by water: lands

at Bankside, Southwark, to view—Account by Evelyn—
Terrific spectacle—Thames covered with barges and boats
laden with goods—Flight to the fields—10,000 houses in
one flame—Burning of St. Paul's—Measures for extinction
—Ruins of St. Paul's: destruction of the stored books in
St. Faith's—Account by Dr. Taswell—Expedition of Bishop
Dolben and the Westminster boys—Melting of the bells—
Reflection in sky seen at Oxford—Excitement of the
people: fury against French and Dutch—Dean Sancroft
—Wren appointed surveyor-general and principal architect
for rebuilding the whole City: fits up part of ruined
Cathedral for worship—Order of the King (January 15, 1667)
for interim repairs, and for walling in the churchyard against
encroachments — Sub-committee for repairs — Striking
sermon of Sancroft, in the temporary structure at the west
end among the ruins, before the King.

CHAPTER XXII

BEGINNING OF THE NEW CATHEDRAL: WREN'S PLANS   220–236

Wren's opposition to patching up—Sancroft's attempts—July
1668, King's warrant for clearing away the old Choir and
Tower—Casing of old piers found useless—1670, total
clearance ordered: lasted till 1674—Wren's favourite
design of a Greek cross, with central dome and portico—
Clerical objections—The Nightmare design: King approves,
"with liberty to make variations"—Wren's unlimited use
of this permission — 1673, Letters-patent for rebuilding
issued to Commission of magnates—The subscriptions—
The accounts—1874, preparations for new foundations:
last portion, west end, not pulled down till 1686—Serviceable remains of old stone sold for rebuilding churches:
ragstone for repaving the streets—Destruction of the tower
by gunpowder—The battering-ram—Examination of the
soil—Difficulty at the north-east corner—Dangers to the
Cathedral from modern burrowings in the soil: deep
sewer averted by Dean Milman and Mr. Cockerell: tube-
railway averted: gigantic sewer recently averted—Wren's
great scheme for the re-arrangement of the City—June 21,
1675, first stone laid—"Resurgam"—Progress: 1678, 1683,
1684, 1694—1685, new Commission of James II.—James
II.'s aims—Wren and the Freemasons—Choir opened for
Thanksgiving for Peace of Ryswick, December 2, 1697.—
Morning Chapel opened February 1, 1698-9—1708, cupola

b 2

covered with lead instead of copper—1710, top stone of lantern laid—The Portland quarries—Edward Strong and Taynton.

CHAPTER XXIII

THE NEW CATHEDRAL 237–258

Dimensions—Comparative areas of seventeen cathedrals—Other comparisons—Guilt's architectural description of St. Paul's: the Latin cross, western chapels, vestries and chambers round the Dome; the Apse; the three arches, attic and domes of the Nave; the same in the Choir, the supports of the Dome, the Clerestory, the Side Aisles, the Vestibule, the Central Area, the eight arches of the Dome, the eight piers above the cornice of the Dome, the inward inclination, the plinth of the inner dome, the two orders of the exterior (Corinthian and composite), the upper of these a screen to hide the flying buttresses; the two western porticoes, the western towers, the cupola: its attic, its vast composite peristyle with balustrade subtended by large plain circular pedestal, supported by the piers and arches of the central space—Wren opposed to an organ-screen: his contest with Father Smith—Grinling Gibbons—Evelyn's account of him—Tijou—Proposed baldacchino—Geometrical Staircase—Whispering Gallery—The flattened arches and curtain walls of the four great supporting spaces of the Dome—Sir James Thornhill—Projected mosaics.

CHAPTER XXIV

THE TREATMENT OF WREN 259–264

Opposition and injustice—A Rump Committee: (1) The organ-screen; (2) Thornhill's paintings; (3) The iron railings; (4) Half the meagre salary to be withheld, in order to hurry Wren—Appeal to House of Commons: (5) Virulent pamphlet; (6) George I.'s Commission and the Balustrade; (7) Dismissal of Wren—Benson, his successor—Wren retires to house at Hampton Court—Steele's sketch of Wren.

CHAPTER XXV

SIR CHRISTOPHER WREN 265–272

Birth and parentage—Westminster School—Sir Charles Scarborough—Wadham College—Fellow of All Souls—Visit

CONTENTS

from Evelyn—Gresham Professor of Astronomy at 24—Savilian Professor of Astronomy at 28—Visits Charles II.—Foundation of Royal Society—Isaac Barrow's tribute—Assistant Surveyor-General—Plans the Sheldonian—Surveyor of St. Paul's—1665 : visits Paris—Emmanuel, Cambridge; Trinity, Oxford; Temple Bar; the Monument; Library and Cloister at Trinity, Cambridge—Marriage—Greenwich Observatory, Kilmainham Hospital, Chelsea Hospital; Winchester Palace—Domestic architecture—Public halls—His fifty-five churches—Hampton Court Palace and Greenwich Hospital—His annual visits to the completed St. Paul's—Peaceful death—Burial in St. Paul's—Epitaph.

CHAPTER XXVI

IN THE DAYS OF WILLIAM III., MARY AND ANNE . 273-281

Bishop Compton: accompanies the flight of Anne: his martial accoutrements: welcomes William to London: supports Comprehension Bill: crowns William and Mary—Dean Tillotson made Primate—Peace of Ryswick—Thanksgiving: Compton's sermon—Eight thanksgivings in Anne's reign for Marlborough's victories and others : (1) Low Countries and destruction of Spanish Fleet at Vigo, (2) Blenheim, (3) Tirlemont, (4) Ramillies and Catalonia, (5) and (6) victories in 1706, (7) Oudenarde, (8) the Peace of Utrecht—The S.P.C.K. and the Charity Children—1710, completion of the fabric by the laying of the top stone (as on p. 235).

CHAPTER XXVII

THE EIGHTEENTH CENTURY AFTER ANNE . . . 282-291

Dean Sancroft succeeded by Stillingfleet, Archdeacon of London—Tillotson dean: succeeded by William Sherlock, Master of the Temple: uproar at his appointment, as he had been a nonjuror—Bishop Robinson—Bishop Gibson : his *Codex*, *Pastoral Letters* and *Preservative against Popery*—Dean Godolphin—Dean Hare : his *Difficulties and Discouragements in the Way of Private Judgment*—Joseph Butler dean—Thomas Sherlock Bishop of London—Bishop Lowth, Hebrew and Latin scholar—Bishop Porteus, supporter of the rising evangelical school—Thomas Secker Dean of St. Paul's—Dean Hume—Dean Cornwallis — Dean Newton — Proposal of Sir Joshua

Reynolds and the Royal Academy to paint pictures for St. Paul's—Dean Thurlow—Dean Pretyman (afterwards Pretyman-Tomline : designed by Pitt for the Primacy : action of George III.—George III.'s thanksgiving for recovery, 1789 : his thanksgiving in 1797 for great naval victories, procession of the Admirals—Burial of Wren in 1723—Burial of Sir Joshua Reynolds in 1793.

CHAPTER XXVIII

ST. PAUL'S IN THE NINETEENTH CENTURY . . . 292–311

The theft of the plate—Description of the lost treasure—Bishop Randolph—Bishop Howley—Bishop Blomfield—Reforms and church-building—Bishop Tait : his institution of Sunday evening services at Westminster Abbey and St. Paul's—Rearrangement of the Choir : removal of the screen—The Special Preachers from 1858 to 1873—Bishop Jackson—Bishop Temple—Bishop Creighton : his *History of the Papacy during the Period of the Reformation*—Bishop Winnington-Ingram—Funeral of Nelson, 1806—Dean Van Mildert—Dean Sumner—Dean Copleston—Dean Milman : his *History of Latin Christianity*, *History of the Jews* and *Annals of St. Paul's*—Funeral of Wellington, 1852 — Dean Mansel : his *Prolegomena Logica*, *Philosophy of Kant*, *Metaphysics*, and *Limits of Religious Thought* — Dean Church : his *Sermons and Essays* — Thanksgiving for the recovery of the Prince of Wales, 1872—Joseph Parkinson's paper in *All the Year Round* (April 4, 1868) on the condition of St. Paul's—Robert Gregory appointed Canon the same year : beginning of reforms—Condition of the music : the choir exhorted—The College of Minor Canons and College of Vicars-choral subjected to the control of the Chapter—Washing and dusting : permanent body of workmen, with skilled foreman—Commutation of the estates—Dr. Stainer and reforms in the music : festival services, oratorios, orchestras—The new Choir School—Liddon's sermons.

CHAPTER XXIX

VERGER GREEN'S DIARY : THE LAST HALF OF THE NINETEENTH CENTURY.—PART I. : 1853–75 . . . 312–330

1853, Heating—1854, Harvest Thanksgiving—1855, Sebastopol—1856, Suicides ; thanksgiving for Peace with Russia—

CONTENTS

1857, Humiliation for Indian Mutiny—1858, First evening service under the Dome—1859, Thanksgiving for end of Indian Mutiny—1860, Alterations in the Choir—1861, *The Messiah*, and Sims Reeves; mourning services for the Prince Consort—1863, Celebrations of the wedding of the Prince of Wales—1864, First mosaic in the Dome—1866, Humiliation for the Cattle Plague—1867, Cathedral closed to visitors through Fenian scare—1868, Installation of Canon Gregory—1869, Alteration of hours of service—1870, Stricter observance of Ascension Day; Lay Helpers' services; Mansion House meeting for decorations (£25,000 subscribed); first consecration of Bishops on record in present Cathedral—1871, Special observance of Dedication Festival; beginning of working-men's Saturday visits; Bishop Jackson revives the cope; beginning of Lectures to Young Men—1872, Thanksgiving for Prince of Wales' recovery; Lowering of the monuments—first Choral Celebration in the Choir; non-communicants allowed to remain during celebration—1873, Large additions to staff of Choir; first rendering of Bach's *Passion-music;* organ to be silent on Fridays; first Hospital Sunday; funeral of Sir Edwin Landseer; first Annual Festival of London Gregorian Association, also of London Church Choir Association—1874, Iron railings round West Front removed; black gown discontinued for external preachers; burial of Foley, R.A.; copies of words of hymns and anthems ordered for afternoon and evening services—1875, George Martin Master of Song; first baptism after 162 years; service for Mayors, Provosts, etc., from the kingdom and abroad.

CHAPTER XXX

VERGER GREEN'S DIARY: THE LAST HALF OF THE NINETEENTH CENTURY.—PART II.: 1876-88 . . . 331-346

1876, "Dettingen Te Deum" sung with orchestra as thanksgiving for safe return of the Prince of Wales from India: Auld Lang Syne—1877, Beginning of Daily Celebrations in N.W. Chapel—Beginning of Lent midday services under the Dome—1878, Plain services in Holy Week—First "Three Hours' Service" on Good Friday; new peal of bells; first rendering of Spohr's *Last Judgment;* mourning for Princess Alice—1879, Churchyard made a garden by Corporation; new buildings in Amen Court—1880, Choral Communion ordered for Saints' Days; first East London

Mission Service; short midday services begun in N.W. Chapel; first scientific peal on new bells—1882, Arrival of "Great Paul"; tolling of "Great Paul" on New Year's Eve, the origin of the annual New Year's crowd—1883, Burial of Professor Palmer, Captain Gill and Lt. Charrington—1884, Mourning for the Duke of Albany; burial of Sir Bartle Frere; centenary of first Bishop of American Church (Seabury)—1885, Memorial Service for General Gordon; burial of Lord Mayor Nottage; first use of Primate's crozier and Bishop's pastoral staff—1886, Service for Delegates of Colonial Exhibition—1887, Visit of Socialists; thanksgiving for Queen Victoria's Jubilee—1888, Dedication of new reredos; new marble steps at entrance to Choir.

CHAPTER XXXI

VERGER GREEN'S DIARY: THE LAST HALF OF THE NINE-TEENTH CENTURY.—PART III.: 1889-1900 . . 347-363

1890, Burial of Lord Napier of Magdala; the first Welsh Service; burial of Canon Liddon; funeral of Dean Church; burial of Sir Edgar Boehm, R.A.—1891, Installation of Dean Gregory; judgment of House of Lords on Reredos Case; Memorial Service for Duke of Clarence; Wellington Monument moved—1893, Great service for Welsh Church Defence; Dedication of new clock—1894, Dedication of Jesus Chapel; jubilee Service of Y.M.C.A.—New large candlesticks (copied from Prince Arthur's tomb) placed in Sacrarium; the eight statues in the Dome completed; mourning for the Emperor of Russia—1896, Death of Prince Henry; burial of Lord Leighton; funeral of Sir Joseph Barnby; unveiling of Choir mosaics; burial of Sir John Millais—1897, Collections for Indian Famine; 1300th anniversary of baptism of King Ethelbert; thanksgiving for 60th Accession-Day of Queen Victoria; great Diamond Jubilee Service at west steps; Memorial Service for the Duchess of Teck; Bi-centenary of opening of Cathedral celebrated by Freemasons—1898, Bi-centenary of S.P.C.K.—Dumb peal for Mr. Gladstone; burial of Sir George Grey—1899, Memorial Service for those fallen in the South African War; intercession for the war; resignation of R. Green.

CHAPTER XXXII

ST. PAUL'S IN THE TWENTIETH CENTURY . . . 364-377

1900, Farewell Services to the City Imperial Volunteers; thanksgivings for the relief of Ladysmith and Mafeking; Bi-centenary of S.P.G.; Memorial Service for Duke of Saxe-Coburg; thanksgiving for the return of C.I.Vs.; burial of Sir Arthur Sullivan; Memorial Service for the victims of the war in 1900—1901, Burial of Bishop Creighton; mourning services for Queen Victoria; Palestrina services; enthronement of Bishop Winnington-Ingram; mourning for the Emperor Frederick; the Chapter agree to instal the Order of St. Michael and St. George in the S.W. Chapel—1902, The Leighton Memorial unveiled; electric lighting given by Mr. Pierpont Morgan; Memorial Service for Cecil Rhodes: Farewell Service for Christ's Hospital; thanksgiving for Peace; intercession for recovery of the King from sudden illness on day fixed for Coronation; thanksgiving for the Coronation; thanksgiving for return of 24th Imperial Yeomanry; thanksgiving for King's recovery, attended by the King, Queen and Royal Family; Memorial Service for Archbishop Temple—1903, Steven's sketch-equestrian figure placed on Wellington Monument for experiment—1904, Centenary Service of Bible Society, attended by Queen and Royal Family; 1300th anniversary of Bishop Mellitus; Memorial Service for G. F. Watts, R.A.; Memorial Service and Monument for Coldstream Guards—1905, First rendering of Allègri's *Miserere;* Princess Louise's Monument to 4200 Colonial Volunteers unveiled by Prince of Wales; Memorial Service for John Hay, U.S.A.; burial of Sir George Williams—1906, Dedication of Chapel of St. Michael and St. George in the presence of the King; Memorial Service for Seddon, Premier of New Zealand; Memorial Service for Canadian and American victims of Salisbury railway disaster; Memorial Service for Miss Beale; Musicians' Company resume Annual Service on St. Cecilia's Day—1907, Jubilee Service of London Diocesan Home Mission; gift of St. Cecilia window by Mr. Crews—1908, King, Queen, etc., present at Memorial Service for King of Portugal and Crown Prince; Thanksgiving Service of Lambeth Conference of Bishops—1909, the Corporation's consent to the Paul's Cross monument.

CONTENTS

CHAPTER XXXIII

THE RICHMOND MOSAICS 378–390

Wren's wish—W. B. Richmond appointed in 1891 to decorate the Choir with mosaics: his generous undertaking: his preparation—Messrs. Powell—Mr. E. J. Harding: skilful scaffolding—Method—The first design completed—Creation of birds, fishes, animals—The figure of Christ in glory—The Latin texts.

CHAPTER XXXIV

THE ORDER OF ST. MICHAEL AND ST. GEORGE . . 391–399

Account of the Order—Beginning of the idea of installation in St. Paul's—Sir Robert Herbert—Difficulties—Mr. Somers Clarke to be architect—Sir Walter Wilkin, K.C.M.G.—Gifts—Dedication Service, June 12, 1906—The Prelate, Bishop Montgomerie—The Annual Commemoration Service on St. George's Day.

CHAPTER XXXV

THE ORGANISTS, ORGAN AND MUSIC AT ST. PAUL'S . 400–421

I. *The Organists:*—List from 1530 to 1909—John Redford—Pressing boys for St. Paul's and the Chapel Royal—Thomas Mulliner, Master of the School—Thomas Tallis—William Bird—Thomas Morley—John Tomkins—Adrian Batten—Albertus Bryne—Michael Wise, Almoner—Jeremiah Clark—John Blow, Almoner—Richard Brind—Handel—Charles King, Almoner—Maurice Greene—John Jones—Jonathan Battishill—Thomas Attwood—Mozart—Mendelssohn—Sir John Goss—Sir John Stainer—Sir George Martin, M.V.O.—Charles Macpherson.

II. *The Organ:*—Julian the Apostate's description—Description by Wulstan, tenth century—Place of Organ in the old Cathedral—Father Smith's Organ: Contest with Wren—The original specification—Additions by Bishop in 1826 and 1849—Placed under middle arch of north arcade in Choir, 1860—Rebuilt and enlarged by Willis in 1871 and placed in present position—Renewals and additions in 1897 by Willis—Details.

III. *The Music:*—Three periods: Motett, Verse and Modern—Gounod—Nathaniel Hawthorne—Bishop Cleveland Cox of New York.

CONTENTS

CHAPTER XXXVI

THE LIBRARY, BELLS AND CLOCK OF ST. PAUL'S . . 422–434

I. *The Library:*—Loss of the ancient collection—Scanty remains—The new Library, over the chapel of St. Michael and St. George: 10,500 books, 10,800 pamphlets—Bishop Compton's bequest—Prebendary Mangey and his son—Dr. Sparrow Simpson's collections—Barham of the *Ingoldsby Legends* Librarian—Charles II.'s subscription-book—Wren's accounts—Luther's Bible—Laud's annotated copy of his controversy—Cranmer's book and signature—Signatures of sovereigns—Casts of seals—Medals.

II. *The Bells:*—The State bell: "Edward of Westminster," or "Westminster Tom"—The old Jesus Tower with four great bells—The new Ring of Twelve—Lists of weights and donors—The College Youths—"Great Paul."

III. *The Clock:*—The old clock—The new: Lord Grimthorpe and Dean Gregory—Messrs. John Smith & Sons, Derby—Varieties of chimes—The legend of the old clock striking thirteen: John Hatfield.

CHAPTER XXXVII

PAUL'S CROSS 435–445

Origin and use of churchyard and other crosses—Activity of Paul's Cross from times before 1191 to 1643—Events in the reigns of Richard I., Henry III., Edward I., Edward II., Richard II., Henry VI., Richard III., Henry VII., Henry VIII., Edward VI., Mary, Elizabeth, James I., Charles I.—Destroyed in 1643 by order of the Long Parliament.

CHAPTER XXXVIII

THE INTERMENTS AND MONUMENTS IN OLD ST. PAUL'S 446–450

1. Royal Persons—2. Men of the State—3. Soldiers—4. Knights, Nobles, Courtiers—5. Bishops of London—6. Lord Mayors of London—7. Deans of St. Paul's—8. Ecclesiastics—9. Doctors—10. Artists—11. Musician.

CHAPTER XXXIX

MEMORIALS AND BURIALS IN THE NEW CATHEDRAL . 451–473

1. Naval—2. Military—3. Statesmen—4. Ecclesiastical—5. Men of Letters—6. Painters, Sculptors, Architects, Engineer—7. Musicians—8. Philanthropists—9. Doctors—10. Explorers—List of sculptors of the monuments.

CHAPTER XL

STRUCTURAL NOTES 474–478

1871, The North-west Chapel—1872, The whole of the monuments lowered—1873, Precautions against fire in the Dome—1876, The oak lobbies added at the west—1877, Crypt made a chapel—1878, Marble floor of choir, whole Crypt opened up and rearranged—1879, Remains of old St. Paul's discovered—1883, Design for decoration by Leighton and Poynter—1886–87, New reredos—The proposed L.C.C. main sewer and the security of St. Paul's.

EPILOGUE 479–482
APPENDIX I 483–486
APPENDIX II 487–488
APPENDIX III 489–490
APPENDIX IV 491–493
BIBLIOGRAPHY 495–496
INDEX 497–512

LIST OF ILLUSTRATIONS

	PAGE
GROUND PLAN OF ST. PAUL'S COMPARED WITH ST. PETERS, ROME (SHADED) . . . . *Facing p.*	vii
OLD DANISH MEMORIAL STONE	11
ARMS OF THE DEAN AND CHAPTER.	26
THE NAVE OF OLD ST. PAUL'S . . . . *Facing p.*	28
OLD ST. PAUL'S, FROM SOUTH-EAST . . . *Facing p.*	50
GROUND PLAN, OLD ST. PAUL'S . . . . *Facing p.*	51
OLD ST. PAUL'S . . . . *Facing p.*	52
OLD ST. PAUL'S . . . . *Facing p.*	55
OLD ST. PAUL'S (WEST ELEVATION) . . . *Facing p.*	57
MONUMENT OF DEAN DONNE	98
CANDELABRUM ON THE ALTAR STEPS	116
MARTIN LUTHER'S BIBLE	121
LONDON AFTER THE FIRE, SHOWING ST. PAUL'S . *Facing p.*	216
ST. PAUL'S FROM FLEET STREET . . . . *Facing p.*	220
THE FIRST DESIGN OF ST. PAUL'S AFTER THE FIRE, FROM THE MODEL IN THE PRESENT CATHEDRAL . . .	222
THE CRYPT, LOOKING EAST	225
THE LAST DESIGN MADE FOR ST. PAUL'S BY SIR CHRISTOPHER WREN . . . . *Facing p.*	226
SIR CHRISTOPHER WREN'S FIRST DESIGN FOR THE CATHEDRAL . . . . *Facing p.*	228
GROUND PLAN OF ST. PAUL'S . . . . . *Facing p.*	229
PLAN OF OLD ST. PAUL'S UPON THE ONE OF THE PRESENT ST. PAUL'S (SHADED) . . . . . *Facing p.*	230
ST. PAUL'S FROM WATERLOO BRIDGE	236

LIST OF ILLUSTRATIONS

	PAGE
THE WEST DOOR, FROM S.E.	238
CHAPEL OF ST. DUNSTAN, OR MORNING CHAPEL (UNDER N.W. TOWER)	240
INTERIOR OF THE NAVE, LOOKING EAST	242
BASE OF COLUMN IN WEST GALLERY	243
THE LORD MAYOR'S VESTRY	244
THE DEAN'S VESTRY AND CHAIR	246
THE CROSS ON THE TOP OF THE DOME	247
THE BISHOP'S THRONE	249
OAK CARVING IN THE LIBRARY	250
TIJOU'S GRILL, LEADING TO S. CHOIR AISLE AND DEAN'S VESTRY	252
IRONWORK AT THE FOOT OF THE GEOMETRICAL STAIRCASE UNDER S.W. TOWER	254
THE EXTERIOR DOME, THE BRICK CONE, AND THE TOP OF THE INNER DOME *Facing p.*	256
OLD PULPIT OF CHOIR	257
THE FONT, BY BIRD *Facing p.*	258
THE WHISPERING GALLERY *Facing p.*	264
THE TOMB OF WREN	272
VIEW FROM THE STONE GALLERY (LOOKING EAST) *Facing p.*	280
OVER THE GRAVE OF NELSON. } *Facing p.*	302
THE SARCOPHAGUS OF WELLINGTON	
NELSON'S TOMB IN THE CRYPT *Facing p.*	303
THE WELLINGTON FUNERAL CAR, WEST END OF CRYPT	318
THE WELLINGTON MONUMENT	334
GREAT PAUL	340
THE REREDOS	350
ALTAR IN THE JESUS CHAPEL (APSE)	353
THE CHOIR, LOOKING EAST *Facing p.*	364
INTERIOR VIEW *Facing p.*	367
THRONES OF KING EDWARD VII. AND QUEEN ALEXANDRA ON NORTH SIDE OF SACRARIUM	370
ABRAHAM AND THE THREE ANGELS *Facing p.*	386
JOB AND HIS THREE FRIENDS *Facing p.*	387

LIST OF ILLUSTRATIONS

	PAGE
CHAPEL OF THE ORDER OF ST. MICHAEL AND ST. GEORGE, FROM E. (FORMERLY WELLINGTON CHAPEL AND CONSISTORY COURT)	392
STALL OF THE SOVEREIGN OF THE ORDER OF ST. MICHAEL AND ST. GEORGE	396
THE SOUTH PORTICO . . . . *Facing p.*	398
THE STATUE OF ST. PAUL, WEST ENTRANCE . . .	399
GAS ENGINE FOR THE ORGAN . . . . *Facing p.*	418
THE LIBRARY, UNDER S.W. TOWER	423
THE BELLS . . . . *Facing p.*	426
THE CLOCK . . . . *Facing p.*	429
THE RODNEY MONUMENT	452
THE NELSON MONUMENT	454
GROUND PLAN OF CRYPT OF ST. PAUL'S . . *Facing p.*	455
GENERAL GORDON'S MONUMENT . . . . *Facing p.*	459
MONUMENTS TO SIR EDWIN LANDSEER AND RANDOLPH CALDECOTT . . . . *Facing p.*	466
W. E. HENLEY	467
THE LEIGHTON MONUMENT	470
PROCESSIONAL CROSS GIVEN BY MRS. BARRY . *Facing p.*	476
ONE OF THE CAMPANILES AT THE WEST ENTRANCE . .	486

MEMORIALS OF
ST. PAUL'S CATHEDRAL

CHAPTER I

ANCIENT LONDON

OBSCURITY as deep as one of its modern fogs broods over the origin of that vast metropolitan area which now extends in all directions round St. Paul's Cathedral for many miles. The first breaking of actual light is the statement of the Roman historian Tacitus that in the reign of Claudius, his general Suetonius made his way to London, not at that time (A.D. 61) dignified with the name of a colony, but widely known for its great throng of merchants, ships and providers of commissariat.[1]

This statement seems to imply that there was a British settlement before the Roman town, for had the place not been previously known and occupied it could hardly have grown to be such an important commercial centre in the few years that followed the conquest of Claudius. Whatever the name of London may mean, there can be little doubt that the word has a Celtic origin; so has Ludgate, the entrance on the west, and Dowgate, that on the east. What a British town was like we learn from Julius Cæsar, who tells us that it was "nothing more than a thick wood,

[1] Tacitus, *Annals*, xiv. 33.

fortified with a ditch and rampart, to serve as a place of retreat against the incursions of enemies."[1] Although, therefore, we must dismiss to the region of imagination the dream of the monkish chronicler, Geoffry of Monmouth, of a great and fair British city on the site of London, Troynovant by name, founded by Brut, grandson of Aeneas, still we may reasonably think of a clearing out of the great forest of Middlesex, extending probably from the site of St. Paul's to that of the Bank of England, with a stockade crowning Ludgate Hill, and the huts of the Britons spread about the higher ground looking down on the broad expanses of the Thames. The mouth of the river was then only a few miles off, and large portions of what are now the counties of Kent and Essex were marshes overflowed with water. The original investigations of Sir Christopher Wren led him to take this view, and he expressed the opinion that "the whole country between Camberwell Hill and the Hill of Essex might have been a great frith or gulf of the sea, and much wider near the mouth of the Thames, which made a large plain of sand at low water, through which the river found its way. This mighty broad sand (now good meadow) was (finally) restrained by large banks still remaining, and reducing the river into its channel; a great work, of which no history gives account; the Britons were too rude to attempt it, the Saxons too much busied with continual wars, he concluded, therefore, it was Roman work."[2]

The actual site of the Roman town is of no great importance; it must have covered part of the present city of London, and must have looked out from the woods, over these broad expanses of water, towards the forests of the Surrey Hills. Roman remains have, from time to time, been discovered in the neighbourhood; a bronze image of Diana, what seem to be sacrificial instruments and vessels,

[1] *De Bello Gallico*, v. 21.
[2] Wren's *Parentalia*, p. 285.

and a great quantity of bones. In 1830, when the foundations of Goldsmiths' Hall were being excavated in Foster Lane, a stone altar was found with a carved representation of Diana. This gives but slight evidence for the story of the existence of a Temple of Diana on the site of St. Paul's Cathedral; but at any rate the worship of the goddess was localized, and was appropriate to a centre from which there must have been abundant opportunities for hunting.

A Roman road, traces of which still exist in Watling Street, ran across the town, in a line from Dover to Newgate Street and the present Marble Arch, where it joined the other road from Westminster. Watling Street does not keep its old route in the City, as it was diverted, probably in the thirteenth century, to make room for an extension of St. Paul's Churchyard. On the south side of the river it was carried on embankments among the shallows, and is recognized in the local names of Stone Street and Newington Causeway.

Suetonius restored order in London after the last struggle of Boadicea. About A.D. 286 it was in the neighbourhood of London that one of the rebel emperors, Allectus, was defeated by Asclepiodotus, the general of Constantius; and under one of the Constantines the place began to be looked upon with favour, and to be extensively fortified. The Roman wall was built between A.D. 350 and 369 and enclosed a space computed at 380 acres. The city was defended several miles off to the east by the River Lea and its extensive marshes, and to the west by the creek of the Fleet River, the waters of which were tidal as far as King's Cross. From 369 to 412 London was reckoned the capital of Britain; about 380 the accurate and impartial Ammianus Marcellinus concedes to her the style and title of Augusta. After the Roman departure in the early years of the fifth century, London disappears from history until 457, when the Britons, fleeing before the victorious Hengest, took refuge behind the Roman wall.

It was in these conditions that Christianity was introduced into Britain, certainly not later than some time in the second century, if not earlier. Its first arrival is as uncertain as the origin of London: the fable of King Lucius and the long list of British Bishops of London must be set aside as pure legend. But there can be no doubt at all that as commerce made its way along the great central Roman road from Marseilles and Lyons, through Gaul, and crossed to Dover, Christianity came with it. In addition to that, during the four centuries of the Roman occupation of Britain the Christian faith was rapidly increasing in Rome in influence and in the number of its adherents, and this change must have been reflected in the army and the social life of the flourishing province. About A.D. 208 Tertullian writes that the Kingdom and Name of Christ were then acknowledged in Britain even in those parts inaccessible to the Romans. Several subsequent writers speak in terms of enthusiasm of the British Church. Unhappily, when the pagan Anglo-Saxon invaders arrived after the departure of the Romans, they so completely destroyed all the records and traces of the British Church that we have little definite information about it, except that it existed, that it was probably founded under Eastern auspices, as Marseilles and Lyons were Greek colonies, and that it was flourishing and was important. In 314, a gleam of light occurs; a Council of Bishops was held at Arles, in the South of Gaul, and was attended by three British Bishops, whose names are inscribed in the records of the Council, and of whom one was Restitutus, Bishop of London. No doubt there was a long line of these Bishops; no doubt they had a Bishop's church, or cathedral; perhaps it may have been on the site of St. Paul's; but that is all that can be said.

At the beginning of the seventh century, the wise and able Pope, Gregory the Great, determined on sending a mission to convert the Anglo-Saxon tribes in Britain. The story of the manner in which his sympathy was aroused by seeing yellow-haired captive boys from Northumbria exposed for sale as slaves in the Roman market, is well known.

The first Roman Bishop of London is thus introduced to us by Bede: "In the year of our Lord 604, Augustine, Archbishop of Britain, consecrated two Bishops, namely, Mellitus and Justus; Mellitus to preach to the province of the East Saxons, who are divided from Kent by the River Thames, and border on the eastern sea. Their metropolis is the City of London, situated on the bank of the aforesaid river, and is the mart of many nations resorting to it by sea and land. At that time Sebert, nephew to Ethelbert (the King of Kent whom Augustine converted) by his sister Ricula, reigned over the nation, though under subjection to Ethelbert, who had command over all the nations of the English as far as the River Humber. But when this province (the East Saxons) also received the word of truth by the preaching of Mellitus, King Ethelbert built the church of St. Paul in the City of London, where he and his successors should have their episcopal seat."[1] Ethelbert not only built the cathedral, but there is also a persistent legend that he endowed it with the Manor of Tillingham, in Essex, as a support for the fabric. The earliest deed may be a copy of his donation: it bears the lines, "And if any one should be tempted to take away this gift, let him be anathema, and excommunicated from all Christian society." There is no rival claimant to Ethelbert in this gift, so that the truthfulness of the tradition may be reasonably accepted. When all the other estates of St. Paul's were handed over to the Ecclesiastical Commissioners for administration on behalf of the Church at large, Tillingham was kept by the Chapter as a sacred charge, and is still used for the same purpose as its original intention thirteen hundred years ago.

The conversion of Sebert, King of the East Saxons, and the building and endowment of a cathedral in London by his uncle and overlord Ethelbert, King of Kent, seemed to

[1] *Eccl. Hist.*, book ii. chap. iii.

promise well for the labours of Mellitus. But Sebert and Ethelbert died, and were succeeded by pagan sons. The kingdom of the East Saxons, including Middlesex, Essex, and Herts, with London, seems to have been ruled jointly by the three sons of Sebert; and their open rejection of Christianity was followed by their people. Entering St. Paul's one day as the Bishop was celebrating the Eucharist, the three openly mocked the sacred rites: "We will not enter into that laver, because we do not know that we stand in need of it; but eat of that bread we will." They gave the Bishop the alternative of compliance or expulsion; so he withdrew in his twelfth year, and retired across the Channel, where he remained some years. Meanwhile Augustine had died, and was succeeded in the Archbishopric of Canterbury by another of his Roman companions, Laurentius. Laurentius entreated Mellitus to return; but "the Londoners would not receive Bishop Mellitus, choosing rather to be under their idolatrous highpriests." Mellitus in the end succeeded Laurentius in the Archbishopric. It may be hoped that his episcopate at Canterbury was more successful than that at London. Bede gives us an interesting glimpse of him in his Archbishopric. He was unfortunately afflicted with the gout: but though his malady sorely hindered his bodily activity, "his mind, with vigorous steps, joyfully leaped up beyond earthly affairs, and flew to love and seek things celestial." There was a terrible conflagration at Canterbury; in those days of wooden buildings such fires were frequent: the whole city was in danger of being burnt; water was thrown upon the flames, but all in vain; they continued to spread with terrific power: the Church of the Four Crowned Martyrs, martyrs who had fallen in the persecution of Diocletian, stood in the place where the fire raged most fiercely: thither the Primate, though weighed down by his infirmities and the pains of sickness, bade his servants carry him. Strong men had laboured to no purpose to put out the flames—he would show them the power of prayer. He prayed fervently; and the wind, which had been blowing from the south, now veered to the north; the flames were beaten back, and presently, the wind ceasing altogether, were entirely extinguished, and the city was saved.[1] Mellitus ruled the Church of Canterbury five years, and died on April 24, 624. London remained pagan. The failure of Mellitus led to an unforeseen result. Gregory the Great had directed Augustine to remove the Primacy to London from Canterbury as soon as the Church in London should be ripe for the change. But the retreat of Mellitus, and the relapse of the East Saxons, were followed by so long an interval, that when at last, under a totally different influence, Christianity was firmly planted in London, it was too late for such a measure: archbishop had succeeded to archbishop in the little city of Canterbury, and prescription prevailed.

It was after nearly half-a-century that Sigebert the Good, King of the East Saxons, on a visit to King Oswy, of Northumbria, was converted by the reasoning of his Christian host, and baptized by Bishop Finan of Lindisfarne. Lindisfarne, or Holy Island, is the largest of a group of islets lying about two miles off the coast of Northumberland between Bamborough and Berwick, and protected by the immediate presence of the Court at the former royal fortress. When St. Aidan came from Iona to convert the wild Teutonic settlers in Northumbria, he chose Lindisfarne as his home and seat of authority, closely following the example of his illustrious chief, St. Columba, in his sacred island amongst the seas of the West Highlands. Iona was the type of a simple and sincere form of Christianity, independent of Rome, which had come to Ireland through Britain, had passed over with St. Columba to Scotland, and was destined to be the source of the greater part of the conversion of the English as well. What Christian eyes

[1] Bede, *Eccl. Hist.*, ii. 7.

can look without emotion on some bright summer day at the little long low island of Lindisfarne, as it lies across the two miles of sand and water, which carts and horses cross as they did in the days of Aidan, with its gleaming sandy banks rising white from the blue sea, over-arched by the vast unbroken vault of heaven, its thick grass brilliant in the sunshine, its fields fertile with a cultivation begun by St. Aidan and his monks, its castle on the rocky hill, the miniature of Bamborough, its beautiful Norman Abbey of red sandstone, built by the Durham monks in miniature of their own cathedral, and in honour of Aidan, Finan, Cuthbert, and other saints; and its honest fisher people, descendants of those to whom Aidan himself preached! Lindisfarne is the real mother of St. Paul's and every church in London; the little Lindis brook, the water from which the baptismal streams of London churches have for twelve centuries and a half derived historically their sacred meaning.

Returning from Bamborough to London, King Sigebert[1] took with him two brothers, disciples of Bishop Finan, and recommended by him for the mission to the East Saxons, English themselves by race. One of the two was Cedd,[2] who was to be the first Anglo-Saxon Bishop of London; a third brother was St. Chad, the illustrious Apostle of Mercia. The two missionaries travelled zealously up and down Essex, Middlesex and Hertfordshire from London, through the forests to the villages and markets, under the protection of Sigebert, and gained so many converts that Bishop Finan felt no difficulty in consecrating Cedd Bishop of the East Saxons. Cedd at once set about training converts, natives of the province, for the priesthood, at two centres—Ythancester, near Tillingham, and at Tilbury.[3] When the Council was held at Whitby to confer on the

---

[1] G is hard, I and E short.
[2] C is hard.
[3] Bishop Browne's *Conversion of the Heptarchy*, p. 154 (S.P.C.K.).

claims of the Church of Rome to supremacy, he acted as interpreter, and was won over with the majority to the Roman method of reckoning Easter. He died of the plague soon after in 664.

Of his successor, Winé, little or nothing is known. Another visitation of the plague is mentioned as having caused half the diocese to relapse, the other half, under King Sebbé, remaining faithful. The overlordship was then in the hands of Wulfere, King of Mercia, who sent his own Bishop Jaruman, who also belonged to the Iona connection, with a number of clergy, who restored the Christianity of the lapsed districts.

Winé's successor was the famous St. Erkonwald, who was himself of the Royal family of the East Saxons. It was he who built the first stone Cathedral of St. Paul's, the previous buildings having been of wood. Erkonwald must have had a strong personality: his legendary Life is full of admiration for his munificence to the Cathedral and of abundant miracles. It was in Bishop Erkonwald's house in London that the great Archbishop Theodore of Canterbury was reconciled to Bishop Wilfrid after their old estrangement. From this meeting may be dated the long series of negotiations which ended in Wilfrid's restoration to his cathedral church and monastery.[1] He was canonized and his tomb became one of the most famous and sacred shrines in England, at which each generation, down to the Reformation, worshipped with devoutest faith and lavish generosity. There is a picturesque story of his death in the old chronicle. He had founded a monastery at Chertsey (near the southern outskirts of Windsor Forest), of which he was himself Abbot. At Barking, in Essex, his sister had established a nunnery, and it was there that he died. The monks of Chertsey hurried to Barking to claim the remains of their Abbot. But the clergy of St. Paul's preferred their claim as well; in the legend they are called

[1] Canon Bright, M.A., *Hist.*, p. 351.

canons, but it is uncertain whether that office existed at this early date. The population of London poured forth with their ecclesiastical leaders, seized the bier, and were bearing it off in triumph to the City. The monks of Chertsey and the nuns of Barking followed in tears, protesting in vain against this unseemly violence, and appealing to Heaven in favour of their right to the revered remains. A terrible storm came on; the River Lea, the boundary between Essex and Middlesex, rose rapidly to a great height, and stopped the procession; there was neither boat nor bridge. In their simple piety, all saw the hand of God in the flood. Each party pleaded its cause with the utmost eloquence. But a man of God addressed the contending disputants, exhorting them to peace, and to leave the debate to the divine decision. The clergy began to intone a litany: the Lea sank to its ordinary level; the procession crossed over to Stratford. There the sun burst out with all its brilliance, and the treasured body passed in glory to the Cathedral.[1]

With the exception of St. Dunstan, who held the See from 959 to 961, St. Erkonwald's twenty-four successors till the period of the Norman Conquest are known merely by their names. That they were in general men in whom the public placed their confidence is shown by the fact of the great estates granted during these three centuries to the Cathedral and the Bishopric. These, with others of a later date, have been for the most part covered with buildings, and are now in the hands of the Ecclesiastical Commissioners, to be administered for the general good of the whole Church. They have become so valuable that they now amount to nearly half of the Commissioners' revenue. The Cathedral receives about a tenth of the income of its ancient property, the Bishop about a twentieth of that which belonged to his predecessors. The rest is most ably distributed by the Commissioners amongst poor or new

Milman's *Annals of St. Paul's*, p. 11 (from Dugdale).

parishes in England and Wales, in providing stipends, in augmenting incomes, in the payment of pensions, and in other admirable ways; so that the whole National Church has now reason to be grateful to the generous benefactors of those early days.

In 962, the year after Dunstan became Primate, St. Paul's was burnt, but was rebuilt the same year. This was the time when London was suffering much from the ravages of the Danes, or Northmen.

In 1014, St. Alphege, or Elphege, the Primate clubbed to death in a drunken rabble by the Danes, was buried in St. Paul's. In 1017 was buried Ethelred the Unready, and nearly half-a-century later, Edward the Outlaw, the representative of the House of Cerdic and Alfred.

OLD DANISH MEMORIAL STONE

CHAPTER II

THE DAYS OF THE NORMANS

THE preponderating Norman influence on the mind of Edward the Confessor is illustrated by the fact that in 1044 he appointed to the Bishopric of London the Norman Robert, Abbot of Jumièges, who six years afterwards was translated to Canterbury. The new Archbishop was, of course, a strong supporter of that influence; and having attained the supreme ecclesiastical dignity, he would not allow King Edward the Confessor to take a step which appeared to him to be retrograde in the nomination of his successor to London. The King favoured the appointment of the Abbot of Abingdon, whose name seems to have been Sperafocus, or the Sparrowhawk (probably from some impressive facial resemblance), who apparently assumed for a time the title and authority of Bishop; but the Primate refused to consecrate him, alleging a positive prohibition from the Pope. By some kind of Council the Abbot was dispossessed, and another Norman, named William, was consecrated in 1051. Next year came the anti-Norman revolution of Earl Godwin, when part of the terms of peace between the Confessor and his victorious kinsman, was that the Primate and all the other foreigners should be banished. The Primate was relegated to the charge of his Abbey of Jumièges; but William of London, beloved on account of his goodness, was allowed to return, and from that time was unmolested in the possession of his Bishopric until his death in 1075. He was one of the most memorable and notable of all the occupants of the

See, beloved by the citizens, the protector of their liberties, honoured and respected even by his adversaries. He had been Chaplain to the Confessor, and after the Conquest in 1066 rose into high favour with the Norman king. This favour he used on behalf of the people; for it was through his intercession that the Conqueror restored and confirmed all the ancient privileges of the City of London. His action and character alike made an indelible impression on succeeding generations of citizens. For centuries they made their annual pilgrimage to the tomb of their revered patron in the nave of St. Paul's. As late as the seventeenth century, A.D. 1622, the Lord Mayor, Edward Barkham, had the following lines set upon the tomb:—

> "Walkers, whosoe'er ye be,
> If it prove you chance to see
> Upon a solemn scarlet day
> The City Senate pass this way,
> Their grateful memory for to show
> Which they the reverend ashes owe
> Of Bishop Norman here inhumed;
> By which this City has assumed
> Large privileges; those obtained
> By him when Conqueror William reigned.
> This being by Barkham's thankful mind renewed
> Call it the monument of gratitude."[1]

In addition to the charters to the city, the Conqueror bestowed valuable privileges on St. Paul's Cathedral. "Some lands I give to God and the Church of St. Paul's in London, and special franchises, because I wish that this Church may be free in all things, as I wish my soul to be on the Day of Judgment." The witnesses to this grant are Lanfranc, Archbishop of Canterbury, Thomas of York, Roger Earl of Shrewsbury, and other magnates. Another grant frees the Church of St. Paul's from Danegelt and other payments, and from all services to the Crown.[2] A

[1] Dugdale, p. 37.
[2] *Ibid.*, pp. 207, 208. Milman is doubtful about the authenticity of these two charters in their present form.

momentous effect of the Conquest on the ecclesiastical condition of England lay in the fact that the Conqueror not only feudalized the realm but also the Church. His gift to the See was a strong castle, that of Bishop's Stortford in Essex, with its military retainers, who did feudal service to the Prelate, and swore homage and fealty to him. But the Bishops of London, living quite near the Royal Tower, and amongst the busy, active and capable citizens, did not attempt a strong political line such as was from time to time adopted by the feudal prelates of the provinces.

In 1075, the last year of Bishop William, a great council was held by the Primate Lanfranc in St. Paul's Cathedral, probably the first full Ecclesiastical Parliament in England. The Saxon Councils had been mostly local synods,[1] the scenes of some of which cannot now be even traced; this was an assemblage of the National Church, in the capital City. Lanfranc was famous throughout Christendom as a theologian; and the Council was attended by almost all the Bishops and greater Abbots of the realm, with the Heads of the Religious Orders. There came Thomas, Archbishop of York; William, Bishop of London; Godfrey, Bishop of Coutances; Walkelin of Winchester; Herman of Sherburne (Salisbury); Wulfstan of Worcester (the one Saxon Prelate whose holiness saved him from dispossession); Walter of Hereford; Giso of Wells; Remigius of Lincoln; Herfast of Elmham (Norwich); Stigand of Selsey (Chichester); Osborn of Exeter; Peter of Lichfield. Rochester was vacant; Lindisfarne (Durham) sent a valid excuse. The Welsh Bishoprics were still independent of England. No mention is made of Ely.

The first question to be settled was the precedence of the Bishops. The Archbishop of York took his seat on the Primate's right, the Bishop of London on the left; next to York came Winchester, as representing the old

[1] Wilkins' *Concilia*; Milman's *St. Paul's*, p. 19.

Saxon capital. The constitutions and canons of this important Council may be read at great length in Wilkins' *Concilia;* they are all conceived in the strictest spirit of the reforms of Clugny, which ruled strongly and sternly in the Norman Abbey of Bec, from which came Lanfranc and afterward Anselm. As an illustration of the Church life of those days, it is interesting to quote from Milman a short summary of some of the decrees. " Permission was granted to remove the See of Selsey to Chichester, of Sherburne to Salisbury, of Lichfield to Chester; but for these rearrangements the assent of the Crown was deemed requisite. No Bishop was to ordain a clerk or monk of another diocese without letters dimissory. To repress the insolent forwardness of some indiscreet ecclesiastics no one except a Bishop or an Abbot was to speak without leave of the Primate. The law against marriage within prohibited degrees, extending to the seventh degree of relationship; against the marriage of the clergy, as against simony of all kinds, had all the austerity of the Hildebrandine school, accepted by the Norman prelates, at least by those from Bec. The Council descended to lower matters. No bones of animals were to be hung up to avert cattle plague; all sortileges, auspices, divinations, and other works of the devil were forbidden under pain of excommunication. No Bishop, Abbot, or clerk was to sit in judgment on, or give his sanction to, any sentence of death or mutilation."

The successor of Bishop William was Hugh de Orivalle, or Orwell, in 1075; he ruled ten years. All that is recollected of him is that he became a leper. In spite of this affliction, which was regarded as a visitation of God, and made its victim an object of commiseration and an outcast of society, he does not appear to have been deposed. It is recorded that a strange and ineffectual remedy was tried: the carrying out of the idea of St. Matt. xix. 12; but he lived and died a leper.

In 1086, he was succeeded by *Mauritius*, chaplain and chancellor to the Conqueror, the builder of the magnificent Norman Cathedral, the nave of which lasted till the time of the Great Fire of 1666. The earlier building, erected originally by St. Erkonwald, had been rebuilt at least twice after fires; and in 1087, the year of the Conqueror's death, a terrible conflagration swept over the whole City, either entirely consuming St. Paul's, or rendering it useless. Of this church, in which Lanfranc had held his great Council, no record survives as to its size, architecture or characteristics. It is not easy to say what an Anglo-Saxon cathedral would be like. A few Anglo-Saxon churches, or parts of churches, remain, such as Bradford-on-Avon, Jarrow, the crypt at Repton (the ancient capital of Mercia), towers at Oxford and Cambridge, a tower and spire at Sompting in Sussex; but these are all on a small scale. Architecture for the Anglo-Saxons was probably brought by Wilfrid and Benedict Biscop from Rome in the seventh century, during the time of their frequent visits, and was Romanesque in character, with semi-circular arches, round pillars of slenderer bulk than those of the Norman style, with thin pilasters and tabernacle work on the walls within and without. There is an eloquent description of Wilfrid's Anglo-Saxon cathedral at Hexham, which seems to have been of nearly the same dimensions as the present Abbey; something of this kind it is left to us to imagine at St. Paul's.

Maurice was appointed at Christmas 1085, and was consecrated at Winchester in 1086. He set about the building of the new Cathedral, with Norman faith and courage, on a superb scale, and with unrivalled design; the preparations were so great that, although he ruled twenty-three years, he did not live to see more than the beginnings of his splendid undertaking. "The new Cathedral must be worthy of the capital city of the kingdom; and the munificence of Maurice kept pace with his architectural vision. The fabric designed by him commanded the admiration of his age, as amongst the noblest churches, not of England only but of Christendom. Many of his contemporaries, such as our authority, William of Malmesbury, must have seen the splendid buildings erected in Normandy at Rouen, and by the Conqueror at Caen. Yet, writes the chronicler, such was the magnificence of its beauty, that it may be accounted among the most famous buildings. So vast was the extent of the crypt, such the capaciousness of the upper structure, that it could contain the utmost conceivable multitude of worshippers."[1] We have almost complete Norman cathedrals at Durham, Peterborough and Norwich; and we have Norman naves at Ely, Gloucester, Rochester, Southwell and Chichester, as well as the monastic churches of Tewkesbury, Romsey, Melbourne and others. From the drawings and measurements of Hollar we arrive at the conviction that these were all surpassed by the design of Bishop Maurice. The nave consisted of twelve bays, and was about 315 feet long; or if the space under the central tower to the entrance of the choir be included, 360; the breadth was 104, the internal height 93, external 130. The choir and transepts, which were finally built on a Gothic plan, were of about the same dimensions.

One of the last acts of the Conqueror was to contribute to the building of the new Cathedral "the ruins of that strong castle then called the Palatine Tower, which stood on the west part of the City, towards that little river of Fleet," then a tidal and navigable stream;[2] Dugdale says it was at the place where afterwards the Priory of Blackfriars was erected. Part of the stone of which the Cathedral was built was, however, fetched from Caen in Normandy.

It was Bishop Maurice of London who crowned King Henry I. at Winchester. He must have grieved to pass

---

[1] Milman's *Annals of St. Paul's*, p. 22; William of Malmesbury, *De Gestis Pontificum*.

[2] Dugdale, p. 6.

C

away before the walls of his enormous church rose higher; but the Norman Cathedral is always connected with his name.

He was succeeded by *Richard de Belmeis*, who also ruled for twenty years, and who, with no less enthusiasm than Maurice, devoted the whole of his official resources to the work, and lived on his own private means. Besides these generous contributions, he gave for the service of the altar the rent of Paul's Wharf, on the riverside below the Cathedral; and, "fearing the wrath of God," he restored to the Canons a wood which he had wrongfully enclosed within his park at Chadenston; he gave also the oblations on the altars of St. Peter and St. Paul on the days when the Canons should officiate; such oblations must obviously have been at the disposal of the Bishop. To the School of St. Paul's he gave a site called the House of Durandus, at the corner of Bell Court. He was a man of large schemes, and did his best to regain for the See of the capital city the dignity to which it had been originally destined by Pope Gregory; he asked the Pope to create an archbishopric of London. It would have been a reasonable and proper step to take: the ecclesiastical chief of the capital ought to possess the highest ecclesiastical station: the Church of France has seven archbishoprics; archbishoprics are numerous in Germany and Italy; in Sicily the Archbishoprics of Palermo and Monreale are within four miles of each other; but Church-life in England has, except in great crises, been extraordinarily conservative in details, and the Archbishops of Canterbury have firmly and consistently opposed any reversal to the original plan of Pope Gregory as a kind of sacrilege. On hearing of the step taken by De Belmeis, St. Anselm wrote to the Pope, urging him by no means to consent to what he regarded as an usurpation.

In the later years of his life, De Belmeis withdrew from the cares of his diocese, and devoted his mind to the foundation of a monastery of regular canons at St. Osyth in Essex. He hoped to retire from his bishopric, and to live in peace as one of the canons. But paralysis seized him: for four years he lingered; in 1128 he died, and was buried at his new foundation.

Of the next Bishop it is not recorded that he did anything for the structure. From his vast and comprehensive learning he was known as *Gilbert the Universal;* he was a Canon of Lyons, and head of the famous School of Nevers. He was charged with covetousness, did not distribute his riches in his diocese, and lived the life of a learned recluse. On his death enormous wealth was found in his treasury, which the Crown seized. His boots, full of gold and silver, were carried to the Exchequer: "wherefore a man," wrote his contemporary, Henry of Huntingdon, "of consummate knowledge was held by the people as the greatest of fools." In the world of scholarship and monasticism he was more highly appreciated, for he is thus addressed by St. Bernard of Clairvaux, the oracle of his times: "All know that thou art truly wise, and hast trampled on the greatest enemy of wisdom in a way worthy of your priestly rank and of your name, that of true wisdom which despiseth base lucre. That Master Gilbert should be a Bishop was not wonderful; but that the Bishop of London should live like a poor man, that is magnificent. . . . What then hast thou dispensed and given to the poor? Money only? But what is money compared with that for which thou hast exchanged it, righteousness which remains for ever and ever?"[1] Gilbert the Universal died on his way to Rome, between 1135 and 1141.

A contest ensued between two sections of the Chapter of St. Paul's as to the appointment of the new Bishop. It was probably partly political, as the struggle between Stephen and the Empress Matilda for the throne of England was beginning about the same period. During the contest, the administration of the See was, by the authority of the

[1] Bernardi Opera, *Epist.* xxiv.

Pope, placed in the hands of Henry of Blois, Bishop of Winchester, Stephen's brother. Part of the canons favoured Anselm, Abbot of St. Edmund's, nephew of St. Anselm the great Archbishop; the party of the Dean supported Robert de Sigillo, a monk of Reading. Both sides sent embassies to the Pope. At length, when in 1141 the Empress Matilda entered London, *Robert de Sigillo* was summoned to be Bishop.

Matthew Paris, the chronicler, tells us that in 1136 another disastrous fire devastated the City. It began at London Bridge and raged as far as St. Clement Danes. He says St. Paul's was burnt; but we do not know how far the building of Maurice had risen, nor what was the effect of the destruction.[1] Bishop Henry of Blois, as guardian of the See, appealed to his own flock on behalf of St. Paul's; collections were to be made throughout all the churches in the diocese of Winchester.

The difficulties of a Bishop of London in these times of trouble, civil war and disputed succession are shown by the fact that when the Londoners, who, on the whole, were strong partisans of King Stephen, and had even proclaimed him in their folk-mote[2] on the ground at the east end of St. Paul's, had to submit to the Empress Matilda on her entrance into the City, the Tower was still held for the King by Geoffry Mandeville, Earl of Essex; and while Bishop Robert was living quietly at his palace at Fulham, Mandeville swooped down upon him, and carried him off to that fortress, whence he was only released by the payment of a heavy fine.[3] Fulham had been the country residence of the Bishops of London since early Anglo-Saxon days.

Bishop Robert de Sigillo instituted the office of Treasurer in the Cathedral; and died of eating poisoned grapes in 1152.[4]

[1] Matt. Paris, *Hist. Minor*, editio Madden, p. 253.
[2] Town's Meeting.   [3] Wharton, p. 57.   [4] Wharton.

There is nothing to say about his successor, *Robert de Belmeis*, except that he was the nephew of the great Bishop of the same name, that he was a man of eloquence, that he ruled ten years, and that he came to a melancholy end in 1162.

Then came another man of note, who ruled the diocese for a quarter of a century, and who passed through very troubled waters, *Gilbert Foliot*, the antagonist and rival of Thomas à Becket. St. Paul's was to witness the extraordinary and unprecedented scene of the formal excommunication of an eminent and highly esteemed Bishop of London at his own high altar by a jealous and vindictive Primate. In his *Latin Christianity* Milman thus describes the Bishop: "Foliot was admitted to be a man of unimpeachable life, of austere habits (he was gently rebuked by Pope Alexander III. for fasting too rigorously), and of great learning. He had been Abbot of Gloucester, then Bishop of Hereford (while Bishop of Hereford Becket accused him of aspiring to the Primacy). He was in correspondence with four successive Popes, Celestine II., Lucius II., Eugenius III., Alexander III., and with a familiarity which implies a high estimate of his ability and experience. He is interfering in matters remote from his own diocese, and commending other Bishops, Lincoln and Salisbury, to the favourable consideration of the Pontiff. All his letters reveal a Churchman as imperious and conscientious as Becket himself. Foliot, under other circumstances, might have resisted the King as inflexibly. He was, in short, a high and stirring ecclesiastic, who did not scruple to wield, as he had done in several instances, the last terrible weapon of the Church, which in the end fell on his own head."[1]

The sudden elevation to the Primacy of the warlike and prodigal chancellor, with no claims but those of a soldier and reckless minister of the Crown, not too respectful of

[1] Milman's *Latin Christianity*, vol. v. p. 37.

Church property, and magnificent in expenditure to the degree of eclipsing the throne itself, must have been a bitter surprise to the leading Churchmen of the day: "The King has wrought a miracle," said Foliot; "he has turned a layman and a soldier into an Archbishop."

Foliot is said to have been the first English Bishop canonically translated from one See to another, other than an archbishopric; and the promotion was sanctioned by Pope Alexander in language of the most profound admiration: "The City of London is the royal residence. The King passes great part of his time there, and there holds the assemblies of his barons and nobles. Forasmuch then as that City is more noble and famous than all other cities of the world, the King would have it ruled by the most honourable and the most learned in divine as well as in human law."[1]

On the retirement of Becket to the Continent, the administration of the estates and diocese of Canterbury fell to Foliot. At the beginning of the strife he had pleaded the King's cause before Pope Alexander; and later on the Pope entrusted the Bishops of London and Hereford with the critical task of remonstrating with Henry II., and bringing about a reconciliation between King and Primate. The audience took place on the borders of Wales, where Henry was fighting the Welsh. In a remarkable letter Foliot relates the story. The King had received the Bishops with courteous deference, and had listened with calm respect to the message of the Pope. He had not, he said, banished Becket. Becket had fled the realm. He had not prohibited or impeded the Primate's return. As soon as Becket would promise to observe the laws and constitutions of the realm, he would be received back with peace and honour. Foliot seems to suggest that no room should be given to the King for obtaining the deposition of Becket. There was an Antipope supported by the Emperor: there might be

[1] *Epist.*, *Alex. III.* Giles, i. 93.

an Archbishop who would accept the pall from that shadow, and there might be Bishops who would follow him.

The enmity between the King and Becket at length advanced to such a height, that Becket determined to excommunicate Foliot for his adherence to Henry and the English law. It was during solemn service at St. Paul's that his representative had the boldness to enter the Cathedral, to advance to the altar, and thrust the roll bearing the sentence into the hands of the officiating priest, proclaiming with a loud voice, "Know all men that Gilbert, Bishop of London, is excommunicated by Thomas, Archbishop of Canterbury." He escaped with some difficulty from the resentment of the people.

The scene in which, on a subsequent day, Foliot vindicated himself was very different. He acted with calm and unshaken dignity. Surrounded by the Dean and Canons, in the presence of the Abbot of Westminster, the Abbot of St. Augustine's, Canterbury, the Abbot of Chertsey, the Priors of many other monasteries, the Archdeacons of the diocese, and the clergy of very many churches, he took his seat before the high altar. Dwelling on the irregularity of the proceeding, he stated that he had been condemned without citation, without commonition, without hearing, without trial, in violation of a well-known canon of Pope Sixtus; and he pronounced his solemn appeal to the Pope, and recommended to His Holiness not only his own case, as that of an innocent man, but that of the Lord King and all the nobles of the realm. The Dean and Chapter joined in the petition, and most of the clergy followed their example.

It is impossible to follow in detail the long contest between Bishop Foliot and Archbishop Becket. For two or three years it was doubtful whether the Pope would confirm the excommunication or not. The Bishop had considerable influence with the Pope as treasurer for the collection, receipt and transmission of Peter's pence to London. And it was not unnatural that he should revive at this time the claims of London to archiepiscopal dignity and even the Primacy; in his appeal against Becket he says: "To him I never made either profession or obedience in the name of the Church of London; and the Church of London demands back that which in old days was wrested from her by the irruption of the pagans, that is that the Archbishopric should be at London; a demand to which we have given our approval."[1] In the end, Foliot submitted to the sentence, and refrained from entering the Cathedral. Becket's complaint against him was overshadowed by the action of Roger, Archbishop of York, in assuming the functions of the absent Primate, and crowning the King's son. We learn from the Archbishop of Rouen that Foliot laboured to promote the final reconciliation with the King, though he himself suffered in consequence, as Becket procured from Rome the condemnation both of Roger and Foliot. After the murder of Becket, Foliot received formal absolution from the excommunication from the Bishops of Nevers and Beauvais, and the Abbot of Pontigny. He took an oath that he had nothing to do with the assassination, and preached a sermon in which he made the same formal declaration on behalf of the King.[2]

How was the building of the great Cathedral proceeding among all these troubles? In one charge to his diocese, Foliot urged the duty of contributing to the completion of the fabric, begun some eighty years before by Bishop Maurice, and lagging for want of funds. In another, he urges all within his jurisdiction, by the labours, sufferings and glorious successes of their patron Saint Paul, to annual contributions and death-bed legacies. He uses that powerful argument in Roman Christianity for church-

[1] Wharton, p. 62.
[2] *Radulph de Diceto*, p. 25.

building and other pious works : liberal indulgences to the living, and masses for the souls of the dead.[1]

Reforming opinions were already being preached by certain weavers in the diocese of Worcester. The Bishop of that See wrote to Foliot to ask what he should do. Foliot recounts the opinions of the Fathers on such questions ; some were for mercy, some for punishment lest religion should perish, some for imprisoning them as madmen, some for capital punishment under the Julian law of high treason, some for burning, some (according to St. Augustine) tempered judgment to scourging and other correction short of death. Foliot offered no personal opinion, but recommended reference of the question to a synod of Bishops. He died November 18, 1187.[2]

[1] Giles, *Foliot's Letters*, i. 330.
[2] Milman's *Annals*, p. 35. Throughout this chapter I have summarized the *Annals*.

CHAPTER III

THE PAPAL LEGATES

FOLIOT'S successor was *Richard de Ely*, or *Fitz Neal*, the son of Nigellus, Bishop of Ely; whether born before or after his father's ordination is uncertain. In 1179, he had been a travelling Justiciary. The King designated him for the Bishopric of London, and summoned the Canons of St. Paul's to Normandy to carry out the election in his presence; as the King was ill, it was deferred from day to day till after his death (December 19, 1188); and the appointment was confirmed by Richard I. Milman calls him the first man of letters on the throne of London, as the author of that famous Dialogue on the Exchequer (*De Scaccario*), which throws vivid light on the history, finances and laws of England. He also wrote a Chronicle called *Tricolumnus* (three columns).

ARMS OF THE DEAN AND CHAPTER

The learned Bishop of London was matched by a learned Dean of St. Paul's, *Radulph de Diceto*. At the coronation of Richard I. at Westminster (September 2, 1189), Foliot being dead and Richard Fitz Neal not yet consecrated, Dean Radulph ministered the holy oil and chrism to the

Archbishop. He was the first Dean of St. Paul's of any note, and the first who was a man of letters. His *Imagines Historiæ* and *Abbreviatio Chronicorum* place him high amongst chroniclers. He wrote long and confidential letters on the affairs of the Church, and his opinion was valued both by the King of France and the King of England.

Milman quotes Dean Radulph on the condition of the clergy of his time, and the relation throws a lurid and terrible light on the Church of the twelfth century: "He rather deprecated the great measure of Gregory VII.—the prohibition of the marriage of the clergy. He condemned especially the licence and encouragement given to the laity to repudiate and despise the Sacraments administered by married ecclesiastics. The Sacraments, he held, had an inherent and inextinguishable virtue, which they did not lose by passing through unworthy hands. They received their mysterious power from the Holy Ghost, and could neither be enhanced by the holiness, nor impaired by the wickedness, of the ministering priest. Few of the clergy, he said, practised continence; some feigned it for the sake of gain or vainglory; on the sin of uncleanness many accumulated perjury and promiscuous adultery. But, worst of all, the laity were tempted to rebel against the clergy, and to throw off all spiritual subjection. The Holy Sacraments were frightfully profaned; marriages celebrated by married priests not held good; tithes paid to such priests wantonly burned. I cannot but suspect that the opinions of the good Dean were in some degree influenced by the state of his own Chapter. There is little doubt that the *focariæ*, so shamefully and cruelly mishandled and imprisoned by the London populace, were, some at least the wives, assuredly the hearth-warmers of the Canons of St. Paul's."[1]

Dean Radulph describes a memorable scene which took

[1] Milman's *Annals of St. Paul's*, p. 38.

place in the nave of St. Paul's on October 8, 1191. King Richard was on his Crusade: Prince John, the Archbishop of Rouen and all the Bishops met there for the arraignment of the Chancellor, William de Longchamp, Bishop of Ely, of many atrocious and tyrannous crimes, especially ill-usage of the Archbishop of York and the Bishop of Durham.

Other occurrences at the Cathedral in Richard's reign were of a very different character. It was a time of heavy exactions, partly for the King's wars, partly for Prince John's exchequer: there were bitter complaints from the poor of the unjust distribution of burthens. The popular leader was William Fitz Osbert; his platform was Paul's Cross, near the north-east wall of the choir. The evil government of John must have roused to extremity the indignation of an orator with popular sympathies: and the oaths which Fitz Osbert administered to his followers were held to be unlawful. The Cathedral itself was invaded by the rioters: frequently the services were disturbed by the cries, clamours and tumults of the discontented populace. Fitz Osbert seized the tower of a church belonging to the Archbishop (he used to have as many as twelve in his gift in the City), and stood a siege. Unable to hold out, he set fire to the church, and it was burned to the ground. Fitz Osbert was dragged from the ruins, carried to the Tower, drawn naked through the City, and burned in chains with some of his followers. The rioters gave hostages for good conduct; peace was restored to City and Cathedral, and no more was heard from Paul's Cross for many years.[1]

Dean Radulph built the Deanery, the tranquil home of many subsequent men of letters: Colet, the pioneer of the Reformation, and founder of the new St. Paul's School; after the Reformation, Alexander Nowell, Donne the Poet, Sancroft, who built the present house after the fire, Stillingfleet, Tillotson, W. Sherlock, Butler of the Analogy, Secker,

[1] Diceto, Hoveden, Lingard and others.

THE NAVE OF OLD ST. PAUL'S

[*To face p.* 28.

Newton of the Prophecies, Van Mildert, founder of Durham University, Copleston, Milman, the historian of Latin Christianity, the Jews, and St. Paul's; and Church, the cultured Tractarian leader, essayist, critic and preacher.

The episcopate of Richard Fitz Neal (or de Ely) was nearly contemporaneous with the reign of Richard I.; he died the year before the King, in 1198. He endowed St. Paul's School with the tithes of two of his manors; and he appointed the celebrated Peter of Blois Archdeacon of London. Peter writes to the Pope that like a dragon he must live on wind, for though London had 40,000 inhabitants and 120 churches, he could get neither tithes, first-fruits nor offerings.

The next Bishop, a Norman, *William de Santa Maria*, was appointed by Richard I. before his death, but his thirty-one years' rule lay chiefly in the dark days of John. He had been Canon of York, Dean of St. Martin's-le-Grand (a magnificent church where the General Post Office now stands) and Canon of St. Paul's. In 1208, he had an awful task to perform, for he was summoned to read the Pope's interdict against the whole realm of England. "He obeyed the mandate, and London with the rest of the kingdom heard the fearful office, which closed all the churches of the land to the devout worshippers, and deprived them of the prayers, the masses, the spiritual blessings and privileges of the Church."[1] Infants received hasty and imperfect baptism; marriages were hurriedly performed in the church porch; the dying were treated with maimed rites; the dead were buried in unconsecrated ground; the bells of St. Paul's were silent over the stricken city.

The one offender who had roused the vengeance of the Pope against the Church of England (the specially cherished province of the Roman obedience), King John, remained at first untouched. Against him Bishop William

[1] Milman's *Annals of St. Paul's*, p. 40.

had scruples about pronouncing the sentence, and retired for five years to the Continent. The Bishops of Ely and Worcester had been courageous enough to remonstrate against the obstinacy of the King; they also fled. Then the King, in his fury, began a fierce persecution of the clergy (1209). The sheriffs were ordered to confiscate all the revenues of refractory Bishops and Abbeys : " The clergy might go and complain to their protector the Pope." The demolition of the Bishop of London's feudal castle at Stortford was specially ordered. " The barns of the clergy were closed, and their contents confiscated to the Treasury. The concubines of the clergy were exposed to every insult and ill-usage. So writes Paris, who bitterly adds that the Bishops, London amongst them, were living abroad in luxurious abundance."[1]

Bishop William de Santa Maria went with Archbishop Langton to Rome, and with him published the sentence of deposition against King John. On John's submission, he returned to England with Langton, received £750 out of the indemnity awarded to the Bishops for their losses during the exile (representing of course a vastly greater sum according to modern value), and with them was met by their repentant Sovereign. John threw himself at their feet, imploring their mercy on himself and the realm, received absolution, and swore on the Gospels fidelity to the laws of England, and to the Lord Pope, Innocent III. Mass was sung, and was followed by a great banquet, at which King and Bishops met in amity.

Three weeks later, July 20, 1219, a great assemblage was convened in St. Paul's Cathedral, of Prelates, Abbots, Deans, Priors and Barons. During the proceedings the Archbishop led aside some of the more important personages, displayed the old charter of Henry I., solemnly urged them to stand fast for the liberties of England, and pledged himself to their support. The scene at St. Paul's

[1] M. Paris, anno 1208; Milman.

was a prelude to Runnymede; William de Santa Maria's signature is on Magna Carta.

But meantime the Pope had veered round, and become the ally of the tyrant. St. Paul's had witnessed the release of the kingdom from the interdict by the Legate, Cardinal Nicolas, Bishop of Tusculum. The Cathedral saw the same Legate ratify and complete the disgraceful scene which had just taken place in the Templars' Church at Dover: the cession of the kingdom as a fief to the Holy See. The King did homage as vassal of the Pope, the Archbishop in vain protesting, privately and in public, and groaning deeply during the ceremony itself. The reign of the Papal Legates had begun.

One more scene before the close of John's infamous reign. At a magnificent mass at St. Paul's, sung by excommunicated prelates and priests, Louis of France was hailed as the Deliverer. Receiving the homage of the citizens of London, he promised to recover to the realm all that had been lost by the pusillanimity of John. It was an unhappy alternative.

Henry III., feeble and inglorious, came to the throne in 1216, and reigned fifty-six years, dying in 1272. The episcopate of Bishop William de Santa Maria lasted till 1221. One of the first acts of the Government was to hold a Council in St. Paul's Cathedral, and to publish the great Charter in a new form (November 6, 1217).[1] On January 26, 1221, Bishop William voluntarily abdicated his See, retaining the power of wearing his episcopal robes in any church to which he might be invited, though his usual dress was that of a canon regular of St. Osyth. A brief from Pope Honorius III. gave permission for this retirement, on a pension, which consisted of three manors.

He was succeeded by *Eustace de Fauconberge*, chiefly distinguished by his descent from one of the old Norman barons, and by the high offices which he had held as

[1] Pearson, *Hist. of England*, ii. 121.

King's Justiciary, twice Ambassador in France and High Treasurer of the realm. He settled a dispute with the Abbot of Westminster about jurisdiction over certain churches, especially St. Margaret's; completed the bell-tower of the Cathedral and laid the foundation of the choir. To his custody was committed Fulk de Beauté, the great freebooting rebel, who played an important part in the wars at the end of John's reign, and in the beginning of that of Henry III. During his time another great Council was held in St. Paul's, under the presidency of Cardinal Stephen Langton as Primate, for the purpose of granting and assessing a subsidy to the King, which the Lord Pope had graciously permitted the Province of Canterbury to vote, and which he had enjoined as an act of goodwill to the Sovereign.[1]

Eustace de Fauconberge was succeeded by *Roger Niger* (the Black), in 1229, described by Matthew Paris as "profound in letters, honourable and praiseworthy in all things, a lover and defender of religion, without pride, venerable for his life, and of admirable sanctity, famous for his knowledge and a perspicuous preacher." He was, says Milman, of the high English party, jealous of all foreign encroachments, jealous above all of the foreigners, who either for their own emolument, or as tribute to Rome, sent abroad the wealth of the land. These were principally bankers, agents of the Pope, branded nevertheless as usurers and extortioners, as all usury, according to ecclesiastical teaching, was wicked and unchristian.

Stowe describes the action of Bishop Roger in strong terms: "Roger Niger admonished the usurers of his time to leave such enormities, as they tendered the salvation of their souls, and to do penance for what they had committed. But after he saw they laughed him to scorn, and also threatened him, the Bishop generally excommunicated and accursed all such, and demanded strictly that such usurers

[1] A.D. 1224, Wilkins, i. 602.

should depart further from the City of London, which had hitherto been ignorant of such mischief and wickedness, lest his diocese should be infected therewithal."[1] In 1230, the people rose and burned the barns and warehouses of the foreigners. The Bishop's hostile attitude to the usurers offended the Pope, under whose protection they lived, and he was compelled to journey to Rome to defend his conduct, nor did he return without a heavy fine. Nothing daunted, he again excommunicated the money-lenders, and was once more involved in troubles with Rome, where they obtained full freedom for plunder.

In 1232, St. Paul's Cathedral witnessed the humiliating scene of a Papal Legate occupying his throne as Dictator over the Clergy of England, with the Bishops and Abbots at his feet. The Legate was Otho the White, Cardinal Deacon of St. Nicolas in Carcere Tulliano, who had been invited by King Henry III., now entirely controlled by the foreigners in his Court, and by a faction of prelates headed by Peter de la Roche, Bishop of Winchester. The Primate, Edmund Rich, had remonstrated in the strongest language, moved by indignation at the growing exactions of the Pope. A more serious cause of complaint was the filling of the richer benefices in England with foreign, chiefly Italian, Churchmen. In earlier days, Rich had sided with Becket against King Henry II.; now he frequently remonstrated with Henry III. for his weakness, subservience and injustice. Finally, like Becket, he fled into exile.

The Legate had been received with the utmost honours. Great bales of scarlet cloth met him at Paris. On the English shore the King met him and did homage. He was loaded with still more costly gifts—palfreys, precious vessels, soft and rich vestments, furs; fifty fat oxen, a hundred measures of fine flour, eight casks of the choicest wines were sent by the Bishop of Winchester.

The Legate ordered a lofty platform to be erected in the

[1] Strype's *Stowe*, vol. ii. p. 119.

nave of St. Paul's; the choir was not yet finished. Here he summoned before him the two Archbishops and all their suffragans, with the Abbots, Priests and Proctors from monasteries and chapters. In those superstitious days omens were closely observed; and the omens were appalling. When, before the opening of the Council, the Legate and ecclesiastics were at their devotions in the Cathedral, the Church was struck by a furious hurricane. It continued in its rage for fifteen days; on the night of the Feast of St. Cecilia clouds like towers rolled over the Church, thunders and lightnings broke over the roof. On a dark and dreary November day (the 20th) the Council met. The first day was occupied with searching the records and statutes; on the second, the Cardinal made his way through the throng of followers and horses which had accompanied the distant travellers and filled the precincts; he was met by sullen discontent, and, in place of acclamations, by hardly suppressed murmurs; two hundred of the King's Guards had been secretly posted for his protection. As the distinguished figure of the Legate, representing the unity and supreme authority of the Western Church, and loaded with rich furs against the chill damp climate, was led to the great west doors, he was met by a long procession, with tapers, music and Litany. He proceeded up the Church, and arrayed himself before the high altar in his gorgeous vestments. Then he ascended the lofty platform in the nave, adorned with splendid tapestry, and took his seat on the throne. On his right was the Primate, next to him Bishop Roger of London; on his left the Archbishop of York, according to a scale of precedence determined by the Legate himself.

Then came the sermon, the first of which we have any report in St. Paul's. The Cardinal lifted up his voice "like a trumpet," and preached on Rev. iv. 6: "In the midst of the throne, and round about the throne were four living creatures, full of eyes before and behind." The living creatures were the prelates of the Church, whose vigilant eyes ought to be everywhere and on all sides. After the sermon, the Legate promulgated the canons which were to form the law of the Church in England. An episode that occurred strongly illustrates the spiritual standpoint of the Bishops of the Middle Ages, and the nature of such opposition as they ventured to offer to the Pope. "When the Legate came to the thirteenth canon, which required a dispensation from the Pope to hold pluralities, there was a low and ominous murmur. Then rose Walter de Cantilupe, Bishop of Worcester. Cantilupe was a high-born, not unworldly, prelate; if judged from his own Constitutions, full of zeal for the authority and discipline of the Church, inclining to austerity rather than to laxity; his noble character was afterwards fully revealed, when he stood by the side of Simon de Montfort in all the vicissitudes of his more glorious and of his adverse fortune. The Bishop of Worcester took off his mitre and, in the name of the clergy of England, made his solemn protest. 'Many of the prelates of England were men of high birth. They had been wont, by holding many benefices, to maintain their dignity, to show generous hospitality, and to be prodigal in almsdeeds. Some were old; they would not consent to be robbed of their income, and reduced to ignominious poverty. Some were young and bold, and would endure a hard struggle before they would surrender their rights. For himself, before he was a Bishop, he had made a firm resolution not to be so plundered. He adhered to his resolution. Let the Pope reconsider this, and be more wisely counselled.' Worcester's speech was received with loud and renewed applause. The Legate, overawed, consented to withdraw the obnoxious canon for the further consideration of the Pope. On a subsequent day the Earl of Lincoln and William Roule, Canon of St. Paul's, protested in the name of the Sovereign against anything being done to the prejudice of the Crown and the royal dignity."[1]

Milman's *Annals*, p. 50.

Other canons were strong against the married clergy, and against the abuse by which benefices, as was common in those days, descended from father to son; and on the dress of the clergy, which had become military rather than ecclesiastical. Otho's Constitutions were before many years superseded by those of another Papal Legate, Cardinal Ottobuoni.

Another story of this powerful Legate must not be omitted, as it ends at St. Paul's. "The Cardinal Legate had taken up his residence in the Abbey of Osney (to deal with the University of Oxford). He was supplied with provisions by the scholars. Certain of these desired to pay their respectful homage to the Legate. The insolent porter shut the door in their faces. The indignant scholars burst in. Just at that moment a poor Irish priest stood soliciting alms. The clerk of the kitchen, instead of alms, threw a bucket of scalding water in his face. The hot blood of a Welsh scholar boiled up. The scholars were armed. The Welshman shot the clerk of the kitchen dead. The clerk was the kinsman, it was said the brother, of the Legate, whose office was to taste the meat before the Cardinal. A fierce fray began; the three nations, Irish, Welsh and English, fell on the Italians. The Legate with difficulty made his escape to Abingdon. Thirty of the ringleaders of the riot were seized by the authorities, and committed to Wallingford jail. But the wrath of the Legate was not appeased. He pronounced his interdict against the University and excommunicated all the guilty scholars. From Abingdon Otho removed to the house of the Bishop of Durham in London. The Mayor was commanded by the King to watch over him as the 'apple of his eye.' The Legate summoned the Bishops, to complain of the affront. The University cowered under the interdict. Probably by the invitation of the Bishop they assembled at St. Paul's, and set forth in sad and solemn array along the streets to the Strand, to throw themselves at the Legate's feet. Many Bishops who had been educated at Oxford joined the procession. They walked, says Fuller, not a short Italian, but a long English, mile on foot, bare-headed, without their cloaks; the Bishops in humble attire. The Legate was appeased, and removed the interdict."[1]

These must have been difficult days for so able and independent a man as Bishop Roger, who forced Henry III. to restore his fallen chancellor, Hubert de Burgh, to the sanctuary from which he had been dragged, and finally to full liberty. His influence consolidated the provisions for the maintenance of the London clergy; he obtained a law, assented to by the Common Council, that the citizens should pay a certain assessment in the pound on their property, as offerings to the clergy. This constitution, more than once confirmed by Primates and Popes, and finally ratified by Pope Nicolas V., was fully maintained till the Fire of London. As many of the churches then destroyed were not revived, an Act of Parliament rearranged these dues.

Bishop Roger earnestly pushed forward the lagging work of the completion and endowment of his vast Cathedral. But the magnificence of the fabric exhausted his resources and those of the Diocese. During the episcopate of his five successors, briefs were issued to the whole of England to ask alms for this great national work, to be repaid by proportional Indulgences.[2] When we admire our sublime cathedrals, amongst other reasons, as monuments of an age of faith now passed away, it is but just to remember this amazing method of providing for their cost. The system culminated in the building of St. Peter's at Rome, when Tetzel's sale of this strange ecclesiastical commodity awoke the spirit of Luther, and brought the Reformation to birth.[3]

[1] Milman's *Annals*, p. 52; Fuller, ii. 170, Oxf. Ed.
[2] Newcourt's *London, Life of Roger*.
[3] I am indebted to Milman for the information in this chapter.

CHAPTER IV

THE PAPAL LEGATES (*continued*)

A GLIMPSE is given of the revenues of the See of London at this time by the fact that during the vacancy after the death of Bishop Roger, out of the funds escheated to the Crown, Henry III. ordered that on the Festival of the Conversion of St. Paul, fifteen hundred poor should be feasted in the churchyard, and fifteen hundred lights offered in the Cathedral. Bishop Roger was canonized by popular acclamation, and his tomb in the south aisle visited by thousands of devout worshippers; for these visits, Indulgences were again granted. He died at his manor of Stepney, September 29, 1241. Stepney, as well as other episcopal manors, was a "peculiar" of the Bishop of London, that is, the ecclesiastical fees were collected for the Bishop by his commissary, and did not pertain to the Archdeacon. An end was put to this anomalous arrangement a few years ago, when an Order in Council placed all the parishes in the diocese on the same footing.

Henry III. now tried to force Peter, Bishop of Hereford, into the vacant See. The Canons, however, proceeded to the election of *Fulk Basset*, of Norman descent, Dean of York. The dispute was not settled for three years, and was ended by the consecration of Fulk Basset on October 29, 1244. In less than two years the new Bishop was called to enforce the tyrannical demand made by Pope Innocent IV., of one-third of their ecclesiastical income from the resident clergy, half from the non-resident. The demand was clenched by what Matthew Paris calls that "detestable" phrase *non obstante*, which swept away all privileges and exceptions. In consequence, Bishop Fulk held a Council at St. Paul's, when it appeared that the Pope's new exaction was too much even for the obsequious Henry III., in whose name appeared Sir John de Lexington and Master Lawrence of St. Martin's, the King's clerk, absolutely prohibiting compliance. A noteworthy reply was returned to Rome: "If the Pope had known the state and condition of the kingdom of England, he would never have promulgated such a statute. In cathedral churches it was the usage that non-resident Canons performed their functions by minor Canons. If half their revenues were cut off, the duties of the Cathedral could not be performed, as they could not maintain the minor Canons, nor with so large a portion of their income in default could they themselves reside. After deducting the expenses of collection and other burdens, hardly a fourth part would remain. So would hospitality altogether become impossible; alms to the poor would cease; those who could not dig and were ashamed to beg, would perish with hunger, or take to robbery and pillage."[1] The remonstrance ended with a significant appeal to a General Council shortly to be held. The Pope was going so far as to rebuke Henry III. for making grants to Bishops and Barons, "to the grave prejudice of the Roman Church, to which the kingdom of England is well known to belong, and to the enormous injury of the same kingdom."[2]

In 1250, Bishop Fulk was brought into violent antagonism with the Primate. After the death of the unworldly and sainted Edmund Rich, the opponent of the Legate Otho, and of Henry III. himself, the King and the Pope had compelled the monks of Canterbury to elect a foreigner, Boniface of Savoy, Lay Bishop of Bellay, uncle to Queen Eleanor of Provence, and brother of Philip of

[1] M. Paris, A.D. 1246; Wilkins' *Concilia*, i. 686.
[2] *MS. Brit. Mus.*, vol. iv. p. 73.

Savoy, the warlike and mitred bodyguard of Innocent IV., who became Archbishop of Lyons. Boniface was elected in 1241, but not confirmed by the Pope till 1244. At the time of his appointment he was not in holy orders. Among the Papal letters in the British Museum is one which authorizes his suffragans to admit him to the diaconate and the priesthood; the Province and Convocation of Canterbury were then under excommunication; the late Primate had fled to Pontigny; on condition of a promise of obedience to this strange successor, the excommunication was relaxed. The newly made ecclesiastic, proud, handsome and worldly, found that Edmund had been a sore saint for the revenues. Canterbury was loaded with an enormous debt, and Boniface had no intention of presiding in an impoverished Primacy. He obtained a grant from the Pope of first-fruits from all the benefices in his province, by which he raised a vast sum. "Six years afterwards, the Primate announced and set forth on a visitation of his province, not, as it was said, and as it too plainly appeared, for the glory of God, but in quest of ungodly gain. Bishops, chapters, monasteries must submit to this unusual discipline, haughtily and rapaciously enforced by a foreigner. From Feversham and Rochester he extorted large sums. He appeared in London, treating the Bishop (Fulk Basset of the old noble Norman house) with contempt. The Dean of St. Paul's (Henry de Cornhill), stood by his Bishop. The Primate appeared with his cuirass gleaming under his episcopal robes. The Dean closed the doors of his Cathedral against him. Boniface solemnly excommunicated the Dean and his Chapter in the name of St. Thomas-the-Martyr of Canterbury. At St. Bartholomew's, Smithfield (the Prior was dead), the Sub-prior fared still worse. He calmly pleaded the rights of the Bishop; the wrathful Primate rushed on the old man, struck him down with his own hand, tore his splendid vestment, and trampled it under foot. The Bishop of London was involved in the excommunication of the Dean and Chapter. On the appeal of the Dean of St. Paul's to the Pope, the excommunication was suspended. But Boniface himself proceeded in great pomp to Rome. The uncle of the Queen of England, the now wealthy Primate, could not but obtain favour with Innocent. The Dean of St. Paul's was compelled to submit to the supreme archiepiscopal authority."[1]

A third contest in which Bishop Fulk was involved was in 1255, with another Legate, the Gascon Rustand. He had to resist almost alone the united authority of Henry III. and the Pope. The Primate, Boniface, was on the continent; the See of York was vacant; Winchester, a Poitevin, was on the King's side, and therefore with Rustand. At a Council in St. Paul's, Rustand exhibited his full powers as Legate. "On learning the exorbitant demand of Rustand, a tenth on England, Scotland and Ireland, Bishop Fulk cried aloud: 'Before I submit the Church to such slavery, I will lay my head on the block.' Bishop Cantilupe of Worcester, in less dignified phrase, said: 'I will be hanged first.' Rustand hastened to the King to denounce the Bishop as a rebel. The King heaped abuse upon the Bishop, and threatened him with Papal censure. The Norman replied, 'The Pope and the King may take away my Bishopric, which, however, they cannot legally do; they may strip me of my mitre, I shall still wear my helmet.'" In his later days he espoused the cause of the Barons, and his name appears affixed to the provisions of the Parliament of Oxford. He died of the plague in A.D. 1259. In that year two Canons, who had been forced into the Chapter of St. Paul's by the Pope, when endeavouring to instal themselves, were killed by the populace. Fulk Basset is described by Matthew Paris as a "man noble, and of great generosity; though

[1] Milman's *Annals*, p. 57; Matt. Paris, A.D. 1241-4, 1250, 1256; *MS. Brit. Mus.*, vi. 347, 383; vol. vii. 16, 57; *ibid.*, A.D. 1242.

he once stumbled, he had been the anchor and shield of stability to the whole kingdom."[1]

The next Bishop was a pluralist on a heroic scale, *Henry de Wingham*, or Wengham, who was Lord Chancellor when the See became vacant. He was obliged to take priest's orders in order to qualify himself for the Bishopric. He had Papal licence to hold the Deanery of St. Martin's-le-Grand in London, the Chancellorship of Exeter, a prebend of Salisbury, and all his other parsonages, even benefices. A month after obtaining this decree, De Wingham, as Bishop of London, petitioned to hold all these preferments, with the See, for five years. He does not seem to have ceased to be Chancellor; but death stepped in, and in less than three years stripped him of everything (1259–1262).

In the weakness of such kings as John and Henry III., the Popes saw their opportunity for riveting an ecclesiastical yoke on England which became intolerable. During the vacancy on the death of De Wingham, a Bull of Pope Urban IV. was read at Paul's Cross, absolving Henry III. from the oaths which he had taken to observe the provisions of the Parliament of Oxford. Orders were sent to the Chapter of St. Paul's to elect an Italian, John de Ebulo, to the Deanery; on the resistance of the Canons, the case was entrusted to the decision of a Cardinal; De Ebulo was satisfied with a Canonry and certain pensions.[2] Paul's Cross, it should be here noted, had become the place for the publication both of civil and ecclesiastical edicts, and of assembly for the citizens of London on their own affairs. The story of Paul's Cross, however, is of such importance that it should be told in a separate chapter.

The successor of Henry de Wingham was *Henry de Sandwith*, elected November 12, 1262. Richard Talbot, Dean of St. Paul's, had previously been elected, but died on the day of his confirmation. The new Bishop needed long

[1] Wharton, p. 94. [2] *MS. Brit. Mus.*, A.D. 1264.

journeys to perform the steps necessary to his appointment, as he had to seek the King in France, and the Primate, Boniface, in Savoy, and was not consecrated till May, 1263. With the Mayor FitzThomas and the citizens of London, he joined Simon de Montfort and the Barons in the great rising in defence of the liberties of England. A new Legate, Ugo Falcodi, who had been dispatched from Rome to deal with the disturbed state of the country, to restore the authority of the King and Pope, and to annul the Provisions of Oxford, was arrested at Boulogne, and forbidden to cross the Channel. He had already launched his excommunication against the Cinque Ports and the City of London, when he was summoned to Rome to become Pope under the title of Clement IV. He never forgot the rebuff which he had received at Boulogne, and in 1265 suspended Henry de Sandwith. "In the following year, the Bishop of London and three other prelates were solemnly excommunicated at Northampton. The Pope ratified the ban. No favour was to be shown to the Bishops of Worcester, London, Lincoln and Ely; they were on no account to be released from excommunication. De Sandwith was obliged to journey to Rome to obtain absolution. He lingered, or was detained there, six years in exile. At length he wrung forth his slow pardon from Pope Gregory V. In the pardon his crimes were duly recited. He had favoured the Barons with his counsel; he had celebrated divine service in London when under suspension by Cardinal Hadrian, and in despite of the excommunication; he had communicated with excommunicated persons. He had lately shown good conduct and devout penitence. Full pardon and absolution were granted by the Holy Father. De Sandwith returned to England in 1273, after the accession of Edward I. He returned to die—not to preside, but to be buried, in his Cathedral."[1] During the suspension the episcopal patronage was in the

[1] Milman's *Annals*, p. 63.

hands of the Archdeacon of Colchester (who afterwards declined the Bishopric) and Godfrey, Canon of St. Dunstan's.

Yet another Legate arrives. "It was during the absence of Bishop Sandwith at Rome, after the battle of Evesham, and the death of Simon de Montfort, at the close of the Baron's War, that the Cardinal Legate Ottobuoni appeared in the greatest pomp at St. Paul's, having summoned all the prelates and dignitaries of the first and second orders throughout the realm. There, in the Cathedral of the metropolis, he promulgated and caused to be read, in the presence of a great multitude, the famous Constitutions. These Constitutions, enlarging and confirming those of Cardinal Otho, became the code of ecclesiastical law in England for several centuries, down to the Reformation. The code was fully and distinctly proclaimed in all its solemnity. The Legate is said to have heard with patience the objections and appeals of the assembled ecclesiastical Parliament or Council. The Legate assumed, in the name of the Pope, full legislative powers, not only over England, but over Wales, Scotland and Ireland."[1]

The next Bishop, *John de Chishull,* was, like Henry de Wingham, an example of pluralism. He had been Provost of Beverley, Archdeacon of London, Dean of St. Paul's, High Treasurer and Chancellor of the Exchequer. He fell into ill-health, and Archbishop Peckham entrusted his patronage partly to the Dean and Treasurer of St. Paul's, partly to the Archdeacon of Colchester. He was Bishop during seven years, from 1273 to 1280.

The Canons, who seem on this occasion to have been left in peace, elected Fulk Lovel, Archdeacon of Colchester, another pluralist. On the same day he refused the Bishopric, alleging bodily weakness and scruples of conscience. Archbishop Peckham, in a letter, rebuked the Archdeacon for his modesty, or his interested motives. He was said to hold no less than twenty benefices.

[1] Milman's *Annals*, p. 64.

On the refusal of Fulk Lovel, *Richard de Gravesend* was appointed, and held the See for twenty-three years, from 1280 to 1303. In his time the Dean of St. Paul's, *William de Montfort*, was appointed to represent the clergy before Edward I. in their resistance to his demand of the moiety of their income as a subsidy. Hardly had he spoken, when he fell dead at the King's feet. In place of the exactions of the Pope the clergy now had to put up with the exactions of the King. "Two years after, when the taxation of the clergy was more imperiously urged, Archbishop Winchelsey, in a letter addressed to Bishop de Gravesend, commanded him to summon a congregation of the whole clergy to St. Paul's. To the Bishop of London, too, the Primate addressed another letter, fiercely denunciatory of all the impious men who, in defiance of the decrees of the Lateran Council, should presume to invade the property of the Church, and of the clergy who should submit to such sacrilegious taxation. He commanded the Bishop to publish in his Cathedral the Bull of the Pope (we are in the high days of Boniface VIII.), which excommunicated all emperors, kings or barons who should dare to exact any payment of any kind on account of Church property, and any ecclesiastic of any rank down to the lowest, who should make any payment whatever, under whatsoever pretext. Having thus declared war against the King in the sermon, before the Pax Domini there were to be special prayers for peace."[1] Edward I. knew how to deal with his refractory clergy, notwithstanding that the Dominican Friars appeared in St. Paul's to challenge all who would contest the Papal authority.

Two years later another sturdy protest was made against the royal demands. "Bishop Richard addressed the Dean and Chapter of St. Paul's, reciting the mandate of Robert, Archbishop of Canterbury, but with a remarkable addition. The King had issued his orders that twice in the year, on

[1] Milman's *Annals*, p. 56.

the Feast of All Souls and on Palm Sunday, should be read in all cathedrals and parish churches the Great Charter and the Forest Charter, with a penalty of the greater excommunication against all who should violate these statutes. The two Archbishops and other Bishops assembled at Westminster had agreed to that publication in the vulgar tongue. After this, the mandate returns to the Lateran Council and the Bull of Pope Boniface, which excommunicated with bell, book and candle all who should lay their impious hands on the property of the Church or the persons of the clergy. Bishop Richard declared that, health permitting, and no obstacle intervening, he himself, on the appointed days, would read the excommunication of the violators of the Charter and the invaders of Church property; and that on those occasions the usual processions would take place in St. Paul's."[1]

Two more letters of the Archbishop to Bishop Richard de Gravesend illustrate the temper of the times. One complains that the Archbishop of York had had the audacity to have his cross borne before him in the province of Canterbury, and to give the people his benediction. The Bishop is enjoined to inhibit all in his diocese from doing honour to, or receiving blessings from, the usurping prelate. The other asks the sanction of the King to close all the synagogues of the Jews in London except one.[2]

The Bishop died December 9, 1306. In the archives of St. Paul's is preserved the catalogue of his property attached to his will, as proved in the Archbishop's Court. It measures twenty-eight feet in length by one in breadth. The value at the time was nearly £3000, and should be multiplied by fifteen to bring it up to the present standard, making about £45,000. The items include plate, the belongings of his chapel, jewels, robes, bed-furniture, carpets, kitchen, butlery, horses, coach, arms (a single sword, not as

---

[1] Milman's *Annals*, p. 67.
[2] Wilkins, ii. pp. 235, 243.

now, two in saltire), wine and wardrobe, which contained his books. The list of the latter is the most interesting part of the inventory, and consisted of about ninety-two volumes, including several Bibles. It was valued at £116, which would now be equivalent to about £1740. He had twenty-seven horses.

During the fifty-six years of the fourteenth century which elapsed from the death of Bishop Richard de Gravesend to that of Bishop Michael de Northburg in 1362, nearly at the end of the reign of Edward III., seven Bishops occupied the See of London, but left little mark. Most of them were benefactors to the Bishopric and the Cathedral, but the annals of St. Paul's are barren of great events. No thanksgiving is recorded for Crecy or Poitiers. *Bishop Ralph de Baldock* (1306-1313) had been Dean of St. Paul's, was Lord Chancellor, and wrote a history of Great Britain from the earliest times to his own day, which had been seen by Leland, and a book on the Statutes and Customs of St. Paul's.[1] In his time (1307) the Dean and Chapter of St. Paul's presented a petition for the canonization of Hugh Grostete, Bishop of Lincoln;[2] and a Provincial Council about the Templars met in St. Paul's (1309); the Bishop afterwards sat in judgment on them. *Gilbert de Segrave*, a theological writer, held the See only four years (1313-1317); *Richard de Newport* only one. *Stephen de Gravesend* (1339-1398) was nephew of Bishop Richard. A list remains of what his seneschal, Almeric, Earl of Pembroke, paid to Archbishop Walter for his consecration: a vast quantity of linen, tapers and candles, 200 loaves, 6 larger barrels of wine, 36 smaller, 1 ox, 1 hog, 4 calves, 24 rabbits, 36 chickens and capons, 50 other articles of food,[3] 200 larks, hay for 160 horses for two nights and other provender.[4] He afterwards protested against the right of the Archbishop of Canterbury to hold a visitation

[1] Wilkins, ii. p. 237.   [2] *Ibid.*, 304.
[3] "*Cercel et beket.*"   [4] Wharton, *Life of Bishop Stephen.*

of St. Paul's, and carried his appeal to Rome, but unsuccessfully.

In Bishop Stephen's time (A.D. 1327), "in the sad days of Edward II.'s reign, St. Paul's witnessed more than one terrible scene, no less than the murder of a Bishop, almost within its walls. The King had committed the custody of the City of London to Walter Stapleton, Bishop of Exeter, the Lord High Treasurer. A letter from the Queen (Isabella of France) was affixed to the Cross in Cheapside, imploring the citizens in pathetic words to rise in the common cause for the defence of their country (against the King's favourites). The Bishop demanded the keys of the City from the Mayor. The citizens seized the Mayor,[1] and compelled him solemnly to swear to obey their orders. A cry rose, 'Death to the Queen's enemies!' They fell on one Marshall, a servant of the younger De Spencer, and cut off his head. Thence to the Bishop of Exeter's palace, burst the gates, and plundered the jewels, plate and household goods. The Bishop had been taking a quiet ride in the fields. He endeavoured to find sanctuary in the Church of St. Paul's. He reached the north door, was torn from his horse, dragged into Cheapside, proclaimed a traitor, and beheaded, and with him two of his servants. The rioters then dragged the body to the foot of a tower which he was building near the Thames, and threw it into the river."[2]

On the deposition of Edward II., Bishop Stephen refused to admit the justice of the sentence, and was ill-used by the populace for his fidelity. After the death of the unhappy King (September 21, 1327), Edmond, Earl of Kent (son of Edward I. by Margaret of France), William, Archbishop

[1] I am indebted to Sir William Soulsby, K.C.B., Secretary to the Lord Mayor, that the first Mayor of London who was granted the prefix of "Lord" was Thomas Legge, ancestor of the Earls of Dartmouth, who served the office in A.D. 1354.
[2] Milman's *Annals*, p. 71.

of York, and Bishop Stephen were accused of conspiring to spread rumours that he was still alive; Edmond was beheaded, and the prelates were convicted of high treason, and only pardoned in 1336 by Act of Parliament.

Great interest attaches to *Simon of Sudbury* (Bishop from 1362 to 1375), as showing an early glimmer of reforming opinions. He had spent many years at the Papal Court at Avignon, under Innocent VI., the best and greatest of the Avignon Popes, when the Papal Court "had thrown off, for a time at least, its evil fame for unrivalled profligacy."[1] Simon had been chaplain to the Pope, and was Archbishop of Canterbury from 1375 to 1381. Wharton quotes William Chartham, a monk of Canterbury, to the effect that in the midst of a vast multitude of pilgrims wending their way in profound devotion to the shrine of St. Thomas in Canterbury, the Bishop rebuked them for their superstitious folly, and told them that their hopes of the promised plenary indulgence were vain and idle. Reproaches were heaped upon Sudbury by the extreme ecclesiastical party of his day, who said that his murder was a just judgment for his lenity to the Wycliffites. He was beheaded on Tower Hill by the rabble in Wat Tyler's rebellion, in his capacity of Chancellor. He died imploring the mercy of God on his assassins.

Milman's *Annals*, p. 72.

CHAPTER V

THE COMPLETION OF OLD ST. PAUL'S

THIS is the proper place to give an account of the progress of the Norman and Gothic building till it was finished about the end of the thirteenth century, in the reign of Edward I. It is difficult to estimate exactly the amount of damage done by "the dreadful fire in the very first year of King Stephen's reign (A.D. 1136), which began at London Bridge and raged as far as the Church of the Danes (St. Clement's)."[1] The chroniclers Matthew Paris and Matthew of Westminster seem to imply total destruction; but though that is probably an exaggeration, the repairs or reconstruction must have caused great delay.

Nearly two hundred years passed from the foundation-stone of Bishop Maurice (about A.D. 1086) to the final triumph. Meantime pointed architecture had been evolved out of Norman, and in its turn increased in charm. "The Quire was not thought beautiful enough," says Dugdale, "though in uniformity of building it suited with the Church; so that, resolving to make a better, they began with the steeple, which was finished in A.D. 1221; and then going on with the Quire, according to the like form of architecture, perfected it in 1240."[2] As at Lincoln, the choir grew in splendour of design as years passed, the finest compartments dating from an addition begun eastwards.

The repairs of the rest of the building seem meanwhile to have made but little progress, for in 1255, one hundred and twenty years after the fire of King Stephen, Bishop

[1] Dugdale, p. 7.   [2] *Ibid.*, p. 12.

OLD ST. PAUL'S, FROM SOUTH-EAST

[*From a drawing by Hollar.*]

[*To face p.* 50.

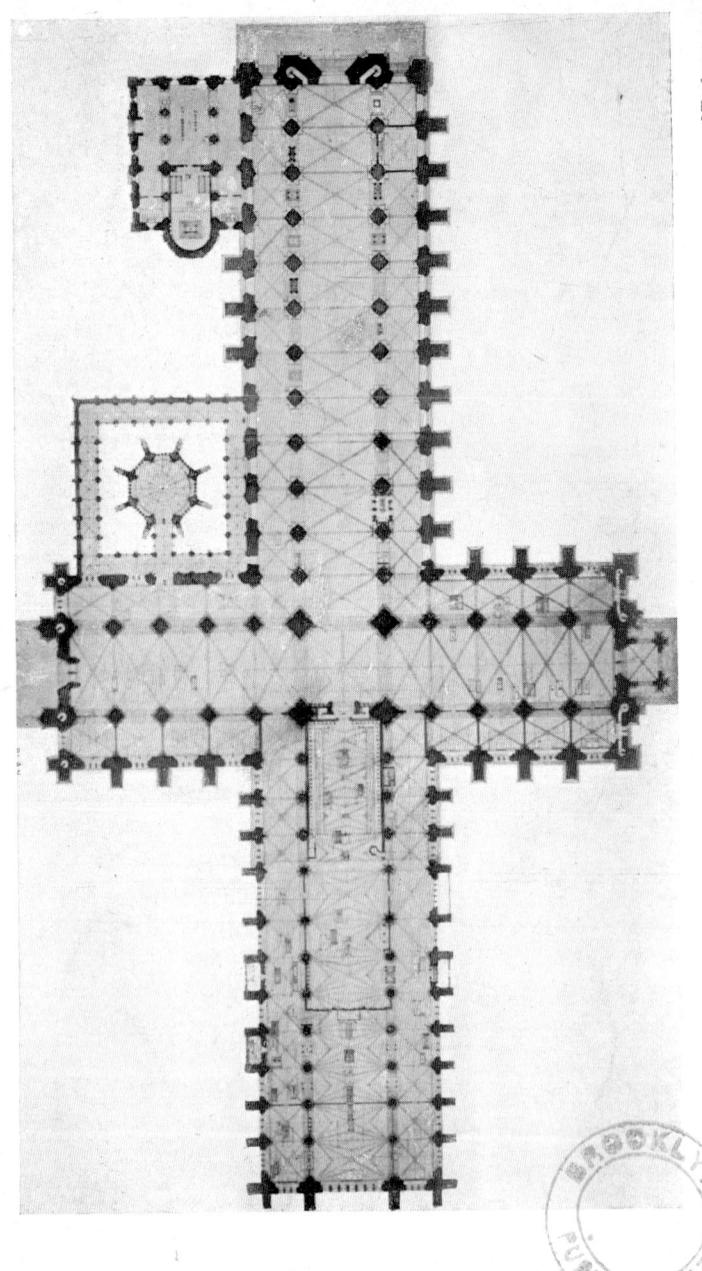

GROUND PLAN, OLD ST. PAUL'S

THE COMPLETION OF OLD ST. PAUL'S

Fulk Basset " issued letters hortatory, to stir up the people to liberal contributions, because that the Church of St. Paul was in time past so shattered by tempests, that the whole roof thereof seemed very ruinous." [1] In consequence of this appeal the roof was made good, and the Cathedral, as Dugdale says, was then lengthened eastward "by the whole extent of that which now bears the name of St. Faith's Church." [2]

Traces of this alteration were found by Sir Christopher Wren when making preparations for the present Cathedral. " Upon demolishing the ruins," says his grandson, " after the last fire, and searching the foundations of this Quire, the surveyor (Wren) discovered nine wells in a row, which no doubt had anciently belonged to a street of houses that lay aslope from the High Street (then Watling Street) to the Roman Causeway (now Cheapside); and this street which was taken away to make room for the new Quire, came so near to the old Presbyterium that the Church could not extend farther that way at first." [3]

At length, about the year 1283, the Cathedral seems to have been nearly completed, for " about this time it seems that the main brunt was over." [4] The pavement of what was called "the New Work," namely, east from the steeple, " made of good and firm marble which cost fivepence the foot" was laid down in 1312, and "within three years afterwards a great part of the spire of timber, covered with lead, being weak and in danger of falling, was taken down, and a new cross, with a pommel, large enough to contain ten bushels of corn, well gilt, set on the top thereof by Gilbert de Segrave, then Bishop of London, with great and solemn procession, and relics of saints were placed within it." [5] This lofty and most magnificent spire (reputed at that time to be the highest in the world), rose from the centre of a great stone tower. According to Wren's

---

[1] Dugdale, p. 14. [2] Ibid. [3] Wren's *Parentalia*, p. 272.
[4] Dugdale, p. 15. [5] *Ibid.*, pp. 16, 17.

measurements before the Great Fire, the tower itself was 260 feet in height, the base of the spire 40 feet, and "therefore according to the usual proportion of spires in Gothick fabricks, which was four diameters, or five at most, it could rise no higher than 200 feet, and make the whole altitude not to exceed 460 feet to the Ball of copper gilt and Cross, upon which, after the first fire by lightning, was added a weathercock representing an eagle, of copper gilt likewise. The Ball was in circumference 9 feet 1 inch; the height of the Cross from the Ball 15 feet 6 inches, and its traverse 5 feet 10 inches. The Eagle from the bill to the tail 4 feet, the breadth over the wings 3 feet and a half."[1] Wren's calculation is by the probability of proportion; Stow and Dugdale make the height considerably greater; but even Wren's estimate is fifty feet higher than the spire of Salisbury.

The difficulty of raising the money was considerable, though the area of contributions included Scotland and Ireland as well as England. "I shall now demonstrate," says Dugdale, "how most of the charge in carrying on so great a work became supported, which, in brief, was by the alms of good people, throughout both the realms of England and Ireland, whose fervent devotion to the advancement of God's service incited them most willingly to further all works of this nature."[2] They were stirred to this by letters of indulgence, "and that this was the way by which they herein proceeded to raise monies, the sundry letters of the several Bishops of both nations to the clergy under their charge, for recommendation of the business to their particular congregations is most evident; a multitude whereof I have seen and read" (a boxful of these is still preserved at St. Paul's): "by which letters there are indulgences extending to a certain number of days for such penance as they had injunction to perform." "Nay, not only the contributors to this glorious structure were thus favoured, but the

---

[1] *Parentalia*, p. 274.   [2] Dugdale, pp. 12, 13.

[*To face p.* 52.

OLD ST. PAUL'S

solicitors for contributions and the very mechanics themselves who laboured therein."[1]

The Cathedral group of buildings was surrounded by a wall of considerable extent. It rose originally from the moat of the Palatine Tower, by leave of Henry I.[2] It passed from the north-eastern corner of Ave Maria Lane, eastward along Paternoster Row to the end of Old Change in Cheapside, whence it ran southward to Carter Lane, and thence to Creed Lane and Ludgate on the west. In the Cathedral wall were six gatehouses, the chief of which stood in Ludgate, near the end of Creed Lane, opening on the west front of the Cathedral; the second was in Paternoster Row at Paul's Alley; the third at Canon Alley; the fourth, called the Little Gate, was an entrance from Cheapside; the fifth, or St. Augustine's Gate, led from Watling Street into the Cathedral precinct by an entry called High Street, which was considered to be the King's Highway; and the sixth gatehouse fronted the south porch of the Church, near what is now called Paul's Chain, from the ponderous chain which once hung across this passage to the entrance. The Bishop's palace stood at the north-west corner of the churchyard,[3] and the Chapter House, built in 1332, which was only 32 feet 6 inches in internal diameter, was on the south side of the body of the Church, in the very centre of the Cloister Garth, on the site of the garden belonging to the Dean and Chapter.[4] On the north side of the churchyard was a burial vault (or charnel house) over which a chapel was built.[5] "The citizens claimed the east part of the churchyard to be the place of assembly to their folk-motes, and that the great steeple there situate was to that use their common bell, which being there rung, all the inhabitants of the City might hear and come together. They also claimed the west side, that they might there assemble themselves

[1] Dugdale, p. 15.   [2] *Ibid.*, p. 7.   [3] Winkle's *Cathedrals*, i. 66.
[4] Dugdale, p. 120.   [5] *Ibid.* p. 131.

together, with the Lord of Baynard's Castle, for the view (review) of their armour (armed bands) in defence of the City." [1]

The wall seems not to have been completed till the year 1285. "Upon information made to King Edward I., that by the lurking of thieves and other bad people, in the night time, within the precincts of the Churchyard, divers robberies, homicides and fornications had been committed therein; for the prevention of the like for the future, the said King, by his patent bearing date at Westminster 10th June, in the thirteenth year of his reign, to the honour of God and Holy Church, and of those saints whose bodies were buried therein, as also for the better security of the Canons and officers belonging thereto, granted unto the said Dean and Canons licence to enclose the said Churchyard with a wall on every side, with fitting Gates and Postern thereto, to be opened every morning and closed every night."

Some of the chapels connected with St. Paul's, which we should have seen if we had been alive before the Reformation and the Fire, deserve mention. One was in Pardon Church Yard, founded by Gilbert à Becket, "Portgrave and principal Magistrate of this City in the reign of King Stephen" (the father of Thomas à Becket), the churchyard of which was enclosed with a large cloister with painted walls. "There was also," says Dugdale, "one great cloister on the north side of the Church, environing a plot of ground of old time called Pardon Church Yard. About this cloister was artificially (exquisitely) and richly painted the Dance of Death, commonly called the Dance of St. Paul's." " In the year 1549, on the 10th of April, the said chapel, by commandment of the Duke of Somerset, was begun to be pulled down with the whole cloister, the Dance of Death, the Tombs and Monuments; so that nothing thereof was left but the bare plot of ground, which is since converted

---

[1] Stow's *Survey*, i. 369. For the account of the Wall, see Longman, p. 15; Milman, p. 155; and Simpson's *Chapters*, p. 62.

RESTORATION OF OLD ST PAVLS CATHEDRAL

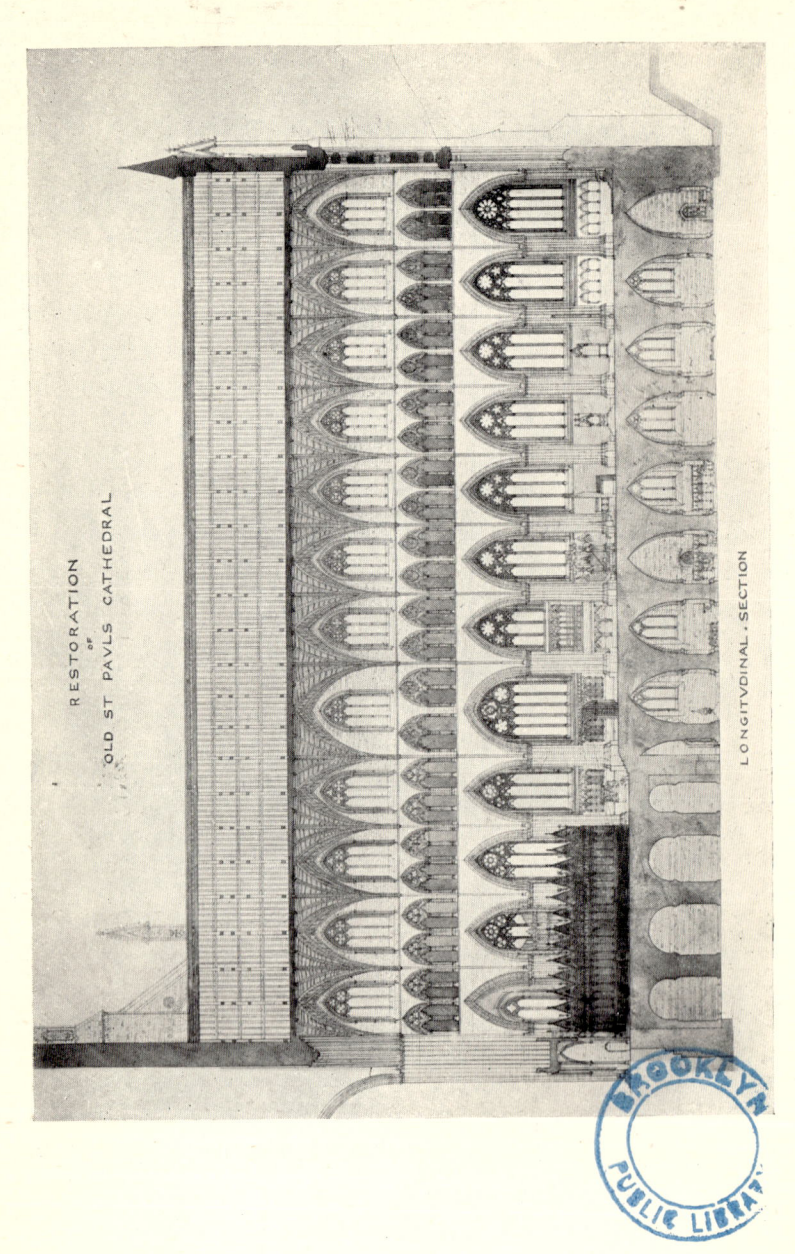

LONGITVDINAL SECTION

[To face p. 55.

OLD ST. PAUL'S

into a garden for the Petty Canons." The Sherrington Chapel stood at the north door, and "was founded by Walter Sherrington, Chancellor of the Duchy of Lancaster, in the reign of Henry VI.": that suffered the same fate as the Pardon Chapel at the hands of the avaricious Protector: "the chapel and library attached to it were pulled down in 1549, and the materials carried into the Strand towards the building of that stately fabric called 'Somerset House,' built by Edward, Duke of Somerset, on his appointment as Lord Protector to King Edward VI."[1] "There was furthermore a fair chapel of the Holy Ghost in St. Paul's Church on the north side, founded in the year 1400 by Roger Holmes, Chancellor and Prebendary of St. Paul's." "Then, under the choir of St. Paul's, is a large chapel, first dedicated to the name of Jesu, in a place called the Shrowds of the Cathedral (part of the crypt), founded, or rather confirmed, the 27th Henry VI."[2]

The most remarkable appendage to the Cathedral was the extremely beautiful parish church of St. Faith, in the crypt. "At the west end of this Jesu's Chapel, under the Choir of St. Paul's, also was a Parish Church of St. Faith, commonly called St. Faith's under St. Paul's, which served for the stationers and others dwelling in St. Paul's Churchyard, Paternoster Row and the places near adjoining." The Church of St. Faith-the-Virgin was originally above ground, and Jesu's Chapel was attached to it. The four great bells belonging to this chapel were hung in a bell-tower on the eastern side of the churchyard. "The bells and the image of St. Paul on the top of the spire were all standing till Sir Miles Partridge, Knight, *temp*. Henry VIII., having won them from the King at one cast of the dice, pulled them down."[3] The Church of St. Faith above ground was demolished in 1256 to enlarge the Cathedral, and part of the undercroft or crypt granted to

---

[1] Dugdale, p. 134.   [2] Stow, i. 640, 641; Dugdale, pp. 132, 133.
[3] Dugdale, p. 130.

the parishioners. Jesu's Chapel was still attached to it, but structurally divided till 1551, when the partition was removed.

"The Parish Church of St. Gregory was built up against the Cathedral at the south-west corner. It was probably in the Norman style, and was removed before 1645; notwithstanding a petition from the parishioners against its demolition,[1] the church was pulled down in regard it was thought to be a blemish to the stately Cathedral whereunto it adjoined."[2]

"The Church (of Old St. Paul's)," writes the architect Guilt, "consisted of a nave and two aisles, running throughout the building, as well in the choir as in the transepts. From the western wall of the nave to its intersection by the transepts were twelve openings, separated by Norman pillars, and crowned with semi-circular arches. Above these was a triforium, in which the circular arch was also employed, but the clerestory windows and vaulting were in the pointed Gothic. Each transept had five arches similar to those in the nave: over their intersection with the choir and nave rose the steeple tower. The entrance to the choir was distinguished by a screen richly ornamented, on each side of whose principal door were four canopies, and to the right and left, just beyond the range of the great pillars, were two doorways, which led to the side aisles of the choir. The whole of the choir was in the most elegant pointed Gothic, with a triforium and clerestory. Over the altar the view extended into the Lady Chapel, whose eastern wall was pierced with a beautiful circular window. On the south side of the Church (towards the west) was a cloister 90 feet square, in the centre of which stood a beautiful octagonal Chapter House."[3]

[1] *Calendar of State Papers, Domestic*, pp. 218, 408; 1637, June 15.
[2] Dugdale, p. 147.
[3] Britton and Pugin's *Illustrations of the Public Buildings of London*, vol. i. p. 3.

WEST ELEVATION

OLD ST. PAUL'S

THE COMPLETION OF OLD ST. PAUL'S

Mr. Ferrey, the architect, has made a very careful calculation of the measurements of Old St. Paul's from ancient surveys in the time of Edward II., and by Hollar. He makes the breadth 104 feet, the height of the roof (west of the choir screen, and up to the ridge of the vaulting), 93 feet; height of the roof (up to the vault ridge) in the choir proper, 101 feet 6 inches; height of roof in the Lady Chapel (the farthest east), 98 feet 6 inches; external height of choir, 142 feet; external height of nave, 130 feet; height of the central tower from the ground, 285 feet; additional height of spire, 208 feet; so that the height of the whole central steeple was nearly 500 feet.

Such was the building, vast, lofty, of enormous length and incomparable beauty, which soared above the City of London in the old days. It had been called "the glory of all Christian lands" and it would have been difficult to surpass it in the dignity of architecture, in the richness of its historical association, and in the splendour and interest of its monuments. The streets were narrow and picturesque, the houses timbered and gabled, the tide of life busy and constant, the dresses of the citizens full of colour and variety; above all this the huge and glorious building must have towered with inconceivable impressiveness, whether on a sunny afternoon, or above the blue mists that filled the streets from the river, or under the mystery of moonlight. It is no depreciation of the perfection of Wren's creation, to lament the lost magnificence of the past.

CHAPTER VI

THE DAYS OF WYCLIFFE

THE star of Wycliffe is now shining over the ecclesiastical horizon in England. He was born about 1324 and died in 1384, aged about sixty. When the new Bishop of London, *William de Courtenay*, was appointed in 1375, the illustrious reformer would be a little over fifty, and had already become conspicuous by his opinions on Papal tributes, the holding of temporal authority and temporal possessions by ecclesiastical persons, and the withholding of tithes and oblations from unworthy pastors. Bishop Courtenay (as we may call him) was the great-grandson of Edward I., his father Hugh, second Earl of Devon, having married Lady Margaret Bohun, daughter of Humphrey, Earl of Hereford (Lord High Constable) and of Lady Elizabeth Plantagenet, daughter of that king. He was a Churchman of the loftiest and boldest views, and of the most inflexible temper. Milman describes him as of the imperial house of Courtenay. The claim is not strong. His ancestor in the fifth degree had a nephew on the French side, a sister's son, named Peter, who became by marriage Emperor of Constantinople, in its decadent state, in 1217. Peter had been succeeded in turn by his two sons, Baldwin and Peter; but the latter was expelled by the Emperor Michael Palæologus in 1261; so that the family held the shadowy throne only a little over forty years, and through two female links.

In his very first year Courtenay showed his immense courage. Edward III., who died the year after, demanded in 1376 a subsidy from the clergy for the expense of his wars. In full convocation at St. Paul's, the Bishop protested against the grant, till the grievances of the clergy and certain wrongs of himself and the Bishop of Worcester should be redressed ; and the clergy refused the King.

Before the end of the year the King had his revenge. "The Pope, Gregory XI., had launched an anathema against the Florentines. The Bull was distributed throughout Christendom. The Florentines, the great merchants of the world in every kingdom of Europe, being under the ban of outlawry, might be plundered with impunity. Bishop Courtenay, without permission from the Crown, caused the Bull to be publicly read at Paul's Cross. This was not only a direct infringement of the Statute of Provisors,[1] but a licence, or rather an incitement to the rabble, to pillage the shops and warehouses of the rich Florentine bankers and traders. The Lord Mayor, as guardian of the public peace and protector of property within the City, took up the affair with a strong hand. He affixed his seal to the chief warehouses and banks, and leading the principal men of the Florentines into the presence of the King, demanded and obtained the royal protection for them and for their property. The Chancellor (the Bishop of Exeter) demanded of Courtenay by what authority he had acted. 'By the Pope's mandate!' It was a clear case of Præmunire.[2] The Chancellor offered the hard alternative (either) the formal revocation of the edict, or the forfeiture of all the Bishop's temporalities to the Crown. With difficulty the Bishop obtained leave to execute the act of revocation by a deputy. His official appeared at Paul's Cross, and with a most contemptible evasion, if not a flagrant falsehood, declared that the Lord Bishop had said nothing of the interdict. 'He wondered that the people,

---

[1] Passed by Parliament in 1351 against Papal encroachments, but without the consent of the Lords Spiritual.

[2] Passed in 1353 against the assumption by the Pope of independent jurisdiction in England.

accustomed to hear so many sermons in that place, should so have misunderstood his words.'"[1]

It was before this haughty ecclesiastic that Wycliffe had to appear: "the earliest champion of religious freedom, the rude apostle of principles which, matured, refined and harmonized, were to make a religious revolution in half Europe, to establish the Church of England as an important branch of the great Catholic Church of Christendom; a revolution which was not confined to any time, to any province, to any nation of the Christian world."[2]

Milman describes the scene, one of the most memorable that ever took place in St. Paul's, in his *History of Latin Christianity*. "Wycliffe, exactly at this time, between the dissolution of the last Parliament and the death of the King, appears summoned to answer at St. Paul's before the Archbishop of Canterbury and the Bishop of London, for opinions deserving ecclesiastical censure. . . . These may be conjectured from those submitted to the Pope, and afterwards brought against him by the Papal mandate. Wycliffe stood before the tribunal, but not alone. He was accompanied by John of Gaunt and the Lord Percy, now Earl Marshal. There was an immense throng to witness this exciting spectacle; Wycliffe could not make his way through. The Earl Marshal assumed the authority of his office to compel the crowd to recede. The Bishop of London, no doubt indignant at the unlooked-for appearance of the nobles, resented the exercise of the Earl Marshal's power in his Church. He haughtily declared that if he had known how Percy would act, he would have inhibited his entrance into the Cathedral. The Duke of Lancaster, in his pride, rejoined that, despite the Bishop, the Earl Marshal would use the authority necessary to maintain order. They reached with difficulty the court in the Lady Chapel. The Earl Marshal demanded a seat for Wycliffe. 'He had many things to answer; he needed a

[1] Milman's *Annals*, p. 74.   [2] *Ibid.*, p. 76.

soft seat.' 'It is contrary,' answered Courtenay, 'to law and reason that one cited before his Ordinary should be seated.' Fierce words ensued between the Earl Marshal and the Bishop. The Duke of Lancaster taunted the family pride of Courtenay. The Bishop replied with specious humility, 'that he trusted not in man but in God alone, who would give him boldness to speak the truth.' Lancaster was overheard, or thought to be overheard, as if he threatened to drag the Bishop out of the Church by the hair of his head. The populace was inflamed by the insult to the Bishop, and the insult to the City of London. The privileges of the City were supposed to be menaced by the Earl Marshal's assumption of authority within the jurisdiction of the Lord Mayor. (Lancaster was afterwards accused of a design to abolish the Lord Mayor, and to appoint a captain under the Crown; and that the Earl Marshal's power should be current in the City as in other parts of the kingdom. Lancaster did turn out the Lord Mayor and Aldermen and appoint others. He also made an attack on the revenues and property of the generous and popular William of Wykeham, Bishop of Winchester.) A wild tumult began. The proceedings were broken up: Wycliffe, who all along had stood silent, retired. Lancaster and the Earl Marshal had doubtless sufficient force to protect their persons. But throughout the City the populace rose; (they were by no means in favour of the reforming and anti-prelatical Duke of Lancaster;) they attacked his magnificent palace, the Savoy; his arms were reversed, like those of a traitor. The palace, but for the Bishop of London, would have been burned down. A luckless clergyman, mistaken for the Earl Marshal, was brutally murdered. The Duke fled to Kennington, where the Princess of Wales was residing with her young son. (She was Joan, the Fair Maid of Kent, daughter of Edmund of Woodstock, Earl of Kent, fifth son of Edward I.) The rioters were appeased by a message from the Princess; but they demanded that the

Bishop of Winchester and Peter de la Mare should have their fair and immediate inquest before their peers, according to the laws of the land."[1] Wycliffe's subsequent conflicts with Courtenay (as Archbishop) were at Oxford, at Lambeth and at the London Monastery of Grey Friars.

In Wat Tyler's rebellion in 1381, St. Paul's and Bishop Courtenay were unmolested, though the Temple, the Savoy and the great house of the Knights Hospitallers at St. John's, Clerkenwell, were in flames, and Archbishop Sudbury was murdered on Tower Hill. Courtenay was his successor both in the Primacy and the Chancellorship.

The new Bishop of London was *Robert De Braybroke*, promoted by a Bull of Pope Urban VI., and consecrated in the chapel at Lambeth Palace (January 5, 1382). King Richard II. was, in 1387, received in great pomp by the Lord Mayor, Sir Nicholas Exton, and escorted to the Cathedral. He was to feast after the service at the house of Sir Nicholas Brember, Lord Chief Justice; and never again to visit St. Paul's, but as a corpse. In the struggle between Richard and his Parliament, De Braybroke took the popular side, and tried with all his famous eloquence to persuade the King to take his uncle, Thomas, Duke of Gloucester, and the Barons who acted with Gloucester, into favour; and denounced the Duke of Ireland, the King's favourite, as his seducer from all good. In 1391, the Bishop of London acted as a mediator between King and City. The City had refused to lend the King money, and had incurred the forfeiture of their privileges. A riot and scenes of violence followed; De Braybroke, on account of his influence in making this peace, was much honoured by the citizens during his life.

In 1395, De Braybroke, with Arundel, Archbishop of York, at the request of the Primate, crossed the sea to the King in Ireland, to obtain powers against the Lollards.

[1] Milman's *History of Latin Christianity*.

The Lollards had advanced so far as to fix on the doors of St. Paul's twelve articles against existing practices and doctrines: the existing priesthood, the celibacy of the clergy, transubstantiation, prayers for the dead, pilgrimages, and other usages which they denounced.

In 1399 appeared a knightly figure in St. Paul's, Henry of Bolingbroke (called after the place of his birth in Lincolnshire), afterwards Henry IV., eldest son of John of Gaunt, Duke of Lancaster, to mourn over the tomb of his father, who had died and been buried in the Cathedral that year, and offer prayers for the dethronement of his ill-fated cousin, and for the success of his own schemes.

Next year the body of Richard II. lay in state three days in St. Paul's after his murder in Pontefract Castle. Seventy years before there had been doubts as to the death of Edward II. under like circumstances; this ceremony was to avoid all uncertainty. It was attended by the utmost pomp, and by prodigal oblations from King and Lords; the body passed on to Westminster, then to Langley, and was finally buried in the Abbey.

De Braybroke, who lived through these troublous times, and died in 1405, was a vigorous reformer of abuses. "He issued a strong rebuke against working on Sundays and Feast-days; especially against shoemakers and cobblers. A prohibition was read at Paul's Cross against barbers shaving on Sundays.[1] There was also the Chapter. "Not thirty years before, King Edward III. had promulgated a tremendous censure against the Dean and Chapter of St. Paul's, even against the Bishop (Sudbury), whom it charged with negligence, if not connivance, in the wicked abuses in the Church of St. Paul, which had been founded and heaped with benefactions by his royal ancestors. Their refectory had become the resort of base mechanics, their inner chambers no better than hired brothels. Where there used and ought to be the daily maintenance and sustentation of

[1] Wilkins, vol. iii. p. 218.

the ministry in holy worship, were all kinds of foul and abominable acts of laymen. The very sacred vessels and ornaments were pilfered and held up for sale. Worse than these abuses, revenues designed for this sacred purpose were wasted, or unequally distributed; some were rolling in affluence, others were miserably poor, the chantries and altars were alienated to other uses. The manors and farms were mismanaged. The King ordered that the establishment should be placed on its old footing. The public table was to be restored; the bakehouse, the brewery, which had gone to ruin, were to be rebuilt, the daily ale and bread distributed. The execution of this stern mandate is committed, not to the Bishop, but to the Lord Mayor and Sheriffs of the City.

"Bishop de Braybroke's reform, which he carried through with difficulty against the opposition of the Canons, was of an abuse which had grown up out of the constitution of the Chapter. The Residentiaryship had formerly been held a burden; the Canons thought it more pleasant to reside each on his separate estate, leaving to others the irksome duty of attending the long and wearisome services of the Church, for which each had his ill-paid deputy. Gradually, however, from the great increase of the common fund (the 'domus') by oblations, obits (payments for masses on the anniversary of deaths) and other sources, shared out to the Residentiaries, this burden became an enviable privilege. There was a rush to become Residentiaries. At this time, too, the Residentiaries had an ingenious device to exclude their eager brethren. The Canon who would become a Residentiary was obliged to pay six or seven hundred marks, to be spent in feastings. So the Residentiary Chapter had sunk down to only two. The affair was brought before the King for his arbitration, and he ordered that residence should be determined according to the usage of the Church of Salisbury.[1]

[1] Wharton, pp. 142, 143.

"But not the Chapter only, the Church itself had fallen into grievous disrepute. . . . Bishop de Braybroke issued letters denouncing the profanation of St. Paul's by marketing and trading in the Church itself. He alleges the example of the Saviour, who cast the buyers and sellers out of the Temple. 'In our Cathedral, not only men, but women also, not on common days alone but especially on festivals, expose their wares as if it was a public market, and buy and sell without reverence for the holy place.' More than this—the Bishop dwells on more horrid abuses. 'Others, too, by the instigation of the devil, do not scruple with stones and arrows to bring down the birds, pigeons and jackdaws which nestle in the walls and crevices of the building; others play at ball or at other unseemly games, both within and without the Church, breaking the beautiful and costly painted windows to the amazement of the spectators.' The Bishop threatens these offenders, if they do not desist on monition from these irreverent practices, to visit them with the greater excommunication."[1]

De Braybroke, who died in 1405, was buried before the high altar of St. Paul's; his body was found entire after the Great Fire, more than 260 years after. It is said that after his death the Mayor, Aldermen and many chief citizens, according to their Companies, went nine times a year in a solemn procession to his burial place, to pray for his soul.[2]

His successor, *Roger de Walden*, held prebends at Salisbury, Exeter and St. Paul's, was Archdeacon of Winchester, Treasurer of Calais, Secretary to King Richard II., and Lord High Treasurer. During an exile of the Primate, Archbishop Arundel, the Pope nominated him Archbishop of Canterbury, and he appears to have been enthroned. Arundel, however, was reinstated, and after waiting five years De Walden was made Bishop of London.

[1] Wilkins, vol. iii.; Milman's *Annals*, p. 83.
[2] Kennet, *Life of Richard II.*, p. 269.

Archbishop Arundel held almost annual Convocations in St. Paul's.[1] It was in St. Paul's that he pronounced the first capital sentence under the terrible writ *De Hæretico comburendo* (on the Duty of Burning Heretics), which he had extorted from the grateful King and obsequious Parliament. The first martyr of Wycliffism was William Sautree, a priest. The form of his degradation may be described as an example of the rest. " He was degraded in St. Paul's, first from the priesthood: the patina and chalice were taken from his hands, he was prohibited from singing mass, and stripped of his chasuble. He was then degraded from the diaconate, the book of the Gospels taken from him, his stole removed, and he was prohibited from reading the Gospels ; then, as sub-deacon, his alb and maniple were torn off; then, as an acolyte, the insignia of that office were taken from him ; then, as an exorcist, the book of exorcisms was wrested from his hands ; then as a reader ; then as a doorkeeper, deprived of the keys of the church and the surplice. The last degradation was the erasure of the tonsure, and setting on his head a layman's cap."[2] In the same Convocation in St. Paul's, John Purvey, who had been almost a successor to Wycliffe, made a recantation of seven opinions : (1) Denial of transubstantiation ; (2) Denial of auricular confession ; (3) Assertion of predestination ; (4) Assertion that clergymen of evil life cannot hold the keys of the Kingdom of Heaven ; (5) Assertion that every clergyman ought to preach the Gospel to the people with or without the Bishop's licence ; (6) Against monastic vows of celibacy, and all such vows; (7) Assertion that the Lateran Council (under Innocent III.) was without authority.

An equally unimportant successor followed De Walden. *Nicholas Bubwith* had been Master of the Rolls, Privy Seal and Lord High Treasurer ; he exchanged the See of London for Salisbury. The next Bishop, *Robert Clifford*

---

[1] Wilkins, vol. iii. 282.   [2] Milman's *Annals*.

(1407–1421), had the distinction of appearing as the representative of the English Church at the great Council of Constance in A.D. 1416. During his time, Archbishop Chicheley held Convocations at St. Paul's with even greater regularity; or the records have been better kept. On King Henry V.'s return from Agincourt, by Chicheley's order, a *Te Deum* was sung at St. Paul's, and a magnificent procession organized from the Cathedral to Westminster. Later on, the Primate addressed a mandate to the Bishop of London, ordering processions and prayers for the success of the King in France, especially against the wicked designs of the necromancers, who were conspiring against his life: his health was already failing. Trials for heresy are now mentioned from time to time. At that of John Claydon, a Skinner of the City of London, in the Chapter House, the Lord Mayor was present. At that of Richard Walker, the culprit, accused of magic, appeared at Paul's Cross, and after an exhortation from the Bishop of Llandaff, solemnly abjured all such arts. His two books were hung, wide open, one on his head, one on his back; and with a special cap on his head he walked all along Cheapside. On his return his books were burned before his face, and he was released.[1] King Henry V. died at Vincennes, August 31, 1422, and one of the most magnificent and picturesque pageants ever seen at St. Paul's was his lying-in-state and funeral.

On Clifford's death, the Canons of St. Paul's, lawfully assembled by royal licence, chose for their prelate Thomas Polton, Bishop of Hereford. But Pope Martin V., who had brought Christendom back to an undivided Papacy at Rome, and was determined that no weakening of the specially close tie between England and the Holy See should be imagined, named *John Kemp*, Bishop of Chester, for London. The claim was admitted, and Thomas of Hereford was promoted to Chester. Next year, Bishop

---

[1] Wilkins, vol. iii. p. 394.

Kemp crossed the Channel as one of the Council of the Regent Duke of Bedford, who was administering the conquests of Henry V. From 1426 to 1432 Kemp was Lord Chancellor, and was then advanced to the Archbishopric of York.

The Pope appointed his successor, *William Gray* (1426–1431), who, after four years, was translated to Lincoln, then a richer See.

Robert FitzHugh, the next Bishop (1431–1436), was Chancellor of the University of Cambridge, and in that capacity made a famous speech, much admired for its Latinity. He had been Ambassador at Venice, and as Bishop of London represented England at the Council of Basel. Elected by the monks to be Bishop of Ely, he died before his translation.

Robert Gilbert was Bishop from 1436–1448. He was appointed by the University of Oxford to examine the suspected writings of Wycliffe, and by the Pope to the somewhat awkward post of Conservator of the liberties of the University against the encroachments of the Archbishop of Canterbury.

CHAPTER VII

BISHOP PECOCK AT ST. PAUL'S

DURING Gilbert's episcopate appeared as preacher at Paul's Cross the most remarkable theologian of his age, Reginald Pecock, Bishop of St. Asaph. He first attracted notice by a brilliant defence of the Bishops against the Lollards; and he ended by having to recant opinions that were liberal and reforming in their character. The sermon in defence of the Bishops was preached at the Cross in 1447, and set forth seven propositions: (1) A Bishop is not necessarily bound to preach to the common people of his diocese; (2) He ought rather to hold himself free from preaching, in order that he may attend to more important matters; (4) A Bishop ought to have greater knowledge in solving important questions than the inferior clergy are bound to have; (4) Bishops are free to preach or not to preach, having regard to the more important functions they are called to perform, and which cannot be done by the lower clergy; (5) A more useful work may be done to the souls of men than by preaching; (6) Bishops may and ought to be non-resident in their dioceses when weighty causes call them away; (7) It is not simoniacal for Bishops to obtain their Sees from the Pope by provision, nor to pay him annates and first-fruits.

The Bishops and the abuses with which they were connected were by this time highly unpopular. Their critics were not only the Lollards, but a growing party of moderate reformers in the Church, represented by Bishop Hallam at the Council of Constance, and Thomas Gascoigne, the author of the *Dictionary of Theology*. Gascoigne mentions seven great contemporary English prelates, appointed by the Pope, whose episcopal duties were null through their Court appointments; in addition to George Nevil, appointed by the Pope to the See of Exeter at the age of twenty-three, and John Delabere to that of St. David's, where he allowed his clergy to keep concubines at a tax of a noble a year. He asserts that from the year 1403 there were none preferred in the Church who knew how in a due manner to do good to souls, or who could or would do it; that at that time in England the care of souls was destroyed by appropriations, the non-residence of incumbents and prelates, the promotion of worthless men, pluralities of benefices, and the very worst conferring of degrees and granting of graces to the unworthy, wicked and vicious persons in Oxford and other universities. Bishop Pecock's sermon was therefore very unpopular with the growth of moderate opinion, as well as with the whole mass of the Lollards; and the Bishops were displeased at their habits being defended in such bold terms and on such questionable grounds. An appeal was made to Archbishop Stafford to censure the sermon; but it was dismissed on the ground that the Bishop's intentions were good. He defended himself in a work published in 1449, called *The Repressor of Over-much Blaming of the Clergy*. Here he upholds six practices of the clergy specially attacked by the Lollards: (1) The use of images; (2) Pilgrimages; (3) The holding of landed possessions by the clergy; (4) The various ranks of the hierarchy; (5) The making of laws by Papal and episcopal authority; (6) The institutions of the religious orders. Bishop Pecock's defence pleased nobody; the Bishops disliked his arguments, and the Lollards the points for which he argued; the book excited great anger and bitterness among Churchmen. His promotion to the See of Chichester in 1450, through the influence of De la Pole, Duke of Suffolk, increased his unpopularity, as his patron was generally detested. The crisis came in 1456, when, with a view of converting the Lollards, the indefatigable Bishop published his *Treatise on Faith*. "In this he quits the ground of the infallibility of the Church, and argues that we ought to listen to authority only so long as the authority is not proved to be wrong. Very remarkably for one of his time he advocates the view that the truth of the Christian religion is not a matter of demonstration, but one of probable argument, and that persecution is not justifiable until the proper means of persuasion have been tried. 'The clergy shall be condemned at the last day if by clear wit they draw not men into consent of true faith otherwise than by fire and sword and hangment, although I will not deny these second means to be lawful, provided the former be first used.' It was a shameful thing for the Christian Church to hold such a faith for substance of its salvation, and yet not suffer it to be examined; it were imputing a villainy to Christ that would give such a faith to His people, into which faith He would His people should turn all other people, and yet could not allow His faith to be full tried. 'The apostles intended not to give any catholic faith necessary to Christian men's salvation by word only, to be kept without writing and remembrance (record, reminder). That they betoken not, out and besides Holy Scripture, any articles to be believed for necessary faiths.' The ceremonies of the Church were ordained not in apostolic times, and therefore do not stand on the same footing as doctrines. The Church and clergy have no power to make new doctrines. Holy Writ is a more worthy ground of our faith than is the clergy of the whole Church on earth. The clergy may only declare and explain; the only authority is in Scripture. But every man is bound to obey the determinations of the Church, unless he can prove them to be wrong. The Church has power to make positive ordinances and to enforce them. There is nothing against the faith in priests having wives, which was permitted by the Apostle Paul; nor is there in Scripture any distinction of meats and drinks, or any authority for eating fish at one season and flesh at another. Too many positive laws are a grievance and a snare. Christ is the Head of the Church which is founded on earth.[1] These views, so entirely alien from those which were held by his contemporary Bishops, this bold quitting of the ground of tradition, and infallible decrees of the Church, and basing all upon Scripture and reason, must have utterly appalled Pecock's brethren. He had begun by defending some of the worst abuses of the Bishops and the Church. He had gradually written himself into clearer views. He now severely commented upon the characters and practices of the clergy. The Friars were 'pulpit-brawlers,' and venters of 'untrue fables.' He had not feared to say that even the great doctors of the Church had no authority, save in so far as their opinions agreed with reason. Milman's judgment is that Pecock took the ground afterwards maintained by Hooker; and 'Hallam has said, with his usual solid wisdom, that in the *Precursor* are passages well worthy of Hooker for weight of matter and dignity of style.'"

At a Council at Westminster, October 22, 1457, a violent attack was made on Bishop Pecock. Opposing divines asked for copies of his works; Pecock promised Archbishop Bouchier to bring them to a meeting at Lambeth on November 11. Numerous examinations were made; the examiners were incapable of understanding Pecock's position, and simply confuted him with sentences from the Schoolmen. He was condemned to recant, or prepare for the stake. There was nothing in dispute which excited the Bishop to be a martyr. On December 3 he abjured the

---

[1] Lewis's *Life of Pecock*, chap. v.; Babington's Introduction to Pecock's *Repressor*, p. xxxiii.; Perry's *Student's English Church History*, p. 477.

condemned propositions at Lambeth in a written form, and the following day being Sunday, at Paul's Cross he made a public recantation in the presence of a vast crowd of people (some said 20,000) and four Bishops. Having recited his alleged errors in Latin, he continued in English, declaring himself to have greatly erred, and that he now solemnly revoked and renounced all the errors aforesaid, and all other heresies and errors contained in his books, and that he submitted himself to the correction of the Church as a contrite and penitent sinner. And he desired that no man should give credence to his false and pernicious doctrines, nor keep any of his books, but bring them all to the Archbishop or his commissaries; and he desired that all his books should be openly burnt. He then himself delivered a parcel of his books to the executioner to throw into the flames. "He retracted," says his latest able biographer, "errors which he had never uttered, and retracted utterances which he knew to be truths. But," he adds kindly, "indeed he seems to have been so confused and bewildered, as scarcely to know what he had said and what he had not said."[1] "What was the state of the Church," says the historian Perry, "when a man in the position of Pecock, who had written temperately, learnedly and with a sincere desire to bring back those who had altogether revolted from the faith of the Church, could be thus ignominiously trampled upon, because he had ventured to doubt the right of the Church to decide all controversies by its own sole fiat?" "It would have been well for the reputation of the Bishops of those days had the forced recantation, with all its falsified items, formed the extent of their persecution inflicted on the liberal-minded Bishop. But in fact they persecuted him to death. Pecock had contrived to interest the Pope in his cause,[2] and had even obtained Bulls of restitution to his Bishopric, of which he had been deprived.

[1] Babington, Introduction to Pecock's *Repressor*.
[2] Pius V. became Pope in 1458.

Whereupon the Archbishop and other prelates went to Henry VI., and represented the enormity of one convicted of heresy obtaining Bulls from the Pope, contrary to the Statutes of Provisors, although all these prelates did, in fact, owe their appointments to the same source. The King induced Pecock to resign his Bishopric, promising that he should be well provided for. The Bishop resigned, and the good provision promised him was found to consist in an imprisonment in Thorney Abbey, where he remained to the day of his death. His biographer and editor's remarks on his character are valuable: 'He would have been remarkable in any age, but was in his own age most remarkable. He was the enlightened advocate of toleration in times most intolerant; he was the acute propounder of a rational piety against unreasoning and most unreasonable opponents. His theological knowledge—scriptural, patristic and scholastic—was for that age very considerable. He was, indeed, by far the most eminent and learned Bishop of the Church of England in his time.'"[1]

[1] Perry's *Student's English Church History*, p. 477.

CHAPTER VIII

THE WARS OF THE ROSES

HENRY VI. reigned from 1422 to 1461, and saw during that time five Bishops of London: John Kempe, Gray, FitzHugh, Gilbert and *Thomas Kempe*. Thomas was Bishop thirty years (1450-1480), and lived through the struggle of the Houses of Lancaster and York, or the Wars of the Roses, to the fourth year of Henry VII. He was nephew of John Kempe, who had been promoted to York, and afterwards to Canterbury. His predecessor's death or resignation had been expected for two years; and the Minister of the day had procured from Pope Nicolas V. a provisor that the succession should be secured to Kempe, Archdeacon of Richmond. In the meantime De la Pole, Duke of Suffolk, had become ascendant at Court, and he applied to Rome to set aside Kempe in favour of the Bishop of Carlisle. Bishop Gilbert died in 1448, and Thomas Kempe's consecration was delayed till next year. It took place in the chapel of York House (afterwards Whitehall), at the hands of his uncle, John Kempe, Archbishop of York.

The fluctuating fortunes of these terrible times were strongly felt in the Cathedral. Here Roger Bolingbroke, necromancer, accused of aiding by diabolic magic the ambitious designs of Humphrey, Duke of Gloucester, the popular brother of Henry V., and Regent during the minority of Henry VI., was exhibited on a platform in front of St. Paul's, together with Southwell, a canon of St.

Paul's, his accomplice. The penance of Eleanor Cobham, Duchess of Gloucester, must have begun or ended in or near the Cathedral, when she was led along, wrapped in a sheet, with a burning taper in her hand—

> "Mailed up in shame, with papers on my back,
> And followed with a rabble, that rejoice
> To see my tears, and hear my deep-felt groans."[1]

By an extraordinary blunder in after days Sir John de Beauchamp's tomb in St. Paul's was mistaken for Duke Humphry's, who was in reality buried at St. Albans.

In March 1452, Richard Duke of York took his oath of fealty in St. Paul's to Henry VI. on the Sacrament, before a numerous assemblage of peers and dignitaries. He was second cousin to Henry V. The oath which he swore is extant; every word condemned him of perjury ere many years had passed:—" I, Richard, Duke of York, confess and beknow that I am, and ought to be, humble subject and liegeman to you, my Sovereign Lord, King Henry VI. I ought, therefore, to bear you faith and truth, to my Sovereign Liege Lord; and shall do all days unto my life's end. . . . I shall not take anything upon me against your royal estate or obeisance, that is due thereto; nor suffer any other man to do as far forth as it shall be in my power to let it (prevent it). . . . I shall never hereafter take upon me to gather any rout, or to make any assembly of your people, without your commandment or licence, even in my lawful defence. I shall report me at all times to your Highness. And over, I agree me and will, if I any time hereafter, as by the grace of our Lord God I never shall, anything attempt by way of feat or otherwise against your royal Majesty, and the obeisance that I owe thereto, or anything take upon me otherwise than as above expressed, I from that time forth be unabled, held and taken as an untrue and openly foresworn man, and unable to all manner

---

[1] *Henry VI.*, Part II., Act II., sc. iv.

of worship, estate and degree, be it such as I now occupy, or any other that might in any wise grow unto me hereafter." On this tremendous oath, in the great national Church, in the presence of the Archbishop, Duke Richard appeals to the sacred Host.

Six years later the oath had been broken, and was to be repaired. In March 1458, the Battle of St. Albans had been fought. "Parliaments and Councils had been held, negotiations endlessly carried on between the contending parties; the poor King had sunk for a time into mental imbecility. He had now recovered. . . . After all this in token of reconciliation, there was a solemn procession to St. Paul's. There was some dread of a collision between the hostile and ill-accordant factions. King Henry and Queen Margaret slept at the Bishop's Palace in the precincts (on the north side of the Cathedral, near the passage known now as London House Yard). The great Lords assembled in the Chapel of that Palace. The King, holding his full Court, surrounded by Yorkists and Lancastrians, sate on a throne. The Archbishop, Bourchier, set the crown on his head. The procession to the Church, preceded by the Archbishop, his cross borne before him by the Bishop of Rochester, was met by the Dean and Chapter. Two and two came those terrible nobles, so soon to meet again in deadly battle— Edmund Beaufort, Duke of Somerset, and the Earl of Salisbury; Henry Holland, Duke of Exeter, and Richard Nevill, Earl of Warwick. Then came the poor King, crowned, with the sceptre in his hand. The Queen followed smiling (oh! the bitterness of that smile!) and 'conversing familiarly' with the Duke of York. They knelt in prayer —one at least, the King on his faldstool, in devout, earnest, Christian prayer. The Nobles were on their knees behind. High Mass was sung; the Archbishop pronounced the benediction—'Go in peace!'—that benediction to have but brief, but very slight, effect! The people no doubt rejoiced at heart, and listened to the service with fond hopes of happier and more peaceful times."[1] A ballad is extant, *Concord and Unity*, describing the service of reconciliation.[2]

Three years later the same oaths have been broken, the same hollow peace patched up, and a like scene is enacted at St. Paul's, but with a change of some of the chief actors. The same Archbishop is again at the west door; he is received as before by Dean and Chapter; he is there once more to receive the unhappy King, coming in full procession from Westminster, as for a solemn thanksgiving. But the battles of Blackheath and Northampton have been now fought, and Henry VI. is virtually a prisoner. Duke Richard has asserted his right to at least the succession to the throne, and the Parliament at Westminster had acknowledged it. "King Henry appeared, still with the crown on his head; but not now with the Queen and half the nobility, or Somerset and Exeter on his side. Somerset had hardly escaped after the defeat at Northampton; Exeter was for the present safe in his own county. The Queen, a fugitive in the north, was busily employed in rallying the depressed Lancastrians. The King was only now accompanied by Salisbury and Warwick. York, Salisbury, Warwick again knelt before the Primate. Bourchier called upon them again to take the oath of fidelity to the King; the oath of allegiance to their prisoner; or to ratify by their homage to the King in the Cathedral the oaths already sworn before the Parliament at Westminster. The Duke of York and his two sons, the Earl of March (afterwards Edward IV.) and young Rutland, swore to maintain the King upon his throne, and not to molest him during his reign. But the succession by the same agreement was to pass away. The Sovereign to whom they swore allegiance had been forced to assent to the decree which, disinheriting his own son, the princely Edward, awarded the succession to the Duke of York.

[1] Milman's *Annals*, p. 102.
[2] *Malcolm*, iii. 151, Cotton Collection.

After this humiliating scene, and after evensong, the King withdrew to the Bishop's Palace.

"Queen Margaret was not there. Ere long she was to efface the memory of this humiliation, and wreak her bloody vengeance. She was to appear at Wakefield (December 31, 1460), with Somerset and Exeter and the northern Lords—Northumberland, Dacre, Clifford—at the head of her army. Young Rutland was to wash out the memory of the oath in his innocent blood. The Duke's head was to wear a paper crown on the walls of York."[1]

Next year (1461) the gates of St. Paul's are again open; again the Archbishop is there, but not to receive King Henry. Homage is now claimed by Edward IV., who has come, with Salisbury and Warwick, to secure the fruits of the second battle of St. Albans (February 2) and Towton (March 29). He has already been acknowledged by the whole realm as the actual monarch. From early days, St. Paul's has known no politics, but given her religious services to all who had the right to claim them.

Ten years later, in 1471, came Tewkesbury and the murder of young Edward, the hapless Prince of Wales. Again in that year the gates of St. Paul's were thrown open, to receive the dead bodies of Salisbury and Warwick and their brother Montagu. For three days the bodies were exposed, with faces bared, to satisfy the people that these grim war-lords, especially the great King-maker, were really dead.

A week after came the sad spectacle of the body of King Henry VI. himself, lying in state in the Cathedral. He died in the Tower, and the cause of his death has remained a mystery. The Yorkists said it was grief; the Lancastrians muttered darker things as loud as they dared. It was commonly reported that both at St. Paul's and at Blackfriars blood gushed from the dead man's nose; and that was held by the people to signify a violent end; that the murderer

[1] Milman's *Annals*, p. 104.

was Richard of Gloucester no one doubted in his heart. That was Shakespeare's opinion. In the terrible scene where the ghosts of his murdered victims rise on the night before the Battle of Bosworth and accuse Richard III., that of Henry VI. appears, and says—

> "When I was mortal, my anointed body
> By thee was punchèd full of deadly holes;
> Think on the Tower and me; despair, and die!
> Harry the Sixth bids thee despair, and die."

The body was afterwards moved towards Chertsey; and, finally, the holy founder of Eton College found fit resting-place at Windsor. In the second scene of the same play, Anne, widow of Henry's son Edward Prince of Wales, in her pathetic lament over the late King's body as it is moved from the Cathedral, says—

> "Come, now, toward Chertsey with your holy load,
> Taken from Paul's to be interrèd there;
> And still, as you are weary of the weight,
> Rest you, while I lament King Henry's corse."

Richard, as Duke of Gloucester, paid a visit to St. Paul's to offer his orisons when, after the death of Edward IV., before the murder of the young children in the Tower, he came up to London to arrest the family of the Queen, the Greys and Lord Hastings. The seals at this crisis were taken from the Archbishop of York and entrusted to Kempe, Bishop of London.

The next step in the tragedy, as far as St. Paul's was concerned, was the infamous sermon at Paul's Cross, in favour of the usurper, and against the heirs to the crown, by Dr. Shaw, brother of the Lord Mayor. "In that sermon he showered imputations of illegitimacy against all who stood in the way of Richard. The preacher openly asserted the bastardy of all the elder brothers of the House of York, Edward and Clarence. 'Bastard slips never take deep root.' Edward and Clarence were born of adultery. The Duchess of York, by his showing, suddenly became virtuous to conceive the Duke of Gloucester—Edward's two sons were certainly bastards, on account of the precontract of Edward (to Lady Butler) before his marriage with Lady Grey (Elizabeth Woodville)." [1]

According to Shakespeare, it was in St. Paul's that the indictment against Lord Hastings, one of Richard's victims, was read. It was in St. Paul's that Jane Shore, accused of sorcery by the tyrant, was ordered to do penance, in a white sheet; "the gaze of the people flushing her pale cheeks with exquisite colour; men were more amorous of her body than curious of her soul; they thought less of her soul than of the cruelty of the Protector." After his accession, and acknowledgment by Parliament, Richard rode solemnly to "the Cathedral Church of London, and was received there with processions, with great congratulation and acclamation of all the people in every place, and by the way that the King was in, that day." [2]

Bishop Thomas Kempe must have been a prudent man. Through the civil wars, the reigns of Henry VI., Edward IV., Edward V., Richard III., down to the fourth year of Henry VII., he remained Bishop of London. Edward IV. protected him against a demand from Rome for 40,000 ducats, alleged to be due from him as Treasurer of the Papal revenues from England. He was able to be munificent; he rebuilt Paul's Cross, which was one of the chief ornaments of the City of London; not the mean structure which fell into decay after the Reformation. The beautiful Divinity School at Oxford also was built at his cost.

Before the close of his long episcopate, the Primate, Morton, with his suffragans, held a notable Convocation at St. Paul's. "There appeared William Symonds, priest, who confessed before the Lord Mayor and Aldermen, that

---

[1] Milman's *Annals*, p. 197.
[2] The official account, Ellis's *Historical Letters*, 2nd series, vol. i. p. 148.

at Oxford he had set up the son of one Originakes as Earl of Warwick, and had conveyed him to Ireland. Symonds made full confession; and at the demand of the Archbishop he was committed by the Mayor and Aldermen to the Tower. King Henry, after his victory over the partisans of Simnel (the pretender), went on two successive days in solemn procession to the Cathedral. On the first day *Te Deum* was sung; on the second there was a sermon at Paul's Cross. The King rode with Lambert Simnel at his side, whose life he spared in contemptuous mercy, and degraded him to a servile office as a scullion in the royal kitchen."[1]

"Archbishop Morton's Convocation proceeded to other business. There was a charge against the Prior of St. John of Jerusalem that certain of his Order had abused their privileges, and preached at Paul's Cross against the Church and Churchmen in the presence of laymen who 'are always hostile to the clergy' (a lamentable admission). On a further day the Prior of St. John's appeared, and promised to amend these errors. On a third day, after a subsidy had been voted, appeared many learned persons, secular as well as regular, accustomed to preach at Paul's Cross 'the Word of God.' They were admonished by the Primate not to preach against ecclesiastical persons. But the next monition rather justified these bold and learned preachers. It was a rebuke to the clergy, especially priests in the City of London, against the evil fame of haunting taverns, hostelries and cookshops."[2]

[1] Lord Verulam, in Kennet, p. 588; Milman's *Annals*, p. 110.
[2] Wilkins' *Concilia*, vol. iii. p. 618; Milman's *Annals*, p. 110.

CHAPTER IX

THE DAWN OF THE REFORMATION

SOME of the successors of Bishop Kempe are mere names. *Thomas Hill* came in 1489, and died in 1496. He was followed by *Thomas Savage*, who was translated to York in 1501. The wise and learned *William Warham*, whose picture is one of the treasures of Lambeth Palace, was appointed by the Pope in October 1501, was not consecrated till 1502, and became Archbishop in 1503. *William Barons*, or *Barnes*, held the See hardly more than ten months, in 1504 and 1505. *Richard FitzJames* was translated from Chichester in 1506. He had been Warden of Merton College and Vice-Chancellor of Oxford, and is extolled by some of the chroniclers as a man of theological learning and goodness; "one of those high-born Churchmen, piously ignorant and conscientiously blind, with whom a hair's-breadth deviation from established usage and opinion is insolence, sin, and worse than sin—heresy."[1] He held the See till 1522, and had three years of Henry VII., and thirteen of Henry VIII., the period of Colet and Erasmus. *Cuthbert Tunstal* succeeded him, a kind, gentle and blameless prelate; he ruled for seven years, and in 1530 accepted the Bishopric of Durham.

The Churchman of these days who had the greatest influence on his times was *John Colet*, the famous Dean of St. Paul's. He was the son of a wealthy London merchant, Master of the Mercers' Company, and at least twice Lord Mayor of London. John was the sole survivor of twenty-

[1] Milman's *Annals*, p. 120.

two children; a fact which concentrated on him his father's wealth, and gave a deeply serious tone to his mind. He might have risen to eminence in the State by his riches, and by devoting himself to public life; but he had early determined to the service of the Christian faith, went young to Oxford, and then travelled for two or three years in France and Italy. In the midst of the full tide of the classical revival, he gave himself up entirely to the study of Holy Scripture and the early Fathers, showing his originality by breaking free from the exclusive reverence in which Augustine was held in Latin Christendom, and paying no less attention to Origen and Jerome. He returned to Oxford to pursue his studies. He was only in sub-deacon's orders, but according to the easy fashion of the day he held a benefice in Suffolk, and prebends in Salisbury, York and St. Martin's-le-Grand. He began his public career with gratuitous lectures on the writings of St. Paul, simply expounding the Greek text, and explaining the general drift and subtleties of the argument. "It was the religion of St. Paul expanded in all its grave and solemn simplicity. But the more the veil is drawn from the mind and character of Colet, the more does he stand out as beyond his age. Besides these lectures on St. Paul, certain others on the Book of Genesis have been unearthed among the treasures of the Cambridge Library. If, on St. Paul, Colet rigidly adhered, not to the letter (he was far beyond the notion of verbal inspiration) but to the sense of the Apostle, we find him in a far more free spirit treating the first chapter of Genesis as a noble poem, designed by its author Moses to impress upon a rude and barbarous people the great truths of the creation of the world by the one Omnific God. The description of the successive acts of creation is followed out with singular ingenuity; and these and the periods of time have in his view a profound religious scope, but in themselves are only pious allegories to commend the great internal truths. I have space only for two passages : 'The day and night were but ingenious figments, not real divisions of time; the resting on the Sabbath-day was partly and chiefly that he might lead the people on to the imitation of God, whom, after the manner of a poet, he had mentioned as working on six days, and resting the seventh, so that they also might devote every seventh day to rest, and to the contemplation of God and of His worship.' According to the theory of Colet, 'Moses, after the manner of a good and pious poet, as Origen against Celsus calls him, was willing to invent some figures, not altogether worthy of God, if only it might be profitable and useful to man; which race of men is so dear to God, that God emptied Himself of His glory, taking the form of a servant, that He might accommodate Himself to the poor heart of man. So all things of God, when given to men, must needs lose something of their sublimity, and be put in a form more palpable and more within the grasp of man. Accordingly the high knowledge of Moses about God and divine things, and the creation of the world, when it came to be submitted to the vulgar apprehension, savoured altogether of the humble and the rustic, so that he had to speak, not according to his own comprehension, but according to the comprehension of the multitude. Thus accommodating himself to their comprehension, Moses endeavoured by this most honest and poetic figure at once to feed them and lead them to the worship of God.'"[1]

At Oxford began the friendship between Colet and Erasmus which lasted for life. Erasmus became one of a circle of kindred spirits: Charnock, Head of St. Mary's College; Grocyn, who first taught Greek at Oxford; Linacre the physician, and young Thomas More, the future Chancellor.

In 1503, after nine years in the University since his return, Colet, who was already Rector of Stepney in the

[1] Seebohm's *Oxford Reformers* and Milman's *Annals*, p. 115.

eastern part of the diocese of London, was made Dean of St. Paul's, and took his degree as Doctor of Divinity.

"As Dean of St. Paul's, Colet stood forth among the Churchmen of his day, with almost all the virtues, few, if any, of the common infirmities of his order: unimpeachable blamelessness of life, generous hospitality, not indiscriminate, though profuse, but delighting in a narrow circle, intellectual as well as religious, in which, according to the fashion of the day, theological readings mingled with the cheerful banquet. Those without this pale taunted him of course as niggardly and covetous, prodigal as he was of the emoluments of his office. This revenue was before long to be augmented by the great wealth of his father, which he entirely devoted to objects of public advantage, and to charity. Colet rapidly worked a complete change, not in the ceremonial or ordinary services of the Cathedral, but as introducing a new system of religious instruction. For the first time the pulpit of the Cathedral, or that of Paul's Cross, freely opened the sacred Scriptures to the people. Colet himself preached regularly on every Sunday and holiday, and obtained the aid of the most learned and eloquent preachers of the day, like himself devoted to the study of the sacred writings and their practical application. He adhered to his famous maxim, 'Keep to the Bible and the Apostles' Creed, and let Divines, if they like, dispute about the rest.' He founded a kind of catechetical lecture for the young, in English, which the chronicler Grafton seems to notice as something altogether new."

Colet's famous sermon at the opening of Convocation is still remembered. It was a calm, powerful, deliberate arraignment of the vices of the clergy, and an earnest exhortation to amendment. The subject was "Conformity to this world, and reformation in newness of mind." The four deadly sins denounced by the Apostle were the pride of life, the lust of the flesh, worldly occupation (the preacher dwelt especially on preferment hunting) and extortionate avarice. A debate followed on the treatment of Lollards. The more merciful asked if there was any text that could justify persecution. "Hereticum hominem post unam et alteram correptionem devita" (a man that is an heretic, after the first and second admonition reject), quoted an old divine, by a gross mistranslation interpreting the last word as "out of life with him." Another astounding quotation was "Suffer not a witch to live," where the Vulgate uses the word "maleficus," an evil practiser. The year before, Bishop FitzJames had forced twenty-three Lollards to abjure, and two at least he had burned at Smithfield. Hunn, a citizen of London, who was furiously opposed to ecclesiastical courts, was judged a heretic because a copy of Wycliffe's Bible was found in his house. One night he was found hanged in the Bishop of London's prison; and the coroner brought in a verdict of wilful murder against the Bishop of London's Chancellor, Dr. Horsey, the summoner and the bellringer of the Cathedral. The King made them pay a fine of £1500 to Hunn's family.

Colet was engaged in building his celebrated school (St. Paul's) on the ground east of the Cathedral, to which he devoted a large part of his patrimonial wealth, endowing it with £30,000 or £40,000 in our money. Bishop FitzJames was filled with the utmost alarm that it was intended to imbue the realm with new, and therefore dangerous, doctrines; he presented to the Primate distinct charges of heresy against the Dean. Warham quietly put these aside without examination or trial. An attempt to arouse Henry VIII. later on against Colet was equally futile. Henry was plunging with youthful ambition into continental wars: Colet, from the pulpit of St. Paul's, preached a bold and powerful sermon against war. The King sent for Colet; instead of rebuke or punishment, he thanked him for the good which he was doing to his people. He, the King, would teach Colet's accusers that they should not assail him with impunity. Colet answered that he would rather surrender his endowments than that any should suffer on his account.

Again, " on Good Friday it was Colet's turn to preach before the King at the Chapel Royal. The King had become more passionately warlike. Colet preached on the victory of Christ. He spoke against wars waged from hate or ambition. Rulers should follow the example of Christ rather than of Cæsar or Alexander. The King again sent for Colet (April 17, 1513); again not to reprimand him, but to consult him 'for the ease of his conscience.' The interview was long: the courtiers watched its issue with undisguised hope. At the close the King said aloud, ' Let every one have his Doctor; this is the Doctor for me.' Latimer says 'that Colet should have been burned if God had not turned the King's heart to the contrarie.' Colet is said to have preached again, admitting the lawfulness of defensive war."[1]

The members of Colet's Cathedral Chapter were not in harmony with him. He left the whole management of the school and its endowments to the Mercers' Company, of which his father was Master. " The Cathedral at that time, as before and after, was a great mart as well as a church. The walls of the nave and the pillars were placarded with advertisements, not only on ecclesiastical matters, but of more worldly character. Men met there in multitudes, and the busy, sometimes loud, hum of business, of barter and sale, was heard, while in the chapels, the aisles, before the altar of the Virgin, before the high altar, masses were being said, and worshippers were kneeling in adoration. Colet does not seem to have interfered to prevent this profanation. We doubt if he had the power over his Chapter to command the suppression of the evil. Over that Chapter he had not certainly the dominant power. He drew up a body of statutes for the Church, rigid, but by no means austere or

[1] Milman's *Annals*, p. 122.

ascetic. But Colet's statutes were never accepted by the Chapter, nor confirmed by the Bishop. FitzJames was not likely to force on a reluctant Chapter statutes framed by Colet. They were then, and remained ever after, a dead letter." [1]

In failing health, Colet determined to retire to a monastery, and chose the house of the Carthusians at Sheen. Before he could remove there, he was carried off by his old enemy the sweating sickness at the age of fifty-three. Erasmus, in a famous letter to Justus Jodocus, describes, with heartfelt eloquence, the two most perfect Christians of his time; one of them was John Colet.

[1] Milman's *Annals*, p. 123.

CHAPTER X

THE INTERIOR OF OLD ST. PAUL'S [1]

THE time chosen by Dr. Sparrow Simpson for his charming description of a walk inside the old Cathedral is 1510, before the Reformation, when the mediæval ritual and arrangements were still complete. The west end has three stately portals, the middle one of which is divided by a great pillar of brass, to which the leaves of the great door are fastened. On the left, as we enter the sublime nave, is the Court of Convocation, at the second bay. Not far is the font, near which Sir John Montacute desired to be buried, "wherein he was baptized." At the sixth bay are two small doors, north and south, offering dangerous facilities for a thoroughfare. A notice against the north door runs thus—

> "All those that shall enter within the Church dore
> With Burthen or Basket must give to the Poore:
> And if there be any aske what they must pay
> To this Box, 'tis a penny ere they pass away."

The whole space between the columns of the tenth bay on the left is filled up with the Chantry Chapel of Bishop Kempe (1448–1489). A large aperture in the roof of the nave is noticeable: the explanation is given by Lombarde, the antiquary, in his *Topographical Dictionary*: [2] "I myself

[1] This chapter is epitomized from one in "Chapters about Old St. Paul's," by my late friend Dr. Sparrow Simpson, the learned Antiquarian and Librarian of the Cathedral, who knew everything that there was to know on the subject.

[2] A.D. 1536–1601.

THE INTERIOR OF OLD ST. PAUL'S

being a child once saw in Paul's Church at London at a feast of Whitsuntide, where the coming down of the Holy Ghost was set forth by a white pigeon that was let fly out of a hole that is yet to be seen in the midst of the roof of the Great Aisle, and by a long censer which, descending out of the same place almost to the very ground, was swung up and down to such a length that it reached at one sweep almost to the west gate of the Church, and with the other to the choir stairs of the same, breathing out over the whole Church and company a most pleasant perfume of such sweet things as were burned therein." It was "a great large censer all silver with many windows and battlements": its weight no less than 15 ounces 3 quarters.

Noticeable, too, are little tables in the nave, where the Twelve Scribes sit for the accommodation of the public, after having taken an oath of fidelity to the Dean and Chapter. They write letters, or prepare legal instruments.

On the right hand of the nave, at the eleventh bay, is a magnificent monument to Sir John de Beauchamp, K.G., son of the famous Guy, Earl of Warwick (*temp.* Edward II.), (whose own tomb is one of exceeding beauty in the Beauchamp Chapel of Warwick Church). Sir John was Constable of the Castles of Dover and London, Warden of the Cinque Ports, Admiral of England and Privy Councillor. He died A.D. 1360, the thirty-fourth year of the reign of Edward III. It is a recumbent effigy in full armour, with armorial bearings on panels at the sides, and a canopy above. By a strange mistake the people call it Duke Humphry's Tomb, though the good Duke of Gloucester lies honourably buried at St. Albans Abbey; "in adoration of which Duke, the vulgar in old times used on St. Andrew's Day, before Christmas, to flock and prostrate themselves before this monument, and have a feast prepared for that purpose, in which they styled themselves several officers appertaining to the said Duke. Moreover, on May-day, a certain rabble of tankard-bearers and mean mechanics used to come early in the morning, strewed flowers and sprinkled water on the said monument ... till within our memory the bell-ringers and door-keepers have debarred them of their superstitious addresses, telling them that if they would visit Duke Humfrey's tomb they should go to St. Albans."[1] A man who goes without his dinner (walking during dinner-time in this nave) is said "to dine with Duke Humfrey"; in reference to this there is a proverb, "Trash and trumpery is the way to Duke Humfrey; that is, folly and idleness is the way to go without dinner."

The small door on the right opens into the cloisters, a beautiful square with seven traceried arches on each side, and of two stories : in the middle rises the lofty octagonal Chapter House with its pointed roof; it was built in 1332.[2]

As you turn back to the interior of the nave, you see an image of the Virgin at the foot of Sir John Beauchamp's tomb, with a light always burning before it; every morning, after matins, a short office is said there. By the north-west pier of the central tower is the Chapel of St. Paul, "built of timber, with stairs mounting thereunto." On the south side of the nave is St. Catherine's Chapel, on the north the chapel of the Holy Trinity; there is also an altar of the Apostles. As we stand under the central tower the great length and beauty of the transepts and their aisles are remarkable; the immense and prolonged choir and its aisles are protected by stone screens with figures and rich canopies. Near the door of the south transept is the Chapel of St. John the Evangelist. In the north transept there is a great crucifix of fabulous age, an object of enthusiastic devotion, with a light burning before it, before which large oblations are made. Near it is the grave of Richard Martin, Bishop of St. David's in the reign of Edward IV., who had special veneration for this crucifix, and left a benefaction for the choristers to sing annually before it. Close to the great

[1] Fisher's *Tombes in Old St. Paul's*, p. 65 ; A.D. 1684.
[2] Dugdale.

north door is a group of chapels dedicated to St. James, St. Thomas, the Holy Ghost, St. John Baptist and St. Margaret.

The choir contains some magnificent brasses: to Bishop FitzHugh near the altar, Dean Evere near the entrance, Canon John Newcourt (1485), Archdeacon Lichfield (1496). In the south aisle stands the image of St. Wilgefort, the chosen burying-place of Dean Colet. Near are two mitred recumbent figures under one canopy, early Bishops of London: Eustace de Fauconberge, Treasurer of the Exchequer, who died 1228, and Henry de Wingham, Chancellor of England, who died 1262. At the east end of the aisle is St. Dunstan's Chapel; the striking altar tomb is that of the famous Henry de Lacy, Earl of Lincoln, Protector of England in the absence of Edward I., and Viceroy of Aquitaine, to whom that King on his deathbed entrusted his son and successor. The figure is cross-legged. He died at his house of Lincoln's Inn. In the north aisle of the choir are many interesting monuments. At the western entrance, under the second window on the left, are two low shrines under deeply recessed arches, the resting-places of King Sebba and King Ethelred. King Sebba's inscription (in Latin) ran thus: " Here lies Sebba, King of the East Saxons, who was converted to the Faith of Christ by that Holy Man Erkonwald Bishop of London, in the year of our Lord 677. This good King was a person frequent in his daily duty and devotion towards God, and seriously intentive on religious exercises, and continual prayer, with the visible fruits of daily almsdeeds, preferring a private and monastic life to all the riches and honours of the kingdom. Who, after he had reigned thirty years, received the religious habit by the benediction of Walter, Bishop of London, who succeeded Erkenwald. Of whom the Venerable Bede writes many things in his History of the Nation of the English." [1]

[1] Fisher's *Tombes in Old St. Paul's*, p. 19.

The inscription to King Ethelred the Unready is also worthy of full transcription: "Here lies Ethelred King of the English, son of King Edgar; to whom on the day of his consecration after the crown was placed on his head St. Dunstan, Archbishop of Canterbury, is reported to have predicted terrible things in these words: 'Because thou hast aspired to the Crown by the death of thy Brother, for whose murder the English have conspired with thine infamous Mother; therefore the sword shall not depart from thine house for ever, but shall cruelly rage against thee all the days of thy life, destroying of thy seed so long till thy Kingdom shall be transferred to a foreign nation, whose customs and language neither thou nor thy people shall understand. Neither shall this thy sin be expiated but by a very long punishment, nor yet the sin of thy mother, nor the sins of all those wicked men who had a hand in that most execrable and pernicious Council.' The which things as they were ominously predicted by this holy man were exactly verified; for King Ethelred being vanquished, and put to flight in several battles by Sweyn and his son Canute, and being at last closely besieged in the City of London, and brought to great extremity, finally ended his days in much tribulation and trouble in the year of our Lord 1017, after reigning six and thirty years in great perplexity."

A few steps further is another deeply recessed tomb, that of John de Chishull, formerly Dean of St. Paul's and afterwards Bishop of London, who died in 1280. On the right is a beautiful tomb with a low canopy and exquisite screen above it; that of Roger Niger, Bishop of London, who died in 1241, and was canonized after his death; the stones are worn by the feet of countless pilgrims; in the sacristy is a cope worn by St. Roger, of red samite, embroidered with stars and roses. Another fine canopied altar-tomb is that of a Knight of the Garter named Burley, Warden of the Cinque Ports, Justice of South Wales, Constable of Windsor and Dover Castles, Vice-chamberlain of the

Household and dearest of the Counsellors of Richard II., beheaded in 1388 during the triumph of one of the factions under the minority of the King. The space between the two columns north of the high altar is occupied by one of the noblest monuments in the Cathedral, that of John of Gaunt and his first wife, Blanche, in her own right Duchess of Lancaster. His second wife, Constance, daughter of Pedro the Cruel, King of Castile and Leon, was also buried beside him, but was not in effigy on the tomb. Passing the low altar-tomb of Canon Ralph de Hengham, Chief Justice of the Common Pleas, we come, at the east end of the aisle, to St. George's Chapel.

Now, having inspected the south and north aisles of the choir, we will go back, and enter the choir itself by its superb carved stone doorway; it is at the top of an ascent of twelve steps. It is a glorious choir, of pure pointed Gothic, and, with the Lady Chapel, which is a mere continuation beyond the reredos, is of the same length as the nave. The delicately carved woodwork of the stalls, like that of Lincoln, strikes the eye; the stalls of the Dean, the Archdeacon of London, the Archdeacon of Middlesex, the Archdeacon of St. Albans, the Archdeacon of Essex, and the Precentor face eastwards. Over each stall of a Canon is the name of his prebend, with the first verse of the portion of the Psalter which he is bound to recite daily. The organ is on the north side. Away to the east in the centre is the straight flat line of the openwork reredos, with the high altar in the centre, dedicated to St. Paul; another altar to the north, dedicated to St. Ethelbert, King and Confessor; and another to the south to St. Mellitus, first Roman Bishop of London. These three altars were originally dedicated by Richard de Bentworth, Bishop of London, March 24, 1339. Over the altar Dugdale speaks of a beautiful tablet, adorned with many precious stones and enamelled work, and divers images of metal; a sort of special reredos; it cost 200 marks in 1309.

On the right is a tabernacle of wood, with a picture of St. Paul richly painted. Above all rises the magnificent rose window, with seven long divisions below it, pouring down a flood of many coloured lights. To reach the sanctuary you ascend six more steps; eastwards of the screen is the famous shrine of St. Erkonwald. He died on April 30, 693, a day sacred to the Cathedral. He was buried in the nave. In the Great Fire of 1087-8, the Cathedral was destroyed, but the saint's resting-place remained. On November 14, 1148, his bones were translated and placed in a very precious tomb. In 1314, Bishop Gilbert de Segrave laid the first stone of a new and more magnificent shrine behind the high altar, to which, on February 1, 1326, the body of the saint was transferred. Canterbury had its shrine of Thomas à Becket, Westminster of Edward the Confessor, Durham of St. Cuthbert, Ely that of St. Etheldreda, St. Albans its twin-shrines of the Proto-martyr and the Roman soldier St. Amphibalus, and St. Paul's has the Anglo-Saxon Prince-Bishop St. Erkonwald. Devotees have vied in their donations: Canon Walter de Thorpe gave all his gold rings and jewels; under Edward II., Dean and Chapter lavished rich store of gold, silver and precious stones; under Edward III., three goldsmiths were at work a whole year; King John of France, when a prisoner, gave twelve nobles; under Richard II., Richard de Preston, citizen and grocer, gave a splendid sapphire, credited with cures for the eyes. There are many images, notably the gilded figure of St. Erkonwald. The lights burning are provided by an endowment of Dean Evere in 1407. The whole effect is superb; besides what has been mentioned, the figures of angels, the Coronation of the Virgin, the crystals, beryls, other jewels, and the sumptuous painting.

The screen which crosses the whole Church behind the altar protects, as we have seen, three chapels: the Lady Chapel in the middle, St. George's north and St. Dunstan's south. In the Lady Chapel the Brethren and Sisters of the Guild of the Minstrels meet for their devotions by Charter of Edward IV. The tomb of one of the greatest of the Bishops of London is near, Richard de Braybroke, who died in 1404, and of whom an account has been given in a former chapter.

In the crypt, a very beautiful structure with four rows of eight columns and a vaulted roof, part of which is known as the Church of St. Faith and part as the Jesus Chapel, are the chapels of St. John Baptist, St. Anne, St. Sebastian and St. Radegund. Over the door into the Jesus Chapel, west of St. Faith's, is a painted picture of Christ; the figure near, wearing her armorial mantle, with her children kneeling around her, is Margaret, Countess of Shrewsbury, whose body lies below the picture; she was daughter of Richard Beauchamp, Earl of Warwick, and second wife of the illustrious John Talbot, Earl of Shrewsbury, general of the English armies in France in the time of Henry VI., and opponent of the Maid of Orleans. She died in 1467. In the Jesus Chapel meets the wealthy Guild of Jesus, for which Colet drew up rules and of which he was Rector.

The earliest guild in the Cathedral was probably that founded by Dean Ralph de Diceto, the members of which meet four times a year for the Mass of the Holy Ghost. Besides the Minstrels' Guild, there are those of St. Catherine, the Annunciation of the Virgin, and of All Saints (which met in the charnel house).

Among tombs later than 1510 are those of Dean Donne the Poet, 1631, in his shroud, the only effigy left whole by the fire; Dean Colet, 1519, with bust above and skeleton below; William Hewit, 1599, a patriotic merchant; Sir William Cokayn, 1626 (with wife and eleven children), the Lord Mayor who received James I., to take counsel about the repairs of St. Paul's, which were afterwards carried out by Inigo Jones; Sir Nicholas Bacon, 1578, twenty years Lord Keeper, and father of the illustrious Lord Bacon;

MONUMENT OF DEAN DONNE (Saved from the Fire)

THE INTERIOR OF OLD ST. PAUL'S

John King, Bishop of London, 1621; the vast monument of Sir Christopher Hatton, 1591, Lord Chancellor, of which it was written—

> "Philip and Francis have no tombe,
> For great Christopher takes all the roome,"

referring to Sir Philip Sidney and Sir Francis Walsingham, whose graves were near; William Herbert, Earl of Pembroke, K.G., 1569, well known in the reigns of Henry VIII., Edward VI., Mary and Elizabeth, who married the sister of Queen Catherine Parr (a very stately monument of marble and alabaster, on the north side); Sir John Mason, 1566, a notable Privy Councillor in the same four reigns; William Aubrey, LL.D., 1595, Regius Professor of Law at Oxford, and Vicar-General, a famous lawyer under Queen Elizabeth; Sir John Wolly, 1595, Privy Councillor and Chancellor of the Garter in the same reign; Sir Thomas Heneage, 1594, Treasurer, Vice-Chamberlain and Chancellor of the Duchy of Lancaster to Queen Elizabeth; Alexander Nowell, Dean of St. Paul's, 1601, author of the celebrated Catechism; Dr. Thomas Linacre, 1557, physician to Henry VIII., founder of the Royal College of Physicians; Sir Anthony Vandyke, the great painter; and others of scarcely less interest too many to mention.

CHAPTER XI

SOURCES OF REVENUE BEFORE THE REFORMATION

THE life of the old Cathedral would be very imperfectly understood, if some account were not given of other characteristic sources of revenue, besides estates and manors, with their rents, tithes, fines and produce.

There were, for instance, public funerals and funeral rites in honour of great personages buried elsewhere. "The benefit was not small which they had by celebrating the obsequies of sundry great persons; as of Queen Anne, wife of Richard II., whose hearse was adorned with the banner of her arms and of the King's; so also of the Earl of St. Paul in the reign of Henry VI.; of Maximilian the Emperor; of the Emperor Charles V.; of Isabel and Joan, wives of the said Emperor; of the Emperor Ferdinand, brother of the said Charles, of Charles VIII., King of France; Anne, Queen of France, Duchess and sole heir of Brittany; of Louis XII., Francis I. and Henry II., Kings likewise of France; as also of Philip, King of Castile, Ferdinand of Aragon, and John, King of Portugal; and sundry eminent men of our own nation, the mention of whom, for brevity's sake, I pass by."[1]

"The state and order in the performance of other obsequies was little inferior to that used at the funerals of these great princes; the Church and quire being hung with black, and escutcheons of their arms; their hearses set up with wonderful magnificence, adorned with rich banner-rolls, pencils, and environed with banners, being chief mourners and assistants, accompanied with divers Bishops

[1] Dugdale, p. vi.

and Abbots *in pontificalibus;* so likewise with ambassadors of foreign princes, and many of our English nobility, the Knights of the Garter, Lord Mayor of London, and the several companies of this great City, and lastly having solemn service and mass on the morrow."[1] All these splendid paraphernalia, on the principle that whatever was brought into the Church belonged to the Church, besides the offerings, went to the treasury of the Chapter.[2]

Then there were the masses for the dead, which were believed to shorten the pains of Purgatory, which awaited all alike, and which only differed from those of hell in point of duration. "The pious prudence of the living, or the desperate devotion of the dying, or the reverence and affection of friends or kindred; in some cases national admiration, eager to do honour to men of renown, provided for the due celebration of these inestimable orisons. The simpler form was that of the *obit*, on the anniversary of the death, performed by the ordinary functionaries of the Church on some especial day;[3] the sums paid for these commemorations were distributed in certain proportions to the clergy and ecclesiastics present; unless otherwise specially provided, the Residentiaries received a double portion. The number of the anniversaries was one hundred and eleven. From this source the Dean and Residentiaries received about £1075 according to present value: the rest was distributed by rule."

To those who believed strongly in the reality of Purgatory and the efficacy of masses for the dead, and who had command of wealth, the foundation of chantries was an obvious step; masses could be said in them for ever, by priests provided by the endowment. None could tell when the soul's release would be finally effected. The number of chantries in St. Paul's is almost beyond calculation: in Dugdale's *St. Paul's* they fill nearly forty pages. They were founded by Kings, Henry IV., Edward IV.; by Bishops,

[1] Dugdale.   [2] Milman, p. 144.   [3] Dugdale, p. 356.

Deans and Canons; by earls and other nobles; by judges and by wealthy citizens of London. "They varied in value with the wealth and munificence of the founders, from lands, manors, messuages and rents, to lamps and candles, and pittances of bread and wine—these chiefly to be distributed to the poor. The chantry founded by King Henry IV. was among the most richly endowed. It was for the souls of his father, John of Gaunt, Duke of Lancaster, specially on February 4, and of Blanche of Castile, his mother, on September 12. It stipulated for the services to be performed on those hallowed days: placebo, dirige, anthems, psalms and lexons. It assigned stipends to the Dean, the Canons, down to the vergers and bellringers; and to the Mayor and Sheriffs of London for their attendance. A house was rented of the Bishop of London in which the chantry priests were to reside (who said the ordinary masses), and due provision made for the repair of this mansion. Besides the gift of chalices, missals, bread, wine, wax and glasses, eighty tapers were to burn for ever on the said anniversaries, and on other great festivals."[1]

Of the Bishops' chantries "the most splendid seems to have been that of Thomas Kempe. King Edward IV., for the singular reverence which he bore unto God and unto the Blessed Virgin Mary, and to the devout Confessors St. Erkonwald and St. Ethelbert, granted license to Thomas Kemp to found a chantry to be served daily by the confessor of the Bishop of London. It was for the good estate of King Edward and Elizabeth his Consort, as also for the Bishop, during their lives in this world, and for the health of their souls after their departure thence, and moreover, for the souls of the said King's progenitors, for the parents and benefactors of the said Bishop, and for all the faithful deceased. The endowment was in land, forest and meadow, 170 acres in Essex. The chantry had a beautiful chapel, between the north aisle and nave of the Church."[2]

[1] Milman, p. 145.   [2] Dugdale and Milman.

The mass priests were a peculiar class and order. The Statutes of St. Paul's recognized a large body of chaplains, outside the corporations of Canons and minor Canons, and rigidly prohibited the holding this office and a benefice with cure of souls.

The mass priests were not held in high reputation. It was probably these that Archbishop Sudbury, following the example of Archbishop Islip, denounced in unmeasured language. "They are so infected with the vice of covetousness that, not content with reasonable stipends, they demand and sometimes receive exhorbitant salaries; and the aforesaid priests, so covetous and delicate, return to their vomit, become uncontrollably mad and unbearable, some of them indulging in gluttony and lust, plunging into the deepest gulfs of evil, to the odious scandal of all ecclesiastics, and most pernicious example to the laity. They are henceforth to be content with five marks a year for those without cure of souls, for those with such cures, with six."[1]

Nor was the work well done. There is a letter of the year 1385, sealed with the mayoralty seal, to the Dean and Chapter of St. Paul's, complaining that many tenements and rents in the same City had been devised for founding and maintaining divers chantries in the same Church, and for offering up prayers and other devotions perpetually for their souls. The foundation deeds were in the Chapter archives and at Guildhall, "and whereas we have fully understood, and also do see it daily with our eyes, when we pass by your Church of St. Paul—the which do we hold to be our Mother Church — that there are but few chaplains to sing there in proportion to the chantries which in the said Church have been founded, to the great peril of your souls, who ought to oversee such chantries, maintain and support the same; we do pray and request you, to the honour of God, and for the profit of the said Church, and of yourselves, and your successors, that you will cause such

[1] Wilkins, vol. iii. p. 136.

fault to be amended and redressed." Let none holding a chantry at St. Paul's hold one elsewhere also, and in St. Paul's only one.[1]

Besides obits and chantries, there were oblations, which were offered at the crucifixes, altars and shrines. There were two great crucifixes, one in the nave and the other, the great popularity of which I have mentioned before, in the north transept. The altars of the Virgin, St. Lawrence, St. John Baptist, St. Mary Magdalene have also been described. The great image of the Virgin in the nave, by the second pillar on the south side, close to the tomb of Sir John Beauchamp, was endowed with a watermill, seventy acres of arable land, five of meadow, three of pasture and eight of wood. The richest shrine of all was that of St. Erkonwald; it was believed that miracles were performed there; "the very dust, mingled with water and drunk, was held to work instantaneous cures." On one occasion the captive King John of France paid his devotions there. "His offerings were those of a king, not of a prisoner. Twelve nobles at the Annunciation, twenty-six at the crucifix near the north door; as he approached the altar he presented four basons of gold. He gave to the Dean five florin nobles; at the shrine of St. Erkonwald twenty-two." The annual offerings at the great cross in the north transept alone are reckoned at £9000 in present value. All the oblations were divided amongst the Dean and Residentiaries.

The exhibition of relics must not be forgotten. Dugdale has preserved two lists, one drawn up by Dean Radulph de Diceto, the other later. In the first list we read of a knife of our Lord, hair of St. Mary Magdalene, the bones and part of the dresses of saints and martyrs, the dust of others. In the second is some of the blood of St. Paul, hair of the Virgin, the hand of St. John the Evangelist. One reliquary contained the milk, the vest and more hair

[1] *Memorials of London Life*, 1868, p. 226, quoted by Milman.

of the Virgin. Another had pieces of the skull and part of the dress of St. Thomas of Canterbury; another the head of St. Ethelbert, King and Martyr. The whole body of St. Mellitus, of which the Cathedral once boasted, dwindled down to dubious proportions, his two arms, one large and one small. The reliquaries were always of exquisite workmanship, in crystal, adorned with gold, silver and precious stones. The two lists fill more than two folio pages and a half. The devotions of the pious at their exhibition was a distinct source of revenue.

Indulgences have been mentioned before in reference to the progress of the building. Here further details must be given from the historian of St. Paul's. In the thirteenth century "began, or rather was opened out in prodigal munificence, a new and unfailing source for the completion, maintenance and adornment of the fabric. The Cathedral of the metropolis was no longer to depend on the episcopal revenues. Of those of the Dean and Chapter, as contributing to the fabric, we find nothing. Not only the City of London; the whole realm, even foreign countries, were laid under tribute to the great national work; a work in which all Churches in England, indeed in Christendom, were to take pride and interest. That fruitful source, the sins of mankind, and the commutation of the days, years centuries of penance established by the Church for the remission of those sins, by alms and contributions, was to pour out in its inexhaustible fulness on the Church of St. Paul. In London, an indulgence of forty days, for all sins duly confessed and repented of, was granted on liberal terms; and this indulgence was to be renewed every year on the anniversary of the dedication."

"But neither were the citizens of London the only class expected to defray the cost of their noble edifice, nor was that the first or the last occasion on which old St. Paul's levied its voluntary tax on the sins and penitence of good Christians. The archives of St. Paul's still contain copies of indulgences issued from the year 1261 to 1387. They extend to almost every diocese in England and Wales, commencing with Bangor. The second in the series is granted by Hugh Foliot, then Bishop of Hereford. The third is from the Archbishop of Canterbury. The Diocese of Canterbury contributed three times; York and the Northern Province only once. Of all the English dioceses Norwich was the most liberal; it contributed seven times.[1] Salisbury, Ely, Hereford, five; Winchester, three times only. Ireland answered freely to the appeal. Seven dioceses appear; Emly and Leighlin twice. There is a solitary contribution from Scotland, from Brechin. Indulgences were not confined to our islands, or to English authorities. Cardinal Otho, in 1260, grants forty days' indulgence to all the faithful of the Province of Canterbury who will devoutly visit the Church of St. Paul: 'he who sows sparingly shall reap sparingly; he who sows plenteously, plenteously, and shall reap eternal life.' In 1235, the Archbishop of Cologne, being in England, is so impressed by the majesty of the Church as to grant an indulgence of fifty days to all who will contribute to it. Cardinal Siran de Sully, Archbishop of Bourges, is even more munificent, and grants an indulgence of one hundred days. The general term ranged from forty days, the usual number, down to twenty. In some few, the particular part of the Cathedral to be repaired, adorned or constructed is specified: as the Chapel of the Virgin, the bell-tower, lights at certain altars. Two of the later indulgences are for Paul's Cross. Sometimes they demand special prayers for the souls of persons named: that from Brechin enjoined devotion for St. Edmond, Martyr and Confessor, King Edward, in the Church of St. Paul, and Isabella Bruce." [2]

[1] The counties of Norfolk and Suffolk, at that time the seat of the woollen trade, were the wealthy part of the kingdom.
[2] Milman's *Annals*.

CHAPTER XII

PERSONAL STAFF OF THE CATHEDRAL IN THE MIDDLE AGES

Dr. Sparrow Simpson, who edited the voluminous Statutes of St. Paul's, has a very interesting account of the staff which served the Cathedral in the days before the Reformation. About A.D. 1450 it consisted of the Bishop, the Dean, the four Archdeacons, the Treasurer, the Precentor and the Chancellor. Besides these there were thirty greater canons, twelve minor canons, a considerable number of chaplains and thirty vicars.

St. Paul's was one of the cathedrals of the Old Foundation, of which there are nine in England: London, York, Salisbury, Lincoln, Lichfield, Hereford, Wells, Exeter and Chichester; all these were served by secular Canons, that is, non-monastic clergy. There are eight cathedrals of what is called the New Foundation: Canterbury, Carlisle, Durham, Ely, Norwich, Rochester, Winchester and Worcester. Five cathedrals were founded by Henry VIII.: Bristol, Chester, Gloucester, Oxford and Peterborough. Two, Manchester and Ripon, were transformed from collegiate into cathedral churches in 1847 and 1836; the Sees of Truro, Liverpool, St. Albans, Southwark, Southwell, Newcastle and Wakefield are still more recent. The cathedrals of the New Foundation were administered by regular clergy (monks living under a regula, or rule), generally the Benedictine. The four Welsh cathedrals were of the Old Foundation.

The connection of the Bishop with St. Paul's was, in early days, very close. The palace was in the precincts, towards the western end of the churchyard, on the north.

Bishop Maurice, Bishop Richard de Belmeis and others charged themselves with the work of building or rebuilding the Church. The withdrawal of the Bishop from the immediate administration of the Cathedral was probably gradual, partly because he so frequently occupied one of the great offices of State, that of Chancellor, High Treasurer, Ambassador and the like; partly because of the attractions of Fulham as a residence. It was the Bishop's duty to be present in the Cathedral on the greater feasts, on Christmas Day, Easter Day, Ascension Day, Whit-Sunday, the Festivals of St. Paul and St. Erkonwald, and on Maundy Thursday and Ash-Wednesday.

Before the Norman Conquest there were no Deans; the earliest Dean in England was the Dean of St. Paul's, A.D. 1086. In earlier days most cathedrals followed the Rule of St. Chrodegang, Bishop of Metz, A.D. 743, which provided a Provost under the Abbot. In cathedral churches which were not monastic, the Archdeacon acted as head of the Chapter under the Bishop. "He had the superintendence of the Cathedral Church and of Divine Service. He was Master of the Ceremonies. As such he had to keep note of the calendar, and to announce the fasts and festivals. He had to correct offences against ecclesiastical order during Divine Service; to see that the arrangements were properly made, and the ritual properly observed; he had also charge of the fabric of the Cathedral Church."[1] The earliest Statutes of St. Paul's embody the Rule of St. Chrodegang; and it is as a survival of this primitive system that Dr. Sparrow Simpson accounts for the unusual precedence accorded by the Statutes of St. Paul's to the Archdeacon of London. "Let the Archdeacon, or Chief Ruler, or Guardian of the Church, provide."[2] "We order therefore that all the Canons should come every day to the Chapter, that their souls may hear the Word of God,

---

[1] *Dictionary of Christian Antiquities:* "Archdeacon."
[2] *Statutes*, chap. 5; Sparrow Simpson's *Registrum*, p. lviii.

and that the Bishop, or the Archdeacon, or any one else who happens to preside, should give them the orders which he has to give."[1] "Let the Porter return the keys to the Archdeacon."

After the Conquest, the Dean became, under the Bishop, the head of the Chapter. The Dean invested the prebendaries, and corrected all offenders of higher rank; the others were left to the Chancellor of the Cathedral. A weekly Saturday Chapter was held for discipline. During vacancies in the See, the Dean and Chapter became guardians of the temporalities of the Bishopric.

Next in dignity to the Dean were the four Archdeacons: London, Essex, Middlesex and Colchester; but the Archdeacon of London was always the Archdeacon of the Cathedral. To the present day, the Archdeacon of London occupies the second stall in the choir, and with the Dean always accompanies the Bishop in processions, and escorts him to his throne. Essex comes next, because London in early days was the capital of the East Saxons. Another Archdeaconry, St. Albans, was added in the time of Henry VIII., but with the ruthless jealousy of ecclesiastical precedent he had no stall nor place in the Chapter.

The Treasurer followed. To him belonged the custody of all the goods of the Church: relics, books, sacred vessels, vestments, altar-cloths, hangings and other items of mediæval ritual. Twenty-six folio pages, each of two columns, in Dugdale's *History of St. Paul's* are filled with an inventory of these things, taken in 1295.

The Treasurer appointed a Sacrist to help him, and under the Sacrist three vergers. The Sacrist had to see that the elements for the mass were duly supplied; the linen and vestments in good condition; the service-books well bound, with clasps; that no one practised singing in the vestibule; and that the doors of the vestibule were opened at the right moment.

[1] *Statutes*, chap. 5; Sparrow Simpson's *Registrum*, p. lviii.

The Precentor was director of music; he had as his deputy the Succentor, and he nominated the Master of the Singing School.

The Chancellor, or Magister Scholarum, was the School Board, or Local Education Authority, of London in his day. From him the schoolmasters of the metropolis received their licence to teach. He composed the letters and deeds of the Chapter, and whatever was read aloud in the Chapter was read by him. He kept the seal, and for sealing any deed he received one pound of pepper. He appointed the Master of the Cathedral Grammar School. He prepared the daily rota of duty.

The Canons, or Prebendaries, were thirty in number, and with the Bishop at their head constituted the Chapter. They elected both Bishop and Dean. Each had an endowment attached to his stall, which are still the titles of the Prebendaries. The number was assigned by a Pope; if ever it should be desirable to increase the number in proportion to the enormous growth of population and interests in the See, it could be done by the Archbishop of Canterbury, who, up to the Reformation, was always Legate of the Pope, and who, after that epoch, was confirmed in his Legatine powers by Act of Parliament. Of these estates, eight were some way off: two in Bedfordshire, five in Essex, one in Middlesex; the rest were near the City. One still bears the curious title of Consumpta per Mare; this unhappy property was at Walton-on-the-Naze, and the predatory innundation occurred at the time of the Conquest. The names are so ancient that they are interesting to record: Cadyngton Major, Cadyngton Minor (Beds.); Sneating, Consumpta per Mare, Ealdland, Weldland, Readnorland and Tillingham (granted by King Ethelbert in 609) in Essex; Chiswick (Middlesex); Willesden, Brondesbury, Brownswood, Chamberlain's Wood, Maplesbury, Neasden, Harlesden, Oxgate, Twyford (all in Willesden); Pancras, Rugnere, Totenhall, Kentish

Town, Isledon (Islington), Newington, Portpool, Finsbury, Hoxton, Wenlock's Barn, Eald Street (a broad belt from Stepney to St. Pancras).

Gradually, says Dean Milman, but by no means slowly, the Canons found the strict residence contemplated by the Statutes (notwithstanding that each had his deputy) irksome; it was more pleasant to each to retire to the enjoyment of his prebendal estate, or the superior office he held. Prebends in those days were lavishly bestowed throughout the Church, with no regard to special duties, and were held by Bishops, dignitaries and foreigners. Thus the splendid company shrank by degrees; the services of the Church devolved on a still diminishing few, who were called Residentiaries. The abuse at length became so flagrant that authority was compelled to interfere, and to enforce the duties of residence: episcopal, Papal, even royal, decrees were necessary to fix a number sufficient to maintain the majesty of the ceremonial. The number seems to have varied from five down to two. Meantime the common fund from demesne lands and from other sources on the spot increased to an enormous extent; and it fell almost exclusively to the share of the Residentiaries. Residence became an object of cupidity. All the thirty were now as eager to avail themselves of their once despised rights as they were before to elude the burdensome duties. Now it was as necessary to limit the numbers, as before to compel residence. Episcopal and Papal decrees determined these, which, nevertheless, floated for a long time in uncertainty. So grew up a Chapter within the Chapter, like the Cabinet within the Privy Council, which undertook to discharge, with some other dignitaries, all the offices of the Church; to administer, and to their own advantage exclusively, the common revenues of the Cathedral.

The Residentiary Canon was to be present at all the canonical hours; to show large and costly hospitality, daily entertaining some of the clergy, and from time to time inviting the Bishop, and the Lord Mayor, Sheriffs and Aldermen, for it was desirable to maintain kindly relations with the City "lest the Cathedral should suffer any detriment." The hospitality is now the other way, for St. Paul's has lost nine-tenths of its lawful revenues, while the City has retained its own. So late as 1843 the shadow of the old hospitality remained, for the Canon-in-Residence, up to the close of that year, still continued to entertain at dinner on Sundays the clergy and vicars-choral of the Church who had attended morning service. At that time the hospitality of Sunday was abolished, and a money payment substituted instead. May I, as a Canon-in-Residence of many years' standing, plead the pleasantness of voluntarily keeping up the old custom?

As each Canon had his vicar, the thirty vicars had their Common Hall. They took rank after the chaplains, who in their turn were inferior to the minor Canons. In Colet's time, the number of vicars-choral had dwindled down to six, and that is the number of the vicars-choral at the present day. The appointment of twelve assistant vicars-choral, to augment the strength of the choir, so that, in addition to the boys, there should be three of each part to each side of the choir, is of recent origin.

The Minor Canons, formerly twelve in number, are of ancient date. They were incorporated as a College by Richard II. in 1394, and still possess that royal charter. A statute issued by the Chapter in 1364 says that they excel all chaplains, and that if the greater Canons do not officiate at the high altar, they are their substitutes. They had estates of their own, and a common seal. On a vacancy in their number, they nominated two to the Chapter, who selected one. One of them was appointed Custos of their College; two were (and are still) called Cardinals, on precisely the same principles, though devoid of the imperial honours, as Cardinals of the Church of Rome, as the pivots of the choir, an office not found in any other church in

England, and in very few abroad; another was called the Pitantiary, whose duties were financial.

The Chantry Priests were a large body, bound not only to say mass at their special altars, but also to attend in choir. Chaucer contrasts the mercenary greed of many of these chantry priests with his own ideal Parson—

> "He setté not his benefice to hire,
> Nor let his sheep, accumbered in the mire,
> To run unto London, unto St. Paul's,
> To seeken him a chantery of souls,
> Or with a Brotherhood to be withold;
> But dwelt at home, and kepte well his fold.
> So that the wolf ne'er made it not miscarry :
> He was a shepherd, and no mercenary."

The Sub-dean was the Dean's deputy, and looked after his interests in the Cathedral in his absence; he was always one of the minor Canons; the office has for some hundreds of years been purely titular. There were also the almoner, the four vergers and their servitors, the surveyor or architect, the twelve scribes in the nave, before alluded to, the book transcriber, the bookbinder, the chamberlain, the rent collector, the baker, the brewer and a host of minor officials.

The brewer alone had no sinecure. The brewings for the Cathedral took place nearly twice a week. "In 1286 there were one hundred brewings in the year. The quantity of grain consumed consisted of 175 quarters of barley, 175 quarters of wheat and 720 quarters of oats. We learn from the account of 1286 that the whole number of gallons brewed was 67,814."[1]

Archdeacon Hale also calculates that the yearly issue of bread amounted to no less than 40,000 loaves. The weight and quality of the loaves, varying according to the rank of the persons supplied, were matters of sufficient importance to be regulated by Statute.[2]

[1] Archdeacon Hale, *Domesday of St. Paul's*, p. 50.
[2] Sparrow Simpson, *Chapters*, p. 37.

CHAPTER XIII

HENRY VIII. AND THE APPROACH OF THE REFORMATION

As the Reformation approached, the sermons at Paul's Cross were perhaps the most influential and characteristic evidence of the conflicting forces. "Latimer was one day thundering against the abuses of the Church; on another Friar Forest was arraigning the King's ministers, and more than covertly glancing at the King himself. In truth, the sermons at Paul's Cross, if they could be recovered and arranged, would be a living and instructive chronicle of the Reformation, from the first murmur about the King's divorce, the almost unanimous rejection of the Papal supremacy, the enactment of the terrible reactionary Six Articles, the stern reassertion of all the Roman doctrines except obedience to the Pope, the rapid progress of the new opinions, even to the iconoclasm under the Protectorate and the reign of Edward VI., the terrible days of Queen Mary, the reorganization and final re-establishment of the Anglican doctrines under Elizabeth."[1]

The Bishops of London were *FitzJames*, the narrow-minded opponent of Colet; the gentle *Tunstall*, who had been advocate of Queen Catherine, and retired to Durham; *John Stokesley*, Ambassador to Rome about the Divorce; *Bonner*, under Henry VIII., strong anti-Papalist, yet eager to execute the stern enactments of the Six Articles, and to light fires in their support; then the kind and learned *Ridley*, the man of the New Testament; then *Bonner* again, now a fierce Papalist, burning Ridley and many others,

[1] Milman, p. 169.

and earning his eternal epithet; then *Grindal*, submitting to imperious Elizabeth, but with the disinclination of a Christian and a Churchman.

The momentous marriage of Catherine of Aragon to Arthur, Prince of Wales, the elder son of Henry VII., took place at St. Paul's Cathedral, on Sunday, November 21, 1501, with the utmost splendour. On her arrival, the Princess was received at the west door of the Cathedral by the Archbishop of Canterbury in full pontificals, the Bishops of Ely, Lincoln, Rochester, Llandaff, Bangor, the Abbots of Stratford, Bermondsey, Tower Hill glittering in their gorgeous attire. She was led to the altar, and made her offering. She was allowed a day's rest after the fatigue of her journey, in the Bishop's Palace. Her Spanish ladies and gentlemen were lodged in the Dean's and Canons' houses. On the following afternoon the Princess went in state, by Paul's Chain, to visit the Queen at Baynard's Castle, down below by the river.

On the day of the marriage the attendance was commanded of the Bishops of Exeter, Hereford, Bath, Lincoln, Carlisle, Chester, Rochester and Norwich; the Abbots of Bury, Westminster, St. Albans, Glastonbury, Abingdon and Reading. The whole Church was to be hung with arras. There was a platform of timber from the west door to the choir, twelve feet broad and four feet in height, with steps on every side, covered with red baize. The platform communicated with the Consistory, to the intent that the King and Queen might secretly (through a door made for the occasion) go out of the Bishop's Palace into the same Consistory, and there to hear and see the ceremonies of the marriage at their pleasure. The Princess was received at the west door, and conducted to the platform by my Lord of York. The ceremony was performed on the platform; afterwards they proceeded to the altar to High Mass. Retiring places were provided on each side of the altar for the Prince and Princess. All the day, at several places in the City, and at the west door of the Cathedral, the conduits ran with white wine and red. The wedded couple were lodged for some nights in the Bishop's Palace. The third day after that, the Court returned by water to Westminster.[1] "Six weeks had not passed when Arthur was in his grave, and the prudent King was meditating the marriage of the high-dowered widow with Prince Henry."

At this period, the marriage of Princess Margaret, Henry VII.'s eldest daughter, to King James IV. of Scotland (1503) was proclaimed at St. Paul's on the Festival of the Conversion of St. Paul. This marriage brought the crown of England to her great-grandson, James VI.

Henry VII. died at Richmond, April 21, 1509; his body was brought over London Bridge to lie in state at St. Paul's, previously to resting some years at Windsor until the splendid chapel at Westminster Abbey should be completed.

The delivery in St. Paul's of a Sword and Cap of

CANDELABRUM ON THE ALTAR STEPS
(Replica of Henry VIII.'s gift to the tomb of his brother, Prince Arthur—sold by Oliver Cromwell to Ghent Cathedral)

[1] Milman, from Dugdale, p. 170.

Maintenance to Henry VIII., in 1514, sent as a compliment by the Pope, is minutely described in a letter of the Venetian Ambassador : "On his entrance into London, preceded by nobles with 400 horses, amid throngs of wondering citizens, and by the Florentine Proto-notary, the Ambassador of the Pope, these insignia were borne aloft by one of his attendants, the cap being on the point of the sword, which was held upright. The weapon was long, with a gilded guard and scabbard, and the cap seemed to be of purple satin, resembling in shape the crown of the caps worn by the Albanian light cavalry; it was a foot long, with a turned-up brim, covered with embroidery and pearls, with sundry small pendant tails of ermine.

"The King was in London, at the Bishop's Palace adjoining St. Paul's Cathedral, the two buildings being separated by a small garth, through which, on Sunday, May 21 (1514), a grand procession moved. The Venetian Ambassador was invited, and on arriving at the Bishop's Palace found the King there, and also the nobility, in their robes of state. Cordial greeting was given to the Papal Ambassador, Badoer, at the head of the stairs by two Lords, who were as familiar with him as if he had been an Englishman. When at length the King came forth, Badoer presented a letter he had just received from the State : but His Majesty said, 'Let us now go to the Holy Procession and Mass, after which we will dine, and then confer together.' So the march commenced accordingly. . . . Either for greater pomp, or to avoid contact with the crowd by reason of the plague, His Majesty went that distance on horseback, riding a most beautiful palfrey as black as velvet, the nobility preceding him in pairs ; the Ambassador Badoer, as a mark of distinction, coming last of all, immediately in advance of the King, arm-in-arm with the Lord High Admiral, Thomas Howard, Earl of Surrey, whose father, then Lord Treasurer, had recently been made Duke of Norfolk.

"On arriving at the portal of St. Paul's, the King dismounted and walked to the high altar, where the Papal envoy stood with the Sword and Cap. Advancing to meet His Majesty, he exhibited his credentials, and then delivered a brief oration in praise of him, which, being ended, the King made a sign to a priest, a doctor (Tunstall, afterwards Bishop of London), to reply, as he did most excellently, on the sudden returning thanks to the Pope.

"The King next knelt at the high altar, and two noblemen girded him with the sword; and on his head they placed the cap, which, by reason of the length, covered his whole face.

"The procession then commenced making the entire circuit of the Church. It was a fine sight to see the King and the handsome nobility of England in most pompous array, with their silk gowns of various sorts, lined with sables and lynx's fur, and egret's down. Some of the nobles wore gowns of another sort, the material resembling silk of two colours in chequers; other gowns slashed in their own fashion. All bore such massive gold chains that some might have served for fetters for felons' ancles, and sufficed their safe custody, so heavy were they, and of such immense value.

"The King wore a gown of purple satin and gold in chequers, and a jewelled collar worth a well of gold, his cap being of purple velvet with two jewelled rosettes, and his doublet of gold brocade.

"After the procession, High Mass commenced, and was performed with great pomp, with vocal and instrumental music, which lasted until 1 P.M., when the King quitted the Church, accompanied by all the nobility, and the Venetian Ambassador, to the palace in pairs, as they came. The whole neighbourhood was crowded with spectators, estimated at 30,000, all anxious to see the King, the Sword and the Cap."[1]

[1] *Calendar of State Papers from the Archives of Venice*, Rawdon Brown, ii. 78.

Next year, October 3, 1515, came a thanksgiving service for the peace. "Last Sunday, the Cardinal of York (Wolsey) sang mass in St. Paul's Cathedral. The occasion was the proclamation of the peace, the Eternal Peace it was declared, between the Kings of France and England, the Pope, the Emperor, and the King of Spain; and the betrothal of Mary, Princess of England, to the Dauphin of France. The large chapel and the choir were hung with gold brocade, wrought with the King's arms. Near the altar was a pew formed of cloth of gold for the King, and in front of it a small altar quite crowded with golden images one foot high, with a cross of pure gold to correspond, all the rest of the ornaments being of silver gilt. At this altar two Low Masses were said before the King whilst High Mass was being sung.

"On the other side of the high altar was a chair, raised six steps from the ground, surmounted by a canopy of stiff brocade, hanging from the wall down to the chair, for the Cardinal of York. On the same side, further removed from the altar, was another chair raised three steps, with a similar canopy, for the Legate Campeggio. In the centre of the Church a wooden platform was raised, reaching well nigh from the great gate to the choir (as at the marriage of Prince Arthur and Princess Catherine).

"The King entered the Cathedral with the two Legates, all the Ambassadors, the Archbishop of Canterbury, and about twelve Bishops, with some six Abbots, besides dukes, marquises and earls. At the mass, all the Bishops and Abbots wore jewelled mitres, taking their place beside the Legates; the Ambassadors with the other great laymen being on the King's side. His Majesty's upper garment was a robe of crimson satin lined with brocade, and he had a tunic of purple velvet powdered with precious stones, namely, a stone and a large pearl alternately, the stones being rubies, sapphires, turquoises and diamonds, all of the best water and sparkling. The King wore a collar thickly studded with the finest carbuncles as large as walnuts.

"Mass being ended, the Legates in their mitres went out of the choir, and from a platform simultaneously gave their benediction to the people, and then, returning to the altar, did the like again to the King and the others; after which, Sir Richard Pace (not yet Dean), made a good and sufficiently long oration, delivering it excellently; whereupon the King, together with the three French Ambassadors, namely, the Admiral of France, the Bishop of Paris and another, flanked by the two Legates, swore at the high altar perpetual peace between the King of France and the King of England, both the King and the Ambassadors taking the oath upon the Gospels, and the Body of Christ."[1]

Four years later there was another splendid ceremony at St. Paul's. "On July 15, 1519, the Venetian Ambassadors were invited to attend the ceremony of the Proclamation of the Emperor (Charles V.) in the Cathedral. They were taken to the appointed place by two knights of the King's Chamber, and found there Cardinals Wolsey and Campeggio, the Ambassador of the Catholic King, and all the chief lords of the kingdom.

"The French Ambassador refused to attend, saying he had received no announcement of the election from his Sovereign.

"When all were assembled in the Church, *Te Deum* was chanted, and Cardinal Wolsey gave the benediction. Then the unanimous election of the Catholic King, as King of the Romans, was proclaimed by two heralds."[2]

In 1521, on May 12, the Pope's sentence against Martin Luther was published at the faithful Cathedral. "The Lord Thomas Wolsey, by the grace of God Legate de Latere, Cardinal of St. Cecilia and Archbishop of York, came unto St. Paul's Church, with the most part of the

---

[1] *Venetian Dispatches*, ii. p. 464.   [2] *Ibid.*, ii. p. 543.

Bishops of the realm, where he was received with procession, and censed by Mr. Richard Pace, the Dean of that Church. He was conducted to the high altar by four Doctors holding a canopy over him, and there made his oblation. He proceeded under his cloth of state, and took his seat on a scaffold near Paul's Cross, with his two crosses; on either side, the Pope's Ambassador, the Archbishop of Canterbury, and the Imperial Ambassador; the Bishop of Durham sat below, with other prelates. Fisher, Bishop of Rochester, preached by the Pope's command against one Martinus Eleutherius and his works, because 'he erred sore and spake against the holy faith,' and denounced them accursed which kept any of his books; and there 'were many burned in the said churchyard of the said books during the sermon.' After that the Lord Cardinal went home to dinner with all the other prelates."[1]

MARTIN LUTHER'S BIBLE
(In the Cathedral Library)

Next year the Emperor Charles V. visited the Cathedral. "On the 9th of June, 1522, the Emperor went to the principal Church of London, where the Pope, which is the Cardinal, said mass. (This is either a mistake or a satirical description of Wolsey.) He was censed by more than twenty mitred prelates, from the one and the other Courts. The festivities were splendid, and some persons wore extraordinarily rich clothes."[2]

[1] *MS. Vitellius*, Malcolm, vol. iii. p. 176.   [2] *Simancas Dispatches*.

It was Wolsey who, as Papal Legate, "deprived St. Paul's of a privilege and distinction no doubt highly estimated in those days. Up to this time, the Convocation of the Province of Canterbury had held its sittings in the Cathedral or Chapter House of St. Paul's. As Archbishop of York Wolsey summoned the Northern Convocation, as Legate the Southern, to meet together in his presence, near his residence at York House, Whitehall. They met by permission of the Abbot of Westminster in the Jerusalem Chamber (and probably the College Hall). This was held by some no less than a robbery of St. Paul's. Since that time, no doubt from convenience,—and so long as the Convocation exercised legislative powers, taxed the clergy, and sate as a branch of the Parliament of England, it was a matter of much convenience—the practice has continued. Since the revival of Convocation in 1852, it assembles at St. Paul's, the Latin sermon is preached, the Prolocutor of the Lower House is chosen, and then Convocation adjourns, for the dispatch of business, to Westminster." [1]

In 1523, came the news of the Battle of Pavia (February 23) and the captivity of Francis I. The event was celebrated by an order of the King to the Lord Mayor that there should be a great bonfire at Paul's Church door, and there to be set a hogshead of red wine, and another of claret, for the people to drink that would, for the good tidings.[2] On the Sunday after, the King, the Queen, the Princess and both Houses of Parliament attended at a solemn *Te Deum* in the Cathedral. On St. Matthew's Day (September 21), there was a great procession of all the religious orders through the City. Wolsey, with his train of Bishops, sang *Te Deum* at the high altar.

In 1527, came news of another imperial victory, the sack of Rome by Charles V.'s general, Bourbon, and the captivity of Pope Clement. There was another solemn procession of Wolsey and the Bishops to St. Paul's. They

---

[1] Milman's *Annals*, p. 178.   [2] *Grey Friars' Chronicle*, p. 27.

HENRY VIII. AND THE REFORMATION

may have rejoiced with the Emperor, but hardly over the Pope.

The story of Dean Colet's brilliant successor, *Richard Pace* (Dean from 1519 to 1532 or 1536), is tragic. The brief facts of Newcourt[1] are supplemented by contemporary writers. When a youth he was secretary to Thomas Langton, Bishop of Winchester, was educated at his charge, and sent by him to Padua. After his return into England he retired to Oxford, where he was received into the service of Dr. Bainbridge, Provost of Queen's, afterwards Bishop of Durham, then Archbishop of York and Cardinal; from his service he passed into the King's, was made Secretary of State, and employed in matters of high concern, largely abroad. In 1514, he became Prebendary of York and Archdeacon of Dorset; in 1519, Vicar of Stepney, Prebendary of Finsbury, and Dean of St. Paul's. He held also a stall in Salisbury, and the Deanery of Exeter. He was sent ambassador to Venice, where he was much commended and admired; he was also employed at Rome about acquiring the Papacy for Wolsey. While at Venice he fell ill, and the Doge wrote urging his recall. He was sent home, and so carefully looked after by physicians, and at the King's command, that he partly recovered. The writer of the preface to the *Calendar of the Simancas Papers* thus writes of him: "Pace is described by all the Imperial ambassadors as the most able and best-informed of English diplomatists. Such disparaging expressions as they so frequently indulge in, when speaking of the other agents of the English government in Italy, were never made use of in connection with his name. Moreover, Pace possessed one of the most necessary qualifications for a good diplomatist. He was of an amiable temper, and succeeded in being on friendly terms with those whom he opposed." After the manner of those times, "he was in the pay of the Emperor, and it was believed that he

[1] *Repertorium*, vol. i. p. 46.

received also a pension of 1000 ducats from Venice. He acted, nevertheless, on the whole, in an upright way."[1] This was after the modern method of the retaining fee.

Professor Brewer speaks of him still more highly. "Pace, the King's secretary, always at Court, a pleasant and versatile companion, a wit, a scholar, a traveller of no small observation and influence, was acquainted with all the distinguished men and potentates of the times, as he had visited every scene of the drama on which the attention of the world was just then fixed. By the brilliancy and charms of his conversation, qualities reflected in his correspondence, he had made his society agreeable to More and Erasmus. He was, besides, a man of the new learning, not so strict or so rigid as the grey headed ecclesiastics whose rank or office held them about the Court. Was it surprising that he should have risen rapidly into favour? that he should have been suspected, though vaguely, of treading too closely on the heels of a great minister?"[2]

That Pace was crushed by a relentless and powerful enemy is matter of historical fact. The question is, whether this was Wolsey or Gardiner. Dates seem to acquit Wolsey, and to inculpate Gardiner. The current tradition, however, was against Wolsey, and it was adopted by Shakespeare, following the chronicle of Holinshed—

Campeius. My Lord of York, was not one Doctor Pace
          In Gardiner's place before him?
Wolsey.   Yes, he was.
Campeius. Was he not held a learned man?
Wolsey.   Yes, surely!
Campeius. Believe me, there's an ill opinion spread then
          Even of yourself, Lord Cardinal.
Wolsey.   How! of me?

[1] Bergenroble, *Calendar of the Simancas Papers*, p. 56.
[2] Brewer, Preface to vol. iii., *Letters and Papers*, p. xiv.

Campeius. They will not stick to say you envied him ;
              And fearing he would rise, he was so virtuous,
              Kept him a foreign man still, which so grieved him
              That he ran mad, and died.
Wolsey.   Heaven's peace be with him !
              That's Christian care enough : for living murmurers
              There's places of rebuke. He was a fool !
              For he would needs be virtuous.[1]

In 1528, there is a sad description of his state, from Skeffington, Bishop of Bangor, to Wolsey (the Bishop had called in physicians). "Yet very little remedy by their promise followeth or none ; by reason whereof I think that he is incurable, or else in them there is great default, or lack of cunning (skill). For in his rage and distemperance, rending and tearing his clothes, no man can rule him, neither will keep him, nor serve him, as this bringer can show unto your Grace."[2] In 1529, Cuthbert Tunstall appoints Sampson the coadjutor of Pace, then, as before, afflicted by imbecility, or rather alienation of mind.[3] Before this date Wolsey had fallen into disgrace.

Pace lived till 1536, and during these years met with cruel usage from some one who had called himself his friend, but was his enemy. "He forcibly ejected him from his own house in a state of poverty, and did not allow him to remain there ; he who not only deserved so well of him, but of all scholars. He was the glory of Englishmen."[4] What a contrast to the life and death of his predecessor, Colet !

With the approach of the Reformation, memorable scenes occurred at St. Paul's, the very kernel of the English history of the day. First, the destruction of Tyndale's Bible, thus described by Froude—

[1] *Henry VIII.*, ii. 2.   [2] Ellis, vol. iii. series ii. 151.
[3] Wharton, p. 239.   [4] Appendix to Knight's *Erasmus*, p. 64.

"On the morning of Shrove Tuesday, A.D. 1527, we are to picture to ourselves a procession moving along London streets, from the Fleet Prison to St. Paul's Cathedral. The Warden of the Fleet was there, and the Knight Marshal and the tipstaffs, with all his company they could make with bills and glaives; and in the midst of these armed officials, six men marching in penitential dresses, one carrying a lighted taper five pounds weight, the others with symbolical fagots, signifying to the lookers-on the fate which their crimes had earned for them, but which at this time in mercy was remitted. One of these was Barnes (burned in 1540); the other five were 'Stillyard men,' undistinguishable by any other name, but detected members of the brotherhood.

"It was eight o'clock when they arrived at St. Paul's. The people had thronged in crowds before them. The public seats and benches were filled. All London had hurried to the spectacle. A platform was erected in the centre of the nave, on the top of which, enthroned in pomp of purple and gold and splendour, sate the great Cardinal, supported on each side with eighteen Bishops, mitred Abbots and Priests—six-and-thirty in all; his chaplains and 'spiritual doctors' sitting also where they could find place 'in gowns of damask and satin.' Opposite the platform, over the north door of the Cathedral, was a great crucifix—a famous image in those days, called the Rood of Northern; and at the foot of it, inside a rail, a fire was burning, with the sinful books, the Tracts and Testaments, ranged round it in baskets, waiting for the execution of the sentence.

"Such was the scene in the midst of which the six prisoners entered. A second platform stood in a conspicuous place in front of the Cardinal's throne, where they could be seen and heard by the crowd; and there, on their knees, with their fagots on their shoulders, they begged pardon of God and the Holy Catholic Church for their high crimes and offences. When the confession was finished, Fisher, Bishop of Rochester, preached a sermon; and, the sermon over, Barnes turned to the people, declaring that he was more charitably handled than he deserved, his heresies were so heinous and detestable.

"There was no other religious service : mass had, perhaps, been said previous to the admission to the Church of heretics lying under censure; and the Knight Marshal led the prisoners down to the fire underneath the crucifix. They were taken within the rails, and three times led round the blazing pile, casting in their fagots as they passed. The contents of the baskets were heaped upon the fagots, and the holocaust was complete. This time an unbloody sacrifice was deemed sufficient. The Church was satisfied with penance, and Fisher pronounced the prisoners absolved, and received back into communion."[1] Meantime the printing of an improved edition went on apace at Antwerp, accelerated by the money the Bishops were paying to buy up the existing copies.[2] Barnes was returned to prison, but escaped, and went beyond sea to Luther.[3] Another holocaust of Bibles took place in 1530, at which Bishop Stokesley presided.

The same year, 1530, occurred a strange scene in the Chapter House, illustrating the working of the extraordinary measure by which all the clergy of the realm were placed under the Act of Præmunire on the plea that they had accepted Wolsey's illegal assumption of Legatine power. In that assumption the King himself had acquiesced; but it was now convenient at once to exact vast sums from the clergy, and to change the supremacy of the Pope into that of the King. The whole of the temporalities of the clergy, from highest to lowest, lay at the mercy of the Crown; the composition for the Province of Canterbury reached the enormous total of £100,000, more than £1,000,000 accord-

---

[1] Froude, vol. ii. pp. 42, 43. [2] Ellis, 3rd series, ii. 91.
[3] *Grey Friars' Chronicle*, p. 33.

ing to present value. The payment was to be accompanied by an acknowledgment of the royal supremacy. The burden was to be divided proportionally amongst the different dioceses, and every ecclesiastic was to contribute his share. When this was known, the indignation of the parish clergy knew no bounds; they had been in no way responsible for the unlawful acquiescence of their superiors, and they determined to resist the iniquitous charge. Bishop Stokesley had appointed September 1 for a meeting at the Chapter House to arrange the assessment. "He was a man of great wit and learning, but of little discretion and humanity, which caused him to be out of favour with the common people." "To his dismay," writes Dean Milman, following Hall's chronicle, "he heard that the whole clergy, at least six hundred, of all ranks and orders, parish priests, stipendiaries, the lowest and humblest, were thronging at the doors of the Chapter House, backed by a great multitude of the people, who crowded round, some perhaps from attachment to their pastors, . . . very many doubtless to enjoy and aggravate the riot. The Bishop's officers called by name the favoured few (who were to consult with the Bishop), but instead of giving way, a great number, thrusting the officers aside, forced the doors, and broke headlong into the chamber. With difficulty the officers succeeded in again closing the doors. This only exasperated the tumult without. 'We will not be left without, our fellows being within. We know not what the Bishop will do with them.' The unclerical multitude goaded them on; there was a rush at the door, which gave way with a crash, and in they all poured, lay and clergy, with a great rending of gowns and cassocks, crushing of caps, and all the wild affray of a London mob. One (it is to be hoped not of the clergy) struck the Bishop's officer on the face. The Chapter House was filled to its utmost corner; it was long before silence could be obtained.

"At length the Bishop's voice was heard: 'I marvel, my

brethren, that ye be so heady, and will not hear what may be said unto you. I pray you keep silence, and listen to me with patience. Friends! we are men, not angels. We have miscarried ourselves towards the King. All our promotions, goods, lands and chattels are forfeit to him, and our bodies liable to imprisonment. The King, on the humble petition of us, the Fathers of the Clergy, has inclined, as he ever does, to mercy. He will release us from the Præmunire on the payment of £100,000 in five years. Therefore, I charitably expect you, brethren, to bear your parts in the payment from your livelihoods and salaries.' The reply was prompt, brief, resolute, not easily answerable. 'My Lord, thirty nobles a year is but bad living for a priest, now that victuals and everything else is so dear; our poverty enforceth us to say, Nay, my Lord, we never offended in the Præmunire, and never meddled in the Cardinal's business. Let the Bishops and Abbots who have offended pay.' High words were uttered, not by the Bishop, but by his officers, no doubt offended at the insolence of these low priests to their lord and master. Blows were struck; the 'temporals' backed the priests, so that the Bishop himself began to quail with apprehension for his sacred person. Pardoning their rude demeanour, giving them a hasty blessing, and entreating them to depart in charity, he withdrew; and the priests, also, thinking all was over, withdrew. The Bishop hastened to the Chancellor, Sir Thomas More; fifteen priests and four laymen were arrested by the Chancellor's order, some committed to the Fleet, some to the Tower; and they paid the penalty for their resistance by a long imprisonment."

The King's divorce had been debated in many a sermon at Paul's Cross. Anne Boleyn, in her magnificent procession from the Tower to her coronation, passed by the Cathedral, at the east end of which she was entertained by the boys of St. Paul's School, with verses in praise of the King and herself, " wherewith she seemed highly delighted."

K

The exposure and degradation of the Nun of Kent, with her accomplices, the Dean of Bocking and the rector of Aldermanbury, whose imposture had inflamed the people in favour of the unfortunate Queen Catherine, took place at Paul's Cross before a vast multitude the year after Anne's marriage; the Bishop of Bangor preached the sermon.

In 1534, after the final determination to abrogate the Pope's supremacy, care was taken to secure Paul's Cross for the new principle. "Orders be taken that such as preach at Paul's Cross (at first it seems they were Bishops) shall henceforth continually, Sunday after Sunday, teach and declare unto the people, that he that now calls himself Pope, and any of his predecessors, is and were only Bishops of Rome, and have no more authority or jurisdiction, by God's laws, within this realm than any other Bishop had, which is nothing at all; and that such authority as he has claimed heretofore has been only by usurpation and sufferance of the Princes of this realm; and that the Bishop of London is bound to suffer none to preach at Paul's Cross, as he will answer, but such as will preach and set forth the same."[1]

Stokesley, like Gardiner (who wrote a long treatise on True Obedience) and Bonner (who wrote a preface to the same), was a supporter of the royal supremacy. He went with Cranmer and Gardiner to Dunstable to cite Queen Catherine to appear. The chronicler gives a curious little scene illustrating his action: "Yesterday we had my Lord of London here (the Nunnery of Sion) in the Chapter House of Women, and the Confessor also, which both took it upon their consciences and the peril of their souls, that the ladies ought, by God's law, to consent to the King's title, his supremacy, whereat they were much comforted."[2]

The Dean and Chapter were on the same side. "An instrument is extant on which, seemingly with entire

---

[1] Strype's *Memorials*, vol. i. p. 151.
[2] *Suppression of Monasteries*, p. 49.

unanimity, they declare their obedience to King Henry, and Anne his wife, and to their offspring. They assert the King to be the head of the Church of England, and that the Bishop of Rome has no more authority than any other foreign Bishop. The document is largely signed by the Dean, four Canons Residentiary, the Sub-dean, the Cardinals and others."[1]

Burning was proceeding. Stokesley burned two Lollards, and forced recantation from many more. "In 1535, nineteen German Anabaptists and five women were examined in the Cathedral; fourteen were condemned; a man and a woman sent to be burned in Smithfield; twelve dispatched to other towns to be sacrificed as an example. To the fate of these poor wretches, the hearts of Papalists and anti-Papalists, of Catholics and Protestants, were sternly sealed. It may be doubted whether in all London, or even in all England, there was a murmur of compassion. Anabaptists were the Ishmaelites of the religious world, against whom was every man's hand, and, unhappily, whose hand, in Germany, had been against every man. The memory of Munster and of John of Leyden pursued them wherever they went. Blameless as some of them may have been, poor ignorant fanatics, they were prescribed by universal abhorrence, not only as heretics, but as lawless socialists."[2]

James Bainham, an accused heretic, "frightened by the cold, stern demeanour of Stokesley, recanted. The next day he recanted his recantation. He was taken to the Bishop of London's coal-cellar at Fulham, the favourite episcopal prison-chamber. There he was ironed, put in the stocks, and left for many days in the chill March weather. Bainham, after repeated whippings, was burned in Smithfield."[3]

At the opening of Convocation, June 1536 (three weeks

[1] Milman, quoting Appendix to Wharton.
[2] Milman's *Annals*, p. 195.   [3] *Ibid.*, p. 197.
K 2

after the execution of Anne Boleyn), sermons were preached morning and afternoon in St. Paul's Cathedral by Hugh Latimer, Bishop of Worcester. They are largely quoted by Froude and by Milman, in whose pages it is well worth while to read the old reformer's words, strongly illustrating the times. Here can only be quoted the description of the scene: "There must have been intense agitation, even wild hopes, raised by that sad event, the Queen's death, which to some might seem a death-blow to the Reformation, had not these hopes been rebuked by the appearance of Latimer in the pulpit. The clergy of all orders crowded the choir; the people the nave and aisles. All the great prelates were there; the Primate, Cranmer, with his heart full of sorrow for the unfortunate Queen, even if that sorrow was not betrayed by his countenance; Stokesley, on his episcopal throne, among the suffragans of Canterbury, Gardiner, Shaxton, Hilsey; Bonner, as yet only Archdeacon. Of Latimer's audience it has been said, I suspect with justice, 'nine-tenths of all those eyes which were fixed on him, would have glistened with delight if they could have looked upon his burning.' The whole multitude were compelled by a changed world to listen quietly while he shot his bitter arrows among them." [1]

A scene which took place in St. Paul's on November 24, 1538, during the episcopate of Stokesley, shows the strength of the rising tide of the Reformation, in spite of the traditional opinions of the older Bishops. The day was Sunday, and the famous "Rood (crucifix) of Boxley in Kent, made to move the eyes and lips, to bow, to seem to speak; which had been working there unquestioned miracles for centuries; having been detected by a clever rationalist of the day, and exposed with all its secret springs and ingenious machinery, at Maidstone, and at Whitehall, was brought to St. Paul's to meet its final discomfiture and doom. To the curious and intelligent

[1] Milman's *Annals*, p. 197; and Froude's *History*.

HENRY VIII. AND THE REFORMATION

citizens of London the whole trickery was shown. Ridley, now Bishop of Rochester, preached a sermon. The holy, wonder-working image was thrown down and broken to pieces amid the jeers and scoffs of the rabble."[1]

In 1539, Stokesley took part in the great debate of the Bishops in the Parliament House at Westminster, under the presidency of Thomas Crumwell. "After an humble acknowledgment of the virtuous exhortation most worthy a Christian King, as delivered in the King's name by Crumwell, then began they to dispute of the Sacraments; and first of all the Bishop of London (Stokesley), who was an earnest defender of the King's part, whom a little before the Lord Crumwell had rebuked by name for defending of unwritten verities; this Bishop of London, I say, went about to defend that there were Seven Sacraments of our Christian religion, which he would go about to prove by certain stinking glosses and old heresy writers. He had upon his side the Archbishop of York (Lee), the Bishop of Lincoln (Longland), Bath (Clerk), Chichester (Saxton), and Norwich (Repps); against him were the Bishop of Salisbury (Shaxton), Ely (Goodrich), Hereford (Fox), Worcester (Latimer), with the Archbishop of Canterbury (Cranmer)." A long speech of Cranmer follows; then an argument by the writer of this account (Alexander Alane Scot), who was interrupted by the Bishop of London, but supported by Fox of Hereford.[2]

In 1539, Stokesley defended the terrible Six Articles against Cranmer, Ridley and other Bishops. In a few weeks he died, September 14, and was buried in St. Paul's.

He was succeeded by *Edmund Bonner*, Bishop of Hereford, then beyond the seas, obviously on the nomination of Henry VIII. Wharton gives the following

---

[1] Milman's *Annals*, p. 102.
[2] *On the Authoritie of the Word of God*, by A. A. Scot, 1542, quoted by Sir Henry Ellis, *Letters*, 3rd series, vol. iii. p. 196.

account of Bonner: "He was natural son to George Savage, priest, by Elizabeth Frodsham, who was the wife (after Bonner had been begotten) of Edmund Bonner, a sawyer, and from him had the name of Bonner. He was born at Elmeley, or at Peter Hanley, in Worcestershire; and about 1512 became a student in Broadgate Hall (now Pembroke College) in Oxon.; took the degree of Doctor of Laws in 1525; he having before that entered into holy orders. He obtained not the least praise for his learning, but much for his skill in other affairs. Hence Cardinal Wolsey made him his Commissary for the Faculties. He had several ecclesiastical benefices, which he held at one and the same time, viz. the rectories of Ripple, Bledon, Cherry Burton and East Dereham, and the prebend of Chiswick in the Cathedral Church of St. Paul; but that he resigned in 1539, as he did his church of East Dereham in 1540. He was likewise Archdeacon of Leicester. He continued firm to the Cardinal as long as he lived; but when he died, he applied himself to the Court, was one of the King's chaplains, a favourer of the Lutherans, and of the divorce between the King and Katherine of Spain, and of the King's proceedings in expelling the Pope's authority here in England. He was employed in several embassies to foreign Princes; and whilst he was ambassador to the King of France, 1538, he was declared Bishop of Hereford; and the temporalities of that See, March 4, 1539, were, in his absence, restored to his proctor; but before his return he was elected, on the 20th of October following, to the Bishopric of London; and after his confirmation, November 12, 1539, took commission from the King for the exercise of his ecclesiastical jurisdiction; and was consecrated in his own Cathedral, April 4, 1540, and enthroned on the 16th of the same month."[1]

In 1540 occurred a sharp contest at Paul's Cross on two

[1] Wharton, quoted by Newcourt, *Repertorium*, vol. i. p. 26.

successive Sundays, and afterwards at St. Mary's, Spittal, between Barnes, who in 1527 had been compelled to burn Bibles in St. Paul's, and who had returned in the time of Anne Boleyn, and Gardiner, Bishop of Winchester, which ended in the burning of Barnes and his two fellow preachers, of whom one was Jerome, Parson of Stepney, as well as three Papalist opponents of the King's supremacy.

In 1542, at the Convocation, Cranmer and Bonner met at St. Paul's, and Bonner celebrated the Mass of the Holy Ghost. Both were engaged in producing the *First Book of Homilies*. The "Exhortation to reading the Holy Scriptures" was written by Cranmer; that on Charity by Bonner.

On June 13, 1546, there was another thanksgiving for peace. It was Whit Monday, and there was a great procession from St. Paul's to St. Peter's-on-Cornhill, with all the children of St. Paul's School, and a cross of every parish church, and "parsons and vicars of every church in new copes, and the choir of St. Paul's in the same manner; and the Bishop (Bonner), bearing the Sacrament under a canopy, met the Mayor in a gown of crimson velvet, the Aldermen, and all the Crafts in their best apparel, and at the Cross was proclaimed, with heralds and pursuivants, universal peace for ever between the Emperor, the King of England, the King of France and all Christian kings for ever."

The last scene of Henry VIII.'s reign at St. Paul's is of the saddest. On July 10, 1546, were burnt a priest of Richmond, the noble Anne Askew, a gentleman of Furnival's Inn named Lascelles and a poor tailor from Colchester. Nicholas Shaxton, who had been Bishop of Salisbury, with two others, was in Newgate with them, and received the same sentence. Shaxton preached at their burning before the Duke of Norfolk, Lord Chancellor Wriothesley, others of the Council, with the Lord Mayor,

Sheriffs and Judge: "and the 1st of August after preached at Paul's Cross the said Nicholas Shaxton, and there recanted and wept sore, and made great lamentation for the offence, and prayed the people to forgive him his mis-example that he had given unto the people."[1] These were difficult times.

[1] *Grey Friars' Chronicle*, pp. 50, 51.

CHAPTER XIV

EDWARD VI. AND THE REFORMATION

THE beginning of the short reign of Edward VI. showed the mingling of the old and new ideas in religion. On January 28, 1547, Edward ascended the throne. On April 1, the English service was heard in King's Chapel. Dr. Glazier preached at Paul's Cross against fasting in Lent as without warrant in Holy Scripture. In another sermon, Dr. Smith, Principal of Whittington College, condemned his own books, written in defence of the old faith. Another preacher, Ridley, Master of Pembroke, Cambridge (soon to be Bishop of London), condemned the worship of pictures, the adoration of saints, and the use of holy water. Barlow, Bishop of St. David's, was very outspoken. On the other hand, the old funereal rites still lingered: a sumptuous hearse was raised in the nave of the Cathedral in honour of the late French King, Francis I. Latin dirges were chanted: Archbishop Cranmer, with eight mitred Bishops, sang the old Requiem Mass. Bishop Gardiner preached the funeral sermon in praise of Francis I., the deadly persecutor of the Reformation. The Lord Mayor and Aldermen were present. The choir and all the body of the Church were hung with black. Every church in London followed suit the same day, all the bells tolling.

The Grey Friars' chronicler describes the royal procession of Edward VI. from the Tower to Westminster: pageants, tapestries, guilds in Cheapside. At the west end of St. Paul's steeple was tied a cable, the other end attached to the anchor of a ship near the doorway of the Deanery, down which a man slid as swift as an arrow from a bow, with his feet and hands abroad, and not touching the rope with them.

Now came orders from the Council. One of these commanded the destruction of images, forbade processions and ordered the discontinuance of all customs held to be superstitious, not in the Cathedral only, but in all the precincts. The Commissioners appeared in St. Paul's in December, and removed the images. On February 14, the Litany was chanted in English, between choir and nave, the singers divided as usual in two sections; the Epistle and Gospel were read in English; all in the presence of Dean May. Bishop Bonner received the Council's injunctions under protest, was committed to the Fleet, made humble submission, and was released after eight days. Vigorous measures were in the air; it must have been unpleasant to the gentle Cranmer to have to summon Gardiner before him at the Deanery of St. Paul's, and commit him to prison. Now was the parting of the ways.

By one determined act all obits and chantries were abolished; unhappily, instead of devoting the ecclesiastical revenue to colleges, religious education in schools, or the increase of poor benefices, which, by the suppression of the monasteries, were exceedingly numerous, the Council swept all these endowments into the hands of themselves and their adherents.

Henry VIII. had confiscated some of the treasures of St. Paul's; the bell-tower on the east side of the churchyard, with the famous Jesus bells, were lost by him on a throw of the dice to Sir Miles Partridge against a stake of £100. Partridge, says the grim Grey Friars' chronicler, was subsequently executed for treason. "In the autumn and winter of 1552–3," says Mr. Froude, "no less than four commissions were appointed with this one object; to go

EDWARD VI. AND THE REFORMATION

over the oft-trodden ground, and share the last spoils which could be gathered from the churches. In the business of plunder the rapacity of the Crown officials had been far distanced hitherto by private peculation. The halls of country houses were hung with altar-cloths; tables and beds were quilted with copes; knights and squires drank their claret out of chalices, and watered their horses in marble coffins. Pious clergy, gentlemen or churchwardens had in many places secreted plate, images or candlesticks, which force might bring to light. Bells rich in silver still hung silent in remote church towers, or were buried in the vaults. Organs still pealed through aisles in notes unsuited to a regenerate worship; and damask napkins, rich robes, consecrated banners, pious offerings of men of another faith, remained in the chests of the vestries." [1] Some of the treasures of St. Paul's are still to be seen in Spain. "Inquire," says Ford's *Handbook*, "particularly in the sacristia of the Cathedral of Valencia, to see the Terno, and complete set of three frontals, or coverings for the altar, which were purchased in London by two Valencian merchants, Andrea and Pedro de Medina, at the sale by Henry VIII. of the Romish decorations at St. Paul's. They are embroidered in gold and silver, are about twelve feet long by four, and represent subjects from the life of the Saviour. In one, Christ in Limbo (Hades), are introduced turrets evidently taken from those of the Tower of London. They are placed on the high altar from Saturday to Monday in Holy Week. In the Cathedral of Saragossa is part of a cope embroidered with Adam and Eve, which was bought at our Reformation from the old Cathedral of St. Paul's, London." [2]

Dugdale records the humble petition of the Dean and Chapter to be permitted to retain a few necessary articles for divine service: "Two pairs of basons for the Communion

[1] Froude, vol. v. p. 458.
[2] Ford's *Handbook of Spain*, vol. i. p. 440; vol. ii. p. 959.

bread, and to receive the offerings for the poor (one pair silver for every day, the other for festivals, gilt); a silver pot for the wine, weighing forty ounces; the written text of the Gospels and Epistles; a large canopy of tissue for His Majesty when he cometh hither; a pall of black velvet for the hearse; a border of black sarcenet, with a fringe of black silk mixed with gold, for the burial of noble persons; baldachins of divers sorts and colours, for garnishing the quire at the King's coming, and for the Bishop's seat, as also at other times when the choir shall be apparelled for the honour of the realm; eight cushions, thirty albs to make surplices for the ministers and the choristers; twenty-four old cushions to kneel on; seven cloths of linen, plain and diaper, for the Communion Table; five towels; two hangings of tapestry for the quire; a Turkey carpet for the Communion Table; a pastoral staff for the Bishop." [1]

Sermons and discussions were now frequent about the Sacrament of the Lord's Supper, often painfully expressed, and distressing to the adherents of the long tradition of the Roman obedience. Such things can hardly be helped at a time of upheaval and transition. Ridley, Bishop of Rochester, rebuked the wranglers in a sermon at Paul's Cross. "In the loftiest tone he asserted the dignity of the Sacrament, in which Christ was present though not in His material or natural body (the bread remained bread), but His presence was felt in the hearts of faithful communicants." [2]

At Easter, 1549, Holy Communion was administered according to the newly revised English form: "confession," the Grey Friar notes, "was only for those who would confess." After Easter, by command of the Dean (William May), began regularly the English service. On St. Martin's Day the sermons began again at Paul's Cross; Ferrar

[1] Dugdale, Appendix, p. 391.
[2] Milman's *Annals*, p. 219.

(Farrar), Bishop of St. David's (afterwards burnt by Queen Mary), was the preacher. "He spake," says the Grey Friar, "against all manner of things, of the Church, and the Sacrament of the Altar, and vestments, and copes, and all other things."

The violence of change met the eye also, not only the ear. Protector Somerset, in building his palace where Somerset House now stands, destroyed a church, the palaces of three Bishops (Llandaff, Chester and Worcester), in the Strand; attempted to demolish St. Margaret's, but his workmen were beaten off by the parishioners; and threw down the fine cloister on the north side of St. Paul's, to provide building materials. The chapel and burial-place in Pardon Churchyard had already been pulled down, and five hundred tons of bones had been carted away and buried in the fields of Finsbury. Processions were forbidden in the streets. The Whitsuntide offices of the Skinners' Company, with their censing in St. Paul's, had been prohibited. The most sacred holiday of the old faith, *Corpus Christi*, had been neglected. On the second Sunday in Lent the Sacrament of the Altar (the Reserved Sacrament and its place) had been pulled down by order of the Dean. On June 26, came an order for the discontinuance of the Apostles' Mass and the Mass of Our Lady. There was to be no communion except at the Holy Table in the chancel. Alas! more Anabaptists! The spirit *De hæretico comburendo* was not yet exorcised. The Archbishop and Commissioners sat in judgment in the Cathedral. One or two recanted, and bore fagots. Jean Bocher, who had imbibed some wild and ignorant opinions on the Incarnation, was burnt, Ridley, alas! taking an active part in her condemnation.

These sudden changes brought about rebellion in many parts of the kingdom, chiefly Devonshire, Cornwall and Norfolk. The City was startled by being suddenly summoned to place itself in a state of defence. Archbishop

Cranmer came hastily to St. Paul's, and gave a terrible account of the insurrection. When it was crushed, he appeared again, on August 10, 1549, arraigning Papal priests as its principal authors.

Bonner was an odd factor as Bishop of London in these times of advancing reform. Two days before the abolition of the Mass of the Apostles, and others of the kind, he received an order from the Council to that effect, which he passed on to the Dean and Chapter. On August 17, he appeared in the Cathedral, and officiated according to the new rites "discreetly and sadly." He was obviously out of sympathy with the new *régime* and was summoned before the Council. "Severe animadversions were made on his unfrequent attendances at the services of the Cathedral, in which he had heretofore officiated with zealous regularity. He was accused of appearing stealthily at foreign masses, and still unreformed ceremonials. He was ordered to reside at his palace near St. Paul's, to discharge all the duties of his function, especially to officiate at the Cathedral on every high festival, and to administer the Communion in the new form. He was to proceed against all who did not frequent Common Prayer and receive the Sacrament, and against those who went to mass. Beyond all this, he was commanded to preach on subjects chosen, with determined ingenuity, to implicate him, if possible, with at least tacit approval of the late rebellion, and to assert those doctrines which he was known, in his heart and conscience, to repudiate. He was to declare the heinousness of wilful rebellion as incurring eternal damnation, especially the guilt of the western insurgents, who were to have their portion with Lucifer, the father and first author of Disobedience, 'whatever masses of holy water soever they went about to pretend.' He was to urge the awful examples of Korah, Dathan and Abiram, and that of Saul, rejected because he spared the sheep for sacrifice, and thereby betrayed his disobedience to God. He was to aver that

EDWARD VI. AND THE REFORMATION

vital religion consisted only in prayer to God, that rites and ceremonies might be altered at the command of the magistrate; therefore, if any man persisted in the Latin service, his devotion was valueless on account of his disobedience."[1]

On September 1, Bonner ascended the pulpit of Paul's Cross in obedience to these directions, with a vast assemblage at his feet. Touching on the chief points of the Council's instruction, he omitted one—that the King was to be implicitly obeyed, as being no less a king when a minor, and not of full age. The rest of the sermon was on the Corporal Presence in the Eucharist, asserting transubstantiation in the strongest terms, with many sharp aspersions of those who held the opposite doctrine.

Bonner was sent to the Tower, and committed a prisoner till the accession of Mary. The See of London was declared vacant. "On the first of November, the Bishop of London was sent for at afternoon to Lambeth, and then the said Archbishop of Canterbury discharged the said Bishop of London as much as lay in his power. But mark what follows. On the 7th day of October (nearly a year later), was proclaimed the Lord Protector traitor."[2]

In April of the following year (1550), the new Bishop of London, *Nicolas Ridley*, Bishop of Rochester, was enthroned in the Cathedral. Ridley was "a gentleman of an ancient house in the county of Northumberland; bred up in school at Newcastle, thence sent to the University of Cambridge, where he studied hard, took the degree of Doctor of Divinity, was some time Fellow of University College in Oxford, but afterwards Master of Pembroke Hall, in Cambridge; and shortly after promoted to the See of Rochester." Before he would enter the choir at his enthronement, he ordered the lights on the Holy Table to be extinguished. He was unmarried. When he took possession of Fulham, he insisted that the mother and

[1] Milman's *Annals*.   [2] *Grey Friars' Chronicle*.

sister of his imprisoned predecessor, Bishop Bonner, should continue to reside at that palace. They were constant and welcome guests at Ridley's hospitable table. The place of honour was always reserved for "our mother, Bonner." Yet Bonner burnt him.

On the night of St. Barnabas' Day, the high altar at St. Paul's was pulled down, the Holy Table set up in its place, and a curtain drawn to exclude non-communicants, according to primitive order. On the following Sunday Holy Communion was administered at the Holy Table. At Christmas the singers' procession was discontinued. On March 24 (1550), the doors at the side of the Holy Table were closed up. The Holy Table was more than once moved. At one time it stood north and south, later on it was moved lower down where the priests sang.

On October 24, there was a general demolition of the altars and chapels throughout the Church; and it should seem, amongst the tombs such as were shrines for public worship. "All the goodly stonework behind the high altar with seats for the Priests, the Dean and the Sub-dean, were remorselessly cut and hacked away. An order from the Court alone saved the magnificent monument of John of Gaunt."[1]

On All Hallows' Day, 1552, began the book of the revised service at St. Paul's, the Second Prayer-book of Edward VI., which has gradually grown into its present form, and was now, if not absolutely, nearly complete.[2] "On this memorable day Bishop Ridley read the prayers and preached in the choir, with no vestment but the rochet and chimere;[3] the Priests, the Dean and the Prebendaries wore their surplices and University caps and hoods. The Bishop preached in the afternoon at Paul's Cross."[4]

On May 25, 1553, came the Commissioners, with the

[1] Grey Friar, p. 76.   [2] Milman's *Annals*, p. 228.
[3] Black satin coat, and white lawn tunic and sleeves.
[4] Milman's *Annals*, p. 220.

EDWARD VI. AND THE REFORMATION

Lord Mayor, to make the last remorseless sweep of the treasures of the Cathedral, leaving but a scanty stock for the simpler service. Bishop Ridley strove, not without success, to rescue endowments for religious and charitable foundations, from the hands of the needy Government and the rapacious nobles. He extorted the foundation and endowment of Bridewell Hospital for the homeless poor, and threw it open to the City, an act (remarkable in those days) of wise charity, which by no means stands alone in these times of prodigal and almost lawless rapine. To the reign of Edward VI., and in great part to the influence of Bishop Ridley, belongs the noble foundation of Christ's Hospital.[1]

Milman's *Annals*, p. 228.

CHAPTER XV

REACTION: QUEEN MARY

THE accession of Mary Tudor was, of course, a complete upheaval of the Reformation arrangements. Bonner was restored, the mass reinstated, Latin revived as the language of worship, sentences of death pronounced against the reformers at Paul's Cross.

Ridley would have been wiser if, like many others, he had retired to the continent and waited for happier days: "If they shall persecute you in one city, flee unto another." He threw himself desperately into the anti-Marian faction, preaching a sermon at Paul's Cross, in which he denounced both Mary and Elizabeth as bastards. How unfortunate it is for the Church when it mixes itself up with politics! Finding there was no chance for Lady Jane Grey, the ideal of beauty and holiness, the pathetic and unwilling Ten Days' Queen of the Protestants, he went to Cambridge to throw himself at the feet of Mary in her victory, was brought back to London, and committed to the Tower.

St. Paul's was now in the hands of the restored Papal Church. At the proclamation of Queen Mary, the unconscious bells rang out in peals; the Lords marched in solemn array to the Cathedral; *Te Deum* was sung; the organ, sometime silenced by the Puritan ideal, burst out into full majestic mass of sound. On the Queen's procession from the Tower to the Coronation at Westminster, a feat was performed at St. Paul's to rival that at the procession of Edward VI.: "a Dutchman stood on the cross, waving a long streamer, and shifting from one foot to another, amid a blaze of torches, which he brandished over his head."[1]

London's acquiescence in the triumph of the Romanist Mary was somewhat superficial. "At the first sermon at Paul's Cross, Dr. Bourne, the preacher, not only prayed for the dead, but denounced the incarceration of Bonner 'in that vile prison, the Marshalsey,' and inveighed strongly against Bishop Ridley. 'There was shouting at the sermon as it were like mad people';[2] cries arose, 'He preaches damnation; pull him down, pull him down.' A dagger was thrown at the preacher, which struck one of the side posts of the pulpit.[3] Happily Bradford, well known as a devout Protestant, stepped forth before the preacher, and reminded the unruly mob of St. Paul's command 'to be subject to the higher powers.' But the fray did not cease; it threatened more violence. The obnoxious preacher was at length rescued by Bradford and Rogers, then a Canon of St. Paul's. He was conveyed in safety to St. Paul's School, hard by. The presence of the Lord Mayor and Lord Courtenay somewhat repressed the tumult."

The Privy Council at the Tower enjoined the Lord Mayor to keep the peace and punish the offenders. Humphrey Pullen was committed to the Compter; Bradford, Veron and Bacon to the Tower, as seditious preachers. Two days later the parson of St. Ethelburga and a barber were set in pillory at Paul's Cross, with their ears nailed to it. At the end of August mass was said in the Cathedral, matins and vespers chanted in Latin, the crucifix was restored; the English service inhibited. On the Sunday before the Coronation, Dr. Feckenham (successively Dean of St. Paul's and Westminster, the gentlest and most learned of the Romanists) preached undisturbed a goodly sermon at Paul's Cross.[4] On October 2, when Dr. Weston, Dean of Windsor, preached, strong barriers had to be

---

[1] Milman's *Annals*, p. 233, from *Chronicle*.　[2] Machyn, p. 41.
[3] August 13: Grafton, Stowe.　[4] Machyn, p. 44.

erected at every entrance into the churchyard, to prevent the crowd of horses and people. On St. Andrew's Day, Dr. Bourne preached safely in the Cathedral, with a great procession, and Latin invocation of the saints. Next day Nicholas Harpsfield did the same. "On the 24th was a very gorgeous procession, while the new Lord Mayor went to Westminster. After dinner, they marched to St. Paul's, banners waving, waits and trumpets blowing, all throughout the Church, and so back to the Lord Mayor's."[1]

On November 25, St. Katherine's Day, was a procession with great lights, following the image of St. Katherine. On January 25, St. Paul's Day, was another goodly procession, with fifty copes of gold, "Hail, festal day!" and a solemn mass. Later on a preacher at Paul's Cross (Dr. Pendleton) was fired at, but the culprit escaped.[2]

One of the first acts of Mary was the release of Bonner. He came forth from the Marshalsea in all the state of a Bishop. Eleven Bishops brought him to his palace at St. Paul's. There was a great concourse of people shouting "Welcome home!" and as many women as could kissed him. He knelt in prayer on the steps of the Cathedral.

On December 8, Bonner ordered a solemn procession at St. Paul's, and afterwards issued his mandate that every parish church should provide a staff and cope, and go in procession every Sunday, Wednesday and Friday, and pray to God for fine weather through London.[3]

On October 18, 1553, on the assembly of Convocation in St. Paul's, Weston, Dean of Westminster, was chosen Prolocutor of the Lower House. He began by denouncing the pestiferous Catechism, and the abominable Book of Common Prayer. Six days there was a long and persistent disputation on the Real Presence. The petition that Ridley and Rogers might be released from prison to sustain the argument on the Reformers' side was refused,

[1] Machyn, p. 66. [2] Ibid., p. 66. [3] Ibid., pp. 49, 50.

and the burden fell on Philpot. The Queen dissolved the Convocation by a mandate addressed to Bonner, Cranmer being in prison.

The marriage of Philip and Mary having taken place, preparation was made for a State reception of the King at St. Paul's: the great Rood must be re-erected. Bonner, in full pomp, and all his prebendaries assembled in the choir. The Rood lay on the pavement, the doors were closed. The Bishop and clergy having chanted certain prayers, they crept to the Cross and kissed it. It was then weighed up, and stood in its accustomed place. *Te Deum* was sung, and the unconscious bells rang out a merry peal.

After the rebellion of Wyatt, a solemn thanksgiving was held for its suppression.

On September 30, Bishop Gardiner preached at Paul's Cross to the largest assemblage ever believed to have been gathered there. He exhorted the people to give a good reception to King Philip, the Queen's husband, that "most perfect Prince," who was to visit the Cathedral on October 18. Philip rode down with a retinue of Lords from Westminster to St. Paul's, Lord Montagu bearing the sword before him. He was received at the west door, and conducted under a canopy up the nave. Mass was sung by a Spaniard.[1]

On the Second Sunday in Advent (A.D. 1554), Cardinal Pole was received at the Cathedral. The Legate, Priests and Clerks were all in most gorgeous attire, with new copes and crosses. The City Guilds were in all their splendour, the Lord Mayor, Sheriffs and Aldermen at their head. The Lord Chancellor (Gardiner, Bishop of Winchester), with the other Bishops, assembled at the Bishop of London's Palace. The Cardinal arrived at Baynard's Castle from Lambeth by water at nine o'clock. He was received by the Lord Mayor, and conducted to the Cathedral preceded by a cross and two magnificent pillars of silver. At the

[1] Machyn, p. 72.

Cathedral he was met by the Lord Chancellor and the Bishops. They moved in procession to the choir, and took their seats. At ten o'clock came the King for the Morning Mass, with 100 English, 100 Spanish, 100 German guards, and a vast retinue of nobles and knights. All listened in the most profound silence. Gardiner preached on the text, " Now it is high time to awake out of sleep." He deplored the recent time of heresies, chief of which was the renunciation of Papal supremacy (to which he and Bonner had contributed); and dwelt on the graciousness of reconciliation through the Legate, and the magnanimity of the great and wealthy King who had come to help restore order to the realm.

A few days after, November 29, Bonner ordered a procession and *Te Deum* in honour of the child about to be born to Mary.[1] Later in the year, when the expected time was approaching, St. Paul's rang with thanksgiving. On January 25 (1555), St. Paul's Day, a procession of ecclesiastics to the number of 160 set forth from St. Paul's, with 90 crosses, chanting, " Hail, festal day ! "[2] On the last of April, came the false tidings that the Queen's Grace was delivered of a son. The bells of St. Paul's clanged in joy, followed by the other churches, and in divers places *Te Deum* was sung. " And on the morrow after it was turned other ways to the pleasure of God, and I trust that He will remember the true servants that put their trust in Him when they call on Him."

" For this consummation more awful offerings, human holocausts, were offered, more terrible manifestations of their faith."[3]

" St. Paul's gave two of the noblest victims to the Marian persecution, her Bishop, Ridley, and a Canon of her Chapter, the worthy Proto-martyr of the Reformed English Church, John Rogers "[4] There is good reason for believ-

---

[1] Machyn, p. 77. [2] *Ibid.*, p. 78.
[3] Milman's *Annals*, p. 241. [4] *Ibid.*, p. 244.

ing that Rogers was the Matthews who finished Tyndale's translation of the Bible. His trial took place in St. Mary Overy (the present Southwark Cathedral). The pathetic details may be read in Foxe. "It was the martyrdom, and the circumstances of that martyrdom, that made so deep, so indelible an impression upon the English mind and soul. So strong was the popular excitement that he was removed by night in secrecy from St. Mary Overy to Newgate. As he was led from his prison to Smithfield, his wife and nine children (another was about to be born) stood watching his 'triumph' almost with joyousness. With wife and children he had been refused a parting interview, by Gardiner first, when in prison, by Bonner afterwards, just before his execution; for what had a consecrated priest to do with wife and children? It was De Noailles, the Romanist French Ambassador, who said that John Rogers passed on, not as to his death, but as to his wedding."[1]

The trial of Bishop Ridley took place with that of Bishop Latimer at Oxford, and they were burned together on October 16, 1555, in front of Balliol College. For that most touching and impressive history we must look once more to the full and simple narrative of Foxe.

Bonner, in the meantime, had emerged from prison in a humour of brutal fury. He wrote insulting letters to Ridley. One day he struck a knight, Sir J. Jocelyn, a violent blow on the ear. The gentle Feckenham, now Dean of St. Paul's, made an apology for the Bishop. "His long imprisonment in the Marshalsea, and the miseries and hardships so altered him, that in these passions he is not master of himself"; to which the knight merely replied, "Now that he is come forth of the Marshalsea, he is ready to go to Bedlam."[2]

Bonner began with a monition to his clergy that none was to be admitted to partake the Sacrament of the Altar without a certificate of auricular confession; altars were

[1] Milman's *Annals*, p. 244.   [2] Machyn, p. 95.

to be prepared with books and vestments for mass. To Bonner the Queen addressed her Articles, inhibiting marriage of the clergy, and ordering the dismissal of the wives of those married. In the spirit of an Inquisitor he appointed commissioners to search out the lives and conduct of every clerk in his diocese: was he a brawler, scolder, hawker, hunter, fornicator, drunkard, blasphemer of God and His saints? was he married? if married, and having put away his wife, did he keep up clandestine intercourse with her? were his sermons orthodox? did he associate with heretics? did he exhort his parishioners to go to mass and confession? No act of a clergyman, dress, tonsure, private moments, almost his thoughts, were free from this tyrannical scrutiny. The Council itself had to interpose; Bonner had acted without their authority. He was at first defiant, but the City of London offered such resistance that reluctantly and sullenly he withdrew his injunctions.[1]

"All the splendid ceremonials and processions with which the Marian Bishops endeavoured to dazzle and win over the not reluctant populace, could not obliterate the feelings excited by those more dismal processions day after day to Smithfield. There is something absolutely appalling in the strange succession, the rapid alternation, of these scenes as they appear in the diary of Robert Machyn, which records whatever took place in St. Paul's and in its neighbourhood. . . . It is appalling enough to read, though at such times mercy could not be expected to such rebels: 'The 7th day of February was commanded by the Queen and the Bishop of London that St. Paul's and every parish church should sing *Te Deum* and ring their bells for the great victory over Wyatt's rebellion. On the 12th, a new pair of gallows were set up, fourteen in number, at each of the gates in London. On the 13th, were hanging on these gallows many bodies, some quartered, some in chains, and

---

[1] Wilkins, iv. p. 105; Froude, vi. p. 257.

those quartered bodies and heads set on the gates of London.' But these were the penalties of unsuccessful rebellion. On the 25th, St. Paul's Day, was the reception of the Legate, already described. 'On the 28th, 29th, and 30th, Hooper, Crome, Rogers, Bradford, Saunders, cast to be burned in divers places. February 14 Rogers was burned in Smithfield. The 9th of February were arraigned before the Lord Mayor and Sheriffs and the Bishop of London and divers Doctors of the Council, six heretics of Essex and Suffolk, to be burned in divers places.' Next, 'March 8, a procession from St. Paul's through Cheapside and Bucklersbury, and so back through Watling Street to St. Paul's, the children of St. Paul's and the Hospital, the Bishop, the Lord Mayor and Aldermen, and all the Crafts, and all the Priests and Clerks singing. On May 25 was arraigned at St. Paul's for heresy, before the Bishop, Master Cardmaker, sometime Vicar of St. Bride's, in Fleet Street, one John Warren, a clothmaker in Walbrook, and cast to be burned, and carried back to Newgate. The 24th of May was a goodly procession of the children of the Hospital (Christ's), and all the schools in London. The 30th May were burned in Smithfield Master Cardmaker and Master Warren. On the 23rd August was burned at Stratford-le-Bow, Middlesex, the wife of John Warren; and the same woman had a son, taken at her burning, and carried to his sister in Newgate. On June 17 were performed at St. Paul's the obsequies of the Queen of Spain. In July went to Smithfield, to be burned, Master Bradford, a great preacher in King Edward's days, and a tallow-chandler's 'prentice, dwelling by Newgate, with a great concourse of people.'"[1]

In the midst of these horrors comes a strange entry. In the reign of Edward I. Sir Walter le Baud gave to the Dean and Chapter of St. Paul's, annually on the Feast of the Conversion of St. Paul (January 25), a fat doe, and on

[1] Machyn, pp. 81, 82, etc.; Milman, pp. 250, 251, 252.

the other day of St. Paul, in the summer, a fat buck from his estate in Essex. These gifts used to be received at the west door, conducted without, about and within the Church, up to the high altar with noisy merriment. Bonner evidently revived the custom. "On the last day of June, St. Paul's Day, was a goodly procession at St. Paul's. There was a priest of each parish in the Diocese of London, with a cope, and the Bishop of London, wearing his mitre, and after came a fat buck, and his head with his horns borne upon a pole, and forty horns blowing before the beast and behind."[1]

On August 15, 1557, yet one more gorgeous procession at St. Paul's, to celebrate Philip's victory at St. Quentin. Orders came for the clergy of all the churches to meet at St. Paul's in their copes. They marched round Paul's Cross, where they were joined by the Lord Mayor and Aldermen, and all went to the Cathedral. The sermon was preached at Paul's Cross by Harpsfield, Archdeacon of London.

Pole was implicated in the burnings. There is a document from his register, signed with his seal, in which five persons, John Cornford of Wrotham, Christopher Browne of Maidstone, John Hurst of Ashford, Catherine Knight of Shoreham, Alice Smith of Beddenden (all in Pole's diocese) are arraigned and made over to the secular arm, to be burned.

Mary kept it up to the last. Four days before she died (November 13, 1558) the Council, of which Pole was the head, issued this royal brief: "Since our Reverend Father in Christ, Edmond, Bishop of London, lawfully proceeding, and according to his office in causes of heretical pravity, has pronounced and declared certain manifest heretics, and delivered them to the secular arm, we do, willing to extirpate root and branch such heretics from our kingdom, adjudge such heretics, according to the law and custom of

[1] Machyn, p. 147, A.D. 1557.

our kingdom, to be burned with fire; we command such heretics to be really burned with fire in public view."[1]

On November 17, Queen Mary died: within twenty-two hours of her death, Cardinal Pole. Nearly at the same time died no less than thirteen Bishops, and a great number of the clergy, from quartan fever, then greatly prevalent. A great barrier to the revival of reforming views was thus removed.

[1] Wilkins, vol. iv. p. 177 (Foxe).

CHAPTER XVI

ST. PAUL'S, QUEEN ELIZABETH AND THE REVIVED REFORMATION

ON November 17, 1558, the day of Queen Mary's death, and of the accession of Queen Elizabeth, Elizabeth's chaplain, Dr. Bill, made a goodly sermon at Paul's Cross, but gave no sign of future policy. From that day, for some months, by the new Queen's prudence, Paul's Cross was silent. It was one of the articles in Cecil's Memorial of the first Acts recommended to the Queen on her accession, to consider the condition of the preacher at Paul's Cross, that no occasion be given by him to stir up any dispute concerning the governance of the realm.[1] "A proclamation was presently set forth, that no man should alter any rites or ceremonies at that time used in the Church; and because, in such divisions of opinions, the pulpits often serve as drums and fifes to inflame fury, proclamation was made that no man should preach but such as should be allowed by authority. . . . Hereupon no sermon was preached at Paul's Cross until the Rehearsal Sermon was made upon the Sunday after Easter."[2] The Marian rites continued for the present in the Cathedral; but another royal proclamation ordered Epistle and Gospel to be in English.

On April 11, Sunday after Easter, Dr. Samson was to preach at the Cross. The keys (after five months' disuse) were not forthcoming; when the Lord Mayor ordered the door to be opened by a smith, the place was found almost

[1] Strype's *Annals*, i. 7.
[2] Hayward's *Annals of Queen Elizabeth*, p. 5.

ST. PAUL'S AND REVIVED REFORMATION 157

too filthy and unclean to be used (the Cathedral pigeons had evidently been in undisturbed occupation).[1] Another day in April appeared Dr. Bill (now the Queen's Almoner), to explain why the recusant Marian Bishops had been sent to the Tower. On May 14, the preacher was the future Bishop of London, Dr. Grindal, before the Queen's Council, the Duke of Norfolk, Lord Northampton, the Lord Treasurer, a great assemblage of nobles and knights, and the Lord Mayor and Aldermen. Next Sunday, the preacher was the future Bishop of Winchester, Dr. Horne, before Lord Mayor, City dignitaries, many judges and serjeants-at-law, and a crowd of people.

A paper drawn up by one of the Council (Sir Thomas Smith or Sir William Cecil) sketches the policy afterwards followed by Elizabeth. "Assuming that it was desirable that the Church of England should be 'reduced to its former purity,' the writer goes on to consider the best means of effecting this. He recommends that those who had weight with Queen Mary should be gradually 'abased,' and those who had been faithful to the interests of Elizabeth advanced to authority. That, under the pressure of the Præmunire statute, the Bishops and clergy who had enriched themselves by the late Queen's concessions should be made to disgorge their wealth to the Crown. That the sheriffs and justices in the counties should be removed. That not too much attention should be paid to the demands of the ultra-reformers, for 'better were it that they should suffer, than her Highness or the Commonwealth should shake and be in danger.' That a Commission of Divines should be at once appointed to revise the English Prayer-book, with a view to its restoration, and that until this was done, a 'strait prohibition' should be made of all innovations."[2]

London and other Bishoprics were not filled up till June 23. The palace of the Bishop of London, by St. Paul's, was assigned for the entertainment of the

[1] Hayward's *Annals*.   [2] Burnet's *Records*, book iii. No. i.

French Ambassadors for the Coronation, the Cardinal of Lorraine, the Duke of Montmorency, the Marquis of Fronsac, the Bishop of Orleans, the Chevalier d'Aubespere. For several days they passed in splendid procession to dine at Court, and after dinner to enjoy music, and the baiting of the bear and the bull.

On June 6, the preacher was Sandys, future Bishop of Worcester, Bishop of London and Archbishop of York. The Lord Mayor and Aldermen were present, the Earl of Bedford and other nobles. The Apostles' Mass was now discontinued, and soon after the mass itself came to an end.

On June 18, a vast congregation heard Jewel, the famous Oxford preacher, afterwards Bishop of Salisbury. On June 23, five Bishops were elected in Bow Church: Parker as Primate, Grindal Bishop of London, Scorey Bishop of Hereford, Barlow Bishop of Chichester, and another. Grindal and the others were not consecrated till the following December.

On August 11 appeared at the Cathedral the Queen's Commissioners to hold their Visitation. Horne, afterwards Bishop of Winchester, was at their head. They took their seats in the Church. The English Litany was read, and Horne preached on "the wise and faithful servant." They then adjourned to the Chapter House. The names of all and singular of the said Church were cited. Bonner had been removed, and Henry Cole, the Dean (formerly Provost of Eton, appointed to St. Paul's in 1556, died 1579), deprived. William May, the Dean previously dispossessed, had escaped burning, but was not re-installed. Of the thirty prebendaries, a considerable number had been appointed by Bonner.

It was by order of the Commissioners that the Cathedral was to be purged of its superstitions. A few days after, the Rood raised with such solemn ceremony by Bonner, fell again. The images disappeared: in St. Paul's, in quiet, with no irreverence. These orders were delivered, in the

ST. PAUL'S AND REVIVED REFORMATION 159

absence of Bishop and Dean, to the Treasurer, Saxey. The Archdeacon of London (John Harpsfield) exhibited the Book of Statutes and Ordinances. Later he was directed to produce a full and faithful inventory of all and singular the jewels, ornaments and whatsoever books belonging to the said Church. Harpsfield, the Archdeacon, and Nicholas Harpsfield, the famous Papal preacher, refused to submit, and were bound to appear. The Treasurer and others were ordered to provide a decent Holy Table for the celebration of the Lord's Supper. Henceforth in the Cathedral none were to use any shaven crowns, amices or vestments called copes. The Harpsfields, Wallerton, four prebendaries and the Archdeacon of Colchester were deprived.

On September 8, 1559, the obsequies of Henry II. of France (who died on July 20, and had been the inexorable persecutor of the Reformers) were performed in the Cathedral with extraordinary magnificence. Elizabeth's aunt, Mary Tudor, had been married to his maternal grandfather, Louis XII. The chronicler is full of "the hearse, scutcheons, coats-of-arms, with great crowns, a great pall of cloth of gold, coat-armour, helmet, and mantle of cloth of gold, target, sword and crest. The choir was hung with black, with armorial bearings. Lord Treasurer Cecil, chief mourner, next my Lord Chamberlain, many nobles, Lords Hunsdon and Abergavenny."[1] Next day, the 9th, all the heralds—Garter, Clarencieux, Norroy, Somerset, Chester, Richmond, York, Windsor, Lancaster, Rouge Croix, Rouge Dragon, Bluemantle and Portcullis—came in their array from the Bishop's Palace. The sermon was preached by Scorey, Bishop of Hereford. The clergy had black gowns and great hoods lined with silk, and drest caps.[2] The expenses amounted to £783 10s. 10d., and were borne by the Queen.[3]

September 30 began the new service in the Cathedral

[1] Machyn.   [2] *Ibid.*   [3] Strype's *Annals*, i. 1.

"at the same time the Apostles' Mass was wont to be sung."

On November 26, Jewel, Bishop-Elect of Salisbury, preached at Paul's Cross, and first uttered his memorable challenge defying the adherents of the old religion to produce a passage from the authoritative Fathers of the first six centuries in favour of the peculiar doctrines of Rome on the Mass. The sermon was enlarged and preached before the Court, March 17, 1560.

On December 17, 1559, Archbishop Parker was consecrated in the Chapel of Lambeth Palace, according to the Ordinal of King Edward's Second Book, by Bishops Barlow, Scorey, Coverdale and Hodgkins; and a few days after, the new Archbishop, with the assistance of some other Bishops, consecrated Grindal to London, Cox to Ely, Sandys to Worcester and Merick to Bangor. In January 1560 five more were consecrated: Young to St. Davids, Bullingham to Lincoln, Jewel to Salisbury, Davis to St. Asaph, and Guest to Rochester. Bonner had been deposed on May 25, 1559. He had presided at Elizabeth's first Convocation, which voted a strong Papal address to the Crown; he, with other Bishops, had stood aloof from Elizabeth's Coronation, though his gorgeous robes had been borrowed for Oglethorpe of Carlisle, the one officiating Bishop. In the House of Lords, with Archbishop Heath of York and other Bishops, he had protested against Elizabeth's Acts in religion. It was not till April 1560, that he was committed to his former prison, the Marshalsea. That imprisonment was for his security against the popular detestation. It "turned to his safety, being so hated by the people, that it would not have been safe to him to have walked in public, lest he should have been stoned or knocked on the head by the enraged friends and acquaintance of those whom he had but a little before so barbarously beaten and butchered. He grew old in prison, and died a natural death in the year 1569, not suffering any want, or

ST. PAUL'S AND REVIVED REFORMATION 161

hunger, or cold. For he lived daintily, and had the use of garden and orchards when he was minded to walk abroad and take the air."[1]

In 1559, on March 31 and April 3, was held a disputation, or great debate, in Westminster Abbey, on the proposed religious changes. The Lord Keeper presided, eight disputants were elected from each side, and Parliament was prorogued that the members might be present. For the Romanists appeared White, Bishop of Winchester; Bayne of Lichfield, Scott of Chester, Watson of Lincoln, Cole, Dean of St. Paul's; Harpsfield, Archdeacon of Canterbury; Langdale, Archdeacon of Lewes; and Chadsey, Prebendary of St. Paul's: for the Reformers, Scorey, formerly Bishop of Chichester; Cox, late Dean of Westminster; Horne, late Dean of Durham; Aylmer, late Archdeacon of Stow, and Whitehead, Grindal, Guest and Jewel. The history of it belongs to Westminster, or the Church at large; it is only mentioned here because of Grindal.

Edmund Grindal was born at St. Bees in Cumberland. He was Fellow and Master of Pembroke College, Cambridge, Doctor of Divinity, and Chaplain to Bishop Ridley. A voluntary exile for the faith during the reign of Queen Mary, he was enthroned Bishop of London on December 23, 1559. Eleven years after, in May 1570, he was translated to York, and in February 1575, he was raised to Canterbury. He hesitated greatly about accepting the See of London, partly on account of the alienation of episcopal estates by the Crown, partly by reason of the Marian vestments, which had not yet been discarded. His friend Peter Martyr, the oracle of the Reformers, reassured him on both these points. Soon after his inauguration (February 2, 1560) there was a riot outside the Deanery, then inhabited by the French Ambassador, because mass had been said in the house. The authority of the Lord Mayor was effective.

It has been well said by Milman that, "of all difficult

[1] Strype's *Annals*.

positions on record in history, few could more severely try Christian temper, wisdom, honesty and piety than that of Elizabeth's Bishops; especially the more prominent, Parker, the Primate, and the Bishop of London. These Bishops, in truth, were the real founders of the (reformed) Church of England. The reforming Bishops of Henry VIII.'s days, even those of Edward VI., were inquirers, searchers for truth, rather than men of fixed and determinate opinions; Cranmer especially, whose whole religious life was a gradual development, on whom new truths dawned successively, and whose creed was therefore in a continual state of change, not undashed with doubt and with seeming contradiction. Elizabeth's Bishops were steadfastly, on reasoning conviction, determined against the old religion, and on certain points were resolute, fixed and fully in unison in their new creed."[1]

Grindal was vexed by the plan of exchanging for the broad lands of the Bishops, the monastic tithes, a possession of uncertain value, of difficult and expensive collection. Fortunately the estates left to the Bishopric of London have now become a fifth part of the whole income of the Ecclesiastical Commissioners, wisely distributed on poor parishes all over the country. "One boon the Bishopric of London received from Queen Elizabeth, of which no one could foresee the future value, what was called 'the Paddington estate,' had been taken from the Abbey of Westminster to endow the short-lived Westminster Bishopric. On the death of the one Bishop of that See, the lands escheated to the Crown. The estate was granted by the Queen to the Bishop of London. In our days this estate, then a few meadows and some wild wastes, is covered with spacious streets and splendid houses, one of the richest quarters of the metropolis."

On August 12, 1560, the first year of Grindal's episcopate, died William May, the reinstated Dean of St. Paul's. He

[1] Milman's *Annals*, p. 266.

had been designated Archbishop of York. He was buried in the Cathedral, and Bishop Grindal preached his funeral sermon.[1] May was succeeded by Alexander Nowell, of Brasenose, Oxford, Archdeacon of Middlesex, a man of the highest character for piety and learning, a consummate master of the controversy with Rome, whose catechisms are accepted and accredited as the authorized expositions of Church of England doctrine.

In 1561, a terrific storm burst over London. The Church of St. Martin's, Ludgate Hill, was struck by lightning; huge stones came toppling down on the roof and on the pavement. The alarm was not over when lightning was seen to flash into an aperture in the steeple of the Cathedral. The spire was of wood covered with lead. The fire burned downwards for four hours with irresistible force, the bells melted, the timber blazed, the stones crumbled and fell. The lead flowed down in sheets of flame, threatening, but happily not damaging, the organ.

There is an interesting and unique Tract in the British Museum on this fire, published six days after, on June 10. It speaks of "a marvellous great fiery lightning, between one and two o'clock in the afternoon, on which immediately ensued a most terrible hideous crack of thunder, such as seldom hath been heard, and that by estimation of sense directly over the City of London. Divers persons being on the River Thames and others in the fields near adjoining to the City affirmed that they saw a long and spear-pointed flame of fire run through the top of the Broche or Shaft of Paul's steeple, from east westward. And some of the parish of St. Martin's then being in the streets did feel a marvellous strong air or whirlwind with a smell like brimstone coming from Paul's Church. Between three and four o'clock a smoke was espied by divers to break out under the bowl of the said shaft of Paul's, and namely by Peter Johnson, Principal Registrar to the Bishop of London, who

[1] Machyn, p. 241.

immediately brought word to the Bishop's home. But suddenly after, as it were in a moment, the flame broke forth in a circle like a garland round about the Broche, about two yards under the bowl of the said shaft, and increased in suchwise that within a quarter of an hour, or little more, the Cross and Eagle on the top fell down upon the south transept. The Lord Mayor being sent for, and his brethren, came with all speed possible, and had a short consultation as in a case might be, with the Bishop of London and others, for the best way of remedy. And thither also came the Lord Keeper and the Lord Treasurer, who by their wisdom and authority directed as good order as in so great a confusion could possibly be. Some counselled that the steeple should be shot down with cannon, to prevent the fire spreading: others were for ladders and axes to be brought, to hew down the parts of the roof nearest to the fire; but before the difficulties of such sudden plans could be overcome (the multitude of idle gazers was not the least), the most part of the highest roof of the Church was on fire. After the fall of the Cross and Eagle, the beams and brands of the steeple fell down on every side, and fired the other three roofs. So that in one hour's space the Broche of the steeple was burnt down to the battlements, and the most part of the highest roof of the Church likewise consumed.

"The state of the steeple and Church seeming both desperate, my Lord Mayor was advised by one Master Winter of the Admiralty to convert the most part of his care and provision to preserve the Bishop's Palace adjoining to the north-west end of the Church; lest, from that house, being large, the fire might spread to the streets adjoining. Whereupon the ladders, buckets and labourers were commanded thither, and by great labour and diligence a piece of the roof of the north aisle was cut down, and the fire so stayed, and by much water that part quenched, and the said Bishop's house preserved. It pleased God also at the same time both to turn and calm the wind, which before was vehement, and continued still high and great in other parts without the City. There were above five hundred persons that laboured in carrying and filling water. Divers substantial citizens took pains as if they had been labourers; so did also divers and sundry gentlemen. In the evening came the Lord Clinton from the Court at Greenwich, whom the Queen's Majesty, as soon as the rage of the fire was espied by Her Majesty and others in the Court, of the pitiful inclination and love that Her Gracious Highness did bear both to the said Church and the City, sent to assist my Lord Mayor for the suppressing of the fire: who with his wisdom, authority and diligent travel did very much good therein.

"About ten o'clock the fierceness of the fire was past, the timber being fallen and lying burning upon the vaults of stone, the yet (God be thanked!) standing unperished; so as only the timber of the whole Church was consumed, and the lead molten, saving the most part of the two low aisles of the choir, and a piece of the north aisle, and another small piece of the south aisle in the body of the Church. In the whole City without the Church absolutely not a stick caught fire, notwithstanding that in divers parts and streets, and within the houses both adjoining, and of a good distance, as in Fleet Street and Newgate Market, by the violence of fire, burning coals of great bigness fell down almost as thick as hailstones, and flakes of lead were blown abroad into the gardens without the City, like flakes of snow in breadth, without hurt, God be thanked! to any house or person.

"On Sunday following, being the 8th day of June, the Reverend Father in God the Bishop of Durham, at Paul's Cross, made a learned and fruitful sermon, exhorting the auditory to a general repentance, and namely to humble obedience to the laws and superior powers, which virtue is much decayed in these our days; seeming to have intelligence from the Queen's Highness that Her Majesty intendeth that more severity of laws shall be executed against persons disobedient, as well in causes of religion as civil, to the great rejoicing of his auditors. He exhorted also his audience to take this as a general warning to the whole realm, and namely to the City of London, of some greater plague to follow if amendment of life in all states did not ensue. He much reproved those persons which would assign the cause of this wrath of God to any particular state of men, or that were diligent to look into other men's lives and could see no faults in themselves; but wished that every man would descend into himself, and say with David, I am he that hath sinned: and so forth to that effect very godly. He also not only reproved the profanation of the said Church of Paul's of long time heretofore abused by walking, jangling, brawling, fighting, bargaining, etc., especially in sermons and service time: but also answered to the objections of such evil-tongued persons which do impute this token of God's deserved ire to alteration, or rather reformation, of religion; declaring out of ancient records and histories the like, yea, and even greater matters had befallen in the time of superstition and ignorance. For in the first year of King Stephen, not only the said Church of Paul's was burnt, but also a great part of the City, that is to say, from London Bridge to St. Clement's without Temple Bar, was by fire consumed. And in the days of King Henry VI., the steeple of Paul's was also fired by lightning, although it was then stayed by the diligence of the citizens, the fire being then by likelihood not so fierce. Many other suchlike common calamities he rehearsed which happened in other countries, both nigh to this realm, and far off, where the Church of Rome hath most authority; and therefore concluded the surest way to be that every man should judge, examine and amend himself, and embrace, believe and truly follow the Word of God; and earnestly to pray to God to turn away from us His deserved wrath and indignation, whereof this His terrible work is a most certain warning, if we repent not unfeignedly."

The fire was held to be a national calamity, and the restoration of the Cathedral a national work. Crown, Church, nobility and commonalty, especially the City of London, were called upon to raise it up again at least to its pristine dignity. The frugal Queen gave one thousand marks in gold, one thousand marks in timber. The City of London gave a great benevolence, and after that three-fifteenths to be speedily paid. The clergy of the Province of Canterbury gave the fortieth part of the income of their benefices charged with first-fruits, the thirtieth of the rest. The total sum raised from the clergy was £1410. The Bishop of London in two donations gave £248; the Dean and Chapter of St. Paul's, £136; the two Chief Justices and Officers of the Court of Common Pleas, £34; of King's Bench, £17; the Bishop of London further for timber, £720.[1]

The Lord Mayor took the lead in the restoration. The flames were hardly extinguished when men were set to work, the most skilful that could be found, to take measures for the immediate repair of the damage. The Lord Mayor personally superintended the works, with "men of knowledge" to overlook the workmen. In one month a false roof was erected to keep out the weather. By the end of the year the aisles were covered in and roofed over with lead. During the next year the great roofs of the west and east ends had been prepared with large timbers framed in Yorkshire, brought by sea, set up and covered with lead. The north and south transepts were covered in by the end of April 1566; one hundred years before the far more terrible and final conflagration under Charles II.

On November 1, 1561, the Lord Mayor and Aldermen, and all the Crafts of London, in their liveries, went to the Cathedral with a vast retinue (eighty men carrying torches);

[1] Strype's edition of Stowe iii. 150.

the Lord Mayor tarried the sermon, which lasted into the night, and returned home by the light of the torches.[1]

The spire, however, remained in ruins, and was never re-erected. The repairs of James I. and Charles I. were confined to another part of the building. The Queen was herself extremely angry that the spire was not restored. The excuse was that Her Majesty's subsidies were pressing so heavily on the City that time was absolutely necessary.

Bishop Pilkington's remonstrance about the traffic in St. Paul's is illustrated by an Act of the Common Council of London, in the first and second years of Philip and Mary, August 1 : " Forasmuch as the material temples of God were first ordained for the lawful and devout assembly of the people, there to lift up their hearts and to laud and praise Almighty God, and to hear the divine service and most Holy Word and Gospel sincerely said, sung and taught, are not to be used as markets or other profane uses."[2] It complains that many of the inhabitants and others were accustomed, unseemly and irreverently, " to make their common carriage of great vessels of ale or beer, great baskets full of bread, fish, flesh and fruit, fardels of stuff and other gross wares, through the Cathedral Church of St. Paul's, and some in leading mules, horses and other beasts irreverently to the great dishonour and displeasure of Almighty God. The Council prohibit all these abuses under fines for the first and second offence ; for the third, imprisonment for two days and nights without bail or mainprize."[2]

Queen Elizabeth, like the City, was determined to bring the old inveterate abuses to an end. She issued a proclamation that " if any person shall make any fray, or draw or put out his hand to any weapon for that purpose, or shoot any hand-gun or dagg within the Cathedral Church of St. Paul, or churchyard adjoining thereto, or within the limits of the boundaries compassing the same, they shall suffer imprison-

[1] Machyn, p. 271.   [2] Stowe, Appendix, p. 937.

ment for two months. Any of Her Majesty's subjects who shall walk up and down, or spend the time in the same, in any bargain or other profane cause, and make any kind of disturbance during the time of preaching, lecturing or other divine service, shall incur the pain of imprisonment and fine, the fine to go to the repair of the Church. No agreement was to be made for the payment of money in the Cathedral; no burden to be carried through the Church; with a reservation for any covenant or bond already made."

An evil with the inveteracy of centuries was hard to cure. Shakespeare makes Falstaff engage Bardolph in Paul's. Dekker, in his *Gull's Handbook*, gives comical details of the gulls and knaves who swarmed in all corners. Ben Jonson lays the scene in the third act of his "Every man out of his Humour" in the middle aisle of St. Paul's. "The knave of the play boasts that he has posted up his bills without observation, and precious bills they were to be read on the walls of a church. The characters which old Ben though a coarse yet not usually an irreverent writer, scruples not to assemble in the Church, is the most vivid illustration of the extent to which the evil had grown."[1]

Bishop Earle describes it wittily in his delightful *Microcosmography*. "Paul's Walk is the land's epitome, as you may call it; the lesser isle of Great Britain. It is more than this; the whole world's map, which you may here discern in its perfected motion, justling and turning. It is a heap of stones and men, with a vast confusion of languages; and were the steeple not sanctified, nothing liker Babel. The noise in it is like that of bees, a strange hum, mixed of walking tongues and feet; it is a kind of still roar or loud whisper. It is the great exchange of all discourse, and no business whatsoever but is here striving and afoot. It is the synod of all parties politic, jointed and laid together, in most serious position, and they are not half so busy at the Parliament. . . . It is the market of young lecturers, who you

[1] Milman's *Annals*, p. 287.

may cheapen here at all rates and sizes. It is the general mint of all famous lies, which are here, like the legends of Popery, first coined and stamped in the Church. All inventions are emptied here and not few pockets. The best sign of a temple in it is that it is the thieves' sanctuary, which rob more safely in a crowd than in a wilderness, whilst every searcher is a bush to hide them. It is the other expense of the day, after plays, taverns, ... and men have some oaths left to swear here. ... The visitants are all men without exceptions, but the principal inhabitants and possessors are stale knights and captains out of service; men of long rapiers and breeches, which after all turn merchants here and traffic for news. Some make it a preface to their dinner, and travel for a stomach; but thriftier men make it their ordinary, and board here very cheap." A melancholy picture!

Restored after the great fire of 1561, St. Paul's received Elizabeth's first reformed Convocation, January 19, 1563. First came the Litany in English, then *Veni Creator*. The sermon, as addressed to the clergy, was preached in Latin (the custom remains to this day), on the text, "Feed My flock," by Day, Provost of Eton. Then the first Psalm in English. Holy Communion was next administered by Archbishop Parker. Nowell, Dean of St. Paul's, was elected Prolocutor. Following the innovation of Wolsey, the Primate then adjourned the Convocation to Westminster, where it held its sittings in Henry VII.'s Chapel.

Having held the Bishopric of London ten years, in May 1570 Grindal was moved to York, ere long to end at Canterbury. Everywhere he bore the character of profound piety and gentleness. His unwillingness to proceed against recalcitrant Puritans is acknowledged. Of him Holinshed wrote: "His book was his bride, and his study his bride-chamber."

His successor in the See of London was *Edwin Sandys*, Bishop of Worcester, installed July 20, 1570. Sandys was

ST. PAUL'S AND REVIVED REFORMATION 171

of gentle birth, Master of Catherine Hall, Cambridge, and Vice-Chancellor when Lady Jane Grey was proclaimed Queen. About this he got into trouble, and was imprisoned for some months. On his release at the intercession of friends, he went into Germany with his wife, and stayed there till the death of Queen Mary. Appointed Bishop of Worcester by Elizabeth, he remained there more than ten years. After six years in London, he followed Grindal at York, where he held the Archbishopric about twelve years, and was buried at Southwell Minster, then in that diocese.

On the night of May 25, 1571, an indignant crowd was gathered round the episcopal gates, reading a great parchment with the Papal arms and signature, the Bull of excommunication and deposition which Pius V. had launched against Queen Elizabeth. Henceforth all English Romanists faithful to the Pope were constrained to regard the Queen as an enemy, and to separate themselves from the Church which she upheld. This action of the Pope is deplored and condemned by all moderate Romanist writers, and it was repudiated by a great number, especially amongst the laity, of the English Romanists at that day. The fanatic who had nailed the Bull to the Bishop's gates seems to have disdained flight. He was arrested, tried, condemned and, on August 8, hanged at the scene of his action.

Puritanism was becoming more active, and was perplexing to Sandys. This is not in any sense a history of the Church of England, but only an attempt to show how, during a long succession of centuries, current movements of thought affected the life of St. Paul's Cathedral. The candid observer of national religious life notices that in every generation there is generally some predominant tide of thought and feeling, often, perhaps, more of feeling than of thought, made up of many contributing influences and causes, which attracts to itself that which is most generous, noble, aspiring and religious among the people. Had Elizabeth herself been really a religious woman, she might have attracted those deep, stirring, religious emotions to the true and beautiful ideals of the reformed and primitive Church of England. As it was, there were two currents throughout her reign, of the same fundamental materials, but flowing in different directions, like the battling tides in the Pentland Firth.

Puritanism appears at Paul's Cross in the person of Crick, from Cambridge, chaplain to the Bishop of Norwich, who attacks the Established Church and upholds Cartwright, afterwards the Puritan opponent of Hooker. Sandys writes to the Council that he has sent a messenger to apprehend him, and that he will not appear again. Then Oxford has her Puritan champion at the Cross in Wake of Christ Church, whom the Bishop's Chancellor warns in vain in the midst of his sermon; and the preacher entrenches himself at Oxford. In the Cathedral itself there was Dering, of an old Kentish family, a preacher of great eloquence and popularity, holding, probably, Bishop de Gravesend's Lectureship in Theology. Preaching before the Queen, he told her that under persecution she was a lamb, now she was an untamed heifer. Dering's Puritanical sermons drew crowds to the Cathedral, but gave offence to the Queen's ministers, and he was deprived. Dering had friends at Court, and wrote to Lord Treasurer Cecil that his chief objection to Bishops was their titles and their civil power; he had submitted to the liturgy, and even to the surplice. Cecil obtained the reinstatement of Dering. Offending again, he was again deprived, and soon after died.

Sandys was succeeded by *John Aylmer*, of an ancient Norfolk family. He was educated both at Oxford and Cambridge, was chaplain to Henry Grey, Duke of Suffolk, and tutor to his daughter, Lady Jane Grey. In 1553, he became Archdeacon of Suffolk, but not conforming to

Queen Mary's Romanism, retired to Germany till the accession of Elizabeth, when he was appointed one of the eight champions of the Reformation in the great debate against the mediævalists. In 1562, he became Archdeacon of Lincoln, and was consecrated Bishop of London on March 24, in 1576. "He was a great enemy to the Puritan faction," says Newcourt, the historian of the Diocese of London, "and much hated by them." "His visitation questions are severe, searching, inquisitorial. On one occasion he suspended thirty-eight of his clergy."[1] The Puritans were now questioning episcopal authority itself, and Aylmer's early writings were capable of quotation. In his answer to Knox's *Monstrous Regimen of Women*, he had written, "Come off, ye Bishops, yield up your superfluities; give up your thousands; be content with hundreds as they be in other reformed Churches, who be as great learned men as ye are. Let your portion be priest-like, not prince-like." Aylmer, as Bishop, showed the weakness, common to not a few other good men, of fondness for money—a story about his dilapidations, a story about felling timber, a story about being forced to pay compensation to an unhappy clergyman improperly condemned, a story about leaving £16,000, a vast sum, equal now to about fifteen times as much. Martin Marprelate was now opening on the Bishops: the chief objects of his satire were Whitgift and Aylmer. He attacked Aylmer for playing bowls on the great lawn at Fulham on Sunday afternoon, and for unfitting words during the heat of the game; he attacked him for his lack of preaching, and called him "Dumb John of London." Aylmer longed for the peace and quiet of the See of Ely, but died in 1594.

His successor was far from a great man. *Richard Fletcher* was Fellow of Corpus, Cambridge, Prebendary of Islington and Dean of Peterborough (1583). He was present with the unhappy Mary Queen of Scots when she

[1] Neal, i. p. 140; Milman, p. 299.

suffered death at Fotheringhay, in February 1586, where he urged her to renounce her religion, contrary to all Christianity and humanity, as it was by many there present so taken, to her great disturbance; and when the Earl of Kent said, "So perish all the Queen's enemies!" he alone replied, "Amen!" He fell under the Queen's displeasure by marrying a second wife, a very handsome widow named Lady Baker (Milman calls her the widow of Sir George Giffard). Fletcher was not only repelled from Court, but wholly suspended from his functions. The suspension was in the end removed, but not the exile from Court. He is said to have died suddenly by excessive smoking of tobacco. He was the father of Fletcher, the dramatist associated with Beaumont.

Fletcher was succeeded by *Richard Bancroft*, of a good Lancashire family; his mother was niece to Dr. Hugh Curwyn, Archbishop of Dublin. Bancroft's steps were rapid—Prebendary of Dublin, chaplain to Bishop Cox of Ely, Rector of Taverham (Norfolk), Rector of St. Andrew's, Holborn, Treasurer of St. Paul's, Prebendary of Brondesbury in St. Paul's, Prebendary of Westminster; and he was at length consecrated Bishop of London, May 8, 1597. In 1604 he became Archbishop of Canterbury, and in 1608 Chancellor of the University of Oxford. He is famous for his sermon at Paul's Cross, A.D. 1588, on the divine right of episcopacy, a view not usually held by the earlier Reformers.

During almost the whole reign of Elizabeth, and for a few years that of James, a man of a far higher stamp was Dean of St. Paul's, *Alexander Nowell*,[1] author of the Catechism. He was Fellow of Brasenose, Oxford, and afterwards principal, and grew very famous for religious learning. When (1595) he became head of his college he was created Doctor of Divinity, with precedence over all the Doctors in the University. For thirty years he preached

[1] Cp. p. 163.

the first and last sermons in Lent before the Queen, dealing very faithfully with her, but without exciting her resentment. "He was a learned man, charitable to the poor, especially if they had anything of a scholar in them, and a great comforter of afflicted consciences."[1]

Nowell had two brushes with the imperious Queen. "Taken with scriptural engravings from Germany, no doubt some of those rude but spirited illustrations of sacred history in which the German reformers took delight, he placed in the Queen's closet at St. Paul's a splendid prayer-book, richly bound and ornamented with these designs, richly illuminated." Somehow the Queen took offence against these unfortunate pictures, though she had hardly given up her crucifix and lighted candles. "'Who placed this book on my cushion?' Her voice bespoke her anger. The trembling Dean acknowledged that he had. 'Wherefore did you so?' 'To present your Majesty with a New Year's gift.' 'You could never present me with a worse.' 'Why so, Madam?' 'In the cuts resembling angels and saints; nay, grosser absurdities. Pictures resembling the Holy Trinity!' The Dean faltered out that he meant no harm. 'You must needs be ignorant, then! Have you forgotten our proclamation against images, pictures and Romish relics in the churches? Was it read in your deanery?' The Dean acknowledged that it was, and again pleaded ignorance. 'If so, Mr. Dean, God grant you His spirit and more wisdom for the future!' The Queen then demanded where the pictures came from. When she heard that they came from Germany, 'It was well it was a stranger. Had it been one of my subjects, we should have questioned the matter.'"[2]

Nowell was for a short time out of favour; but we find him before long preaching at Court, and seemingly high in the Queen's esteem. Again he was preaching before her on Ash Wednesday, 1572. A book had been dedicated to

[1] Newcourt, p. 50. [2] Strype, vol. i. p. 409.

her as *Principe e Virgine*. This irreverent "impudency," as it seemed to Nowell, roused his indignation. He inveighed against certain superstitions and Popish customs in the book. In the warmth of his harangue he touched on the sign of the Cross. The Queen's voice was heard from the Royal closet commanding him to return from his ungodly digression and revert to his text. The Dean was so utterly dismayed that the Archbishop, to console him, carried him home to dinner.[1]

Nowell was summoned to attend the execution of the Duke of Norfolk on June 2, 1572, and, with the Dean of Windsor, to visit the famous Jesuit missionary, Campian, in his dungeon in the Tower, and hold argument with him. Other conferences with the prisoner were held, in which Nowell does not seem to have taken part. Before these latter Campian was tortured to make him betray the hiding-place of his more dangerous colleague, Allen, who escaped to the Continent.

Nowell had the happiness of celebrating the deliverance of Queen and country from the Armada. The victory took place on July 29; on September 8, the preacher at Paul's Cross moved the people to give thanks to God for the overthrow of the Spaniards. Eleven ensigns taken from ships were set on the lower battlements of the Church, except one streamer representing the Virgin with the Saviour in her arms, which waved over the preacher. On Sunday, November 24, the Queen came in state to the Cathedral, with the Privy Council, the nobility, the French Ambassadors, the judges and heralds. The Queen was carried, amid a blare of trumpets, in a chariot "like a throne" drawn by four stately white horses. The sermon was preached by the Bishop of Salisbury, the Queen's Almoner. The procession returned through the Church to Bishop Aylmer's palace, who had the honour of entertaining Her Majesty at dinner. The captured banners,

---

[1] Churton's *Life of Nowell*, p. 111; Milman's *Annals*, p. 305.

which for some days floated over the Cathedral, were finally suspended in the interior.[1]

Elizabeth died on March 24, 1603, in the seventieth year of her age and forty-fifth of her reign, and was buried in the chapel of her grandfather, Henry VII., at Westminster Abbey.

[1] Stowe's *Annals*, p. 751 ; Milman's *Annals*, p. 310.

CHAPTER XVII

JAMES I.

WHEN James I. acceded to the throne of Elizabeth he found Bancroft Bishop of London, Nowell Dean of St. Paul's, and the admirable Whitgift Archbishop of Canterbury. "Bancroft, at the Hampton Court conference, bore the brunt of the collision between 'the right divine of episcopacy' and 'the right divine of the Book of Discipline.' Both parties were firmly and profoundly convinced that God and the Gospel were clearly, decisively on their side. Neither had the slightest inclination to respect the right of conscience in the other. Sacerdotal tyranny, whether of Bishop or Presbyter, was alike irreclaimably despotic (so honest Neal, the historian of the Puritans, acknowledges), alike determined to compel their adversaries to come into their peculiar notions. It was Bancroft who, in an agony of wrath against the obstinate objections urged by the Puritans, fell on his knees before the King, citing an ancient canon that schismatics are not to be heard before their Bishops. King James had never seen a Churchman at his feet before. How different had been the attitude of the clergy in his native land! their feet had been constantly on his neck. He gently rebuked the passion of Bancroft; but from that hour the Solomon of his day embraced in his heart the text, 'No Bishop, no King!' . . . He treated the Puritan divines with more determined repugnancy; his language was not coarse only, it was absolutely indecent; but Bancroft fell on his knees again, not now in wrath, but in an ecstasy of admiration, and declared that his heart melted with joy that 'Almighty God of His singular mercy had granted us such a king as since Christ's time had not been.' A few weeks after Whitgift, a great and good Primate, died, and Bancroft moved upward to Canterbury."[1]

In 1605, there was a dreary scene in front of the west end of St. Paul's Cathedral. Four of the conspirators of Gunpowder Treason were hanged, drawn and quartered: Sir Everard Digby, Winter, Grant and Bates. Guy Fawkes and others met their fate at Westminster. Garnet the Jesuit suffered the same penalty in St. Paul's Churchyard the following year.[2]

The repairs of the Cathedral after the fire of 1561 had never been completed in Elizabeth's time, and nothing had been done to the great central tower. Bancroft had been succeeded by *Richard Vaughan*, chaplain and cousin to Bishop Aylmer, Archdeacon of Middlesex, Bishop of Bangor and Bishop of Chester. He died when he had held the See of London little more than two years, and left a reputation for learning and readiness in preaching. Vaughan had been followed by *Thomas Ravis*, of Westminster School and Christ Church, Oxford. His eminent learning, gravity and prudence induced King James to appoint him Bishop of Gloucester in 1604, a diocese "overstocked with such ignorants as could scarce brook the name of a Bishop"; he obtained their love, and in 1607 was translated to London, where he died after two years. It was to him that King James addressed a letter on the state of the restoration of St. Paul's. The Crown, being poor, declined altogether the burden of repairs. "Among the possessions that belong to that See there be lands especially appropriated to the fabric of the Church, which, if they had been continually employed to this use, these decays would not have gone so far."

[1] Milman's *Annals*, p. 315; *Nugæ Antiquæ*, i. 181.
[2] Fuller, v. pp. 351, 360.

Nothing was done, however, till the eighteenth year of King James's reign; "but then, having been frequently solicited by one Master Henry Farley (for the space of eight years before, who, though a private man, was so extremely zealous to promote the work, that he ceased not by sundry to importune that King therein) his princely heart was moved with such compassion to this decayed fabric, that for prevention of its near approaching ruin (by the corroding quality of the coal smoke, especially in moist weather, whereunto it had been so long subject), considering with himself how vast the charge would be; as also that without very great and public help it could not be borne; to beget the more venerable regard towards so worthy an enterprise, and more effectually to put it forwards, he came in great state thither, upon Sunday the 26th of March, anno 1620, with all the lords and great officers of his Court, Sir William Cokain being then Lord Mayor; who, with the City in their liveries, then also gave their attendance—(it must have been a procession of magnificent and national impressiveness: the details are given in the appendix to Dugdale's *History of St. Paul's*)—where, alighting at the west door, having kneeled near the brazen pillar, and prayed for good success to this his pious intention, he was received under a canopy, supported by the Dean and Residentiaries, the rest of the prebendaries and dignitaries, with the whole company of singing men, going before.

"And having thus proceeded to the choir, which was adorned with his own hangings for that occasion, and there heard an anthem, he went to the Cross, where the then Reverend Bishop of London (Doctor John King) preached a learned sermon upon a text given him by His Majesty as pertinent to the business in hand, namely Ps. cii. verses 13 and 14 ('Thou shalt arise and have mercy upon Sion: for it is time that thou have mercy upon her, yea, the time is come. And why? thy servants think upon her stones:

and it pitieth them to see her in the dust'); and when the sermon was ended, repaired to the Bishop's Palace, with his said nobles, and the whole train of his servants attending him, where they were magnificently entertained with several set banquets"[1] (that is, there would be too many to sit down in one hall or at one table).

A Royal Commission was appointed, and it is interesting to note whom it included : the Lord Mayor (Sir Francis Jones), Archbishop Abbot, the Lord Chancellor (Francis Bacon, Lord Verulam), the Earl of Worcester (Lord Privy Seal), the Duke of Lennox (Lord Steward), George Villiers, Marquess of Buckingham (Lord High Admiral), the Marquess of Hamilton, the Earls of Nottingham, Pembroke, Arundel, Southampton, Exeter, Dunfermline, Mar, Kelly and Melrose; Viscounts Wallingford and Doncaster; the Bishops of London, Durham, Winchester and Lincoln; Lords Zouche (Cinque Ports), Wolton, Stanhope, Carew and Digby; and above forty other influential persons, including Inigo Jones, Surveyor of His Majesty's Works.

Before this Commission it was admitted that the Bishop of London had peculiar care of the whole body of the Church, the Dean and Chapter of the choir; "but that which each of them enjoyed as to this purpose was so little as that they yearly expended double as much upon the roof and other parts decayed, to preserve them from present ruin. The Church from its foundation had been supported partly out of the large oblations of those that visited the shrines and oratories therein, partly from public contributions." It is said that some of the Commissioners aimed "at the wreck" of the Bishop and the clergy of the Church. Lord Southampton and other zealous Churchmen interposed for their protection. Grindal had, in his day, bestowed on the repairs of the Cathedral £1184. Aylmer had claimed of his predecessor, Sandys, £309 for dilapidations on the Church. On Bancroft's appointment the estimate for repairs

[1] Dugdale's *History of St. Paul's*, p. 101.

was over £4000. The Commissioners agreed that the chargeable estates were altogether inadequate; St. Paul's was national, and must be repaired by public contributions.

"Whereupon the King himself, to give example unto others, began the subscription, most of the nobility, and many more, following very cheerfully therein; the then Bishop (King) giving £100 (all these figures must be multiplied to give present value), and subscribing for so much annually, as long as he should continue in that See; which was but a short time, for the next ensuing year he died (1621).

"Unto whom succeeded Dr. George Mountaine; which Bishop, being no less zealous to promote the work, disbursed a considerable sum of money to provide stone from Portland for that purpose. But the collection of moneys went so slowly forwards as that, though a good proportion of stone was brought in by the said Bishop, the prosecution of the work became wholly neglected; so that part of the said stone lying useless, was after borrowed by the Duke of Buckingham for the building of the water-gate at York House; and there employed for that use, as I have heard." (Buckingham's water-gate of pilfered stone is still standing, near the Adelphi.)

The estimate was—

		£	s.	d.
For the choir	. . . .	1,619	4	1
,, ,, tower	. . . .	12,015	15	0
,, ,, nave and aisles	. .	6,891	19	4
,, ,, transepts	. . .	1,647	4	5
,, ,, chapter house	. .	361	19	5
		£22,536	2	3 [1]

Bishop Ravis had been commemorated by a beautiful poetical epitaph by Corbet, Dean of Christ Church, afterwards Bishop of Norwich, who subsequently contributed

[1] Malcolm, *Londinium Redivivum*, iii. pp. 74, 75.

£400 (in Laud's time) to the restoration of St. Paul's. He was succeeded by *George Abbot*, 1609, promoted to Canterbury the year after. The next Bishop was *John King*, nephew of Robert King, the first Bishop of Oxford. Like Bishop Ravis, he was educated at Westminster and Christ Church, Oxford, of which he became Dean in 1605. He was chaplain to Queen Elizabeth and King James, and to Lord Keeper Egerton. For several years together he was Vice-Chancellor of Oxford. King James, punning, called him King of Preachers. He was had in great reverence by all people, as a solid and profound divine, of great gravity and piety, and of a most excellent volubility of speech.[1] " He omitted no Sunday when he did not mount the pulpit in London or near it." [2] Sad to say for him, but fortunately for the Church of England, he was the last of our Bishops " who (with another, the Bishop of Lichfield) put in force the statute for the burning of heretics. It was in the Consistory Court of the Bishop of London that Bartholomew Leggatt, accused of Arianism, was made over to the civil power and burned at the stake. For the last time the atmosphere of London was tainted with the reek of a holocaust on such a charge. Leggatt was offered a pardon on recantation, refused it, and died a martyr for his faith. A Spaniard, accused on the same suspicion, escaped, the popular feeling being so strong against his execution." [3]

King was succeeded by *George Montaigne*,[4] notable for the rapidity of his promotions : Master of the Savoy, Dean of Westminster, Bishop of Lincoln (1617), Bishop of London (1621), Bishop of Durham (1627), Archbishop of York (1628); soon after this last step he died.

The Deans of this period were notable men, worthy successors of the learned Ralph de Diceto, the admirable Colet and the statesmanlike Pace. Nowell has already

[1] Newcourt's *Repertorium*. [2] Fuller, v. p. 499.
[3] Milman's *Annals*, p. 321; Fuller's *History*.
[4] The name is spelt in different ways.

been mentioned. He died in 1602, and was succeeded by *John Overall*, Fellow of Trinity, Cambridge, Master of St. Katherine's in that University, Dean of St. Paul's, Fellow of Chelsea College, Prolocutor of the Lower House of Convocation of Canterbury, where he drew up in three books of manuscript the Acts and Canons then passed, afterwards published by Archbishop Sancroft as Bishop Overall's Convocation-book. He became successively Bishop of Coventry and Lichfield, and Bishop of Norwich, where he died and was buried in 1619. The celebrated Bishop Cosin of Durham, who had been his secretary, erected his monument.

His successor, *Valentine Carey*, became Bishop of Exeter, and was followed by the famous poet *John Donne*. Of him Newcourt writes : " His life is incomparably well written by Mr. Isaac Walton, published 1670, to which I refer the reader, and therefore out of it shall only give this short account of it. 'He was born in London, of good and virtuous parents (Roman Catholics), had his first breeding in his father's house under a private tutor until he was nine years old ; when ten, he was sent to the University of Oxford, where he remained in Hart Hall till the fourteenth year of his age ; and then was translated to Cambridge, where he stayed till his seventeenth year, about which time he was removed to Lincoln's Inn. About the nineteenth year of his age he resolved to travel, and therefore took the advantage of waiting on the Earl of Essex, going first to Calais, and afterwards the Island Voyages; but returned not back to England till he had stayed some years first in Italy, then in Spain. Not long after his return Lord Chancellor Ellesmere took him to be his chief secretary, which employment he continued for five years ; from whose service he was discharged for marrying Lady Ellesmere's niece, daughter to Sir George Moor, Chancellor of the Garter and Lieutenant of the Tower, without the allowance of her friends ; but after some time his father-in-law was reconciled, and would have gotten him readmitted into the Lord Chancellor's service, but could not prevail. Dr. Moreton (afterwards Bishop of Durham) both importuned and encouraged him to enter into holy orders, but he thankfully declined the offer. In the meanwhile he and his family lived with his noble and courteous kinsman Sir Francis Wolly (his monument, like Donne's, is one of the few relics of the fire of 1666), at Pyrford, in Surrey, till the death of the said Sir Francis; after that at Wickham for about two years, then at London, where Sir Robert Drury assigned him a house rent free, next his own in Drury Lane. His Majesty had formerly both known and put a value on his company, and had given him some hopes of State employment; and about this time, there growing many disputes about the oaths of supremacy and allegiance, in which the King had engaged himself by his public writings, he commanded Donne to draw the arguments into a method, and then write his answers to them; he accordingly, in six weeks' time, performed it, and brought them to His Majesty under his own handwriting, as they are now printed, *Pseudo-Martyr*. When the King had read and considered that book, he persuaded Mr. Donne to enter into the ministry, to which at that time he appeared unwilling; and though he did not then deny, yet he deferred it for almost three years; but at last yielded, and was in 1614, in the forty-second year of his age, ordained both deacon and priest by Dr. John King, Bishop of London; presently after which the King made him his Chaplain-in-Ordinary; and that summer, attending His Majesty in his progress, who was entertained at Cambridge by the University; Mr. Donne, at His Majesty's recommendation, was there made Doctor of Divinity the same month that he entered into orders. Within the first year after his ordination he had fourteen advowsons presented to him; but they were in the country, and he could not leave his beloved London. Immediately after his return from Cambridge, his wife died, leaving him a man of an unsettled estate, and father of seven children then living;

upon which he betook himself unto a retired and solitary life; but at length was prevailed upon by the importunity of his friends the Benchers of Lincoln's Inn, to accept of their lecture; where he continued for two years, faithfully and contentedly preaching to them, and they liberally requiting him. About which time he was appointed by His Majesty's special command to attend the Earl of Doncaster, his ambassador, into Germany, and about fourteen months afterwards returned to his friends in Lincoln's Inn. About a year after which the King gave him the Deanery of St. Paul's. This year he was chosen Prolocutor to the Convocation. He was made Dean in the fiftieth year of his age; which honour he enjoyed upwards of ten years. He died of consumption in 1631. His monument, executed after his orders in his own lifetime escaped the fire and is in the south aisle of the choir of Wren's Cathedral: he is represented in his shroud, standing on his own urn.'"

Donne in his own day was esteemed a greater preacher than poet. "Coleridge, perhaps almost alone of modern readers, delighted to wander in the wide and intricate mazes of Donne's theology. In one of his caprices of orthodoxy he sets up Donne above one of his great quaternion of English writers—Shakespeare, Hooker, Bacon, Jeremy Taylor. Yet, not carrying admiration quite so far, he who will give himself to the work will find in Donne a wonderful solidity of thought, a sustained majesty, an earnest force, almost unrivalled, with passages occasionally of splendid, almost impassioned, devotion. The learning of Donne is in general singularly apposite, and rarely obtrusive or ostentatious; the theology masculine, but not scholastically logical. Even what in those days was esteemed wit, which ran wild in his poetry, and suffocated the graceful and passionate thoughts, is in his prose under constraint and discipline."[1]

[1] Milman's *Annals*, p. 329.

CHAPTER XVIII

CHARLES I.

WHEN Charles I. succeeded his father in 1625, Montaigne was Bishop of London and Abbot Archbishop of Canterbury. On Montaigne's translation to Durham at the end of 1627, the famous *Laud* became Bishop of London in 1628. His character and career are so well known, and are so largely the property of the Church of England itself, that it is only needful here to sketch his rise, and to note his relation to St. Paul's. He was Fellow of St. John's 1593, Proctor of the University 1603, Chaplain to the Earl of Devonshire the same year, Vicar of Stamford 1607, received the advowson of North Kilworth 1608, D.D. and chaplain to the Bishop of Rochester the same year, exchanged North Kilworth for West Tilbury in 1609, Rector of Cuckstone 1610, left Cuckstone for Norton the same year, President of St. John's 1611, King's Chaplain the same year, Prebendary of Bugden 1614, Archdeacon of Huntington 1615, Dean of Gloucester 1616, left Norton for Ibstock 1617, Prebendary of Westminster 1620, Bishop of St. Davids 1621 (resigning the Presidency of St. John's), Vicar of Creek *in commendam* 1622, Bishop of Bath and Wells 1626, Dean of the Chapel Royal the same year, translated to London 1628, Chancellor of Oxford University 1630. This wonderful list throws a curious light on the ideals of clerical and episcopal duty in those days. He held the Bishopric of St. Davids for six years, and the Bishopric of Bath and Wells for two; but his diary shows that he only visited St. Davids twice, and contains no record of a visit to Bath and Wells. Confirmation also seems to have fallen into disuse. But the debt of St. Paul's to the new Bishop was great. " One of his first objects was the restoration of the Cathedral. With his influence it was not difficult to work for such an object on the congenial mind of the King. . . . Inigo Jones was now at the height of his renown. He had already designed the great palace of Whitehall, one part alone of which, alas! he was to achieve, the Banqueting House; yet that alone was enough for his fame. He was surveyor to the King; he had been included in the original commission of King James for the repair of the Cathedral. He was not only at the summit of, but stood almost alone in the noble profession of architecture. It is curious that he was born in the immediate neighbourhood of St. Paul's, just as Sir Charles Barry in Bridge Street close upon the site of his incomparable Houses of Parliament. The funds flowed rapidly in. When the design for Inigo's portico appeared, the King expressed his determination himself to defray the cost of that part of the work. Laud, as appears from his own statement, and he was not a man to boast of his munificence, contributed first and last £1200, in those days a great sum. But he loaded the fund with a very productive, but highly unpopular, source of revenue. The High Commission Court had assumed the power of inflicting heavy mulcts, not for recusancy only, but for all kinds of moral delinquencies, and these fines were imposed with no sparing hand. . . . The common saying spread abroad again that, in another sense, St. Paul's was restored out of the sins of the people.

"The works commenced without delay, and were carried on with a high hand. The mean shops and houses which crowded on the Church, especially on the west front, disappeared. The owners and tenants were compelled to accept what the authorities thought adequate, they of course inadequate, compensation. The demolition of these houses, and the ejection of their inhabitants, were among the charges against Laud at his trial. Laud excused himself by alleging that it was done by Commissioners under the authority of the Council. He threw, too, the chief blame on the Dean and Chapter, who (in old days) had allowed these houses to be built on consecrated ground. By an extraordinary, and it should seem most iniquitous, stretch of power, the Parliamentary Government made the innocent architect, Inigo Jones, pay largely towards the compensation. . . . The Church of St. Gregory, which stood in the way, abutting on the Cathedral at the south-west corner, was removed without scruple, and rebuilt on a more convenient site. The removal of this church was another of the charges brought against Laud at his trial.

"'In the restoration of St. Paul's,' writes Horace Walpole, 'Inigo made two capital faults. He first renewed the sides with very bad Gothic, and then added a Roman portico, magnificent and beautiful indeed, but which had no affinity with the ancient parts that remained, and made the Gothic appear ten times heavier.' The first of these capital faults was inevitable. Throughout Christendom the feeling, the skill, the tradition of Gothic architecture had entirely died out. . . . Inigo Jones was an Italian in all but birth : he had studied in Italy ; in Italy imbibed his principles, his tastes, his feelings. . . . His studies had been chiefly at Rome, where there was but one, and that a very inferior, Gothic church ; in Florence, in Vicenza. In Italy, the name Gothic, of the same import as barbarous, was now looked upon, spoken of, written of, with utter contempt."[1]

As Inigo Jones's work was to be laid level with the ground by the Great Fire of 1666, less than a quarter of a century after the end of the process of restoration, it is unnecessary to describe it in detail. Among the individual contributors none was so generous as a citizen of London, a Turkey merchant, Sir Paul Pindar, who had been the English Ambassador at Constantinople in the reign of

[1] Milman's *Annals*, p. 337.

James II. "At his own charge he repaired the end of the choir, adorning the front thereof, outwards, with fair pillars of black marble and statues of those Saxon kings which had been founders or benefactors to the Church, beautified the inner part thereof with figures of angels, and all wainscote work of the choir with excellent carving," and "afterwards bestowed £4000 in repairing of the south cross (probably transept)."[1] The total sum thus contributed by this princely merchant is said to have amounted to about £10,000.

The accounts given by Dugdale and Stow of the amounts received and paid on this great work of renovation are not quite complete, but give a general idea of the scale (when multiplied to represent present money value). The Chamberlain of the City of London was treasurer of the fund. Up to October 29, when the accounts were audited, he had received £89,489. Of this they paid £9628 for houses demolished, £1452 to the Clerk of the Works for a similar purpose, and £68,000 for the repair of the body of the Church, the choir and west end. This left the Chamberlain £10,400 in hand. When the accounts were audited, the Clerk of the Works had in hand £6730, which, added to the surplus in the hand of the Chamberlain, left £17,100 for further repairs.

Money flowed in copiously till the end of 1640, but in 1641, when the nation's troubles began, contributions suddenly dropped from £10,000, received in 1640, to less than £2000; in 1642, £2000 was received, but in 1643, £15 was the whole amount received. "In October 1642," says Stow, "the flames of our civil dissensions broke violently out; so that there was not only an unhappy period put to this good and praiseworthy work, but by the votes of Parliament, made September 10, anno 1642, the very foundation of this famous Cathedral was utterly shaken in pieces." "The famous Cross in the churchyard, which had been for many ages the most solemn place in this nation

[1] Dugdale, p. 143; Stow, i. 646.

for the greatest divines and most eminent scholars to preach at, was pulled down to the ground," "but its site was long denoted by a tall elm-tree."[1] "In the month of March ensuing, the houses and revenues belonging to the Dean and Chapter of the Cathedral were seized on by order likewise of the said Parliament, together with all money, goods or materials, bought or given, for repairing or finishing of this Church, were seized on and disposed of."[2]

"Laud filled the See of London for five years—from July 15, 1628, to September 19, 1633—he then passed upwards to his fatal eminence, the Primacy. One act of his as Bishop of London must be commemorated with due honour and acknowledgment of his quick recognition of the highest genius and purest piety. Of all divines in the Church of England, none perhaps has excited so much deep Christian emotion, or spoken so penetratingly and forcibly to the religious heart of England, as Jeremy Taylor. He appeals to every power and faculty of the soul with almost equal force: to the imagination in his *Life of Christ*, and in some of his Sermons; to the religious emotions, which he almost works up to asceticism, in his *Holy Living and Dying*, and in others of his Sermons; to the reason in the severe logic which underlies his most imaginative prose, and in the *Ductor Dubitantium*, which with all the depth and subtlety of a schoolman almost enlivens and quickens arid casuistry; to the loftiest Christian charity, in its Pauline sense, in his *Liberty of Prophesying*. Jeremy Taylor began his career as Divinity Lecturer at St. Paul's. Laud either heard him, or heard of him from those whose judgment he could trust. He took him at once under his patronage, and by Laud's influence, Taylor obtained his first preferment, a Fellowship at All Souls, Oxford."[3]

Laud's diary records the remonstrances and threats which his policy evoked from many quarters, both in

[1] Timb's *Curiosities of London*, 8vo, p. 105.   Stow, i. 647.
[3] Milman's *Annals*, p. 344; Wood's *Athenæ Oxonienses*, iii. 782.

London and the Primacy. On March 29, 1629, soon after his appointment to London, "two papers were found in the Deanery of St. Paul's, his yard, before his house, 'Laud, look to thyself. Be assured thy life is sought, as thou art the fountain of all wickedness. Repent thee thy monstrous sins before thou art taken out of the world.... Assure thyself that neither God nor the world can endure such a vile counsellor to live, or such a whisperer.'" Laud's note is: "Lord, I am a grievous sinner; but I beseech Thee deliver my soul from them that hate me without a cause." On July 9, 1637, a short label was pasted on the Cross in Cheapside, that the Arch-wolf of Canterbury had his hand in persecuting the saints and shedding the blood of the martyrs. On August 20, and again on May 9, 1640, when the High Commission was sitting at St. Paul's because of the troubles of the times, very near 2000 Brownists (Congregationalists) made a tumult at the end of the court, tore down all the benches in the consistory, and cried out, "We will have no Bishop, and no High Commission."[1]

When Laud was translated to Canterbury he secured as his successor in London *William Juxon*, a moderate High Churchman, of a gentle and Christian character, and a zealous loyalist, round whose name his faithful and sympathetic attendance on Charles I. on the scaffold, has lit a special halo. Though not a man of learning, he was blameless, unworldly and unambitious; prudent and conciliatory beyond most Churchmen of his time. Laud was anxious to revive the time when the greatest offices of state were held by ecclesiastics, and he got the new Bishop of London made Lord High Treasurer. One of Laud's chief defects was that he could not see the signs of the times; over this act, at which it is clear that Clarendon stood aghast, he exulted. On March 6, 1636, he writes in his diary: "William Juxon, Lord Bishop of London, made Lord High Treasurer of England. No Churchman

[1] Laud's *Diary*: Dates.

had it since Henry VII.'s time. I pray God to bless him, and carry it so that the Church may have honour, and the King and the State service and contentment by it. And now if the Church will not hold themselves up, I can do no more." Five years later he was done to death by the vindictive Commons, now completely under Puritan and Scottish influence. As the trial lasted long, a Bill of Attainder was brought into the Commons and passed; only six peers could be got to agree with them. "From Canterbury he descended to Tower Hill," says Milman, "to be the victim of the most barbarous crime of those dark days; a crime because it was an act of wanton, unnecessary revenge. As long as Strafford was alive, Strafford might be dangerous. Laud in the Tower was as harmless (to the cause of the Parliament) as Laud in his grave. He died (he was above seventy years old) with calm resignation. His body was decently interred in the neighbouring Church of All Hallows, Barking (next the Tower), and the burial service of the Church of England was read over his grave."

Juxon, on the first opportunity, when it was supposed that the High Treasurership might win over the Earl of Bedford, retired willingly and gladly from the perilous office. Retiring to Fulham, he was allowed to live in peace and respect without disturbance till 1647. On January 30, 1649, he was permitted to take his honourable part in the lamentable scene on the scaffold at Whitehall.

Until a few years ago the Chapter of St. Paul's had in their possession a pathetic document in the handwriting of Charles I., registering a vow that he would give a large benefaction to the Cathedral, if he should be victorious over his enemies. It was thought, however, that a paper of such value should be in the Record Office, and it was offered to that department and accepted. The Chapter retained a photographic copy, which is in the glass case in the Cathedral library.

o

CHAPTER XIX

ST. PAUL'S UNDER THE COMMONWEALTH

By the Puritans " St. Paul's was considered a vast useless pile, the lair of old superstition and idolatry. . . . The Cathedral was not destroyed, for it would have been a work of cost and labour to destroy it (and probably the citizens would have defended it). . . . One of the first acts, however, of the triumphant Parliament was to seize and appropriate to other uses the sum remaining out of the subscription for the repairs of the Church in the hands of the Chamberlain of the City. This sum amounted to above £17,000. The scaffolding erected round the central tower was assigned to Colonel Jephson's regiment for £1746, due as arrears of pay. On removing the scaffolding, part of the south transept, with its roof, came down."[1]

Disendowment was in the air. Even as early as the summer of 1641, the year of Strafford's execution, there was a debate in Parliament on the abolition of Cathedral Chapters, and for the appropriation of their revenues to more utilitarian purposes. The Universities petitioned in their favour; they were defended before the Commission by Dr. Hacket, Archdeacon of Bedford and Prebendary of St. Paul's. The Bill passed the Commons, but the Bishops had not yet been expelled from the House of Lords, and it dropped. In 1642 appeared the Ordinance for the removal of crucifixes and other " monuments of superstition " from churches. St. Paul's is named with other cathedrals. Ordered May 31, "That the Committee for pulling down

[1] Milman's *Annals*, p. 347.

and abolishing all monuments of superstition and idolatry do take into their custody the copes in the Cathedrals of Westminster, Paul's and Lambeth; and give order that they be burnt (the gold separated from the gilt by fire), and converted to the relief of the poor in Ireland." December 15, ordered, "That the Committee for taking away superstitious ornaments do open Paul's Church, and that they shall have power to remove out of the said Church all such matters as are justly offensive to godly men."[1]

In January 1644–5, came an order "that my Lord Powys's house in Aldersgate Street, and the Deanery of St. Paul's should be prepared for the reception of certain prisoners from Chichester or elsewhere." In April came more violent signs of spoliation. It was ordered that the chest of silver vessels in St. Paul's shall be sold for the best advantage, towards the providing of necessaries for the train of Artillery, by the Committee at Grocers' Hall. The Deanery had probably been vacated by Dr. Winnif, who had received the empty nomination to the Bishopric of Lincoln; Dr. Steward, appointed to the Deanery, had not yet appeared. In May of the same year came the fatal mandate to the Lord Mayor and the Court of Aldermen to seize and sequestrate all the revenues of the Dean and Chapter of St. Paul's, with the sole reservation of £400, to be paid quarterly to Dr. Cornelius Burgess, as Lecturer in the Cathedral. The Dean, Steward, mentioned in a later Act as in possession of the Deanery, had not yet been installed. The Cathedral clergy, unless they would sign the Covenant, were scattered about to their respective places of retirement. A second Act followed on April 23, constituting Cornelius Burgess Lecturer of St. Paul's, and putting him in possession of the Deanery. A part of the eastern end of the Church was walled in for his services and congregations.

Two pictures are given us of this Puritan tenant of St.

[1] Milman's *Annals*, p. 347.

Paul's, one by the Puritan Neal, the other by the Loyalist Wood. In Neal, he is among the most moderate of the Parliamentary divines; as Vicar of Watford, he declined to sign the Covenant until threatened with ejection. As the antagonist of Hacket in the debate about the abolition of Chapters, he complained of their unprofitableness, of the "debauchery of singing men, and of their vicious conversation," and spoke against music in churches as useless and hurtful; but he summed up with declaring that he held it necessary to apply these foundations to better purposes; it was by no means lawful to alienate them from pious uses, or to convert them to any private personal profit. According to Wood, he began some years before by preaching a Latin sermon at St. Alphege, London Wall, before the London clergy, in which he spoke strongly of the connivance of the Bishops at the growth of Arminianism and Popery. He was summoned before the High Commission Court, and from that time became implacable against the Bishops. With his friend Captain Venn, he exercised great authority over the populace of London. It was usual for Burgess and Venn to lead the tumult of the City apprentices and the rest to the Parliament doors to see that the "godly party" in the House (so their faction was called) were not outvoted; and then, turning back to the rabble, Burgess would say, "These are my bandogs, and I can set them on, and I can take them off." This was done with special violence at Strafford's trial. Hence his popularity in London, and his nomination at St. Paul's. The lecture in the evening at the Cathedral was appointed at the desire of some of the Aldermen of London, who were unwilling that St. Paul's should be altogether silenced. The Aldermen were probably responding, according to Wood, to a demand from the Militiamen of London among whom the Doctor was wont to ride with a case of pistols, being called Colonel, and sharing the gains. These were queer times. It was to the credit of Burgess that he headed the daring petition of the London clergy against the execution of the King. The petition ended with the memorable prayer, "That God would restrain the violence of men, that they may not dare to draw upon themselves and the kingdom the blood of their Sovereign."[1]

This Parliamentarian minister of St. Paul's, Burgess, was a man of some power. "His sermons rank high, for vigour and something at times bordering on the eloquence of his age, among the preachers of the day. He is somewhat proud of his small Hebrew, which he inflicts at length on the patient House of Commons. There is one sermon before the House on November 5, 1641, rising to terrific invective against the conspirators in the Gunpowder Plot, and on those in high places in the Roman Catholic world, who vindicated, excused, admired, made martyrs of those wretched assassins. 'What measures will the wisdom of Parliament adopt against perilous Popery? But if anything may be added,—for the taking away of their children, and training them up (at the parents' cost if they have wherewithal) in the nurture and fear of the Lord, that so there may not still be new generations of Papists; I presume it would be a noble and pious service, for which the souls of many thousands would for ever bless you, by whose mercy they should be delivered out of the power of that Ægyptian darkness, and translated into the Kingdom of Jesus Christ.'[2] Fanaticism speaks the same language in Papal Rome and in Inquisitorial Madrid, and in Puritan London. Everywhere it tramples remorselessly on the holiest rights and duties of human nature, and outrages the deepest and most sacred feelings of the heart of man."[3]

"Burgess came to a wretched end. He had written a pamphlet to prove that it was no sin to purchase Bishops' lands. In the conviction of its sinlessness he left St. Paul's

[1] Neal, iii. 536; Milman's *Annals*, p. 349.
[2] Wood, *Cornelius Burgess*.
[3] *Parl. Sermons*, p. 35; Milman's *Annals*, p. 350.

(he did not purchase any of our estates), and obtained the benefice of St. Andrew's, in Wells, Somerset. He invested all his gains in the lands of that See, for which investment he was said to have been offered £12,000. At the Restoration he was forced to disgorge; lived in miserable poverty, and lingered on, writing dismal letters imploring charity to keep him alive. He died and was buried at his old benefice in Watford."[1]

"The Act for the sale of Bishops' lands, November 16, 1646, disturbed Juxon in his peaceful retreat at Fulham, where he had lived unmolested, to the credit of his own virtue and prudence, and, as Warburton observes, showing the moderation of the Parliamentary leaders up to that time.[2] A committee was appointed to assess the allowances to be made to the deprived Bishops. Mr. Hallam cites an Order (May 1, 1647) that, whereas divers of the tenants of the late Bishop of London at or before the 1st November last, have refused to pay the rents or other sums due to him as Bishop of London at or before the 1st November last, the trustees of Bishops' lands are directed to receive the same and pay them over to Dr. Juxon. 'Though this was only justice, it shows that justice was done, at least in this instance, to a Bishop.'[3] Fulham passed into the possession of Richard Harvey, a decayed silk-mercer, whether as a reward of his services (and he had rendered great services in putting down an insurrection in London at the time of Walker's plot), or by purchase from spoils obtained in the war.[4]

"The Cathedral was left to chance, exposed at least to neglect, too often to wanton or inevitable mischief. There is a strange story that Cromwell had determined to sell the useless building to the Jews. . . . This may have originated in one of those grim pleasantries in which Oliver took

---

[1] Milman's *Annals*, p. 351.   [2] Notes to Clarendon.
[3] *Constit. Hist.* i. 597, note.
[4] Clarendon, p. 418; Walker's *Hist. of Independence*, vol. i. p. 176.

delight. . . . As it was, the only part secure was the east end, set apart for the congregation of Burgess. From Inigo Jones's noble portico the statues of the two kings (James I. and Charles I.) were tumbled ignominiously down, and dashed to pieces. The portico was let out for mean shops, to sempstresses and hucksters, with chambers above and staircases leading to them. The body of the Church, Dugdale, who saw it, declares, with sorrow and bitterness of heart, became a cavalry barrack and stable. The pavement was trampled by horses, the tombs left to the idle amusement of the rude soldiers, who, even if religious, were not much disposed to reverence the remains of a Popish edifice. Sir H. Ellis has quoted a curious notice from a printed paper in the British Museum, dated May 27, 1651: 'Forasmuch as the inhabitants of St. Paul's Churchyard are much disturbed by the soldiers and others, calling out to passengers and examining them, though they go peaceably and civilly along, and by playing at nine-pins at unseasonable hours: they are therefore to command all soldiers and others, that hereafter there shall be no examining and calling out to persons that go peaceably on their way, unless they do approach the guards; and likewise to forbear playing at nine-pins and other sports from the hours of nine o'clock in the evening till six in the morning, that so persons as are weak and indisposed to rest may not be disturbed.'"[1] Barrack-rooms are very much the same at all times: smoking, drinking, joking, the cleaning of accoutrements, the combined smell of steaming joints and vegetables, and of pipe-clay; strict discipline and a certain amount of order. The Parliamentary soldiers were sternly religious, according to their standards; but the sacredness of a cathedral did not enter into the circle of their religious ideas, any more than modern Christians would respect the old-world sanctity of a ruined pagan temple. St. Paul's was to them a thing of the past, an anachronism from

[1] Ellis's *Dugdale*, p. 115.

which all interest, life and importance had for ever departed.

"The famous adjunct to the Cathedral was not left to slow decay. It might have been supposed that Paul's Cross, from which so many sermons had been preached in the course of years, some, as has appeared, as fiercely condemnatory of Popish superstition as the most devout Puritan could have wished; that the famous pulpit, which we might have expected Presbyterian and Independent divines, the most powerful and popular, would have aspired to fill, and from thence hoped to sway to their own purposes, and to guide to assured salvation, the devout citizens of London, would have been preserved as a tower of strength to the good cause. But it was (called) a cross, and a cross was obstinately, irreclaimably Popish. (It had quite lost its original appearance and shape, and had in the course of time become a kind of octagonal garden-house or booth, with open sides, and steps leading up to it, and a bulging roof, all of decadent architecture.—W. M. S.) Down it went. . . . Its place knew it no more; tradition alone pointed to where it had stood; it never rose again. In later times it had lost something of its influence and authority. It is certain that James I. heard sermons there; it is not so certain whether Charles did. Only two sermons of Laud's are recorded there: not yet Bishop of London, he preached at the Cross in April 1624; as Bishop of London, April 1631."[1]

[1] Laud's *Diary;* Milman's *Annals*, p. 354.

CHAPTER XX

THE RESTORATION OF MONARCHY

AT the Restoration, Bishop Juxon was restored to his See, becoming later on Archbishop of Canterbury, in recognition of his faithful loyalty to Charles I. His successor in London was *Gilbert Sheldon*, who, in conjunction with Hammond, had done much to support the suffering clergy during the Protectorate; and as Juxon was more than seventy, and very infirm, the initiative and authority which belong to Canterbury fell in large measure to Sheldon. "To Sheldon we owe the St. Bartholomew Act, the Act of Uniformity, with those rigid clauses which we have but now shaken off, and all those stern measures which made Puritanism a permanent and perpetual schism. Then some of those who might have been the most powerful, as they were amongst the most pious, of the servants of the Church of England became her irreconcilable antagonists."[1] After three years of the See of London, Sheldon became Archbishop of Canterbury, August 31, 1663. He was the builder of the beautiful Sheldonian Theatre (the public hall of the University) at Oxford.

The next Bishop of London was a quiet man, of whom very little is heard: *Humphrey Henchman*, Bishop of Salisbury. When holding a benefice in the neighbourhood of Salisbury, the Boscobel Tracts state that he was engaged in the escape of Charles II. after the Battle of Worcester. His name rarely occurs either in the affairs of the State, or of the Church, or of the diocese, or in the annals of

[1] Milman's *Annals*, p. 355.

St. Paul's, except as a liberal contributor to Wren's new Cathedral. He filled the See for twelve years, and died in 1675, nine years after the Great Fire.

Of the Deans of St. Paul's during this period, the first, *William Nicholas*, brother of King Charles's faithful Secretary of State, lived only a month; installed July 10, he died August 14, 1662.

The life and adventures of the next Dean, *John Barwick*, told by himself in his autobiography, read like a vivid romance.[1] They are thus summarized by Milman: "If conscientious fidelity to his Sovereign, daring, dangerous, indefatigable labours in his cause, might deserve reward from that King, John Barwick's claims were surpassed by few, probably by none, of the clergy. Barwick must have been a man of rare ability and courage. For eight years he carried on the correspondence of the King's friends in London with Oxford and the Royalist camp.[2] At the breaking out of the Civil War, Barwick was a Fellow of St. John's, Cambridge. He was noted in the College chapel as turning to the east during the Creed; he was warned against leaning to 'the infamous errors of Arminianism and Papal superstition.' Barwick was a Churchman and loyalist to his heart's core. To him Strafford and Laud were the pillars of the State; Charles the best of princes, 'high beyond all praise.'

"Barwick's first act at the commencement of the troubles was to take possession of all the money in the hands of the college, and all the college plate; and with the other loyalists of the University to transmit the proceeds to the Royal camp. This was no easy affair. Cromwell, in command of the neighbourhood, was on the watch, and had stationed troops to intercept the convoy. Barwick, by his knowledge of the country, contrived to baffle the vigilant general, and to convey the treasure by circuitous by-ways in safety to the King. The expedition was conducted by

---

[1] Vita Johannis Barwick.
[2] Compare the character of Dr. Rochecliffe in Scott's *Woodstock*.

Barnabas Oley of Clare Hall, a well-known man. The hand of Cromwell soon after fell heavily on the University. The 'Complaint of Cambridge' was addressed to deaf ears. The loyalists fled from their colleges; some made their way to the Royal camp. Barwick took refuge in the crowded solitude of London. He became chaplain to Morton, Bishop of Durham, and from Morton's spacious house which held many inhabitants, issued the letters which passed from the London loyalists and the Royal camp. Something passed besides letters: supplies, even military supplies, were smuggled through the Parliamentary army to Oxford. Barwick mentions the important personages whose wavering loyalty he confirmed, as Sir Thomas Middleton and Thomas Pope. From the press of one Royston, in close connection with Barwick, came forth Royalist publications, which were actively disseminated throughout the country. They were embarked as merchandise on the Thames, and landed at convenient places. All this was done at fearful hazard.

" Barwick continued fearlessly, yet it must have been with consummate caution, his desperate intrigues. Among his most important services was his saving the life of Lord Langdale, who, after his utter defeat in the north, found his way to London. He was disguised by Barwick in the dress of a clergyman, and so stole over to the Continent.

" When King Charles I. was at Holdenby, not a letter passed between the King and the Queen, or any of the Royal family, or the more faithful loyalists, but through the agency of Barwick, or that of one of his friends, who pretended himself a follower of Lord Pembroke. After the seizure of the King at Holdenby by Cornet Joyce, and his removal to the army, the hopes of the false and misguided King rose high. He thought to play the opposing parties on the Parliamentary side one against the other—a fatal game! His faithful friends, full of hope, flocked to the King in the Isle of Wight, among them Barwick. But Barwick was too useful in London: he was sent back to watch the King's interests there. Of the King's insincerity, and of its perilous consequences, he must have been fully aware; but obedience was his duty; he closed his eyes to what must have appeared folly as well as treachery to a less zealous partisan.

"It was not till after eight years that the Parliamentary police got clear evidence of the subtle agency of Barwick. A warrant was issued by President Bradshaw for his arrest and committal to what was then, no doubt justly, called the loathsome prison of Westminster, the Gate House. But even then Barwick had the forethought and the time to burn all papers or ciphers which could compromise him. His brother, Edward Barwick, was arrested with him as implicated in his offences. They agreed to answer truly all questions which they could safely answer, on all others to refuse to answer at all.

"Just at that time Barwick was seized with a malady which threatened to be fatal—disease of the lungs, spitting of blood and other symptoms of rapid decline. It seemed that his wasted frame must soon give away. He was saved by what he thought the cruelty of his enemies. He was treated with great harshness in Westminster, and at the Tower, after his removal thither. But that which seemed at first to aggravate his malady, proved the best remedy. The meagre diet, entirely vegetable, with no drink but pure water (when he could command it); the total abstinence from animal food, and no doubt constrained quiet, wrought the cure. His attenuated frame recovered its health, and to a certain extent its vigour.

"Even after the execution of the King, Barwick did not despair of the Royal cause; but having obtained his release, remained quiet. After the death of Cromwell he resumed his activity. He was in busy correspondence with Charles II. and with Hyde, chiefly on money matters, which seemed to be conducted in a strange loose way, and by their slender amount show the utter destitution of the exiled King. Barwick was sent by the surviving Bishops to Breda, as best able to represent the state and condition of the Church, and to advise about its re-establishment.

"At the Restoration, Barwick was spoken of for the Bishopric of Carlisle; he was appointed Dean of Durham, and set to work on the repairs of that noble Cathedral, which had suffered much, not only from the neglect of the Puritans, but from the ravages of the Scots, whose hatred of England combining with their fanatic Presbyterianism, had done much wanton mischief. After a year at Durham, Barwick was summoned to the Deanery of St. Paul's; there to consult (as yet only to consult) on the restoration of the ruined Cathedral. He found all in confusion. Among other difficulties, the College of Minor Canons had dwindled to one, who had contrived to lease for his own benefit, and so to alienate, the estates of the College of Minor Canons. Barwick did not live to see the utter destruction of the Cathedral by the Great Fire; he died December 15, 1664. In his younger days, he had shown a great fondness for music; his knowledge of it enabled him to restore the choir of St. Paul's, so long silent, to some order and efficiency."[1] The estates of the Cathedral seem to have been recovered without difficulty.

Now came the great question about the Cathedral. "The damage which it had suffered from the Commonwealth was not easily repaired. The public services were recommenced, and some kind of order restored. At first, finding that the stalls in the choir, with the organ-loft, were entirely destroyed, the east end of the Church (the Lady Chapel), which had been fitted up as a preaching-place for Dr. Burgess, was enlarged by taking in one bay of the choir; and there for a time the services went on. But the whole fabric was seen to be insecure, if not dangerous. What was to be done was the question anxiously debated

[1] Milman's *Annals*, p. 356, etc.

for two or three years." A commission had been appointed by Charles II., on April 18, 1663, to consider what should be attempted. Large sums were soon collected, and the work was begun in August of the same year. What the Commissioners did consisted chiefly in taking down the houses which still encroached on the Cathedral, in ascertaining the extent of its decay, in examining the quality of the stone from the Isle of Portland—the crews of the ships carrying it being freed from imprisonment—and from Beer in Devonshire, in making other preparations, and in repairing the portico. Between August 1663 and August 1666, they spent £3600.

Under the King's instructions Dean Barwick had prepared a book for the receipt of subscriptions, "like unto those which were kept in the time of our dear grandfather and father." This book is still preserved in the Cathedral library, and is called "A Booke of Subscriptions towards the Repaire of the Cathedral Church of St. Paul's in London." Many of the signatures are of great interest. Charles II. gives £1000 a year, to be paid quarterly; James, Duke of York, £200 a year. Archbishop Sheldon contributes handsomely: he writes on July 2, 1664, "Because I have been Bishop of London, and thereby have received more than ordinary Profits, I doe subscribe to give freely towards the Repayre of the Cathedrall Church of that See the sum of £2000 to be payd if the work shall be undertaken and goe on uninterrupted." Lord Clarendon, whose writing is almost illegible, gives £50 on condition "if I live and hold the place I now have." Lord Southampton, who gives £50 a year, and Lord Anglesey £20, make the same condition. The Duke of Albemarle signs his name for £40 annually, the Duke of Ormonde £50, the Earl of Sandwich £30, the Archbishop of York £100, and the Bishops of London and Winchester each £100 as long as they receive the revenues of their Bishoprics.[1]

[1] Longman's *Three Cathedrals of St. Paul's*, p. 77.

THE RESTORATION OF MONARCHY

Here appears the immortal Wren. He is about this time appointed one of the Commissioners.[1] His report on the defects of the old building, and his ideas as to how the damage should be repaired, were laid before the Commissioners about May 1, 1666. At that time Evelyn, in the dedication of his *Account of Architecture* to Wren, says, "You will not, I am sure, forget the struggle we had with some for patching it up anyhow (so the steeple might stand), instead of new building which is altogether needed." [2]

"Some may aim at too great magnificence," says Wren, in his report on the old structure, "which the disposition of the age will not bear. Others may fall so low as to think of piecing up the old fabric, here with stone, there with brick, and cover all faults with a coat of plaister, leaving it still to posterity as a further object of charity. The Cathedral is a pile for ornament and for use. It demands a choir, consistory, chapter house, library, preaching auditory (which might be furnished at less expense, but which would want grandeur). It was a monument of power and mighty zeal in our ancestors in public works in those times, when the City had neither a fifth part of the wealth it now boasts of."

He then criticizes at length the Norman and Gothic work, and proceeds: "The middle part is most defective both in beauty and firmness, both within and without, for the tower leans manifestly by the settling of one of the ancient pillars that supported it. Four new arches were therefore of later years incorporated within the old ones, which both straightened and hindered the room, and the clear thorough view of the nave, in that part where it had been more graceful to have been rather wider than the rest, . . . without, the three buttresses (the fourth is wanting) are so irregular that the tower, from the top to the bottom, with

---
[1] Elmes' *Life*, p. 219.
[2] Evelyn's *Miscellaneous Works*, p. 351.

the next adjacent parts, is a heap of deformities, that no judicious architect will think it corrigible.

"I cannot propose a better remedy than by cutting off the inner corners of the cross, to reduce this middle part into a spacious dome or rotundo, with a cupola or hemispherical roof, and upon the cupola a lantern with a spiring top to rise proportionably."

CHAPTER XXI

THE GREAT FIRE OF 1666

THE schemes of Evelyn and his friends for the repair of St. Paul's were brought to a sudden close. The plans and estimates were ordered on Monday, August 27, 1666; on Sunday, September 2, the Great Fire broke out. At three o'clock in the morning, Pepys, who lived in Seething Lane, near the Tower, was awoke by the alarm. The mischief had begun at the King's bakehouse in Pudding Lane, near Fish Street, Eastcheap, Lower Thames Street and London Bridge. Pepys walked to the Tower, and from a high point saw houses burning at both ends of the bridge, and an infinite great fire at the north side. He got a boat, passed under the bridge, with the blazing houses above it, and hastened to Whitehall to be the first to carry the news to the King and the Duke of York. From Whitehall he drove in Captain Cook's coach, without difficulty, to St. Paul's, which seemed as yet perfectly secure. In Watling Street the people were already removing their goods. In Watling Street he met the Lord Mayor, who was quite exhausted, and seemed to have lost his head. He had ordered houses to be pulled down, nobody obeyed, so he went "quietly home and to bed." In the afternoon Pepys went down again to Paul's, walking through the City, "the streets full of nothing but people and horses and carts laden with goods, ready to run over one another, and removing goods from one burning house to another. Cannon Street, which received goods in the morning was now removing its goods to Lombard Street." Pepys had a boat waiting for him at Paul's Wharf; on the river he encountered the King's barge, and followed the royal party. "In the evening, when we could endure no more upon the water, we landed at Bankside (Southwark) at a small public-house, and there stood and saw the fire grow, and as it grew darker appeared more and more, and in corners, and upon steeples, and between churches and houses, as far as we could see up the City, in a most horrid bloody malicious flame, not like the flame of an ordinary fire. We stood still, it being darkish; we saw the fire as only one entire arch of fire from this to the other side of the Bridge, and on a bow up the hill for an area of above a mile long."

Evelyn describes the night of the 3rd: "(If I may call that night which was light as day for ten miles round about, after a dreadful manner), when conspiring with a fierce Eastern wind in a very dry season; I went on foot to (Bankside) and saw the whole south parts of the City burning from Cheapside to the Thames, and all along Cornhill (for it likewise kindled back against the wind as well as forward), Tower Street, Fenchurch Street, Gracechurch Street, and so along to Baynard's Castle, and was now taking hold of St. Paul's Church, to which the scaffolds (for repairs) contributed exceedingly. The conflagration was so universal, and the people so astonished, that from the beginning, I know not by what despondency or fate, they hardly stirred to quench it, so that there was nothing heard or seen but crying out and lamentation, running about like distracted creatures, without at all attempting to save even their goods; such a strange consternation there was upon them, so as it burned both in breadth and length, the churches, public halls, Exchange, hospitals, monuments and ornaments, leaping after a prodigious manner from house to house, and street to street, at great distance one from the other; for the heat, with a long set of fair and warm weather, had even ignited the air and prepared the materials to conceive the fire, which devoured after an incredible manner, houses, furniture and everything. Here we saw the Thames covered with goods floating, all the barges and boats laden with what some had time and courage to save, as, on the other, the carts, etc., carrying out to the fields, which for many miles were strewed with moveables of all sorts, and tents erected to shelter both people and what goods they could get away. Oh, the miserable and calamitous spectacle! such as haply the world has not seen the like since the foundation of it, nor be outdone till the universal conflagration of it. All the sky was of a fiery aspect, like the top of a burning oven, and the light seen above forty miles round about for many nights. God grant mine eyes may never behold the like, who now saw above 10,000 houses all in one flame; the noise and cracking and thunder of the impetuous flames, the shrieking of women and children, the hurry of people, the fall of towers, houses and churches, was like an hideous storm, and the air all about so hot and inflamed that at the last one was not able to approach it, so that they were forced to stand still and let the flames burn on, which they did for near two miles in length, and one in breadth. The clouds also of smoke were dismal, and reached upon computation near fifty-six miles in length.

"September 4. The burning still rages, and it was now gotten as far as the Inner Temple; all that street, the Old Bailey, Ludgate Hill, Warwick Lane, Newgate, Paul's Chain, Watling Street now flaming, and most of it reduced to ashes; the stones of Paul's flew like grenades, the melting lead running down the streets in a stream, and the very pavements glowing with fiery redness, so as no horse nor man was able to tread on them, and the demolition had stopped all the passages, so that no help could be applied. The Eastern wind still more impetuously driving the flames forward, nothing but the Almighty power of God was able to stop them, for vain was the help of man.

"September 5. It crossed towards Whitehall; but oh, the confusion there was then at that Court! It pleased His Majesty to command me amongst the rest to look after the quenching of Fetter Lane end, to preserve if possible that part of Holborn, whilst the rest of the gentlemen took their several posts, some at one part, some at another (for now they began to bestir themselves, and not till now, who hitherto had stood as men intoxicated, with their hands across), and began to consider that nothing was likely to put a stop but the blowing up of so many houses as might make a wider gap than any had yet been made by the ordinary method of pulling them down with engines; this some stout seamen proposed early enough to have saved nearly the whole City; but this some tenacious and avaricious men, aldermen, etc., would not permit, because their houses must have been of the first. It was therefore now commanded to be practised, and my concern being particularly for the Hospital of St. Bartholomew near Smithfield, where I had my wounded and sick men, made me the more diligent to promote it; nor was my care for the Savoy less. It now pleased God by the abating of the wind, and by the industry of the people, when almost all was lost, infusing a new spirit into them, that the fury of it began sensibly to abate about noon, so as it came no farther than the Temple westward, nor than the entrance of Smithfield north; but continued all this day and night so impetuous toward Cripplegate and the Tower as made us all despair; it also broke out again in the Temple, but the courage of the multitude persisting, and many houses being blown up, such gaps and desolations were soon made, as with the former three days' consumption, the back fire did not so vehemently urge upon the rest as formerly. There was yet no standing near the burning and glowing ruins by near a furlong's space.

"September 7. I went this morning on foot from Whitehall as far as London Bridge, through the late Fleet

Street, Ludgate Hill, by St. Paul's, Cheapside, Exchange, Bishopsgate, Aldersgate, and out to Moorfields, thence through Cornhill, etc.; with extraordinary difficulty, clambering over heaps of yet smoking rubbish, and frequently mistaking where I was; the ground under my feet so hot that it even burnt the soles of my shoes. In the meantime His Majesty got to the Tower by water, to demolish the houses about the graff, which being entirely built about it, had they taken fire and attacked the White Tower where the magazine of powder lay, would undoubtedly not only have beaten down and destroyed all the bridge, but sunk and torn the vessels in the river, and rendered the demolition beyond all expression for several miles about the country.

"At my return I was infinitely concerned to find that goodly Church St. Paul's now a sad ruin, and that beautiful portico (for structure comparable to any in Europe, as not long before repaired by the late King), now rent in pieces, flakes of vast stone split asunder, and nothing remaining entire but the inscription in the architrave, showing by whom it was built, which had not one letter of it defaced. It was astonishing to see what immense stones the heat had in a manner calcined, so that all the ornaments, columns, friezes, capitals and projectures of massy Portland stone flew off, even to the very roof, where a sheet of lead covering a great space (no less than six acres by measure) was totally melted; the ruins of the vaulted roof falling broke into St. Faith's, which being filled with the magazines (stores) of books belonging to the Stationers, and carried thither for safety, they were all consumed, burning for a week following. It is also observable that the lead over the altar at the east end was untouched, and among the divers monuments the body of one Bishop remained entire. Thus lay in ashes that most venerable Church, one of the most antient pieces of early piety in the Christian world, besides near 100 more."[1]

[1] Evelyn's *Diary* (Newnes), pp. 392-396.

There is a third account, written by Dr. Taswell from his recollections as a boy, for the fire occurred between his election and admission as a King's Scholar at Westminster. "On Sunday between ten and eleven, just as I was standing upon the steps leading up to the pulpit of Westminster Abbey, I discovered some people below me running to and fro in a seeming inquietude and consternation; immediately almost a report reached my ears that London was in a conflagration. Without any ceremony I took leave of the preacher, and having ascended the Parliament steps near the Thames, I soon perceived four boats, crowded with objects of distress. These had escaped from the fire scarce under any covering but that of a blanket."[1]

The next day, Monday, September 3, the Dean of Westminster (Dolben, Bishop of Rochester) set forth at the head of the Westminster boys (Taswell says that in the Civil Wars Dolben had frequently mounted guard as sentinel), to do what they could to help stay the fire. They got as far as St. Dunstan's-in-the-East (near Tower Hill), which they aided in saving by fetching water from the back sides of the building. "The people who lived contiguous to St. Paul's Church raised their expectations greatly concerning the absolute security of that place, upon account of the immense thickness of its walls and its situation, built on a large piece of ground on every side remote from houses." Upon that account they filled it with all sorts of goods; and besides, in the Church of St. Faith, under that of St. Paul, they deposited libraries of books, because it was entirely arched over; and with great caution and prudence even the least avenue, through which the smallest spark could penetrate, was stopped up. "But this precaution availed them little. As I stood upon the bridge (a small one over a creek at the foot of what is now Westminster Bridge), among many others (on Tuesday the 4th), I could not but observe the progress of the fire towards that

[1] Camden's *Miscellany*, vol. ii. p. 12.

venerable fabric. About eight o'clock it broke out on the top of St. Paul's Church, almost scorched up by the violent heat of the air and lightning too; and before nine blazed so conspicuous as to enable me to read very clearly a 16mo edition of Terence, which I carried in my pocket." On Thursday the 6th, soon after sunrise, Taswell tried to reach St. Paul's. "The ground was so hot as almost to scorch my shoes, and the air so intensely warm that unless I had stopped some time upon Fleet Bridge to rest myself, I must have fainted under the extreme languor of my spirits. After giving myself a little time to breathe, I made the best of my way to St. Paul's.

"And now let any person judge of the extreme emotion I was in, when I perceived the metal belonging to the bells melting; the ruinous condition of the walls, with heaps of stones of large circumference tumbling down with a great noise just upon my feet, ready to crush me to death. I prepared myself for retiring back again, having first loaded my pockets with several pieces of bell metal.

"I forgot to mention that near the east end of St. Paul's a human body presented itself to me, parched up as it were with the flames, white as to skin, meagre as to flesh, yellow as to colour. This was an old decrepit woman who fled here for safety, imagining the flames would not have reached her there; her clothes were burned, and every limb reduced to a coal. In my way home I saw several engines which were bringing up to its assistance, all on fire, and those engaged with them escaping with all eagerness from the flames, which spread instantaneous, almost like a wildfire, and at last, accoutred with my sword and helmet, I traversed the torrid zone back again." He relates that the papers from the books in St. Faith's were carried with the wind as far as Eton. The Oxonians noticed the rays of the sun tinged with an unusual kind of redness, while a black darkness seemed to cover the whole hemisphere.

Mere accident did not seem enough to the people to

account for so stupendous a conflagration. "In the midst of all this calamity and confusion," says Evelyn, "there was, I know not how, an alarm begun that the French and Dutch, with whom we were now in hostilities, were not only landed, but even entering the City. There was in truth some days before great suspicion of those two nations joining; and now that they had been the occasion of firing the town. This report did so terrify, that on a sudden there was such an uproar and tumult that they ran from their goods, and taking what weapons they could come at, they could not be stopped from falling on some of those nations whom they casually met, without sense or reason. The clamour and peril grew so excessive, that it made the whole Court amazed, and they did, with infinite pains and great difficulty reduce and appease the people, sending troops of soldiers and guards to cause them to retire into the fields again, where they were watched all this night."[1] Taswell also describes the fury of the ignorant and excited mob, hurried, while the fire was still raging, into frenzy against foreigners or Roman Catholics, imagining that they actually saw such incendiaries throwing red-hot balls into the houses. He saw a blacksmith fall on an innocent Frenchman, "whose blood flowed down to his heels." In another place he saw a French painter's house plundered and levelled to the ground. His brother saw a Frenchman in Moorfields almost torn to pieces; the poor man had a box of what they asserted to be fire-balls, which turned out to be tennis-balls. These unfounded suspicions were afterwards engraved in the inscription on the Monument, reluctantly and after much resistance erased under James II.; restored at the Revolution, and only in later days finally blotted out.

At the time of the fire, the Dean was *William Sancroft*. Of the Bishop, Henchman, we know little,[2] except that at

[1] *Diary*, p. 397.   [2] Cp. p. 201.

[*To face p.* 216.

LONDON AFTER THE FIRE, SHOWING ST. PAUL'S
(*From an old print in the possession of Chas. T. Veasey, Esq., Baldock, Herts*)

THE GREAT FIRE OF 1666

a later date he rebuilt, at his own cost, the palace of the Bishops of London, at that time in Aldersgate, and contributed generously to the new Cathedral. At the outbreak of the Civil Wars Sancroft was at Cambridge. His college was Puritan, Emmanuel, and after some delay he was ejected from his fellowship, and lived in retirement. After the execution of Charles he went to the Continent, where he not only supported himself but assisted others with great liberality; among these was Cosin, afterwards Bishop of Durham. At the Restoration, Sancroft returned to England, and Cosin was in a position to show his gratitude. He conferred on his benefactor a rich prebend, and the benefice of Houghton-le-Spring, then held to be one of the best and pleasantest in England. Sancroft became Master of Emmanuel, Dean of York in 1662, and two years later Dean of St. Paul's.[1]

Very soon after the fire, Dr. Wren, who had previously distinguished himself as a member of the Royal Society, was appointed deputy surveyor general and principal architect for rebuilding the whole City; having been previously appointed architect and one of the Commissioners for the reparation of St. Paul's.[2] He immediately set to work to fit up a portion of the dilapidated Cathedral for temporary use in divine service.[3] Having been consulted relatively to the state of the Cathedral before the fire, "he was prepared with plans, elevations and sections of every part, which he had but just finished to a large scale on vellum when that event occurred."[4] In the meantime it was indispensable to keep the building in some state of repair. Accordingly, on January 15, 1667, the King issued an order: "It being thought necessary in the meantime (till it shall please God to bless us with a more favourable juncture for doing something more lasting and magnificent) that some part of the venerable pile be forth-

[1] Milman's *Annals*, p. 385.
[2] Elmes' *Life*, p. 219.
[3] Dugdale (1716), p. 153.
[4] Elmes' *Life*, p. 220.

with restored to its religious use—it was this day ordered that a choir and auditory for present use be forthwith set out."[1] On the same day it was ordered, "for the suppressing of present and future annoyances and encroachments, the churchyard be forthwith walled in, or otherwise enclosed at such distance from the Church on all sides, that the public way without the said enclosure be left at least as broad in all places as the late Act of Parliament for the rebuilding of the City requires." On March 5, a sub-committee was appointed for the repairs.

The whole management of this work was left to the care and direction of the Archbishop of Canterbury, the Earl of Manchester, the Lord Chamberlain, the Bishops of London, Rochester, Winchester and Ely, Sir Richard Chaworth (Vicar-general of the Province of Canterbury) and the Dean and Chapter of St. Paul's. The temporary choir was hastily fitted up at the west end, which was thought the safest part of the ruins, the east being utterly desolate. About £3500 were spent on these temporary repairs.

On October 10, 1667, Sancroft preached on the fire before the King in this part of the ruined Cathedral. "Therefore dream no longer (he said) of grenades or fireballs, or the rest of those witty [2] mischiefs. Search no more for *bout-feus*, or incendiaries, Dutch or French. The Dutch intemperance, and the French pride and vanity, and the rest of their sins, which we are so fond of, are infinitely more dangerous to us than the enmity of either nation, for we have made God our enemy too; or if you will needs find out the incendiary, 'Intus hostis, intus periculum' (within is the enemy, within is the danger), saith St. Jerome. Turn your eyes inward into your own bosoms. There lurks the great *make-bate*, the grand *bout-feu*, between earth and us. . . . Thanks be to the Lord who has so long showed us marvellously great kindness. I say not with the Psalm, 'In the strong city' (though the strongest without Him is

[1] Dugdale's *St. Paul's* (Ellis), p. 127. [2] Imaginary.

weakness), but in a very weak one, a city in the meanness of its materials, the oldness of the buildings, the straitness of some streets, the ill-situation of others, and many like inconveniences, so exposed to this dismal accident, that it must have been long since in ashes, had not His miraculous mercy preserved it : Who so long as He pleaseth, and that is just so long as we please Him, continues the *fire* to us, useful and safe, serviceable and yet innocent, with as much ease as He lays it asleep and quiet in the bosom of a flint. . . . His compassions fail not, that God hath left us yet a holy place to assemble in, solemnly to acknowledge, as we do this day, that most miraculous mercy, that before all our wit was puzzled, and all our industry tired out, when the wind was at the highest, and the fire at the hottest, when all our hope was now giving up the ghost, then He . . . restrained also on the sudden the fury of that merciless and unruly element." [1]

[1] Sancroft's *Life* (D'Oyley), p. 377.

CHAPTER XXII

BEGINNING OF THE NEW CATHEDRAL: WREN'S PLANS

IN spite of providing temporary accommodation, Wren saw that a new Cathedral was necessary. He consequently strenuously opposed all patching-up of the Cathedral, while Sancroft and the committee appear to have attempted to do this, notwithstanding his protests. About a year after the appointment of the sub-committee, Sancroft wrote to Wren at Oxford (April 25, 1668): "What you last whispered in my ear at your last coming hither, is now come to pass. Our work at the west end of St. Paul's is fallen about our ears. Your quick eye discerned the walls and pillars gone off from their perpendicular, and, I believe, other defects too, which are now exposed to every common observer. The third pillar from the west, at the south side, which they had new cased with stone, fell with a sudden crash; the next, bigger than the rest, stood alone, certain to fall, yet so unsafe that they dared not venture to take it down. In short, the whole work of Inigo Jones was so overloaded as to threaten a total wreck. . . . What we are to do next is the present deliberation, in which you are so absolutely and indispensably necessary to us that we can do nothing, resolve nothing, without you."[1] Sancroft begged Wren to come to London with all possible speed, and to bring with him the drawings and designs he had already made. The patching, however, still went on, notwithstanding a remonstrance from him; but on July 2 the Dean wrote to Wren again, to tell him that, "yesterday my Lords of Can-

[1] Elmes' *Wren*, p. 245.

ST. PAUL'S FROM FLEET STREET

terbury, London and Oxford met on purpose to hear your letter read once more, and to consider what is now to be done in order to the repair of St. Paul's. They unanimously resolved that it is fit immediately to attempt something, and that without you they can do nothing. I am therefore commanded to give you an invitation hither in His Grace's name and the rest of the Commissioners, with all speed; that we may prepare something to be proposed to His Majesty (the desire of such a choir, at least, as may be a congruous part of a greater and more magnificent work to follow). . . . And then, for the procuring of contributions to defray this, we are so sanguine as not to doubt of it if we could but once resolve what we would do, and what that would cost. So that the only part of your letter that we demur to is the method you propose of declaring, first, what money we would bestow, and then designing something just of that expense; for, quite otherwise, the way their Lordships resolve upon is to frame a design handsome and noble, and suitable to all the ends of it, and to the reputation of the City and the nation, and to take it for granted that money will be had to accomplish it."

On the 25th of the same month, July, the King issued a warrant for taking down the walls and clearing the ground to the foundation of the east end, the old choir, and the tower, so as to make room for a new choir as part of a possible new Cathedral.[1] The tentative works continued for nearly two years, when at last the necessity for an entirely new church was demonstrated. "Towards the latter end of which two years," says Wren's grandson, "they fell to casing some of those great and massy pillars which stood between the middle aisle and the side aisles; beginning with those below the little north door towards the west; but before the third pillar was perfectly cased they were found to be incapable of any substantial repair.

[1] Elmes, p. 253.

THE FIRST DESIGN OF ST. PAUL'S AFTER THE FIRE, FROM THE MODEL IN THE PRESENT CATHEDRAL.

It was therefore fully concluded that in order to a new fabric, the foundations of the old Cathedral, thus made ruinous, should be totally cleared; and preparation of materials and all things needful made ready, conducing to a new fabric, which work continued until the last of April, 1674, at a total cost of £10,909."[1]

Besides the one made before the fire, Wren made several plans for a classic dome in the middle of the old Gothic Cathedral; the earlier were sketches "merely for discourse' sake, to find out what might satisfy the world." Then came Wren's own favourite design, one of incomparable beauty, in the form of a Greek cross, with a vast vestibule and portico surmounted by a lesser dome, the points of the Greek cross being connected by superb concave façades. The King ordered a model to be made of it, which still exists; it is on a huge scale, was lent for some years to the South Kensington Museum, and is now again in a corridor near the west gallery of St. Paul's. But the Chapter and some others of the clergy thought the model not enough of a cathedral fashion, to instance particularly, in that the choir was designed circular, and that there were no regular aisles or nave.[2]

Wren, therefore, prepared another drawing, sometimes called "the Nightmare design." Out of a vast reversed pudding-dish arises a neat but small cupola, resting on a sufficiently handsome drum with pillars and windows; but from the top of the cupola soars up a lofty spire like that of St. Bride's, Fleet Street; while the western front resembles very closely that left by Inigo Jones, and destroyed by the fire. The King endorsed this plan as "very artificial (artistic), proper and useful"; but he most fortunately gave him "liberty, in the prosecution of his work, to make some variations, rather ornamental than essential, as from time to time he should see proper, and to leave the whole to his management."[3] "Wren availed himself of this per-

[1] *Parentalia*, p. 278.   [2] Elmes, p. 319.   [3] *Parentalia*, p. 283.

mission to an incredible extent, and constructed a building almost as different from the approved plan as St. Paul's Cathedral is from that of Salisbury."[1]

On November 12, 1673, letters-patent, under the Great Seal of England, were issued, announcing the determination to erect a new Cathedral: "Inasmuch as it is now become absolutely necessary totally to demolish and to raze to the ground all the relics of the former building, and in the same place, and on new foundations, to erect a new church; wherefore, that it may be done to the glory of God, and for the promotion of the divine service therein to be celebrated, and to the end that the same may equal, if not exceed, the splendour and magnificence of the former Cathedral Church when it was in its best estate, and so become, much more than formerly, the principal ornament of our royal City, to the honour of our Government and this our realm . . . we have caused *several designs* to that purpose to be prepared by Dr. Christopher Wren, Surveyor-General of all our works and buildings, which we have seen, and *one of which* we do more especially approve, and have commanded a *model thereof* to be made after so large and exact a manner, that it may remain as a perpetual and unchangeable rule and direction for the conduct of the whole work." (This was Wren's favourite plan, that of the Greek cross, for which, in order to please the clergy, was afterwards substituted that of the Latin cross, with the small cupola and the lofty spire on the top.)

The warrant was addressed to the Lord Mayor of the City of London for the time being, Archbishop Sheldon of Canterbury, Lord Chancellor Shaftesbury, Archbishop Sterne of York, all the great Officers of State,[2] the Bishop of London and other Bishops, the Judges, and the Dean and Chapter of St. Paul's. These, with others, were Commissioners for the rebuilding, new erecting and *adorning*

[1] Longman's *Three Cathedrals*, p. 114.
[2] James, Duke of York, was President of the Commission.

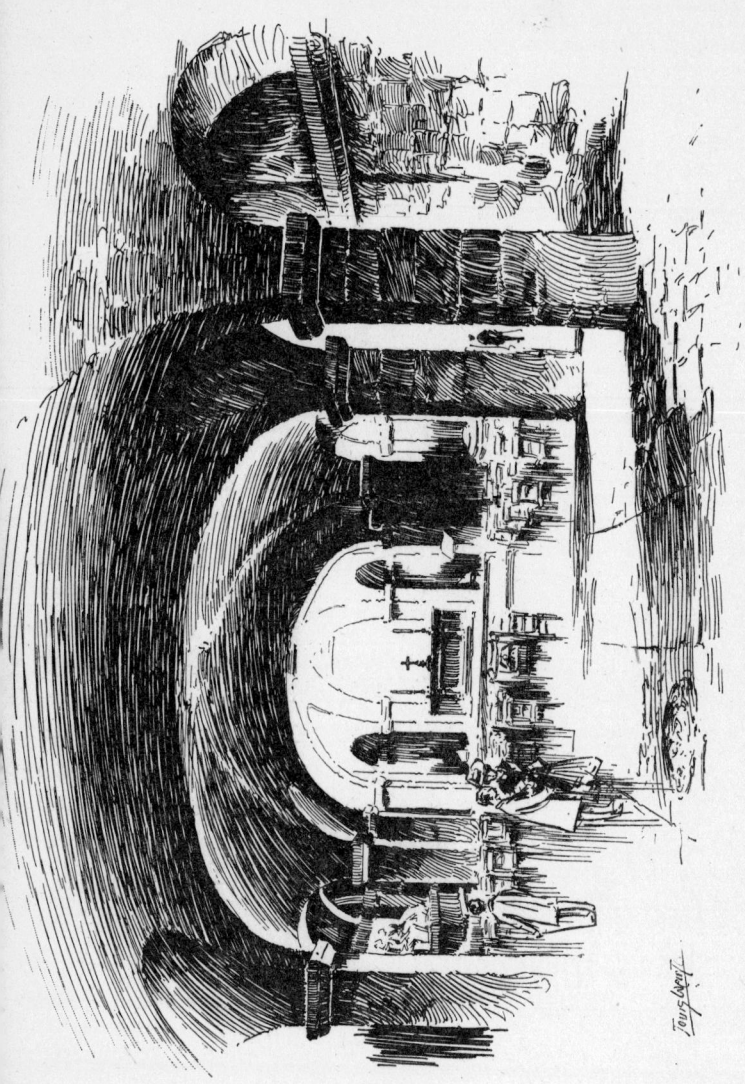

THE CRYPT, LOOKING EAST

the said Cathedral Church of St. Paul in London. Six Commissioners were to be a quorum, of which the Bishop of London, or the Dean of St. Paul's for the time being was to be one. Amongst other ample provisions was one to frame orders "for the better preservation and maintenance of the said Cathedral Church in time to come, and for the preventing and suppressing of all present and future annoyances, purprestures and encroachments which do, shall or may in any way tend to the damage or hurt, blemishing or disgrace of the same."

The Commission indicated the means for providing the vast expenditure needed; it was to be a national, not a diocesan, undertaking. Charles II. continued the promise of £1000 which he had made in 1664, but there is no trace of any payment; all that he gave was £527 out of fines and forfeitures, commonly called Green Wax Money, and £1627 out of impropriations due to him and not pardoned. The total amount of the Primate's subscription was £2000. Bishop Henchman subscribed largely, and left a considerable bequest; Bishop Morley of Winchester and Bishop Crewe of Durham were liberal; those three represented the wealthiest Sees. In 1678, an Order in Council was issued that Bishops, instead of giving expensive entertainments at their consecrations, should send £50 for the new Cathedral; until this was paid, the Archbishop was not to consecrate. It was followed by another order that another sum of £50 was to be paid by each new Bishop instead of the gloves that used to be given to all who attended his consecration. The ecclesiastical judges were to assign a proportion of commutations of penance. A special form of brief, enjoining subscriptions, was sent round to cathedrals and churches. All classes contributed; various private persons gave handsome sums and left liberal legacies. Collections were made over the whole country in parish churches, and were continued for ten years. Christopher Wren himself gave £60. So great was

[*To face p.* 226.

THE LAST DESIGN MADE FOR ST. PAUL'S BY SIR CHRISTOPHER WREN

BEGINNING OF THE NEW CATHEDRAL

the fervour that the coal-dues in the Port of London were granted to the City of London for rebuilding the City churches, for St. Paul's and for general purposes. The successive Acts for this purpose are given in Dugdale. In the second Act one-half of three shillings per chaldron went to the City; of the other half, $13\frac{1}{2}d.$ went to the City churches, and $4\frac{1}{2}d.$ to St. Paul's. It is difficult to fix accurately the total cost of the new Cathedral up to its final opening in the reign of Queen Anne; for, by a fire at Guildhall, the later subscription-lists, copies of which had not been sent to the muniment-room at St. Paul's, were lost. The total receipts from 1663 to 1685 amounted to £126,604; the total disbursements to £124,261. Of this, a sum of £3586 was spent on repairs before the Great Fire; and £10,909 on the preparations for the new Cathedral. After 1684 (or 1685) to September 29, 1700, the expenditure was £615,986; and from 1700 to 1723, in additional embellishments, £11,000. Thus the expenditure would appear to be £747,661. This total is obtained by subtracting £3586 (spent before the Fire) from £124,261 (disbursements before 1685), and adding £615,986 and £11,000.

This, however, is not all. The total money received up to September 29, 1700, including money borrowed, amounted to £1,167,474. Of this sum the enormous amount of £83,744 was paid for interest on money borrowed because the funds did not come in fast enough. The sums borrowed amounted to £288,951, and at the above date (September 29, 1700) only £279,290 has been paid off. The sum of £14,808 was paid for houses demolished; and there remained in hand £49,384.

It was on May 1, 1674, that Wren began to clear the ground for the new foundation.[1] It was a slow process, for the last portion removed, the west end, was not pulled down till 1686.[2] He began at the east end, and demolished

[1] Stow's *London*, i. 649.   [2] *Parentalia*, p. 293.

as he proceeded. The timber, rag, freestone and chalk, and the smaller and less serviceable freestone and rubble, were ordered to be sold for use in rebuilding the parish churches, and the surplus ragstone for repairing the streets.[1] It is said also that a large amount of the more serviceable stone was employed for filling up the interior cores of the vast walls and pillars of the new Cathedral. When Wren came to the great central tower, which formerly bore the spire, and which still stood more than two hundred feet above the ground, he found it so strongly built that he determined to blow it up with gunpowder. "Digging a hole about four feet square beside the great north-west pier, which, standing at the angle of nave and transept, had formed one of the main supports, he bored another hole half-way through the masonry of the pier itself, a distance of some seven feet. In this latter cavity he placed a box containing eighteen pounds of gunpowder. Setting a fuse, the surveyor waited, only to find the result exactly as he had anticipated. The charge sufficed to raise the great pier bodily; and with a shock which the Londoners compared to that of an earthquake, it fell, carrying with it a part of the ruins of the nave. So careful had been the preparation, so nicely calculated the force of the explosion, that no one was injured; and the same means would have sufficed to break up the remaining sides of the tower. The King's commands, however, drew Wren away from London just then, and the completion of the demolition was left to a subordinate, who, thinking to hasten matters and to outdo his master's achievement, used more powder and less wit. 'Too wise in his own conceit he put in a greater quantity of powder, and neither went low enough, nor sufficiently fortified the mouth of the mine.' The wall fell, indeed, but the carelessly laid charge projected a great fragment of stone into a room in a neighbouring house, in which some women were sitting at work. No one was

[1] Elmes, p. 308.

SIR CHRISTOPHER WREN'S FIRST DESIGN FOR THE CATHEDRAL (AFTER THE FIRE)

[*To face p.* 228.

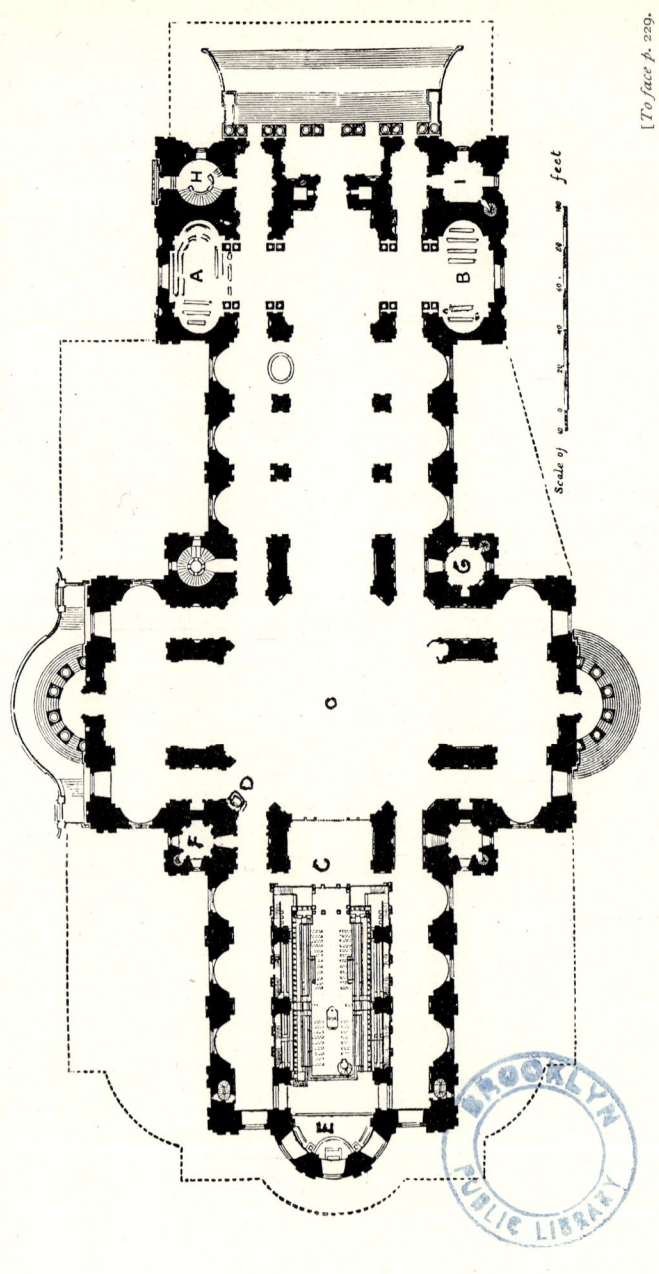

GROUND PLAN OF ST. PAUL'S

(The dotted line shows Sir Christopher Wren's original plan for the railings.)

A. Chapel of St. Michael and St. George. B. Vestry Chapel. C. Choir. D. Pulpit. E. Jesus Chapel. F. Dean's Vestry. G. Lord Mayor's Vestry. H. Clock Tower. I. Belfry.

[To face p. 229.

BEGINNING OF THE NEW CATHEDRAL

hurt, but the citizens, sharing the sempstresses' panic, implored that the use of any further gunpowder might be prohibited."[1] Wren determined to make a battering-ram instead. "He took a strong mast of about forty feet long, arming the bigger end with a great spike of iron, fortified with bars along the masts, and ferrels. This mast in two places was hung up to one iron ring with strong tackle, and so suspended lead to a triangular prop, such as they weigh great guns with; thirty men, fifteen on a side, vibrated this machine to and again, and beat in one place against the wall the whole day; they believed it was to little purpose, not discerning any immediate effect; he bid them not despair, but proceed another day; on the second day the wall was perceived to tremble at the top, and in a few hours it fell." He used the same means for beating down the rest of the walls.

Before beginning to build, Wren had to explore the ground for his new foundations; for various reasons he was determined to avoid the old, an aim which he dexterously accomplished by directing the axis of the new Cathedral slightly more to the north than that of the former. "The surveyor observed that the foundation of the old Church stood upon a layer of very close and hard pot-earth, and concluded that the same ground which had borne so weighty a building would do so again. However, he had the curiosity to search further, and accordingly dug wells in several places, and discerned this hard pot-earth to be, on the north side of the churchyard about six feet thick and more, but thinner and thinner towards the south, till it was, upon the declining of the hill, scarce four feet; still he searched lower, and found nothing but dry sand, mixed sometimes unequally, but loose, so that it would run through the fingers. He went on till he came to water and sand mixed with periwinkles and other sea-shells: these were about the level of low-water mark. He con-

[1] Lena Milman's *Life of Wren*, p. 120; *Parentalia*, p. 293.

tinued boring till he came to hard beach, and still under that till he came to the natural hard clay which lies under the City and country and Thames also far and wide."[1] "The pot-earth as described by Dean Milman—on the authority of Sir Charles Lyell and Mr. Prestwick, whom he consulted—is the loam or brick-earth which often forms the upper layer of the great bed of gravel covering the London clay; the two beds of sand, the sea-shells, and the old sea-beach are not marine, but fresh-water, foundations resting on the London clay. Wren apparently built on the pot-earth, which he now calls brick-earth, the 'natural hard clay' lying too deep, probably at least forty feet down." This seems evident from Wren's account of the failure of the ground at the north-east end. "He began to lay the foundations from the west end, and had proceeded successfully through the dome to the east end, where the brick-earth bottom was yet very good. But as he went on to the north-east corner, which was the last, and where nothing was expected to interrupt, he fell, in prosecuting the design, upon a pit where all the pot-earth had been robbed by the potters of old time. It was no little perplexity to fall into this pit at last. He wanted but six or seven feet to complete the design, and this fell into the very angle north-east. He knew very well that under the layer of pot-earth there was no other good ground to be found till he came to the low-water mark of the Thames, at least forty feet lower. His artificers proposed to him to pile, but this he refused, for though piles may last for ever where always in water (otherwise London Bridge would fall), yet if they are driven through dry sand, though sometimes moist, they will rot. His endeavours were to build for eternity. He therefore sank a pit of about eighteen feet square, wharfing up the sand with timber, till he came forty feet lower into water and ... shells. He bored through this beach till he came to the

[1] *Parentalia.*

[*To face p.* 230.

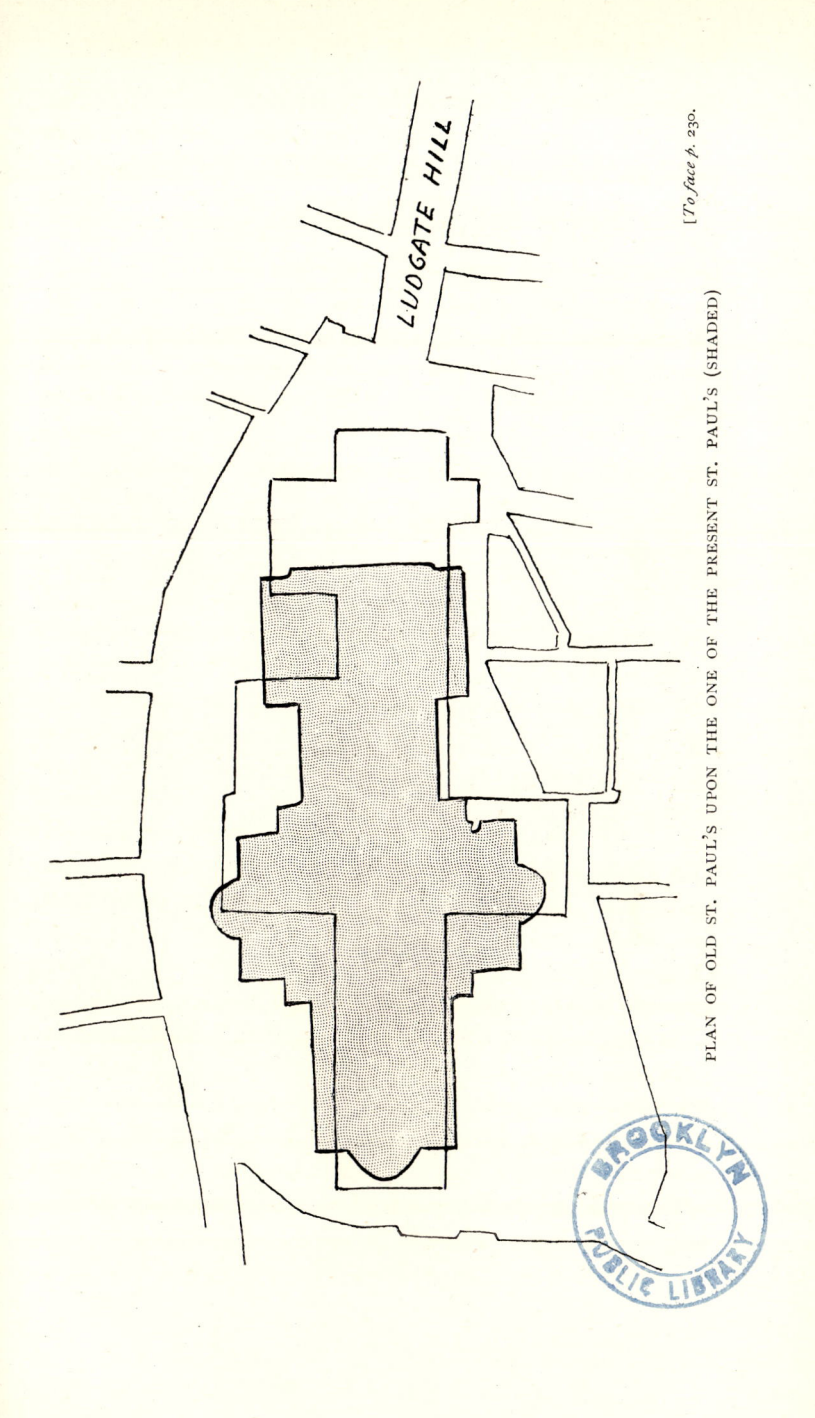

PLAN OF OLD ST. PAUL'S UPON THE ONE OF THE PRESENT ST. PAUL'S (SHADED)

original clay. Being then satisfied, he began from the beach a square pier of solid good masonry, ten feet square, till he came within fifteen feet of the present ground; then he turned a short arch underground to the former foundation, which was broken off by the untoward accident of the pit. Thus this north-east coin of the choir stands very firm, and no doubt will stand."[1] As a matter of fact, all these questions have been tested lately[2] in connection with the public interest in the stability of St. Paul's, and the north-east angle has been found to be the most stable point of the whole Cathedral: for whereas in the course of two hundred years the entire building has sunk evenly to an almost imperceptible degree, perhaps an inch, this portion remains absolutely unchanged.

Dean Milman, in his full work on St. Paul's, has worked out the question of the underlying strata, and the questions which they suggest, with great completeness. "It is clear that this layer of loose sand underlies the firm pot-earth or loam which thins out towards the south. This cannot be too widely known, and the possible consequences of its oozing out cannot be too jealously watched. It fully justifies the apprehension of our late accomplished and scientific surveyor, Mr. R. Cockerell, who, when a deep sewer was commenced on the south side of the Cathedral, came to the Dean in much alarm. On the representation of the Dean and Mr. Cockerell, the work was stopped by the authorities of the City."[3] Twice in more recent times has the same danger threatened and been averted; in the first case by the proposal of a new tube railway between Carter Lane and the District Railway, which was abandoned; in the second, by the proposal of the London County Council to drive a huge sewer below the church-yard, within forty feet of the south-west tower. The alteration of the scheme by the next London County

[1] *Parentalia*, 236. [2] 1908.
[3] Milman's *Annals*, p. 408.

Council deserves the gratitude of all lovers of architecture all the world over.

Wren, having been appointed surveyor for the rebuilding of the whole City, drew up an admirable plan for its reconstruction after the fire. He took two great centres, St. Paul's and the Royal Exchange, and proposed to surround each of them with great circular piazzas, from which should extend with geometrical precision straight broad streets like the spokes of a wheel, to be prolonged as far as might be possible. This he was not able to effect. The Commissioners for rebuilding the City had in the first place marked and staked out the streets, and Parliament had confirmed their report, before anything had been fully determined about the design for the new fabric (though Evelyn, writing on September 27, 1666, says that Wren had already presented his scheme for the City to the King). The proprietors of the ground with much eagerness and haste had begun to build accordingly; an incredible progress had been made in a very short time; many large and fair houses erected; and every foot of ground in that trading and populous part of the town was highly estimated.[1] "Thus was lost, it is to be feared for ever, the opportunity of placing the Cathedral of London on an esplanade worthy of its consummate design; an esplanade which, we may almost say, Nature, by leaving a spacious level on the summit of the hill, had designated for a commanding and noble edifice."[2] Think what it would have been if the unequalled splendours of St. Paul's had been approached by a broad straight avenue from Fleet Street; if a new Cheapside had led straight up to the East End; and if similar avenues had led up to it from the river on the south, and from Aldersgate on the north!

On May 14, 1675, the King ordered the work to begin. On June 21 of the same month the first stone was laid, with little or no ceremony; neither King, Court, Primate,

---

[1] *Parentalia.*   [2] Milman's *Annals*, p. 410.

BEGINNING OF THE NEW CATHEDRAL 233

Bishop, Dean or Lord Mayor seems to have been present. Milman says the stone was laid by Wren; Longman, quoting Stow and Ellis, says that the first stone was laid at the south-east corner of the choir by Mr. Strong, the foreman, and the second by Mr. Longland.

A story quoted by Milman from the *Parentalia* is worth repeating, as it was noticed at the time as an encouraging omen in the vastness of the undertaking. When the surveyor in person had set out on the site the dimensions of the great dome, a labourer was ordered to bring a flat stone from the heaps of rubbish, the first that might come to hand, to be laid for a mark and direction to the masons; the stone which he immediately brought and laid down for the purpose happened to be part of a monument, with nothing remaining of the inscription but this single word, "RESURGAM." This has been asserted to have been the origin of the emblem, a phœnix on its fiery nest, sculptured by Abber over the south portico, and inscribed with the same word.[1]

We have little information of the progress of the building. Wren's biographer tells us that in 1678 "the Cathedral of St. Paul continued with undeviating progress, the eastern part, or choir, being the principal care of its architect."[2] And, again, "the year 1683 of Wren's life passed much the same as the last, superintending and designing for St. Paul's Cathedral."[3] "In 1684, St. Paul's continued with undeviating progress towards completion."[4] "The year 1687 passed as the preceding. St. Paul's was continued with unabated activity."[5] We get one little note from Evelyn's *Diary*, October 5, 1694: "I went to St. Paul's to see the new choir, now finished as to the stonework, and the scaffolds struck, both without and within, in that part. Some exception might perhaps be taken as to the placing columns on pilasters at the eastern tribunal.

---

[1] *Parentalia*, p. 292; Elmes' *Life*, p. 384.   [2] Elmes, p. 384.
[3] *Ibid.*, p. 419.   [4] *Ibid.*, p. 437.   [5] *Ibid.*, p. 445.

As to the rest, it is a piece of architecture without reproach."

In 1685, on the death of Charles II., a new Commission was ordered by James II. for continuing the work at St. Paul's; this was the year before the disappearance of the last remains of the ancient Gothic Cathedral, for the order gives authority "to demolish and take down what is yet remaining of the old fabric, and to carry on the new work."[1]

It is recorded that the recesses or chapels along the aisles of nave, choir and transepts were insisted upon by James II., whether as Duke of York or King. He looked forward with certainty to the time when the old Roman Catholic worship would take possession of the new Cathedral; and then the line of chapels, wanting only their altar, would be ready for the daily masses.[2]

It is well known that Wren was a Freemason, and that he was one of the earlier pioneers which converted the craft of practical and working Freemasonry, in his day no longer needed, into its modern form of a speculative and ideal fellowship. St. Paul's was probably the last great building erected by Freemasons; it is believed that many of his workmen belonged to the craft, and held their lodges in the neighbourhood.

In 1688 or 1689, a fire broke out at the west end of the north aisle of the choir, in a room prepared for the organ-builder to work in, when the choir was nearly finished. But the communication between the workroom and the organ-gallery being broken down, the fire was got under, doing no other damage but to two pillars and an arch with enrichments. The repair cost more than £700.[3]

The choir was opened for divine service on December 2, 1697, on the Thanksgiving Day for the Peace of Ryswick; but of that a special account must be given. The Morning Chapel, now St. Dunstan's, at the north-west end of the

---

[1] Ellis's *Dugdale*, p. 170.   [2] Milman's *Annals*, p. 403.
[3] Ellis's *Dugdale*, p. 172.

nave, was opened on February 1, 1698 or 1699. At length, in 1708, St. Paul's had proceeded so far towards completion that the best mode of covering the cupola was taken into consideration, and it was finally decided by the committee to cover it with copper at the cost of £3050. This decision was overruled, and it was covered with lead at the cost of £2500.[1]

In 1710, when Wren was in his seventy-eighth year, his son laid the highest stone of the lantern on the cupola, in the presence of his father, and "that excellent artificer Mr. Strong, his son, and other Free and Accepted Masons, chiefly employed in the execution of the work."[2]

All these years the quarries of Portland supplied their excellent stone in abundance, and the long procession of ships laden with the future Cathedral sailed along the south coast to the mouth of the Thames. "Wren might seem as if he ruled over the vassal island;[3] roads were made to convey the stone with the greatest facility to the port. An admirable and obedient regiment of masons and workmen was organized."[4] Thomas Strong, of Taynton, in Oxfordshire, was Master of the Masons at the beginning; on his death, his brother Edward, who had from the first been associated with him, took up his office, and continued it to the completion. This is recorded on Edward's monument in St. Peter's Church, St. Albans, and in Conder's *Hole Craft and Fellowship of Masonry*, p. 241. It is often carelessly repeated that it was Thomas who lived and worked all through the years of the building of St. Paul's. Thomas was owner of the famous quarries of Taynton, in Oxfordshire, which, renowned as early as 1474, and used for the erection of St. George's Chapel, Windsor, provided a great quantity of stone for the rebuilding of the City of London: at Taynton it is believed, also, for St. Paul's itself.

[1] Elmes, p. 491. [2] *Parentalia*, p. 393.
[3] Elmes, p. 269: "Royal Proclamation."
[4] Milman's *Annals*, p. 410.

236 MEMORIALS OF ST. PAUL'S CATHEDRAL

ST. PAUL'S FROM WATERLOO BRIDGE

CHAPTER XXIII

THE NEW CATHEDRAL

The dimensions of the new building are as follows:—

Exterior length	515 feet.
Interior ,,	479 ,,
Width of transepts from door to door	250 ,,
,, across nave and aisles	102 ,,
,, between the piers	41 ,,
Length of west front	180 ,,
Diameter of area at crossing of nave and transept	107 ,,
,, of drum beneath the dome	112 ,,
,, of dome	102 ,,
Height of central aisle	89 ,,
Total height from pavement to top of cross	365 ,,
,, ,, of western towers	221 ,,

The comparative size of the building may be gathered from the following table of dimensions of areas:—

St. Peter's, Rome	227,000 sq. feet.
Milan	108,277 ,,
Seville (about)	100,000 ,,
Florence	84,802 ,,
St. Paul's	84,311 ,,
Cologne	81,464 ,,
York	72,860 ,,
Amiens	71,208 ,,
Antwerp (about)	70,000 ,,

THE WEST DOOR, FROM S.E.

THE NEW CATHEDRAL

St. Isaac's	68,845 sq. feet.
Chartres	68,261 ,,
Rheims	67,475 ,,
Lincoln	66,900 ,,
Winchester	64,200 ,,
Nôtre Dame, Paris	64,108 ,,
Westminster Abbey	61,729 ,,
Canterbury	56,280 ,,

Old St. Paul's was a little less in area than its successor; but its length exceeded that of every church except St. Peter's, which measures 680 feet. The present St. Paul's is exceeded in length by Winchester, Ely, York and Canterbury. The length of Old St. Paul's was about 100 feet less than that of St. Peter's, and about the same amount greater than that of the present Cathedral. St. Peter's is a little less than three times the size of St. Paul's. The cross of St. Paul's would rise a little above the middle of the dome of St. Peter's.

The best architectural account of St. Paul's is by a former surveyor of the Cathedral, Joseph Guilt.[1]

"The plan of St. Paul's is a Latin cross: to the foot or western end of which projections are added northward and southward, which, while they serve the purpose of a morning chapel and consistory court, are expedients for elongating and giving importance to the west front. At the internal angles of the cross are square bastion-like adjuncts, whose real use is to strengthen the piers of the dome, but they become internally serviceable as vestries and a staircase. The nave and choir are separated by the area over which the cupola rises. From this area the transepts diverge north and south, each extending one arch in length. The choir is terminated eastward by a semi-circular tribune, whose diameter is in general terms equal to the width of the choir itself.

[1] *Illustrations of the Public Buildings of London*, by J. Brittain and A. Pugin, 1825.

CHAPEL OF ST. DUNSTAN, OR MORNING CHAPEL (UNDER N.W. TOWER)

"The interior may be considered with respect to its nave and choir, and their side aisles, and the transepts (of which a sufficient account has been already given), the morning chapel and consistory, and last, by the cupola and its sub-order.

"The nave and choir are each flanked by three arches, springing from piers, which are strengthened as well as decorated on their inner faces by pilasters of the Corinthian order; these are crowned by an entablature whose cornice reigns throughout the Church. Over this order rises a tall attic, which breaks with the entablature over each pilaster, and by its break forms an abutment pier for the springing of semi-circular arches, between each of which pendentives gather over from their springing points, and at their extreme height receive a cornice. Above the cornice a small cupola springs up, spherical in form, but rising vertically much less than its semi-diameter. The eastern piers of the nave serve at the same time for the support of the cupola; they are wider than the other piers, and are flanked by pilasters at their angles, with a square recess in the intercolumniation.

"The western end of the choir is terminated with piers similar to those just described, uniform with which there are at its eastern end, piers of the same length and form, except that they are pierced for a communication with the side aisles. In other respects the leading features of the choir resemble those of the nave, with the addition of the tribune in which an altar stands, which is domed over from the top of the attic order.

"In the upright plane space on the walls, evolved from the piercing of the pendentives, a clerestory is introduced over the attic order.

"The side aisles, which are extremely low in respect of the nave, are vaulted from the small pilasters, and terminated in a manner similar to that of the vaultings of the nave and choir.

R

INTERIOR OF THE NAVE, LOOKING EAST

"The nave, it has been seen, is to a certain extent (viz. three arches westward) similar to the choir. At their termination the north and south extension of the foot of the cross begins. In the other spaces, from pilaster to pilaster, the length is not equal to the breadth of the nave, but the fourth or western severy of the nave is square on the plan. The side arches spring from insulated columns coupled with pilasters attached to the piers, and on the north and south exhibit the morning chapel and consistory court, which are both parallelograms on the plan, and are terminated at the eastern and western ends by semi-circular tribunes.

"The central area, under the cupola, is circumscribed by eight large piers, equal in size, but not equidistant; the four large openings of course occur where the choir, nave and transepts diverge from the great circle, the lesser between them. These latter are surmounted by arches

BASE OF COLUMN IN WEST GALLERY

which spring from the architrave of the main order; but by extending the springing-point above in the attic, so as to break over the re-entering angular pilaster below, such an increase of opening is acquired in the attic that the eight arches which receive the cornice of the Whispering Gallery are all equal. Above this cornice a tall pedestal rises up for the reception of the order immediately under the dome. The order is composite. The periphery is divided into eight portions of three intercolumniations each, pierced for windows, each of these divisions being

THE LORD MAYOR'S VESTRY

separated from that adjoining it by a solid pier, one intercolumniation wide, decorated with a niche. The piers so formed connect the wall of the inner order with the external peristyle, and thus serve as counterforts to resist the thrust of the inner brick cupola; as well as that of the conical wall which carries the stone lantern, neither of which are more than two bricks thick. The pedestal and order just described incline inwards as they rise, and it is worthy of remark that their bearing is solely on the great arches and their piers, without any false bearing on the pendentives—a precaution which evinces great judgment. A plinth over the order receives the *inner* dome (named above, 'inner brick cupola'), which is of brick plastered, the paintings on the plaster being the work of Sir James Thornhill. The inner dome is pierced with an eye in its vertex, through which a vista is carried up to the small cupola in which the great cone terminates.

"The *exterior* of the fabric consists of two orders—the lower one Corinthian, the upper composite. In both stories, except at the north and south doors, which are decorated with semi-circular porticoes, and in the west front, the whole of the entablatures rest on coupled pilasters, between which, in the lower order, a range of semi-circular-headed windows is introduced; but in the order above the corresponding spaces are occupied by dressed niches, standing on pedestals, pierced with openings to light the passages in the roof over the side aisles. The upper order is nothing but a screen to hide the flying buttresses carried across from the outer walls to resist the thrust of the great vaulting. In the west front are two porticoes, one above the other. The lower consists of twelve coupled columns; that above has only eight, which bear an entablature and pediment, whose tympanum is sculptured in bas-relief, representing the Conversion of St. Paul. The transepts are terminated upwards by pediments over coupled pilasters at the quoins, and two single pilasters in the intermediate space.

THE DEAN'S VESTRY AND CHAIR

"On each side of the upper western portico a square pedestal rises over the upper order, and on each pedestal a steeple of two orders in light pierced work; these are covered with domes shaped like bells.

"The cupola, which is by far the most magnificent and elegant feature in the building, rises from the body of the Church in great majesty. The dome itself stands on an attic order whose detail is extremely simple and appropriate, and its profile excellent. Below the attic, whose exterior circuit is flanked by a balustrade of considerably larger diameter, a peristyle of a composite order, with an unbroken entablature, encloses the interior order. It may be safely affirmed that for dignity and elegance no church in Europe affords an example worthy of comparison with this cupola. The order of the peristyle stands on a large circular pedestal, which in its turn is supported on the piers and great arches of the central space."

THE CROSS ON THE TOP OF THE DOME

Wren intended the dome to be the central feature of the Church, as well in the interior as in the outside elevation. The choir, nave and transepts all consist of sections of exactly the same design, proportion and ornamentation; the arcade of three arches in the choir is precisely the same as the arcade of three arches in the nave, and that of one arch in the two transepts. The arcade of the choir is completed by the apse; that of the nave by a magnificent and stately vestibule, flanked by the north-west and south-west chapels;[1] the arcade of each transept ends in a flat ornamental wall, with a superb semi-circular porch outside. Each arm of the Church is attached to the dome by walls with vast panels supporting a barrel arch of identical pattern: a similar barrel arch joins the choir to the apse. The whole interior is extraordinarily harmonious.

Wren intended no organ-screen, shutting off the choir. The account of the erection of such a screen against his wishes is given in Dr. Rimbault's *History of the Organ.* "In consequence of the reputation which Father Smith had acquired, he was made choice of to build an organ for St. Paul's Cathedral, then in course of erection. A place was accordingly fitted up for him in the Cathedral to do the work in, but it was a long time before he could proceed with it, owing to a contention between Sir Christopher Wren and the Dean and Chapter. Sir Christopher Wren wished the organ to be placed on one side of the choir as it was in the old Cathedral, that the whole extent and beauty of the building might be had at one view. The Dean, on the contrary, wished to have it at the west end of the choir; and Sir Christopher, after using every effort and argument to gain his point, was at last obliged to yield. Smith, according to his instructions, began the organ, and when the pipes were finished found that the case was not spacious enough to contain them all; and Sir Christopher, tender of his architectural proportions, would not let the case be enlarged to receive them, declaring the beauty of the building to be spoilt by the box of whistles." The screen stood about the middle of the western arch of the choir. The stalls of the Dean and the Archdeacon of Essex on the south side, and of the Archdeacon of London and the Precentor on the north, faced eastwards. There were at that time five

---

[1] Now the Chapel of St. Dunstan, and the Chapel of the Order of St. Michael and St. George.

THE NEW CATHEDRAL

Archdeaconries in the diocese : London, Essex, Middlesex, Colchester and St. Albans.

Among the most valued assistants to the new Cathedral was the illustrious sculptor in wood, Grinling Gibbons. Evelyn writes on December 18, 1670: "This day I first acquainted His Majesty with that incomparable young man Gibbon,[1] whom I had lately met with in an obscure place by mere accident as I was walking near a poor solitary thatched house near Sayes Court. I found him shut in; but looking in at the window I perceived him carving that large cartoon or crucifix(ion) of Tintoret, a copy of which I had myself brought from Venice, where the original painting remains. I asked if I might enter; he opened the door civilly to me, and I saw him about such a work as for the curiosity of handling, drawing and studious exactness, I never had before seen in all my travels. I questioned

THE BISHOP'S THRONE : GRINLING GIBBONS

[1] Evelyn always spells the name Gibbon; but the final *s* is now universal.

250 MEMORIALS OF ST. PAUL'S CATHEDRAL

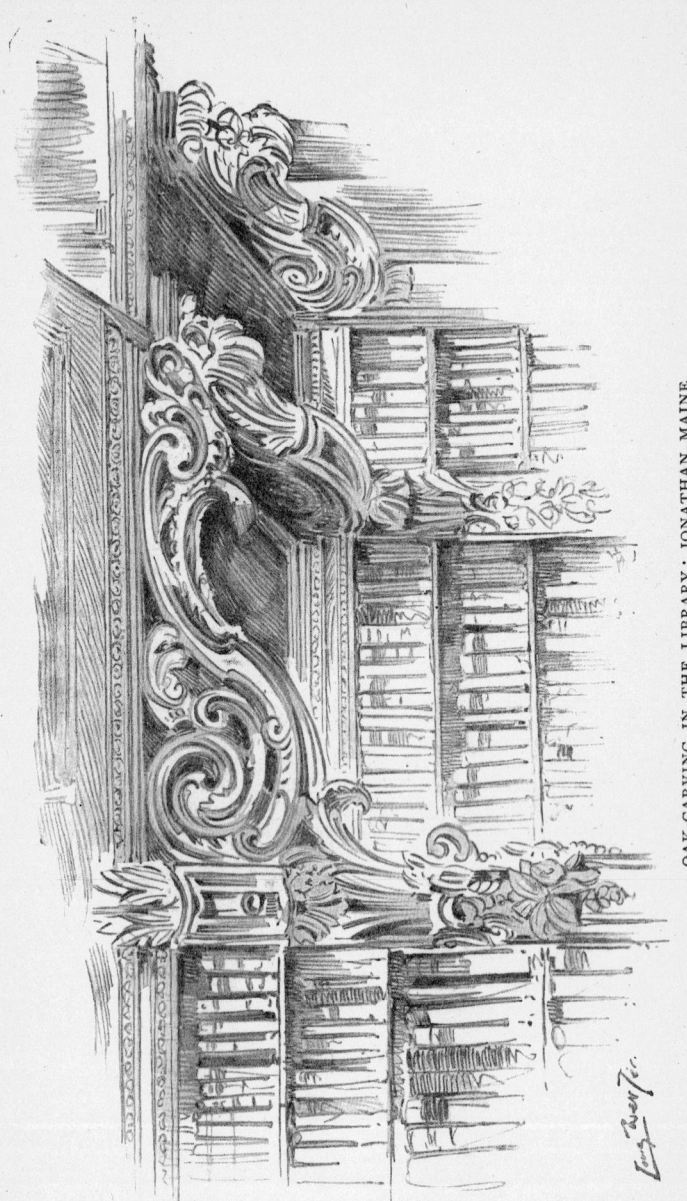

OAK-CARVING IN THE LIBRARY : JONATHAN MAINE

him why he worked in such an obscure and lonely place; he told me that it was that he might apply himself to his profession without interruption, and wondered not a little how I had found him out. I asked if he was unwilling to be made known to some great man, for that I believed it might turn to his profit; he answered he was yet but a beginner, but would not be sorry to sell off that piece; on demanding the price, he said £100. In good earnest the very frame was worth the money, there being nothing in nature so tender and delicate as the flowers and festoons about it, and yet the work was very strong; in the piece were more than one hundred figures of men, etc. I found he was likewise musical, and very civil, sober and discreet in his discourse. There was only an old woman in the house. So, desiring leave to visit him sometimes, I went away.

"Of this young artist, together with my manner of finding him, I acquainted the King, and begged that he would give me leave to bring him and his work to Whitehall, for that I would adventure my reputation with His Majesty that he had never seen anything approach it, and that he would be exceedingly pleased, and employ him. The King said he would himself go see him." Horace Walpole says that Gibbon was employed by Betterton in decorating the theatre in Dorset Garden. Charles gave him a place in the Board of Works, and employed his hand on ornaments of most taste in his palaces, particularly at Windsor. Many of the City churches and halls contain specimens of his skill; some of his best work is at Chatsworth and Petworth.

"The fame of Grinling Gibbons," says Wren's latest biographer, Lena Milman, "whose delicate carvings decorate not St. Paul's alone, but many of the great houses of England, has tended to rob Wren of the credit due to him for designing what are certainly the finest late Renaissance choir stalls not only in England, but in

TIJOU'S GRILL, LEADING TO S. CHOIR AISLE AND DEAN'S VESTRY

Europe. There is a drawing extant by Wren's own hand, which proves the general arrangement to be as exclusively his as the details are Grinling Gibbons's. The amazing delicacy of Grinling Gibbons's lime-wood carving has left the masterly spacing and designing of the oaken stalls which they adorn generally disregarded, and indeed the architect, by suggesting such prodigal decoration, willingly subordinated his own share in the scheme. In the panels and columns, however, of the back elevation, those that abut upon the ambulatory, Wren is supreme, blending panels and mouldings in masterly fashion with grilles of Tijou's ironwork."[1]

Tijou was a French artist in metal of whom Wren had heard, and to engage whom he went over to Paris himself. The ironwork gates and grilles in the choir, the railing of the geometrical staircase of the west gallery, and of the four galleries in the dome, are the monuments of his exquisite genius. The low railing which now fences the choir is also his work, and was originally made for the sacrarium. Tijou used only charcoal-smelted iron, which came from the Sussex forges: when more ironwork was wanted in the adaptation of his creations to the recent changes in the choir, it was found that coal-smelted metal split, and was useless for the finer work; Tijou's method was discovered in the records, and charcoal-smelted iron was procured from Norway.

At the east end of the apse, Wren proposed to place a Baldacchino, the design for which is in the collection of his drawings at All Souls' College, Oxford. It was to consist of rich marble columns, "writhéd, etc., in some manner like that of St. Peter's at Rome." The *Parentalia* tells us that "the painting and gilding of the architecture at the east end of the Church, over the communion table, was intended only to serve the present occasion, till such time as materials could have been procured for a magnificent

[1] *Sir Christopher Wren*, p. 214.

IRONWORK AT THE FOOT OF THE GEOMETRICAL STAIRCASE
UNDER S.W. TOWER

design of an altar, consisting of four pillars wreathed (writhed?) of the richest Greek marbles, supporting a canopy hemispherical, with proper decorations of architecture and sculpture, for which the respective drawings and a model were prepared. Information and particular descriptions of certain blocks of marble were once sent to the Right Rev. Dr. Compton, Bishop of London, from a Levantine merchant in Holland, and communicated to the surveyor, but unluckily the colour and scantlings did not answer his purpose, so it rested in expectance of a fitter opportunity, else probably this curious and stately design had been finished at the same time with the main fabric."

The Geometrical Staircase in the south tower is a circular ascent, of a diameter of twenty-five feet, with steps nearly six feet broad at their outer edge. The steps at one end are imbedded in the wall, at the other they rest mathematically on each other without any support from below, but connected above by Tijou's iron railing.

The Whispering Gallery is almost exactly one hundred feet from the pavement, and about the same distance across. The curious acoustic effect is produced partly by the circular shape of the wall, partly by its smoothness, partly by the fact that the whole wall of the dome slopes inwards from the eight great supporting arches with a view to avoiding any outward thrust from the stupendous weight above, and partly perhaps by the nearness of the overhanging concave hemisphere.

With regard to the dome, it would be unwise to blame Wren for having so great a space between the interior and exterior covering. Construction apart, if the interior had risen to the great height of the exterior, it would have been out of proportion to the space below. The interior surface is of the exact height for the satisfaction of the eye in point of harmonious relation to the rest of the Cathedral. The lantern, in itself a very large structure, said to weigh

700 tons, rests on the invisible cone of brick, which is itself secured by the vast supports and abutments which rise from the central portion of the crypt; and the exterior dome, which is of timber covered with lead, resting on a forest of timber beams, is supported in the same way. The weak point of the construction, about which Wren himself was not satisfied, is to be found in the flattened arches and curtain walls of the four great intermediate arches of the dome. The solid filling up of these spaces at St. Peter's avoids these difficulties.

The painting of the interior of the dome was given, in spite of Wren's remonstrances, to Sir James Thornhill, who decorated it with scenes from the life of St. Paul in monochrome. Wren desired to cover that vast and important space with brilliant mosaics, lightening instead of darkening the huge canopy. The architectural divisions of Thornhill's design do not harmonize with the lines of the building, and in the opinion of Mr. Penrose, the late learned and accomplished surveyor of St. Paul's, tend to give the thirty-two Corinthian pilasters of the dome the appearance of leaning forward.

"The judgment of the surveyor," writes his grandson in the *Parentalia*, "was originally, instead of painting in the manner it is now performed, to have beautified the inside of the cupola with the more durable ornament of mosaic work, as is nobly executed in the cupola of St. Peter's in Rome, which strikes the eye of the beholder with a most magnificent and splendid appearance, and which, without the least decay of colours, is as lasting as marble or the building itself. For this purpose he had projected to have procured from Italy four of the most eminent artists in that profession; but as this art was a great novelty in England, and not generally apprehended, it did not receive the encouragement it deserved. It was imagined also that the expense would be too great, and the time very long in the execution. But though these and all objections were

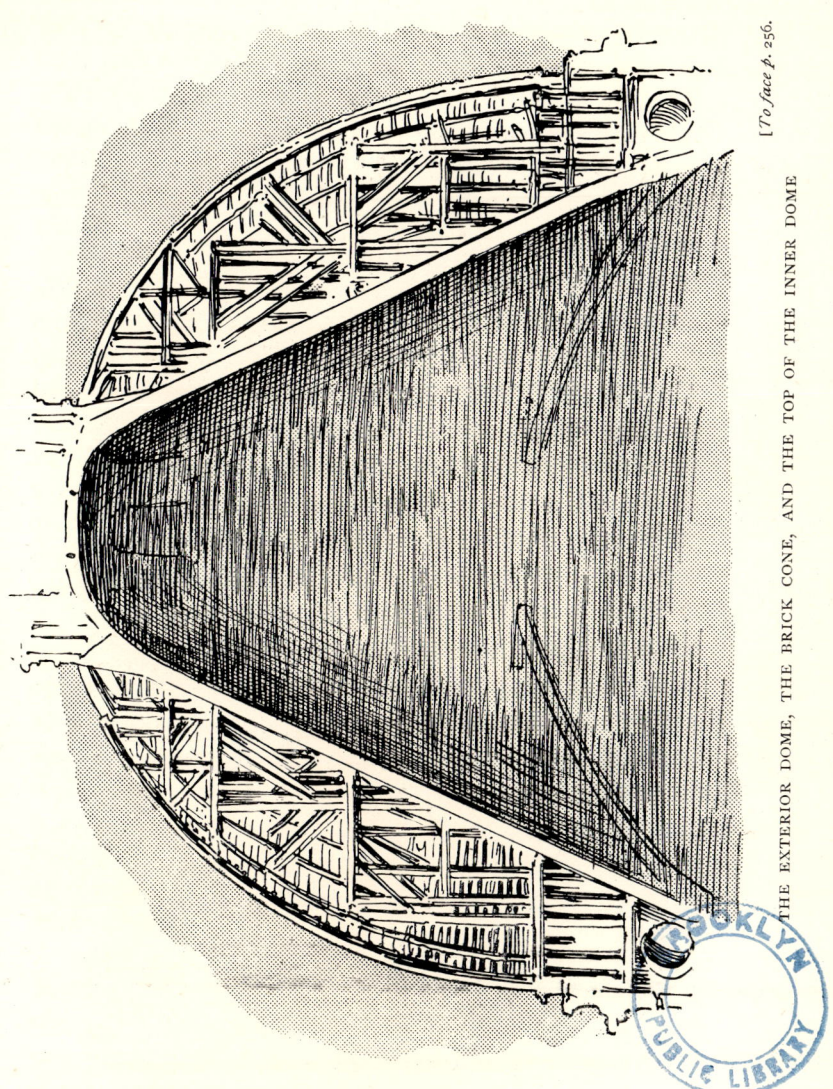

THE EXTERIOR DOME, THE BRICK CONE, AND THE TOP OF THE INNER DOME

[*To face p.* 256.

fully answered, yet this excellent design was no further pursued." [1]

The lectern was finished in 1720 by Jacob Sutton, at a cost of £241 15s., which, like all the other figures of that date, must be multiplied by five to give the modern value. The font, of veined Carrara marble, was the work of the sculptor Bird. Bird also carved the group of the Conversion of St. Paul in the pediment of the west front. The Phœnix

OLD PULPIT OF CHOIR (used at the opening of Convocation)

over the southern portico was the work of Caius Gabriel Cibber. The statue of Queen Anne with the four attendant figures in front of the west end of the Cathedral was by Bird.

The windows were left plain. In a classical building, the windows form no part of architectural decoration as such, as they are in a Gothic cathedral, and are only stately apertures at distant intervals for the admission of light.

[1] *Parentalia*, p. 292, note (*a*).

The area of windows in Westminster Abbey is proportionally about three times that of St. Paul's. A classical building requires no shadowy recesses, or distant depths of dim religious light. Every part is equally balanced, and the harmonious proportions and ornamentation of the whole require an equal distribution of light. Light cannot enter except by windows; and as the exact number necessary for this purpose has been accurately calculated by the consummate genius of Wren, it is a mistake to be led by the Gothic habit of thought and association to darken the windows with heavy tinted glass. Colour is needed, and must come by painting, marble or mosaic. If the windows are darkened, however much painting, marble or mosaic may enrich the walls, it will not be seen. And the need of light is much greater than in Wren's day, for the surrounding buildings are vastly higher, the skies greyer and more smoke-laden, the fogs more frequent.

[*To face p.* 258.

THE FONT, BY BIRD

CHAPTER XXIV

THE TREATMENT OF WREN

In the latter years of the long period of building, Wren met with opposition and injustice at the hands of an altered and dwindled committee. Bishop Compton lived to see the completion, but was too old for an active share in deliberation; Sherlock also died at a great age, in 1707. Evelyn was dead. The active Commissioners shrank to six or seven; the Dean, one of the Residentiaries, and the civilians from Doctors' Commons. The ruling spirits were Dr. Battesworth, Dean of the Arches; Sir Thomas Meeres, Queen's Advocate; Dr. Nathaniel Lloyd, Dr. Harwood and one other.

After the initial struggle between the forms of a Greek and Latin cross as a model for the building, but at a long interval, came the question of the organ-screen with the organ on the top, cutting off the choir from the greater part of the Church, and confining the space for worship to accommodation for only three or four hundred persons. Wren's urgent opposition to this was abundantly justified by the removal of the whole screen in 1870, and the erection of the organ in two parts above the stalls of the dignitaries. The next vexatious action was placing the decoration of the dome, contrary to Wren's judgment, in the hands of Sir James Thornhill.

Worse was to come. There had been some murmurs in Parliament at the slow progress of the Cathedral. "There seems to have been a notion that a vast building like St. Paul's, with all its accessories, all its countless details, all its infinite variety of exterior and interior ornamentation, its works of all kinds, and of every kind of material, might be finished off like an elegant Italian villa, or a small church, like St. Stephen's, Walbrook. However this may be, a clause had crept into an Act of Parliament that, until the work should be finished, half his salary should be withheld from the surveyor. The Commissioners proceeded at once to carry this hard clause into effect. This was not only a hardship, but a tacit imputation that the architect was delaying the completion of the work for his own emolument. It is indeed stated plainly in one of the Commissioners' papers that Sir Christopher, or some employed by him, who, by many affidavits, have been proved guilty of great corruption, may be supposed to have found their advantage in this delay. Wren presented a petition to the Queen, 'beseeching Her Majesty to interpose her royal authority, so that he may be suffered to finish the said building in such a manner and after such designs as shall be approved by your Majesty, or such persons as your Majesty shall be pleased to appoint for that purpose.' Wren addressed also the Archbishop of Canterbury and the Bishop of London. These petitions stated two of the points in dispute: the painting of the cupola and the enclosure of the exterior by high, stiff, disfiguring railings."[1]

Wren's appeal was submitted to the Attorney-General, Sir E. Northey, who acknowledged the case to be hard, but considered the Act to be explicit. Wren accordingly petitioned the House of Commons: "Wherefore (he wrote) that honourable and august assembly so considered the case, and were so well satisfied with the justice and reasonableness of it, as to declare the Church to be finished so far as may be required to be performed and done by him as Surveyor-General." The salary was to be paid up to a specified date.

In the year 1712, the dispute was embittered. A virulent

[1] Milman's *Annals*, p. 437.

pamphlet appeared, " Frauds and abuses at St. Paul's, in a letter to a Member of Parliament." It took the side of the Chapter and the Commissioners, and was obviously aimed at Wren, though the persons attacked by name were the foreman of the carpenters, Jennings, and the head superintendent, Bateman. In 1713, Wren himself replied, " stood by his officers, and fully justified their proceedings. His case, to his friends, it should seem to the public of the day, as it has seemed to later inquirers, came off triumphant."[1] Wren complained of the dissolution of the old Commission of twenty-eight persons; the new one was cut down to fifteen: the two Archbishops, the Bishop of London, the Dean (no Residentiaries), the Lord Mayor, the Attorney-General and certain great Officers of State.

With the accession of George I. there came a new Parliament and yet another Commission. Milman expresses himself with just indignation about their proceedings: " that they should presume to dictate to the architect, and such an architect, on matters purely architectural; that they should conceive that they could finish Wren's glorious building better than Wren himself; that they should issue their peremptory mandate, giving Wren but a fortnight for consideration and reply to their dictates, is scarcely to be credited except from their own words."[2] " I have considered," writes Wren, " the resolution of the honourable Commissioners for adorning St. Paul's Cathedral, dated October 15, 1717, and brought to me on the 21st, importing that a balustrade of stone be set up on the top of the Church, unless Sir Christopher Wren do, in writing under his own hand, set forth that it is contrary to the principles of architecture, and give his opinion in a fortnight's time; and if he doth not, then the resolution of a balustrade is to be proceeded with." (The reply is dated on the 28th): " In observance of this resolution, I take leave to declare I never designed a balustrade. Persons of

[1] Milman's *Annals*, p. 440.   [2] *Ibid.*, p. 442.

little skill in architecture did expect, I believe, to see something they had been used to in Gothic structures, and ladies think nothing well without an edging. I should gladly have complied with the vulgar taste, but I suspended for the reasons following." After giving his reasons he continues: "I am further to observe, that there is already over the entablature a proper plinth, which regularly terminates the building, and, as no provisions were originally made for a balustrade, the setting up one in such a confused manner over the plinth, must apparently break into the harmony of the whole machine, and in this particular case be contrary to the principles of architecture." Nevertheless, the balustrade was made, and is still in position.

Last came the crowning act. "It can hardly have been without the sanction, if not through the direct influence of the Commissioners, that, the following year, Wren, in the eighty-sixth year of his age, the forty-ninth of his office, being still in possession of his wonderful faculties, was ignominiously dismissed from his office of Surveyor of Public Works. The appointment of his successor was attributed to German intrigue."[1]

"Benson, unhappily for him set over the head of Wren, paid dearly for his two acts of presumption—the occupation of the office of Wren, the inscription of his own name on Milton's monument in Westminster Abbey. Instead of his rightful obscurity during life, and utter oblivion after death, he lives and has obtained an infamous immortality in Pope's lines, which appear with variations in the *Dunciad*—

"'Benson, sole judge of architecture sit,
And namby-pamby be preferred to wit.'

"The later version is—

"'On poets' tombs see Benson's titles writ,
Lo! Ambrose Phillips is preferred for wit.'

"Benson indeed was not only held up to merited ridicule

[1] Milman's *Annals*, p. 443.

by the satirist, he had to undergo an humilation no doubt far more galling to so presumptuous a man. He was publicly convicted of ignorance and incapacity. He was called on to survey the House of Lords, and made a report that the House and the Painted Chamber were in danger of falling. The prudent peers demanded further inquiry. The result was an address to the Crown to remove and prosecute Benson. The King's gracious answer was, that he should be removed and prosecuted according to law. It might be thought that the Lords would have arraigned more justly those who appointed a man so incompetent to such an office, rather than the man himself for his incompetency. But Benson had influence enough to obtain a grant of Whitehall Wharf, worth £1500 per annum, the assignment of a Crown debt in Ireland, and the reversion of another lucrative place." [1]

"He (Wren) then betook himself to a country retirement (a house at Hampton Court), saying only with the Stoic, 'Nunc me jubet fortuna expeditius philosophari' (Now fortune bids me study philosophy more unhindered)." "Free from worldly cares, he passed the greatest part of the five last following years of his life (he lived to ninety-two) in contemplation and studies, and principally in the consolation of the Holy Scriptures, cheerful in solitude, and well pleased to die in the shade as in the light." [2]

"The beginning and completion of St. Paul's by Sir Christopher Wren are a fabric and an event which, we cannot wonder, left such an impression of content on the mind of the good old man that, being carried to see it once a year, it seemed to recall a memory which was almost deadened to every other use." [3]

Wren was sketched by Steele in the *Tatler* under the name of Nestor: "Nestor in Athens was an unhappy instance of this truth, for he was not only in his profession

[1] Milman's *Annals*, p. 444; Chalmers' *Dictionary:* "Benson."
[2] *Parentalia*.   [3] Horace Walpole.

the greatest man of our age, but had given more proofs of it than any man ever did; yet from want of that natural freedom and audacity which is necessary in commerce with men, his personal modesty overthrew all his public actions. Nestor was in those days a skilful architect, and in a manner the inventor of the use of mechanic powers, which he brought to so great perfection, that he knew to an atom what foundation would bear such a superstructure; and they record of him that he was so prodigiously exact that, for the experiment's sake, he built an edifice of great beauty and seeming strength; but contrived so as to bear only its own weight, and not to admit the addition of the least particle. This building was beheld with much admiration by the virtuosi of the time; but fell down with no other pressure but the setting of a wren upon the top of it. Yet Nestor's modesty was such, that his art and skill were soon disregarded for want of that manner, with which men of the world support and assert the merit of their own performances. Soon after this instance of his art, Athens was, by the treachery of her enemies, burned to the ground. This gave Nestor the greatest occasion that ever builder had to render his name immortal, and his person venerable; for all the new city arose according to his disposition, and all the monuments of the glories and distresses of that people were erected by that sole artist. Nay, all the temples, as well as their houses, were the effects of his study and labour; insomuch that it was said by an old sage, 'Surely Nestor will now be famous, for the habitations of gods as well as men are built by his contrivance.' But this bashful quality still put a damp upon his great knowledge, which has as fatal an effect upon men's reputations as poverty, for as it is said, 'The poor man saved the city, and the poor man's labour was forgot,' so here we find the modest man built the city, and the modest man's skill was unknown." [1]

[1] *Tatler*, No. 52, quoted by Milman.

THE WHISPERING GALLERY   [*To face p.* 264.

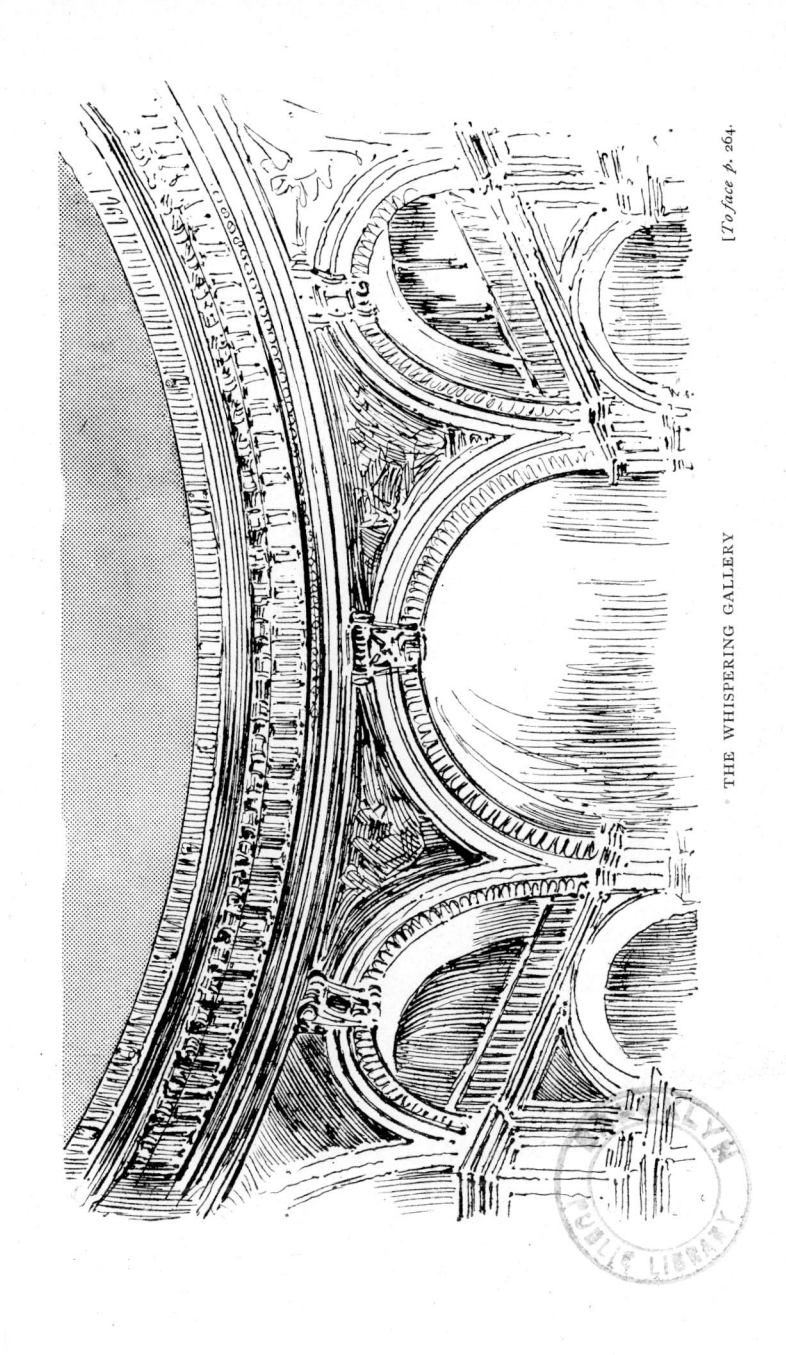

CHAPTER XXV

SIR CHRISTOPHER WREN

WREN was born (probably) on October 20, 1632, at East Knoyle, Wilts, of which his father Christopher was rector, afterwards becoming Dean of Windsor. His mother was Mary Cox, of Fonthill Abbey, in the same county. His uncle was Dr. Matthew Wren, Bishop of Ely; his grandfather, Francis Wren, citizen and mercer of London; his grandfather's grandfather, William Wren, of Sherborn House, Durham, who died between 1527 and 1539. The family were staunch Royalists, and Bishop Wren suffered eighteen years' imprisonment for his opinions; Wren, at the age of nine (1641), was entered at Westminster School, under the uncompromising Royalist Dr. Busby. While at school, he invented an astronomical instrument which came into general use. It was in the time of the Civil Wars, the home at Windsor was twice rifled, and the Dean at last ejected. During the three years that passed between leaving school and going up to Oxford, Wren studied mathematics in London under a famous physician, Sir Charles Scarborough, ejected from his fellowship at Caius College, Cambridge. In 1649-50 Wren entered as a Gentleman-Commoner at Wadham College, Oxford, under Dr. Wilkins, the Parliamentary Warden, to whom cavaliers gladly sent their sons, as he strove to be tolerant. Wren continued his mathematical studies as well as his love of ingenious inventions. In July 1654, John Evelyn records, during a visit to Oxford, that he " visited that miracle of a youth, Mr. Christopher Wren, nephew of the Bishop of Ely," who had recently been made a Fellow of All Souls.

In 1657, when only twenty-four, he was offered the Professorship of Astronomy at Gresham College, London, which he modestly declined at first on account of his youth, but was afterwards persuaded to accept. In 1661, the year after the Restoration, Wren resigned his Gresham chair, where his lectures had after Cromwell's death been interrupted by the fact that soldiers were quartered there, and was appointed Savilian Professor of Astronomy at Oxford, in succession to his friend Seth Ward, just made Bishop of Salisbury. The fame of the lunar globe which he now constructed came to the ears of Charles II. and Wren was invited to present it to the King in person at Whitehall. An informal association which Wren and his friends had gathered round Gresham College led to the foundation of the Royal Society by Charter on July 15, 1662. In the same year Isaac Barrow, succeeding to the Gresham Chair of Astronomy, paid the following tribute to Wren in his inaugural oration: "One there is whose name common gratitude forbids me to pass over, whom I know not whether most to admire for his divine genius or for the sweetness of his disposition (though this I dare assert that no one's promise ever raised such hopes whose performance so little disappointed), once a prodigy of a boy, now a miracle of a man; and, lest I seem to exaggerate, it will suffice I name the great and good Christopher Wren, of whom I will say no more, since his merit attracts the eyes of the whole world, and is known best of all to you, so that his fame is diminished rather than enhanced by praises by which I may chance to offend the modesty of a living man, and, in dealing with so great a subject, but display my own shortcoming." In the same year, on Charles II.'s marriage with Catherine of Braganza, the King asked Wren to survey and report on the condition of the harbour and fortifications of Tangier (then in so ruinous a condition as to invite inroads by the Moors), which formed part of the dowry of the new Queen. Wren excused himself on the score of health, when the King appointed him assistant to the Surveyor-General, Sir John Denham, who held the office in succession to Inigo Jones, and was, as Evelyn said, more of a poet than an architect. It was also in 1662 that Archbishop Sheldon, in order to free the University Church at Oxford from the secular parts of the academical arrangements, determined to spend £16,000 on the erection of the Sheldonian Theatre, and asked Wren for plans. Bishop Wren had already asked him to design a door at Ely Cathedral, and a chapel at Pembroke College, Oxford (finished in 1665). In the same year, 1662, on the invitation of the Dean and Chapter, he undertook to survey St. Paul's Cathedral.

In 1665, the chief year of the plague, when all places of assembly were closed, and Parliament did not meet, Wren availed himself of an introduction to Henry Jermyn, Earl of St. Albans, British Ambassador at Paris, to visit that city, in the splendid times of Louis XIV., where he found the Louvre in process of completion, and Versailles being built.

On his return at the end of February 1666, he presented his report on St. Paul's, about May 1, to the Dean and Chapter; an account of this has been given already. He was then only thirty-three years of age. Then came the Great Fire, and the years of discussion as to what was to be done.

In 1668, he began a new chapel and Italian cloister for Emmanuel College, Cambridge, of which Sancroft, Dean of St. Paul's, had been master. The Sheldonian Theatre was opened in 1669; Wren's new buildings at Trinity College, Oxford, in 1668. Temple Bar was undertaken in 1670, and completed in two years; it was taken down in 1878, on account of the increasing traffic, and re-erected at Theobald's Park, Herts. Between 1671 and 1677 was built the monument to commemorate the spot where the Great Fire first broke out; the brass flaming ornament on the top is not Wren's.

Between 1673–79 he built the magnificent library and

cloister at Trinity College, Cambridge, at the request of his friend Dr. Isaac Barrow, who had become master; and about the same time the Honeywood Library at Lincoln Cathedral, on the ruined side of a Gothic cloister.

On December 7, 1669, Wren had married Faith, daughter of Sir John Coghill, of Bletchingdon, Oxford, the village of which Susan Wren's husband, W. Holder, was rector, and where Dean Wren had died. The issue of this marriage, Christopher, compiled an incomplete chronology of his father's life, and the materials for the *Parentalia* published by Stephen, the architect's grandson. In 1672, Wren was knighted, and in 1675 his first wife died; in the following year, at the Chapel Royal, St. James's, he married Jane FitzWilliams, daughter of Lord Lifford. The second Lady Wren had two children, Jane born in 1677, and William in 1679; she died in giving him birth. William survived his father; Jane, during her short life of twenty-six years, was her father's constant companion, and was buried twenty years before him in the crypt of St. Paul's; the inscription on her monument records the sweetness of her disposition, and her skill in music.

In 1675, came Greenwich Observatory; between 1680–86, the Royal Hospital, Kilmainham, Dublin, which was projected for disabled soldiers by Lord Granard, the Commander-in-Chief in Ireland, and supported by the Duke of Ormonde; and between 1682–92, for a like purpose rose the stately fabric of Chelsea Hospital. Charles II. had granted the property of old Chelsea College to the Royal Society when homeless through the Great Fire, and Wren now suggested to Sir Stephen Fox, who proposed to get an asylum for old soldiers established in London, that the estate should be sold back to the Government with that object. Between 1683 and 1685, splendid plans were made for a Royal Palace at Winchester, and the building was begun; but it was neglected after Charles II.'s death, and finally turned into barracks.

SIR CHRISTOPHER WREN 269

With regard to his domestic architecture, Wren's modesty prevented him from preserving plans and records, and accordingly it is difficult to determine what is his work. The finest and most characteristic country house remaining is Belton Hall, Grantham (1685-9); there were also Bishop's Hostel, Cambridge (1670); Mercers' Hall, Cheapside (1670, re-erected at Swanage in 1882); Brewers' Hall (1670); Arbury House (1674, the stables only now remaining); King's Bench Walk, Temple (1678); Fawley Court, near Henley (1684); Kensington Palace (1690-1706); Appleby School, Leicestershire (1693); Morden College, Kent (1695); Marlborough House (1698); and the Orangery at Kensington (1704-6).

Of a different class were the Ashmolean Museum, Oxford (1681-3); the Great Schoolroom at Winchester College (1684); the Guildhall at Rochester (1687); and the Town Hall at Windsor (1688).

It is impossible in a brief summary to describe his numerous churches. They come in a long and striking list: St. Mary-le-Bow, Cheapside (1671-3, the beautiful steeple in 1680); St. Mary-at-Hill (1672-7); St. Michael, Cornhill (1672, the tower in 1721); St. Stephen's, Walbrook (1672-9, the tower in 1681); St. Benet, Fink (1673-6, destroyed in 1843 for the new Royal Exchange); St. Olave Jewry (1673-6, destroyed in 1887 under the Union of City Benefices Act); St. Dionis, Backchurch (1674, destroyed in 1876 under the same Act); St. George, Botolph Lane (1674-7, destroyed in 1905 under the same Act); St. Michael, Wood Street (1675, destroyed under the same Act); St. Magnus, London Bridge (1676, the steeple in 1705); Ingestre Parish Church (1676); St. Mildred's Poultry (1676-7, destroyed in 1872 under the Act); St. Stephen, Coleman Street (1676); St. Lawrence, Jewry (1676); St. James, Garlickhithe (1677-83); St. Nicholas, Cole Abbey (1677); St. Michael, Queenhithe (1677, destroyed in 1876 under the Act); St. Mary, Aldermanbury (1677); St. Swithin, London Stone (1678-9); St. Michael, Bassishaw (1678-9, destroyed under the Act); St. Bartholomew, Exchange (removed in 1841 to Moorfields, to make way for the Sun Fire Office, and finally destroyed under the Act); St. Anne and St. Agnes, Aldersgate (1679-80); St. Clement Danes, Strand (1680, steeple by Wren's pupil Gibbs, 1719); All Hallows, Bread Street (1681-4, destroyed under the Act); St. Peter, Cornhill (1681-2); St. Antholin, Watling Street (1682, destroyed in 1875 under the Act); St. Mary, Aldermary (1682, tower rebuilt 1711); St. James, Piccadilly (1683, the tower was not Wren's); St. Mildred, Bread Street (1683); St. Augustine and St. Faith, Watling Street (1683, spire in 1695); St. Clement, Eastcheap (1683-6); All Hallows the Great, Upper Thames Street (1683, destroyed in 1896 under the Act); St. Benet, Paul's Wharf (1683-4, now the Welsh Church); St. Martin, Ludgate Hill (1684-5); St. Alban, Wood Street (1685); St. Mary Magdalen, Knightrider Street (1685, injured by fire in 1886 and removed); St. Benet, Gracechurch Street (1685, destroyed in 1867 under the Act); St. Matthew, Friday Street (1685, destroyed in 1886 under the Act); St. Mary, Abchurch (1686); St. Margaret Pattens, Eastcheap (1687); St. Andrew, Holborn (1687); St. Michael, Crooked Lane (1688, destroyed in 1831 for an approach to new London Bridge); St. Edmund King and Martyr, Lombard Street (1689-90); St. Margaret, Lothbury (1690); St. Andrew by the Wardrobe (1692); All Hallows, Lombard Street (1693); Chapel of Trinity College, Oxford (1691-4); St. Michael Royal, College Hill (1694); tower of St. Mary's Church, Warwick (1695); St. Vedast, Foster Lane (1695); St. Mary Somerset, Thames Street (1695, destroyed in 1872 under the Act, the tower left standing); spire of St. Dunstan-in-the-East (1698-9); St. Bride's steeple (1700); and All Saints, Isleworth (1701-5).

Of his Gothic work, the best-known specimen is Tom

Tower, Christ Church, Oxford (1681–2). The church of St. Mary, Aldermary, is rich and beautiful; the towers of St. Michael, Cornhill, St. Dunstan-in-the-East, and St. Alban, Wood Street, are interesting examples.

The noblest of his secular works are Hampton Court Palace and Greenwich Hospital.

Wren's troubles have been detailed in another chapter. His death was one of entire peace. "Once a year it was Wren's custom to drive to St. Paul's and spend some time sitting under the dome he had built; and on one of these occasions he caught cold. Having returned to his house at Hampton Court, he had been dining in the bow-windowed room of the ground floor, when his servant, wondering at his lingering so long, found him dead in his chair, his features in no way disturbed, having apparently passed away in his sleep. So, on February 25, 1723, died Christopher Wren, and was laid to rest a few days later, near his daughter in the crypt of St. Paul's. For nearly a century and a half there was no memorial to Sir Christopher Wren in the great Cathedral of his building, and the famous epitaph—

SUBTUS CONDITUR HUJUS ECCLESIÆ ET URBIS CONDITOR CHRISTOPHORUS WREN QUI VIXIT ANNOS ULTRA NONAGINTA, NON SIBI, SED BONO PUBLICO. LECTOR, SI MONUMENTUM REQUIRIS, CIRCUMSPICE,

(Underneath lies buried the builder of this Church and City, Christopher Wren, who lived more than ninety years, not for himself, but for the public good. Reader if you ask for a monument, look round),

the composition of his son, was but inscribed on the plain tablet which marks his burial-place in the crypt. Now, at last, it has a worthy place above the door of the north transept."[1]

[1] *Sir Christopher Wren*, by Lena Milman, p. 297.

272 MEMORIALS OF ST. PAUL'S CATHEDRAL

THE TOMB OF WREN

CHAPTER XXVI

IN THE DAYS OF WILLIAM III., MARY AND ANNE

HENRY COMPTON, who held the See of London thirty-eight years (1675-1713), was sixth son of Spencer Compton, second Earl of Northampton, one of the most heroic of the Cavalier commanders, who fell at the Battle of Hopton Heath, near Stafford, in 1642-3. Henry's brother, the third earl, was also a Royalist leader, and at the entry of Charles II. into London led a band of two hundred mounted gentlemen arrayed in grey and blue. Another brother, Sir Charles, was famous for the surprise of Beeston Castle; the third, Sir William, was also a Cavalier leader; the fourth, Sir Spencer, accompanied Charles II. into exile; the fifth, Sir Francis, became a general after the Restoration. The grandfather, the first earl, married the daughter and heiress of Sir John Spencer, Lord Mayor of London. "Compton was not famous for intense piety or profound learning, but was a fine example of the high-born, high-minded prelate, who, blameless in life, sustained the authority of his office with simple dignity, performed all its duties with quiet industry, trod his arduous path not without prudence, but with conscientious courage, never wantonly defying, but encountering the King's aggressions with resolute firmness."[1] On April 17, 1673, Evelyn heard a sermon from him at Court: "Dr. Compton, brother to the Earl of Northampton, preached on 1 Cor. 11-16, showing the Church's power in ordaining things indifferent; this worthy person's talent is not preaching, but he is like to make a

[1] Milman's *Annals*, p. 411.

grave and serious good man." In another place in his *Diary* (September 3, 1676), he says: "The Bishop had once been a soldier (he was a Cornet in Lord Oxford's Regiment of Guards), had also travelled in Italy, and became a most sober, grave and excellent prelate." He was originally of Queen's College, Oxford, afterwards Master of Arts of Cambridge, and incorporated in the same degree at Oxford in 1666. He became Canon of Christ Church, Master of St. Cross's Hospital, near Winchester, Doctor of Divinity 1669, Bishop of Oxford 1674 and Bishop of London December 18, 1675. He had been entrusted with the religious education of the two future Queens, Mary and Anne, the daughters of James, Duke of York. In 1685 he seconded William, Earl of Devonshire, in his proposal to take into full consideration the speech of James II., in which he had avowed his determination to protect his Roman Catholic officers from the Test Act, and was in consequence deposed by the King from his office of Dean of the Chapel Royal; and his name was struck out of the list of Privy Councillors. Later on in the year James forbade the clergy to touch on controversy in their sermons. The spirit of the whole order rose against this attempted despotism, and amongst others, Sharp, Dean of Norwich and Rector of St. Giles's-in-the-Fields, preached a strong sermon against the Roman faith. Compton received orders from James's minister, Sunderland, to suspend Sharp. He represented to the King the difficulty of such a proceeding in the existing temper of the country, and at the same time asked Sharp not to appear in his pulpit for a time. James at once created a new Court of High Commission, to which the whole Church of England was subjected; it consisted of seven members, of whom Jeffreys, the Lord Chancellor, was the chief. Compton was ordered before this illegal tribunal, rudely and brutally browbeaten by Jeffreys, and suspended from all spiritual functions, the charge of his diocese being committed to two of his judges, Crewe, Bishop of Durham, and

Sprat of Rochester. He continued to live at Fulham Palace, and to receive his revenues. It was during this retirement that he planted those noble trees in the grounds at Fulham, of which a few still remain, but which about thirty years ago were still in the glory of a splendid old age. As he was still suspended, he did not take part in the remonstrance of Archbishop Sancroft and his six colleagues against the Declaration of Indulgence in 1688; but in the medal which was afterwards struck his head occupies the centre of one side (as he had always suffered for his courage), with those of the six Bishops round him, while the Primate's effigy occupies the obverse. With Shrewsbury, Devonshire, Danby, Lumley, Russell and Sidney he signed the invitation to the Prince of Orange. When the Princess Anne fled from her father her hackney-coach was guarded by the Earl of Dorset and the Bishop of London. The first night she spent in the Bishop's Palace in Aldersgate Street. Next morning they rode to Dorset's house in Epping Forest. Equally unsafe if they remained there, or attempted to join the Prince of Orange at Salisbury, they took refuge with the northern insurgents. To ensure the safety of his royal pupil, the Bishop for the moment put off his episcopal costume, and resumed that of his youth in the Life Guards, riding before the carriage in a buff coat and jack-boots, with a sword at his side and pistols in his holsters. Arriving at Nottingham, he consented to act as colonel to the troop of gentlemen who mustered round the Princess. It was uncanonical; but the liberties of England, civil and religious, were at stake, and every leader was of moment.

On the entry of William into London, Compton welcomed him at the head of the London clergy, who were followed by a hundred Nonconformist ministers. When the Comprehension Bill was under discussion Compton was its zealous supporter. It was Compton who crowned William and Mary; the Primate Sancroft had taken the lead of the nonjuring party, and retired to an estate in Suffolk. When the Primacy became vacant in 1691 Compton fully expected it; but it was felt that at such a crisis a leading theologian was needed; and it was given to Tillotson, the gentle and learned Dean of St. Paul's, formerly Dean of Canterbury, who in 1689 had succeeded Stillingfleet when the latter was made Bishop of Worcester. "Tillotson was a man of acknowledged learning; he was the most popular preacher of his day. He was endeared to the Whigs by his connection with the martyr of their party: he had attended Lord Russell at his death; he had been the comforter, the spiritual adviser of his incomparable wife. No one could fulfil more entirely the apostolic precept, 'Let your moderation be known unto all men.'"[1] Compton was at first mortified and disappointed, and showed coldness; but he was not unforgiving, and Birch, in his *Life of Tillotson*, shows that the intercourse between them at Lambeth was friendly. In 1691 Compton, with Norfolk, Ormond, Devonshire, Dorset, Portland, Monmouth and others, attended William on his first visit as King of England to Holland, when a Congress took place at the Hague, and further preparations were made for the war with France.

The Peace of Ryswick was signed in September 1697. On the 16th November King William made his triumphant entry into London from Margate and Greenwich, passing by the new Cathedral, which was surrounded by three regiments of Londoners, and at the east end of which were drawn up the boys of Christ's Hospital. December 2 was appointed to be the day of national thanksgiving for the peace. "The Chapter of St. Paul's resolved that on that day their new Cathedral, which had long been slowly rising on the ruins of a succession of pagan and Christian temples, should be opened for public worship. William announced his intention of being one of the congregation. But it was represented to him that if he

[1] Milman's *Annals*, p. 416.

persisted in that intention, three hundred thousand people would assemble to see him pass, and all the parish churches of London would be left empty. He therefore attended the service in his own chapel at Whitehall, and heard Burnet preach a sermon somewhat too eulogistic for the gravity of the pulpit. At St. Paul's the magistrates of the City appeared in all their state. Compton was, for the first time, seated on a throne rich with the sculpture of Gibbons. When the prayers were over, the Bishop exhorted the numerous and splendid assembly. His discourse has not been preserved, but its purport may be easily guessed; for he took for his text that noble song: 'I was glad when they said unto me, Let us go into the house of the Lord.' . . . Throughout London, and in every part of the realm, even to the remotest parishes of Cumberland and Cornwall, the churches were filled on the morning of that day; and the evening was an evening of festivity."[1] St. Paul's must indeed have presented an appearance of wonderful beauty, clean and fair in all the freshness of the stone from Portland. No consecration was needed, for the building stood on the hallowed ground of the superb cathedral of past ages.

In the glorious reign of Anne, the services of special thanksgiving were numerous. Year after year she went in solemn procession to commemorate brilliant victories; seven times she fulfilled this welcome duty; from the eighth she was only prevented from being present in person by increasing bodily infirmity. Blenheim, Gibraltar, Ramillies, Majorca, Minorca, Oudenarde, Malplaquet and the rest made indeed a glowing record for a reign of twelve years. The first was on November 12, in Anne's first year. Milman quotes a full description of it from the contemporary records, as it was the model for so many others. It was "for the success of John, Earl of Marlborough, in the Low Countries, and for the destruction of the Spanish fleet in

[1] Macaulay's *History*, vol. iv. p. 809.

the Port of Vigo by the Duke of Ormonde and Sir George Rooke; 'burning, sinking, and taking many ships of war, and great riches of their enemies.' The Council declared that the Cathedral being for that day the Queen's Chapel Royal, the seats were to be disposed of, and all the arrangements made by the Lord Chamberlain. The Queen's throne was 'exactly as in the House of Lords,' about three feet higher than the floor of the choir, covered with a Persian carpet, and a canopy upheld by iron rods fastened to the organ-loft above, fifteen feet high; 'with an armed-chair on the throne, with a faldstool before it, and a desk for the Queen's book covered with crimson velvet, richly embroidered and fringed with gold, with a cushion thereon of the same. Some distance behind were stools for the Countess of Marlborough, Groom of the Stole, the Countess of Sunderland, Lady of the Bedchamber-in-waiting. Further behind stood the Vice-Chamberlain, with other Officers of State.' The two Houses of Parliament determined to assist at the ceremony: the Lords, in the area or body of the choir as a House of Lords. The Commons were called over, the Speaker sitting on the seat often occupied by the Bishop of London in the middle of the south side of the choir, with the Serjeant-at-Arms and officers just below him, the members in the stalls and galleries on each side. The Lord Mayor, Sheriffs and Aldermen sat in the furthermost lower galleries towards the altar; foreign ministers and their ladies in the middle gallery on the north side. Compton sat in his official seat at the south-east end of the choir; the Dean, Canons and Prebendaries on chairs within the rails of the altar; the choirs (Chapels Royal and others) and their music in the upper galleries on each side of the organ.

"In the procession to the Cathedral the House of Commons led the way. At eight o'clock they proceeded to St. James's Palace, then along Pall Mall, and so to the Cathedral. The Lords met at ten; the procession, prethe forcing of the French lines at Tirlemont by the Duke of Marlborough; the sermon was by Dr. Willis, Dean of Lincoln.

On July 1, 1706, the thanksgiving was for the Battle of Ramillies, and for Peterborough's successes in Catalonia; the preacher was Stanhope, Dean of Canterbury.

At the national service on January 1, 1707, for fresh success, the preacher was the Bishop of Salisbury; at that in May of the same year the Bishop of Oxford.

On August 23, 1708, the national gratitude was expressed for the victory of Oudenarde; the preacher was the Bishop of St. Asaph.

On July 7, 1713, thanks were returned for the Peace of Utrecht, both Houses of Parliament attending in full state. This was six months before the death of Anne, and she was already too unwell to be present in person. It was on this day that the children of the newly formed Charity Schools first made a feature in the streets. In 1698 had been founded the Society for Promoting Christian Knowledge; and under its auspices these Charity Schools began to spring up everywhere. In about eight years five hundred were established. In many of these schools the children were clothed and fed, as well as taught. Special care was given to their religious instruction. They became famous on the Continent, and accounts of them, translated into German, led to the formation of similar institutions in Germany and Switzerland. Later on, the Charity children in London had an annual service under the dome of St. Paul's, which was not discontinued till the rearrangement of the choir enabled daily service to be held in that vast area, a practice which not even the wooden galleries for the Charity children could be allowed to disturb.

In the year 1710, Sir Christopher Wren, perhaps in person (as seems implied by the Wren MS.), perhaps by the hands of his son, with Mr. Edward Strong in attendance, the mason who had executed the whole work from the ceded by the officers of the House, consisted of Masters in Chancery, Judges, Peers under age, then Barons, Bishops, and the other nobles according to rank; then the great Officers of State, the Archbishops, and Sir Nathan Wright, Keeper of the Great Seal. All the while till the arrival of the Queen the organ continued playing voluntaries. At eleven the Queen took coach at St. James's; at Temple Bar she was received, according to custom, by the Lord Mayor, Sheriffs and Aldermen on horseback. The Lord Mayor presented the sword with a short speech; the Queen returned it, and the Lord Mayor bore it before her to the Cathedral. On her arrival at the west door the Queen was met by the peers and principal officers of state, and conducted up the nave to her throne. She knelt at her faldstool, and after a short ejaculation rose and seated herself. The music ceased. Dr. Stanley, Residentiary, read the first part of the service, after which the *Te Deum* was sung with vocal and instrumental music. The old Whig Bishop of Exeter, Sir Jonathan Trelawney, one of the Seven in the Tower, preached an 'excellent' sermon on Joshua xxiii. 9: 'But as for you, no man hath been able to stand before you unto this day.' It lasted about half-an-hour; then came the anthem, prayers and benediction. The Queen led the way back; and the Tower guns, those on the river and those in St. James's Park, were fired three times. Such was the model and precedent for royal processions and receptions at St. Paul's in the eighteenth century."

The second thanksgiving was on September 7, 1704, to celebrate the victory of Blenheim. Parliament was not sitting, but the Peers, Privy Councillors, and great Officers of State were in attendance. There was full service, with ante-communion. The preacher was the Dean of St. Paul's, Sherlock, the text Ps. lviii. 11: "Doubtless there is a God that judgeth in the earth."

The third occasion was August 27, 1705, commemorating

VIEW FROM THE STONE GALLERY, LOOKING EAST

[*To face p.* 280.

beginning, first as worker, then as master, and the whole body of the Freemasons, of which the great architect was an active member, laid the last and highest stone of the lantern of the cupola, with humble prayers for the divine blessing on the work. Wondering and admiring crowds thronged the streets below. Everywhere around, as far as the eye could see from that great height were the noble evidences of the multiplied achievements of that illustrious genius.

CHAPTER XXVII

THE EIGHTEENTH CENTURY AFTER ANNE

Two Deans of St. Paul's were about this time promoted directly to the Archbishopric of Canterbury: Sancroft in 1677 and Tillotson in 1691. Sancroft had been succeeded by the famous *Edward Stillingfleet*, Rector of St. Andrew's, Holborn; he held with the Deanery the Archdeaconry of London, which had been vacant three years. At the age of twenty-four he published his celebrated *Irenicon*, with a view to peace with the Nonconformists. Twenty years later, in 1682, he wrote his *Unreasonableness of Separation*, a very able work; he was still in favour of some concessions, and wished for a further review of the Prayer Book. He refused to read James II.'s Declaration of Indulgence, and in 1689 was appointed by William III. to the Bishopric of Worcester; on the vacancy at Canterbury, Tillotson strongly advised his appointment to the Primacy. Stillingfleet's controversial writings, his *Origines Sacrae*, his *Antiquities of the British Church*, his criticisms on the philosophy of Locke, were long held to be standard works.

His successor, Tillotson (November 19, 1689—June 12, 1691), held the Deanery too short a time to make his mark in that position, especially as St. Paul's was still unfinished. He "had the ambition of establishing in the weary, worn-out, distracted, perplexed mind and heart of England, a Christianity of calm reason, of plain, practical English good sense."[1] He was the foremost leader of the school of toleration, the most popular preacher of his day, and a master of English prose. The Lower House of Convocation was against any concessions. "When he observed," wrote

[1] Milman's *Annals*, p. 420.

THE EIGHTEENTH CENTURY AFTER ANNE 283

Calamy, "with what resolution the body of them from the very first declared against any alterations, and how they fortified and strengthened their confederacies and combinations, he was convinced that the method he had been for was really impracticable as things then stood, and therefore was not for repeating the dangerous experiment, or having any more to do with Convocations all the while he continued Archbishop."[1] He endeavoured to govern the Church by royal injunctions; and in the disturbed condition of that time, and with such a king as William on the throne, no policy could have been more unfortunate.

The successor of Tillotson in the Deanery of St. Paul's was *Dr. William Sherlock*, Master of the Temple. He had advocated the very highest notions of nonjuring loyalty in his *Case of Resistance*, but having incurred suspension, he changed his mind, and published to the world his reason for doing so in a work called *The Case of Allegiance due to a Sovereign Power*. In this he declared that his acceptance of the *de facto* government was greatly influenced by the publication of the canons passed by the first Convocation of James II., which had lately been made known for the first time by Archbishop Sancroft. In these Sherlock discovered some that were strongly for a government *de facto*. Six Bishops, including the Primate, and about 400 beneficed clergy, were deprived by the operation of the Act on February 1, 1690: to all of these Sherlock would appear a renegade. Macaulay has given a long description of the appointment of Sherlock: "As soon as the name of the new Dean was known, a clamour broke forth such as perhaps no ecclesiastical appointment has ever produced: a clamour made up of yells of hatred, of hisses of contempt, and of shouts of triumphant and half-exulting welcome." The passage is too long for insertion, but part of the source of the uproar must be indicated: "The popular belief (this probably was most galling to the Dean) was that his retractation was the effect of the tears, expostulations and

[1] Calamy's *Autobiography*, p. 210.

reproaches of his wife. The lady's spirit was high; her authority in the family was great; and she cared much more about her house and carriage, the plenty of her table, and the prospects of her children, than about the patriarchal origin of government, or the meaning of the word 'abdication.' She had, it was said, given her husband no peace by day or by night till he had got over his scruples. In letters, fables, songs, dialogues without number, her powers of seduction and intimidation were malignantly extolled. She was Xanthippe pouring water on the head of Socrates. She was Delilah shearing Samson. She was Eve forcing the forbidden fruit into Adam's mouth. She was Job's wife, imploring her ruined lord, who sate scraping himself among the ashes, not to curse and die, but to swear and live."[1]

During the eighteenth century there were eight Bishops of London: Robinson, Gibson, Thomas Sherlock, Hayter, Osbaldeston, Terrick, Lowth and Porteus. Three of these have left a name: Gibson, Thomas Sherlock and Lowth.

John Robinson succeeded Compton in 1713; he had been ambassador at Warsaw, and a plenipotentiary at the Peace of Utrecht. He had held a deanery, and the Bishopric of Bristol.

He was followed in 1723 by *Edmund Gibson*, who held the See a quarter of a century. He will be always remembered as the learned compiler of the vast *Codex Juris Ecclesiastici Anglicani*. He was born at Bampton, in Westmoreland, in 1669, and went up to Queen's College, Oxford, where, at the early age of twenty-two, he distinguished himself by the publication of a valuable edition of the *Saxon Chronicle*. In 1694 came a translation of Camden's *Britannia*, with additions. The same year he was appointed chaplain and librarian to Archbishop Tenison; and, later on, Rector of Lambeth and Archdeacon of Surrey. In the disputes about Convocation he warmly supported the right of the Archbishop to continue to prorogue it. The *Codex* followed in 1713, a work which

[1] Macaulay, iv. 44-50.

THE EIGHTEENTH CENTURY AFTER ANNE 285

discusses more learnedly and comprehensively than any other the legal rights and duties of the English clergy, and the constitutions, canons and articles of the English Church. In 1715 he became Bishop of Lincoln, in 1725 Bishop of London, where, during the long illness of Archbishop Wake, he was practically Primate. A conservative in Church politics, he respected the various forms of dissent, and discouraged all attempts to prevent dissenters from worshipping in the manner and according to the principles which they preferred. He exercised a vigilant oversight over the morals of all ranks and classes of his diocese; and his fearless denunciation of the licentious masquerades which had become highly popular at Court finally lost him the royal favour. In later years he wrote a series of *Pastoral Letters* in defence of "Gospel Revelation," and against "lukewarmness" and "enthusiasm" (excitement), as well as a *Preservative against Popery* in three folio volumes (1738), which is still printed. He died September 6, 1748.

Sherlock's successor as Dean of St. Paul's, *Henry Godolphin*, was uncle by marriage to one of Marlborough's daughters, and brother of the famous minister of William III. and Anne. His name at St. Paul's is marred by his conduct to the illustrious Wren. In 1726 he resigned the Deanery for the Provostship of Eton, where he is remembered as a munificent benefactor. He was succeeded by the tutor of Marlborough's son, *Francis Hare*, who had also been Chaplain-General and Dean of Salisbury, and as Canon-Residentiary of St. Paul's had been equally obnoxious to Wren. Hare is remembered for his witty and sagacious dissuasive from Biblical criticism, which had been censured by Convocation. He became Bishop of St. Asaph, and of Chichester, and was the ancestor of Augustus and Julius Hare, two remarkable clergymen in the nineteenth century.

Joseph Butler, the philosopher, became Dean of St. Paul's in 1740, and held the office for ten years. In 1738 he had been made Bishop of Bristol, the income of which was only £400, so that the See was always held with other preferment.

Butler kept it till he was translated to Durham in 1750. It was in 1736 that he published the *Analogy*, and in 1726 the famous *Fifteen Sermons*, which he had preached at the Rolls Chapel. In 1746 he was made Clerk of the Closet to George II., and in 1747 he received the offer of the Primacy. A nephew, John Butler, a rich bachelor, came up to town prepared to advance £20,000 for the heavy expenses necessary to taking up that exalted and responsible position in Church and State, in first-fruits, tenths, and the furniture and apparatus of so vast a house as Lambeth. Butler, however, who was naturally of a melancholy and desponding disposition, was deeply impressed with the worldliness, viciousness and scepticism of the age: he replied that "it was too late for him to try to support a falling Church." It is unnecessary to say more about him, as his name belongs to English literature and theology.

Gibson was succeeded in the Bishopric of London by *Thomas Sherlock*, son of the former Dean. Born in London, he was educated at Catherine Hall, Cambridge, and in 1704, at the early age of twenty-six, succeeded his father as Master of the Temple. He took a prominent part in the Bangorian controversy against Hoadley, who had impugned the notion of the existence of any visible Church, and scoffed at the maintenance of tests of orthodoxy, and the claims of ecclesiastical government. In 1728 he succeeded him as Bishop of Bangor; was translated to Salisbury in 1734, and to London in 1738. His skill in business and the affairs of his university earned him from Bentley the name of "a little Alberoni." In controversy he was considered powerful against Hoadley, the Deists, Tindal and Woolston. His sermons were long held to be the model of English pulpit eloquence; not merely from his masculine vigour and sustained force, but because, in harmony with the English taste of the age, he aimed at no flights of rhetoric.

Three uneventful episcopates followed: that of *Thomas Hayter* (1761),[1] *Richard Osbaldiston*, of a landed family in

---
[1] Preceptor to George III. and the Duke of York; Bishop of Norwich.

THE EIGHTEENTH CENTURY AFTER ANNE

Yorkshire (1762),[1] *R. Terrick* (1764).[2] *Robert Lowth*, who succeeded, held the See thirteen years; he was a great Hebrew scholar for his day, and master of a Latin style rarely surpassed in purity and elegance. His lectures on Hebrew poetry, as Professor of Poetry at Oxford, are regarded by Milman as making an epoch in Biblical criticism by suggesting how large a part of Biblical language is poetical, and belongs to the metaphors, apologues, and the allegories of the imaginative East. Lowth was also known as the successful combatant with the literary tyrant of the day, Bishop Warburton. His exquisite epitaph on his daughter must once more be quoted :—

> Cara vale, ingenio praestans, pietate, pudore,
> Et plus quam natae nomine, cara vale.
> Cara Maria vale ! at veniet felicius aevum,
> Quando iterum tecum, sim modo dignus, ero.
> Cara redi : laeta tum dicam voce, paternos
> Eja age in amplexus ! cara Maria redi.

Bishop Porteus[3] closes the episcopal list at St. Paul's in the eighteenth century. He held the See from 1787 to 1809. He is described by Milman (who could recollect him) as "a man of no great learning or power, but of singular sweetness of character and amenity of manners, suitable perhaps for the rough and turbulent age in which he lived (the era of the French Revolution)." He was gifted with a voice the beauty of the tones of which could never be forgotten. He also bequeathed to Fulham Palace what is still known as the Porteus Library, which he placed in what had been the chapel, using the hall of the palace for the purposes of worship. Bishop Tait restored the hall, and built a new chapel.

[1] Dean of York, Bishop of Carlisle.
[2] Vicar of Twickenham, Canon of Windsor, Canon of St. Paul's, Bishop of Peterborough.
[3] Bishop of Chester; supported the rising Evangelical party in both his Sees; an early patron of the Church Missionary Society and of the Bible Society.

There were five Deans of St. Paul's during the latter half of the eighteenth century: Secker, Hume, Cornwallis, Thurlow, Pretyman; two of them Primates, three Bishops. *Thomas Secker* (1750-58) was son of a Nonconformist. His writings were respected in his own day, but his history belongs rather to the Archbishops of Canterbury; in 1735 he was Bishop of Bristol; 1737, Bishop of Oxford; and in 1758 Primate. *John Hume* was Dean from 1758-66, and successively Bishop of Bristol, Oxford and Salisbury. *Frederick Cornwallis*, seventh son of Charles fourth Lord Cornwallis, was Dean from 1766 to 1768, Bishop of Lichfield 1749, and became Primate in 1768. Thomas Newton was Dean from 1768 to 1782; he held also the Bishopric of Bristol, which frequently was given with the Deanery, as its stipend was only £400 a year. He was known as the author of a book on the interpretation of Old Testament prophecy, which was never on a critical basis, and is now quite obsolete; he also wrote an amusing autobiography illustrative of the manners and customs of the day, and, amongst other things, of the eagerness for preferment which is characteristic of worldly times, and which has been not unknown in earlier ages. He was a man of letters, accomplished, with a taste for pictures and prints. It was in his day that Sir Joshua Reynolds, and the other members of the Royal Academy, then recently founded, proposed to paint Scriptural pictures for the adornment of St. Paul's. The project was overruled by Bishop Terrick, who was alarmed on Protestant grounds. Even Newton's own suggestion that Sir Joshua and West (his successor in the presidency) should fill two compartments over the doors north and south of the apse was rejected. West was to have painted the " Giving of the Law," Sir Joshua " Christ in the Manger." The latter idea was afterwards utilized by Sir Joshua in his window at New College, Oxford. Newton died at the Deanery in 1782; the monument which he had designed for himself at St. Paul's was rejected by his colleagues, and may be seen at St. Mary-le-Bow in Cheapside.

His successor, *Thomas Thurlow*, was brother of Lord Chancellor Thurlow, and father of the second peer. Amongst other honours, he became Master of the Temple, Dean of Rochester (1775-79), Bishop of Lincoln (1779), Dean of St. Paul's (1782) and Bishop of Durham in 1787. He died in 1791.

He was followed by *Sir George Pretyman-Tomline*, tutor of William Pitt (Dean from 1787 to 1820). He held the Bishopric of Lincoln with the Deanery (consecrated 1787) and resigned the latter on being promoted to Winchester in 1820. Pitt intended him to succeed Archbishop Moore as Primate in 1805, but George III., hearing in the hunting-field of the vacancy, galloped many miles to Windsor to effect the immediate appointment of Manners Sutton, the Dean of Windsor. He insisted on being shown up *incognito* into the Dean's dressing-room, where he was preparing for dinner, and announced his intentions to the astonished dignitary by saying, "What a lot of boots you've got, my Lord Archbishop!"

There was little of a memorable character in St. Paul's during the greater part of the Georgian era. "After the accession of the House of Brunswick, and the procession of George I. to St. Paul's, the royal presence was not vouchsafed for more than seventy years in the Cathedral."[1] George II. never paid it an official visit. On April 25, 1789, there was a solemn procession for George III. to return thanks for his recovery from his grievous illness. "The nation, with whom the sorrows (and virtues) of the King had rendered him highly popular, beheld him, with the Queen, the Prince of Wales, the Duke of York, and others of rank, in royal state, along the streets. There was the usual ceremony at Temple Bar, the Lord Mayor and the civic authorities performing their usual functions.

[1] Milman's *Annals*, p. 473.

The King, followed by his family, drove through the open space, was received at the west door, and conducted up the nave by Bishop Porteus and Dean Pretyman. Both Houses of Parliament were in attendance; the Peers filled the body of the choir, the Commons the stalls. The sermon was preached by the Bishop of London. With the choir were the Charity children (6000), who joined in parts of the service." [1]

"A second time George III. went in procession with all the royal family, December 23, 1797, in thanksgiving for the naval victories. Both Houses of Parliament were present. The distinguishing and imposing part of that ceremonial was the bearing the French, and Spanish, and Dutch flags captured in the several actions. The French flag, taken on June 1 (by Lord Howe in the English Channel), was borne by Admiral Caldwell, with eight admirals and captains—Sir Thomas Pasley, Sir Roger Curtis, Admiral Bazely, Admiral Gambier, Lord Hugh Seymour, Captain Payne, Captain Domett, Captain Elphinstone. Admiral Goodall, with three others—Linzee, Young, Holloway—bore the flag of March 14, 1795. Sir Alan Gardner, with Admiral Hamilton and four others, carried that of June 23, 1795; Sir Charles Thompson that of February 14, 1797; Admiral Waldegrave that of February 18, 1797, at the head of a famous group—Sir Horatio Nelson and six captains. Captain Douglas bore the flag of Admiral Lucas, taken August 17, 1796. Then appeared the Dutch trophies of Camperdown, October 11, 1797: Lord Duncan bearing the flag of De Winter, Sir Richard Onslow that of Admiral Reinjies; ten captains of the fleet followed." [2]

Towards the close of the reign of George I. (1723) came the quiet funeral procession of Sir Christopher Wren, when his remains were laid in the south-east corner of the crypt, beside those of his beloved daughter. Round him are the graves of the great painters and sculptors who

[1] Milman's *Annals*, p. 473. [2] *Ibid.*, p. 474.

have given Artists' Corner at St. Paul's a fame like that of Poets' Corner in Westminster Abbey.

On March 3, 1793, with a procession of nearly one hundred carriages, the body of Sir Joshua Reynolds was conveyed to the Cathedral. The most distinguished peers begged for the honour of being his pall-bearers: the Dukes of Dorset, Leeds and Portland, Marquis Townshend, the Marquis of Abercorn, the Earls of Inchiquin and Upper-Ossory, Viscount Palmerston, Lord Eliot. The colleagues and disciples whose remains in after years were laid to rest in that sacred space will be mentioned in the chapter on the burials and monuments of St. Paul's.

CHAPTER XXVIII

ST. PAUL'S IN THE NINETEENTH CENTURY

AT the beginning of the nineteenth century St. Paul's suffered a grievous loss from thieves, aided, it was feared, though never proved, by accomplices from within. The *Gentleman's Magazine* thus describes the misfortune: "Sunday, December 23, 1810.—This morning the sacrist of St. Paul's Cathedral, on approaching the repository where the sacramental plate is kept, in order to take it to the altar, found the iron door had been double-locked. As his key could only open it when single-locked, he concluded the officer who kept the master-key had done it; he accordingly went to him, and they both repaired to the spot, when, on opening the door, a most affecting scene presented itself. The two large chests had been forced open, and emptied of their valuable contents; a magnificent edition of the Bible and Common Prayer in two volumes, the covers of which were of solid silver, most beautifully chased with Scripture history, was deprived of its ornaments; and the whole of the immense booty, amounting to 1761 ounces, was carried off. The villains seem to have acted with the most cool deliberation. To effect their purpose they had to pass eight doors before they reached the repository; each of these doors they opened, and on their return carefully relocked, excepting the iron door, which they double-locked. The large chests were each secured by two immense padlocks, besides the principal chest-locks; the padlocks they opened, but the locks baffling their exertions, they contrived to force the chests open. The robbery must certainly have been committed on the night of Friday or Saturday, as on the former day the plate was used at an Ordination. The intrinsic value of the plunder is not the only thing to be lamented; as a great part of it was of the most curious antique workmanship, being presents from different Deans and other pious persons, and might be considered as exquisite specimens of the workmanship of the different ages in which they lived, and could not now be executed at less than £2000. Every precaution and means have been taken to discover the depredators, but hitherto without effect."[1]

Malcolm, who wrote in 1803, some years before the robbery, gives a description of the plate—

"The great Bible (1640) with a silver-gilt cover, representing a temple, with Moses and Aaron between the columns, and Jacob's Dream on one side; with the inscription, 'Verbum Domini manet in æternum.' On the other side, Elijah fed by Ravens, with the words, 'Habent Mosen et Prophetas: audiant illos.'

"A most superb silver-gilt and embossed prayer-book, adorned with angels, a Glory, pillars, etc., inscribed: 'Oculi Domini super istos et aures ejus in preces eorum,' and ' Fiant orationes pro omnibus hominibus, pro regibus.'

"Two silver-gilt chalices with patens, embossed with a saint, bearing 'Agnus Dei.'

"A pair of patens.

"Two large silver-gilt plates, the gift of Charles Smith, late Prebendary of St. Paul's and Archdeacon of Colchester. The bottoms of these plates embossed with representations of the Lord's Supper, and the widow giving her mite; the rims with the donor's arms and crest, cherubim and scrolls.

"Two enormous tankards, finely embossed, given by the same.

"A very large silver-gilt plate with the Lord's Supper, cornucopiae and emblematical figures.

[1] *Gentleman's Magazine*, vol. lxxx. pt. ii. p. 655.

"Two large tankards of silver-gilt, very much embossed.

"A large silver-gilt plate.

"A pair of silver-gilt candlesticks, two feet nine inches; a second pair, a little shorter."

Since that time St. Paul's has been presented with a set of gold plate, of the value of about £1500, by Canon Scott Holland.

The Bishops of London in the nineteenth century were eight: John Randolph, William Howley, Charles James Blomfield, Archibald Campbell Tait, John Jackson, Frederick Temple, Mandell Creighton and Arthur Foley Winnington-Ingram.

John Randolph (1809–13) was a distinguished Oxford scholar, Professor of Poetry, Professor of Greek, Professor of Moral Philosophy and of Divinity. He held the Sees successively of Oxford, Bangor and London.

William Howley (1813–28) was Regius Professor of Divinity at Oxford. While at Fulham, he encased the picturesque old garden court, with its red-brick towers and battlements of the time of Henry VI. with plain yellow-brick Georgian walls. In 1828 he was translated to Canterbury and rebuilt a large part of Lambeth Palace in the Gothic of that period. His architect was his brother-in-law, Mr. Belli.

Charles James Blomfield (1829–56) was the son of a schoolmaster at Bury St. Edmund's. He was Fellow of Trinity, Cambridge, held one or two country rectories, and then the important parish of St. Botolph's, Bishopsgate. In 1822 he was Archdeacon of Colchester, in 1824 Bishop of Chester, and after five years was translated to London. He resigned from ill health in 1856, and died next year at Fulham. He was one of the most active Bishops of his day: started funds in various parts of London for building new churches, and consecrated more than two hundred during his tenure of the See. He was the last who received the unrestricted revenue of the Bishopric, and gave more than

£100,000 to the cause of church-building. He was an ardent Church-reformer, and passed the Pluralities Act, which put an end to an old and grievous scandal. He was also mainly instrumental in establishing the Ecclesiastical Commission, which receives and administers the superfluous estates of the Bishoprics and Cathedral Chapters. The incomes of Archbishops, Bishops and Chapters were arranged on a more reasonable scale, and great sums were liberated for founding new parishes, endowing poor churches, and other practical Church objects throughout the country. To speak roughly, the income of the Commissioners is about £1,000,000 a year, two-fifths of which they receive from the old estates of the Bishopric of London and the Chapter of St. Paul's. This reform has been incalculably to the advantage of the Church and country. Bishop Blomfield was the first prelate to appear at Court without the official wig. Sir George Sinclair was a friend both of William IV. and the Bishop: after a visit at Fulham, he was driving off to stay with the King at Windsor, and asked his host if he could convey any message. The Bishop, with a laugh, said that as the weather was so warm he would be glad to be allowed to leave off his wig. The King, with his usual bluff good-humour, settled the question at once; and gradually the Bishops left off the emblem of dignity still worn by judges and barristers. The last Archbishop who wore it was Sumner.

Archibald Campbell Tait (1856–69) was Fellow and Tutor of Balliol College, Oxford, and one of the Four Tutors who protested against Newman's Tract No. XC. He was a man of robust good sense, strong humour and every statesmanlike quality, as well as of the deepest and most earnest piety, and even in the estimation of those who disagreed from his opinions, he was one of the very ablest of the long line of Bishops of London and Primates. He succeeded Arnold as headmaster of Rugby, where he remained seven years, and he was seven years Dean of

Carlisle. In 1850 he was one of the Royal Commission on the University of Oxford; in 1856 he became Bishop of London. He gathered Bishop Blomfield's various church-building associations into one great Bishop of London's Fund for providing for the spiritual wants of the diocese, which has achieved inestimable good, and was in every way an indefatigable leader in the development of Church work in London. He had the full confidence of the laity, and no member of the House of Lords was listened to with deeper attention than he received as Primate. He was translated to Canterbury in 1869, and died in 1883. One of his permanent results must be given in detail: the account is taken from his *Life*, by Benham and Davidson.

"Ever since his consecration in 1856, he had been throwing himself into every kind of open-air and mission preaching. He would go off from the House of Lords to speak to a shipload of emigrants in the docks, from the Convocation discussions on Church discipline to address the Ragged School children in Golden-lane, or the omnibus drivers in their great yard at Islington. He preached to the costermongers in Covent Garden Market, to railway porters from the platform of a locomotive, to a colony of gipsies on the common at Shepherd's Bush, and this without in any way relaxing the accustomed round of Confirmations, sermons and committees which must always occupy a Bishop's time in addition to his huge correspondence. At the same time the impulse came to Lord Shaftesbury and his friends to have Sunday evening services for non-Churchgoers in Exeter Hall, which were attended by vast multitudes. The excitement aroused by the Exeter Hall addresses had the happy result of strengthening Bishop Tait's hands in his determination to secure the opening of Westminster Abbey and St. Paul's Cathedral for Sunday evening services for the people. From the very day of his consecration he had been in communication upon the subject with his friend Dean

Trench, of Westminster, and it was by their joint effort that one by one the many lions in the path were conquered, and at last, on January 3, 1858, the first great Sunday evening service was held in the Abbey in the presence of an overflowing congregation.

"The Westminster difficulties overcome, the Bishop had to face obstacles still graver at St. Paul's. It was at first in vain that he pressed upon the eminent Dean of that day and his colleagues the imperative necessity of utilizing the great space at their command. The impossibilities were endless. 'The want of such services,' wrote the eminent Dean, 'is not felt in the City, where so many churches are available, and it is extremely doubtful whether a sufficient congregation would attend to justify so costly an experiment;' and further, 'there is no fabric fund to provide for the expenses.' The Bishop replied by issuing an appeal for public subscriptions, heading the list himself with a donation of £100. The funds were soon forthcoming, and after further correspondence the space under the dome was at last thrown open to the public on the evening of Advent Sunday, 1858, when the Bishop himself was the preacher. The excitement of the occasion was immense, and Ludgate Hill was for the time completely blocked by the crowd. An hour before the time of service every seat was occupied, and enormous numbers (variously estimated in the newspapers at from 10,000 to 100,000) were turned away for want of room. The services were well attended throughout the winter, and the Bishop exhausted every effort in the endeavour to persuade the Chapter of St. Paul's of fifty years ago to continue them in spring and summer. He promised to make a further appeal for funds, and to undertake, if desired, the entire responsibility of finding preachers for the Sunday evenings, but the Chapter of those days, to his openly expressed disappointment, unanimously declined to accede to his request, and although the services were resumed every winter, it was not till long afterwards that they were maintained throughout the year."

A direct result of the happy innovation of evening services under the dome, was in after days the rearrangement of the chancel. That was in the period of the present Dean, then our reforming Canon. Up till this time there was a heavy oak screen right across the choir, fixed at about a quarter the length of that part of the Cathedral from the dome. On the top of the screen stood the organ. About the year 1858 I visited the Church, and well remember that heavy and gloomy arrangement. All the regular services were conducted behind the screen, and there was only room for 300 or 400 worshippers. Well might Bishop Blomfield stand at the top of Ludgate Hill and exclaim of those times, 'Of what use is that vast and magnificent building?' Under Bishop Tait it was to be altered. In consequence of the extraordinary popularity of the evening services under the dome, it was felt that choir and dome should be drawn as close as possible together. The heavy screen was pulled down, the organ was placed on each side of the chancel arch, instead of the monuments to Captain Cooke, of the *Bellerophon*, and Captain Duff, of the *Mars*, two naval heroes who died at the Battle of Trafalgar, now in the crypt. Nelson himself was moved to the south transept. The choir-stalls were transported from the eastern part of the chancel to the west, so that they should touch the dome, and the singers and clergy should be close to that vast auditory. The Holy Table was brought forward from the end of the aisle to its present position, and curtains were hung behind it, so that the voice of the officiating clergy should not be lost. The whole choir was raised two or three feet from the absolute level on which Wren had constructed it, so that the congregation should be able to see and hear the better.

I have before me the Book of the Special Preachers from 1858 to 1873, compiled by the Dean's verger, from the

ST. PAUL'S IN THE NINETEENTH CENTURY 299

Penny Pulpit. As these services were extra, no record of them was kept by the Chapter. After Bishop Tait followed Dean Milman : Bishop Bickersteth, of Ripon ; Dr. Hook, of Leeds ; Canon Cadman ; Rev. Hampden Gurney ; Canon Dale, of St. Paul's ; Canon Hugh McNeile ; Dr. Vaughan, of Harrow ; Dr. Stanley, afterwards Dean of Westminster ; Bishop Villiers, of Carlisle ; Dr. Goulburn (author of *Personal Religion*) ; Mr. Eyre, of Marylebone ; Bishop Samuel Wilberforce, of Oxford ; Canon Champneys, of St. Paul's ; Canon Miller, of Birmingham ; Dean Alford, of Canterbury ; Dean Harvey Goodwin, of Ely ; Archdeacon Hale, of London ; Canon Boyd, of Cheltenham, afterwards Dean of Exeter ; Archdeacon Sinclair, of Middlesex ; and Bishop Tait himself concluded the first series on Easter Day. Well-known and honoured names, all of them with many associations. How would a list of five months of evening preachers at the present day compare with these?

Amongst other names in succeeding years I see Whewell, Master of Trinity ; Canon Melvill, the modern Chrysostom ; Thomson, afterwards Archbishop of York ; Magee, also afterwards Archbishop of York ; Bishop Waldegrave, of Carlisle ; Sir Emilius Bayley ; Wordsworth, afterwards Bishop of Lincoln ; Woodford, afterwards Bishop of Ely ; Trench, afterwards Archbishop of Dublin ; Moberley, afterwards Bishop of Salisbury ; Fulford, Bishop of Montreal ; Moorhouse, afterwards Bishop of Manchester ; Hugh Stowell ; a young student of Christ Church named Liddon ; Dean Close, Milman, afterwards Bishop of Calcutta ; Howson, Dean of Chester ; Temple, Headmaster of Rugby, and afterwards Bishop of London and Archbishop of Canterbury ; Merivale, Dean of Ely ; Monsell, the Church poet ; Falloon, of Liverpool ; Barry, afterwards Bishop of Sydney ; Alexander, afterwards Archbishop of Armagh ; Gregory, of Lambeth, afterwards Canon and Dean ; Jackson, Bishop of London ; Mansel, Dean of St. Paul's, and many others whom I should like to mention in such a retrospect as this; but I have said enough to show that in those days the evening pulpit commanded the best, the choicest, the most influential names in the whole Church of England. After 1873, when they had lasted fifteen years, the services ceased to be special, and were continued the whole year round.

The great Scotsman was succeeded by a man of deep piety, humble mind, resolute will and sound learning—*John Jackson* (1869–85). After a successful career at Oxford he came into prominence as Rector of St. James's, Piccadilly, where his sermons on personal Christian life attracted many of the most prominent and able men of the day. In 1853 he became Bishop of Lincoln. The great respect in which he was held, and his unhesitating firmness enabled him to rule his dioceses with distinguished success.

Frederic Temple (1885–96), was Fellow and Tutor of Balliol, a Double First-Class-man (his natural bent was mathematical), Headmaster of Rugby, Bishop of Exeter 1869, Archbishop of Canterbury 1896. He was one of those who wrote in *Essays and Reviews,* a volume expounding liberal theology. Each writer was independent of the rest, and his essay, "On the Education of the World," contained nothing unorthodox. But he was involved in the storm that the volume produced; and it is a strong tribute to his high moral character, his genuine and unaffected Christian belief, and his undaunted courage, that the opponents of his appointment to Exeter were so soon won over, and that after singularly happy years in Devonshire, he became profoundly revered by the whole Church, both as Bishop of London and Archbishop of Canterbury. One of his last acts was to crown King Edward VII.

Mandell Creighton, Fellow and Tutor of Merton, Oxford, and a brilliant historical scholar, had been Professor of Ecclesiastical History at Cambridge, and had honorary degrees from Oxford, Cambridge, Durham, Dublin,

Harvard, besides other like distinctions. He was Professor of Ancient Literature at the Royal Academy, Canon of Worcester, Canon of Windsor, and, in 1891, became Bishop of Peterborough. He wrote many important books, but his great work was the *History of the Papacy during the Period of the Reformation*. His brilliant conversation, bright and caustic humour, and appreciation of the many-sided aspects of modern life, brought him great influence with men of every class. He was unfailingly ready both as a speaker and preacher. Though he was the first Bishop to introduce a mitre into St. Paul's since the Reformation, nobody could say to what school of thought in the Church he belonged. He was Bishop of London from 1897–1901; and his influence was becoming so great that his premature death was felt to be a universal loss.

The present Bishop of London (*Arthur Foley Winnington-Ingram*, Bishop of Stepney and Canon of St. Paul's) was brought into the See by that unprecedented wave of popularity and affection which has only increased in volume with the years.

On January 9, 1806, in the time of Dean Pretyman, were deposited in St. Paul's the remains of Nelson, the greatest of naval heroes. The funeral of Nelson created quite as great an impression at the time as that of Wellington forty-six years afterwards. "The Cathedral opened wide her doors to receive the remains of the great admiral, followed, it might almost be said, by the whole nation as mourners. The death of Nelson in the hour of victory, of Nelson, whose victories of Aboukir and Copenhagen had raised his name above any other in our naval history, had stirred the English heart to its depths, its depths of pride and sorrow. The manifest result of that splendid victory at Trafalgar was the annihilation of the fleets of France and Spain, and it might seem the absolute conquest of the ocean, held for many years as a subject province of Great Britain. The procession, first by water, then by land, was, of course, magnificent, as far as generous cost could command magnificence.

"The body was preceded to St. Paul's by all that was noble and distinguished in the land; more immediately by all the Princes of the Blood, headed by the Prince of Wales (afterwards George IV.). The chief mourner was Admiral of the Fleet Sir Peter Parker.

"The place of interment was under the centre of the dome. As a youth I was present, and remember the solemn effect of the sinking of the coffin. I heard, or fancied that I heard, the low wail of the sailors who bore and encircled the remains of their admiral.

"By a singular chance, the body of Nelson is deposited (beneath) a sarcophagus in which Cardinal Wolsey expected to repose."[1] It has been conclusively proved by Alfred Higgins, F.S.A., in a paper read at the annual meeting of the Archæological Institute, in 1893, that this tomb was not, as alleged, by the Italian sculptor Torregiano, but by Benedetto da Rovezzano, also a Florentine sculptor. The same writer gives an account of how it was utilized for a monument to Henry VIII. by having a brass figure of that king placed on the top. The figure remained there until Windsor Castle was taken by Oliver Cromwell, and it was melted down to contribute to the pay of his soldiers. Again it became tenantless. When George III. was preparing to make Wolsey's Chapel a burial-place for the royal family, in reference to the fact that Westminster Abbey was becoming overcrowded, having more than two thousand bodies below its floor, it became a question what was to be done with the monument of Cardinal Wolsey and Henry VIII. It is probable that Wyatt, the architect of the Castle, suggested it as fit to surmount the coffin of Nelson. So it commemorates three incongruous notabilities: Cardinal Wolsey, Henry VIII. and the Great Captain.

Besides Dr. Pretyman-Tomline, there were in the nine-

[1] Milman's *Annals*, p. 484.

OVER THE GRAVE OF NELSON

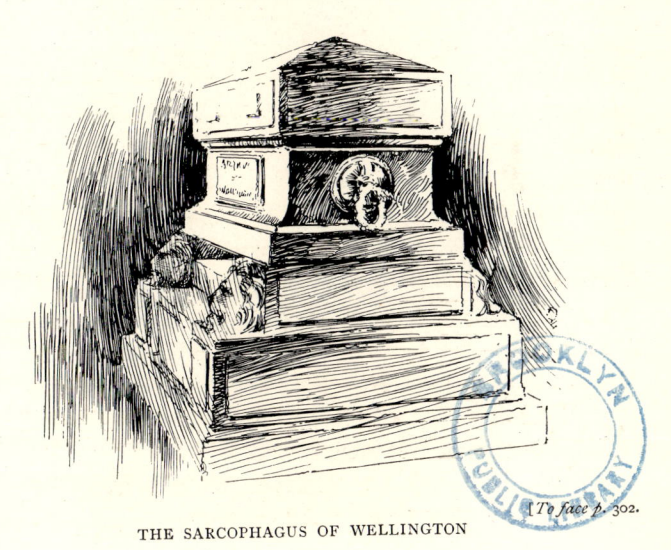

THE SARCOPHAGUS OF WELLINGTON

[*To face p.* 302.

[To face p. 303

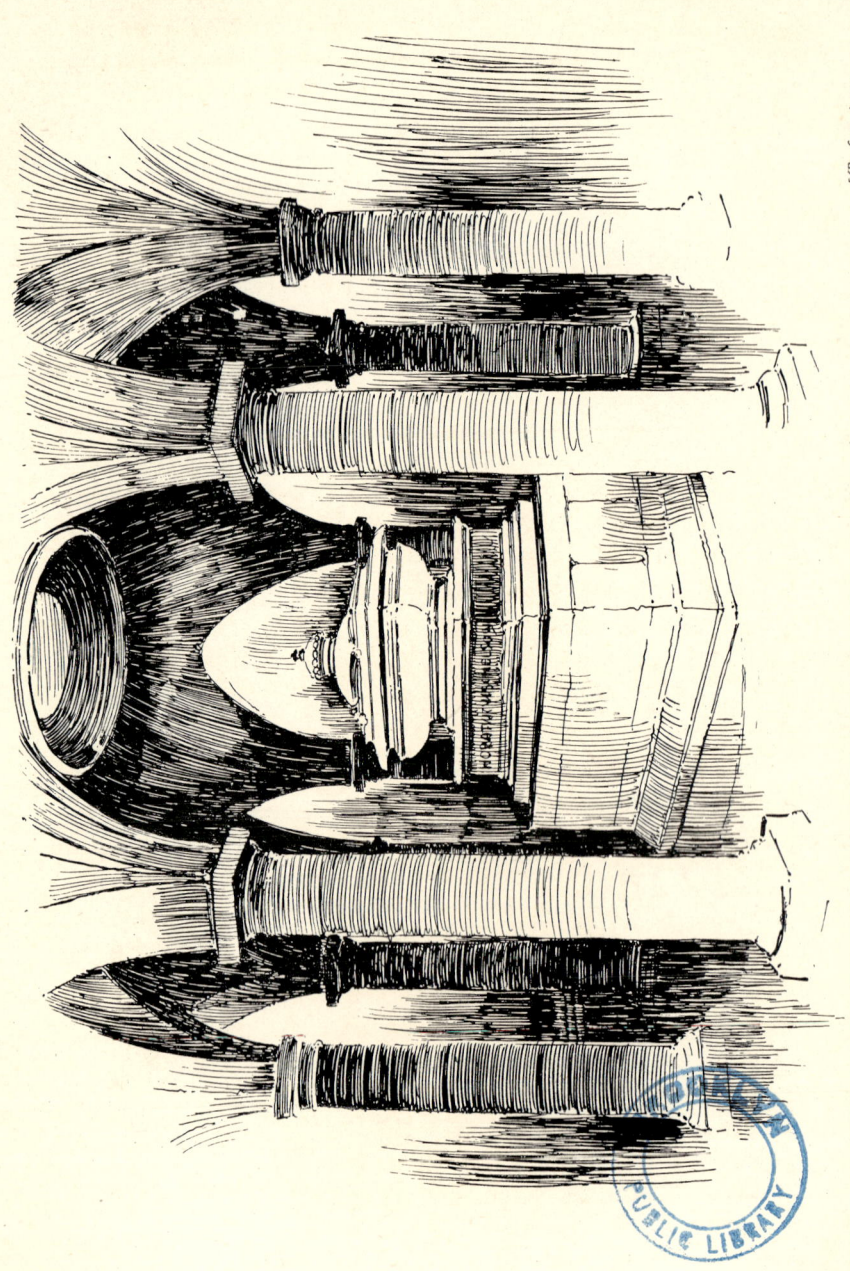

teenth century seven Deans of St. Paul's: William Van Mildert, Charles Richard Sumner, Edward Coplestone, Henry Hart Milman, Henry Longueville Mansel, Richard William Church and Robert Gregory.

William Van Mildert (1820-6) was Rector of St. Mary-le-Bow, Canon Residentiary of St. Paul's and, in 1819, Bishop of Llandaff. He held the Bishopric with the Deanery until, in 1826, he was made Bishop of Durham. He was the founder of the University of Durham, surrendering the historic castle for that purpose, and reserving a suite of rooms for the Bishop. It had been the duty of the Bishops of Durham, as Palatines of the county, to keep hounds for the laity; he was the last who complied with this custom.

Charles Richard Sumner (1826-7) was also Canon Residentiary of St. Paul's and Bishop of Llandaff. He had been tutor in the family of the Marquess Conyngham in the time of the Prince Regent, was brother of Archbishop Sumner of Canterbury, father of the Bishop of Guildford, and grandfather of the Bishop of Gloucester. After a year at the Deanery, he became Bishop of Winchester.

Edward Coplestone (1827-49) was well known at Oxford as Provost of Oriel, Vicar of St. Mary's (the university church) and Professor of Poetry. Like his two predecessors, he was Canon Residentiary of St. Paul's and Bishop of Landaff.

Henry Hart Milman (1849-68), to whose admirable *Annals of St. Paul's* this lesser volume is so greatly indebted, the eminent Church historian, was the youngest son of Sir Francis Milman, Bart., Physician to George III. After being Rector of St. Margaret's, Westminster, and Canon of the Abbey, he became one of the most notable of the Deans of St. Paul's. His *History of Latin Christianity* and *History of the Jews* have given him a permanent place in English literature. Master of a massive and eloquent prose style, he was also no mean poet, and enriched English hymnody with the well-known lyrics, "O help us, Lord, each hour of need," "Ride on, ride on in majesty" and "When our heads are bowed with woe." It was in his time that schemes were first mooted for the decoration of St. Paul's.

In Dean Milman's time took place the ever-memorable funeral of the Duke of Wellington. I must quote the account of the Dean himself: "In the Cathedral, time had not been allowed to carry out the design as proposed by the authorities. The interior was to have been entirely dark, except from artificial light, lines of which were to trace out all the lines of the architecture. This was thought far more impressive than the dull, dubious light of a November day. But the daylight was, from haste, but imperfectly excluded, and the solemn effect of illuminating the whole building, with every arch, and the dome in its majestic circle, was in some degree marred. So ill indeed had the time been measured, that on the morning of the funeral hundreds of workmen had to be dismissed from the Cathedral.

"Yet the scene under the dome (for under the dome was the ceremony to take place) was in the highest degree imposing. The two Houses of Parliament assembled in full numbers: on the north side of the area the House of Commons, behind these the civic authorities, the City companies and the members of the Corporation: on the south side of the area the peers, behind them the clergy of the Cathedral and their friends. The foreign ambassadors sat on seats extending (from the entrance of the choir) to the organ gallery (across the chancel). Every arcade, every available space, was crowded; from 12,000 to 15,000 persons (it was difficult closely to calculate) were present. The body was received by the Bishop, and the Dean, and the clergy, with the choir, at the west door, and conducted to the central area under the dome, on which shone down the graceful coronal of light which enriched it under the

Whispering Gallery. The pall was borne by eight of the most distinguished general officers who had survived the wars of their great commander, or other glorious wars in which their country had been engaged.

"The chief mourner was, of course, the Duke of Wellington, with the Prince Consort, and others of the Royal Family.

"The service was the simple burial office of the Church of England, with the fine music of Croft and Purcell wedded to that office, and other music, including an anthem of a very high order, composed by the organist, Mr. Goss.

"The prayers and lesson were read by the Dean. . . Nothing could be imagined more solemn than the responses of all the thousands present, who repeated, as had been suggested, the words of the Lord's Prayer. It fulfilled the sublime Biblical phrase, 'Like the roar of many waters'; only that it was clear and distinct: the sad combined prayer, as it were, of the whole nation.

"The gradual disappearance of the coffin, as it slowly sank into the vault below, was a sight which will hardly pass from the memory of those who witnessed it.

"The sarcophagus which, after some time, was prepared to receive the remains of Wellington, was in perfect character with that great man. A mass of Cornish porphyry (weighing 17 tons) wrought in the severest and simplest style, unadorned, and because unadorned more grand and impressive; in its grave splendour, and, it might seem, time-defying solidity, it is emblematic of him who, unlike most great men, the more he is revealed to posterity, shows more substantial, unboastful, unquestionable greatness."[1]

Henry Longueville Mansel (1868–71), the keenest metaphysician of his time, came from St. John's College, Oxford, and was Professor of Moral Philosophy and Ecclesiastical History. He was a disciple of Sir William Hamilton and the Scottish School, and was best known by his

[1] Milman's *Annals*, p. 492.

Prolegomena Logica, Philosophy of Kant, Metaphysics, and *Limits of Religious Thought* (Bampton Lectures). His wit was also famous; his satirical poem, "Phrontisterion," on modern German philosophy was keenly appreciated, and his squibs were circulated through the University. One may be quoted on a change in the method of conferring the degree of Doctor of Divinity, according to which two theological papers were to be submitted in future by the candidate—

> " The degree of D.D.
> We propose to convey
> On an A double S,
> For a double Es-say."

Richard William Church (1871–90), Fellow of Oriel, was one of the Tractarian writers, and in the very front rank of the intellectual men of his day. His literary taste and knowledge, purity of style, keen critical faculty and exalted Christian character gave him great ascendency over the clergy, and attracted to him the friendship of the foremost men of the day. Of a singularly retiring disposition, he was contented for eighteen years (1853–71) to be rector of the small village of Whatley, in Somersetshire, preaching to rustics. As Dean, he suffered a good deal from weak health, and left much of the business of the Cathedral to Canon Gregory, his successor, who was treasurer to the Chapter. His *Sermons and Essays* gave him a high place in the literature of the nineteenth century. He was supported by a very able Chapter, which besides Canon Gregory, included at different times Lightfoot (afterwards Bishop of Durham), Stubbs (afterwards Bishop of Oxford), Liddon, Henry Scott Holland and Archdeacon Gifford (formerly Headmaster of Birmingham School, at which had been educated three of the greatest of modern prelates: Benson, Lightfoot and Westcott).

In Dean Church's time occurred the great national thanksgiving service for the recovery of the Prince of

Wales (afterwards King Edward VII.) from his almost fatal attack of typhoid fever. I take the account from the notes of the famous verger, Robert Green, who began his service on the day of the funeral of the Duke of Wellington: "1872, Monday, February 5.—Preparations for the Thanksgiving Service began, on the recovery of the Prince of Wales from his serious illness; the Cathedral closed to visitors on the 7th; the services discontinued (except the 8.0 a.m. service in the N.W. chapel, and one service on week-days and two services on Sunday (11.0 a.m. and 3.15 p.m.) at Christ Church, Newgate Street). The special Sunday evening services were discontinued. Sunday, February 11.—The Fire Brigade on duty at the Cathedral during the Thanksgiving preparations. Tuesday, February 27.—Thanksgiving Service. The Queen and most of the members of the Royal Family attended. A pew was erected just under the great arch towards the nave. The Dean (Church) received Her Majesty at the west entrance. The day was fine, but cold." The sermon was preached by Archbishop Tait on Family Life. "Wednesday afternoon, February 28.—The Cathedral open to the public to view the fittings: great crowds present. On the 29th, and March 1 and 2, the Cathedral was open to special visitors by cards from the Dean: great crowds attended."

To Dean Church and his earlier colleagues, on the initiative chiefly of the great reformer Canon Gregory (who became Dean in 1890), the alterations in St. Paul's are owing, which have changed it from a condition of motionless decorum into the most active centre of religious life in England.

I have an amusing paper before me in *All the Year Round*, of April 4, 1868, by my old friend Joseph Parkinson, a collaborateur of Charles Dickens, who died last year (1908). "'You'll find it horribly dirty,' exclaimed the friend I met on Ludgate Hill, in reply to the intelligence that I was about to go over St. Paul's for the first time.

'Horribly dirty,' I repeated to myself. 'Is *that* all the creature can find to say concerning Wren's masterpiece?' But, having now been from crypt to ball, and round galleries, and about nave, dirt and neglect are, I find, the most prominent characteristics of the handsomest edifice of the wealthiest city in the world. The most prominent fact connected with an inspection of the monuments is their filth. Dust which is black in its thickness rests undisturbed upon the handiwork of Chantrey and Flaxman, converting classic groups into piebald monstrosities, turning white black, and reading a bitter lesson of neglect and indifference to the looker-on. It would be ludicrous if it were not sad to note the strange metamorphoses effected by simple dirt. Black angels are conveying Ethiopian heroes to their long rest. Smutty-faced Britannias vie with much-besoiled Glories and Fames in doing honour to English worthies to whom soap and a scrubbing-brush are a first necessity. . . . A few amateur cleaners might relieve the City of London of a grave scandal and reproach by giving up an hour once a month to the Cathedral. . . . Surely in these days of voluntary effort, it would not be difficult to organize a little staff of Churchmen who would each undertake to keep a statue clean; or if this were too much labour, who would take a leg or an arm, or a cherub or an animal under his individual care. Few tasks would be more immediately effective, and I beg to throw out, as a suggestion to the gentlemen of London, that an amateur cleaning society be formed for the restoration of the statues of St. Paul's."

In that very year, 1868, Gregory was appointed Canon, and the reforms began. The appointment was not popular with the Chapter, who suspected energy, and their displeasure was shown by the fact that his installation took place by the light of a farthing dip. Before his time the members of the choir were most irregular in their attendance. Like the Minor Canons, the Vicars-choral were an independent college. Sometimes the daily attendance was very scanty, and it was difficult to perform the music. There is a legend that on one occasion, when the " Hallelujah Chorus" was to be sung, a message was sent up to Sir John Goss, the organist, that there was only one tenor and one bass. " Do your best," he replied, " and I will do the rest with the organ." The choirmen used to straggle in with the procession, and sometimes led their children by the hand. One day the storm broke. Gregory was canon-in-residence, and after evensong he addressed to the choir a severe and peremptory exhortation. The older choirmen flew to the newspaper offices, and the evening papers had large headings on their placards : " Scene in St. Paul's." Gregory persisted, and instituted a system of fines for non-attendance and unpunctuality, reviving the old Saturday Chapter for Discipline. One of the senior choirmen remonstrated. " My dear sir," replied the determined reformer, " if you were to die on the steps of the Cathedral on your way to attend a service, I should fine your widow for your non-appearance." Gradually opposition quailed before such stern resolution. The attendance of the choir soon became as regular as clockwork. The College of Minor Canons and the College of Vicars-choral, while retaining certain rights, were both subjected to the authority of the Chapter. A system of regular washing and dusting was begun, and perfected as the years went on, till St. Paul's, although daily thronged by thousands of visitors, has become a model of cleanliness. A large body of workmen were engaged, and a foreman of works appointed, who should always be engaged in the duties of renovation and ablution. In 1871 came the time for commuting the estates of the Cathedral, and here again the business-like head and firm hand of Gregory were of the greatest importance in calculating and weighing with the Ecclesiastical Commissioners the claims of the various interests concerned in the vast machinery of St. Paul's. The composition was thought to be on the whole on a liberal scale; but as the fabric fund was to be chiefly drawn from King Ethelbert's estates in Essex, and these have since fallen to half their value, the allowance made for repairs has proved wholly insufficient. Nothing like enough, again, was granted for fire insurance, which, as St. Paul's is surrounded by vast warehouses, has become a matter of great importance. The Chapter have lately increased their premiums on a large scale.

The reforms in the music of St. Paul's date from the appointment of Dr. Stainer in 1872. The reconstruction of the choir was no less necessary than that of the organ; and every change was carried out by that admirable musician and devout Churchman with consummate tact, good humour, courage and firmness. He could do anything he liked with the choir. The splendid choral midday celebration, for which St. Paul's has become famous, was introduced. Festival services and oratorios, with full orchestral accompaniments, became part of the regular routine: Bach's *Passion-music*, Spohr's *Last Judgment*, Mendelssohn's *St. Paul* and *Elijah* were regularly heard. A choir school was built for the boys, and the numbers increased: and much is due to the care of the successive masters, Barff, Russell, Morgan-Brown. From 1871 to 1888, when he resigned on account of failing eyesight, Stainer was an ideal coadjutor of the reforming Chapter in the development of the musical forces of St. Paul's.

The revival of the preaching reputation of the Cathedral is owing to the illustrious Liddon (1870–90). Who can forget those unprecedented and unrivalled congregations, when the nave was full, and men stood in serried ranks round the dome, with the huge figure of Ruthven Pym and other wardsmen keeping order? that high silvery tenor voice, ringing in impassioned tones through every corner of the building? the sustained logical eloquence, the glowing faith, the wide reading, the familiarity with every phase of philosophy and science, the reminiscence of the classical eloquence of the great French preachers of the eighteenth century, the atmosphere of culture, distinction and extraordinary personal charm? The sermons were long, sometimes more than an hour, but none of the audience was sensible to the flight of time. Liddon was an incomparable factor in the revival of St. Paul's.

CHAPTER XXIX

VERGER GREEN'S DIARY: THE LAST HALF OF THE NINETEENTH CENTURY.—PART I.: 1853-75

THE life of the Cathedral during the last half of the nineteenth century may be illustrated very happily from the *Diary* of the able and venerable verger, Mr. Robert Green, which has been placed in my hands by his son; he did duty for the first time on November 18, 1852, at the Duke of Wellington's funeral, and retired on November 13, 1899, and died December 15, 1901, in his eightieth year. The entries are selected from the *Diary*. Some may appear unimportant; but, like the flowers in a garden, or the threads in a tapestry, they help to make up the whole effect.

1853.

February. Much snow and hard frost this month; Cathedral very cold; thermometer inside down to freezing point, 32 degr.; at this time there were no means of heating the Cathedral. (We may compare the note in December, 1858): "Various plans for warming the Cathedral had been made from time to time; Archdeacon Hale had a sort of wagon drawn about the floor, filled with red-hot coke; but after the Gurney stoves were introduced and placed in different parts of the Crypt, the hot air passing the gratings in the floor, with the thermometer reaching over 60 degrees in the winter frequently, and seldom below 55 degrees, made a vast difference in the temperature all the year round." (The temperature now is usually about 64 degrees both summer and winter.)

Nov. 22. The Duke's coffin removed from off Nelson's tomb, where it had rested since the funeral, in the presence of the Dean (Milman), the Duke of Wellington, Miss Burdett-Coutts, and others.

1854.

Sunday, Oct. 1st. Thanksgiving Service for a plentiful harvest. (These services had not then become universal.)

1855.

Sunday afternoon, Feb. 4th. Canon Dale preached in commemoration of John Rogers the martyr.

April 19th. The Emperor and Empress of the French visited the City: people were admitted to the South Portico to see them pass. The same on Dec. 4th with the King of Sardinia.

Sept. 30th. Thanksgiving Day for the capture of Sebastopol.

1856.

Jan. 26th. Sir Edmund Lyons (the victorious admiral of the Black Sea Fleet, afterwards commemorated by a statue in the south transept) visited the Cathedral, also the Crypt. I may note here that previously to the Duke's funeral, the Crypt was shown to visitors by the light of a lantern; there was no gas as there is now; each Verger had his lantern handed down as he came into office, and their assistant Vergers had to explain the monuments to the visitors; but only a portion of the Crypt was open, nothing west of Nelson's tomb.

March 14th. A man named Smart committed suicide from the Whispering Gallery. 1869, Aug. 12th.—A man attempted to commit suicide by running an iron spike into his throat at Sir John Moore's monument. 1878, Jan. 10th, 3 p.m.—A man named Stevens committed suicide from the Whispering Gallery. A lady and two children had a narrow escape, for he fell amongst the chairs close to where they were sitting. He died on the way to the Hospital, whilst in the cab. He had previously been confined as a lunatic. The Gallery was closed for some time, whilst an extra guard-rail was erected. 1890, Sunday morning, Sept. 28th.—A man named Edward Easton committed suicide during the service by shooting himself with a revolver whilst the Rev. Prebendary Eyton was preaching, about 10 m. before 12.0. An inquest was held at St. Bartholomew's Hospital: verdict, temporary insanity. On Monday, Oct. 13th, 5 p.m., the Bishop of London, Dr. Temple, held a Reconciliation service on account of the above suicide. (Dean Church considered this unnecessary, but there was a movement in the *Church Times*, and Canon Gregory considered it important.— W. M. S.)

April 21st. The Princess Royal and the Princess Alice visited the Cathedral. Dean Milman and Canon Champneys (afterwards Dean of Lichfield) were in attendance.

April 29th. Peace proclaimed in the City and elsewhere after the war with Russia. Sunday, May 4th.—Thanksgiving Service for peace.

June 3rd. The Prince of Baden visited the Cathedral.

June 23rd. Prince Oscar of Sweden visited the Cathedral (the late King Oscar; he was then hoping for a marriage with Princess Mary of Cambridge).

June 29th. Great Peace rejoicings: grand fireworks in the Parks at night. Dean Milman and friends, Charles Dickens, Archdeacon Hale and friends went up to the Golden Gallery at 11 p.m. to view.

July. Monument to the Coldstream Guards erected near the Dean's entrance with their colours. (Other monuments to the same regiment have since been erected in the same place.)

VERGER GREEN'S DIARY.—PART I.

Sept. 2nd. The Prime Minister (Lord Palmerston) and the Prince Consort came to the Cathedral respecting a site for the Duke's Monument.

Dec. 4th. Enthronement of Dr. Tait as Bishop of London. A very cold day, and sharp frost.

1857.

Sunday morning, Jan. 25th. General Tom Thumb and his attendant came to the service.

April 30th. Duchess of Gloucester died: the great Bell was tolled.

June 15th. The Archduke of Austria visited the Cathedral.

Oct. 7th. Day of Humiliation for the Rebellion in India. The Rev. Morgan Cowie preached in the morning, and Canon Dale in the afternoon, when Lord Mayor Finnis and the Corporation attended the service.

1858.

August. The Duke of Wellington's tomb in the Crypt finished, with the surroundings. For some time after the public were admitted to the Crypt free of charge, on Mondays, Thursdays, and Saturdays.

Nov. 11th. Bishop Tait's first Visitation began. He delivered his Charge on the 17th under the Dome, which took him 4 hours and 20 minutes.

Nov. 28th, Advent Sunday. The first special evening service under the Dome. Bishop Tait preached: the Cathedral crowded: a great number of people outside unable to get in.

1859.

Sunday, Feb. 27th. The Duchess of Cambridge and Princess Mary at the evening service. Bishop of Oxford (Samuel Wilberforce) preached.

Sunday, May 1st. Thanksgiving Service this afternoon for the suppression of the Indian Mutiny: the Lord Mayor and Corporation attended.

Wednesday, June 8th. The remains of General Sir Thomas Picton (a Waterloo hero) brought on a gun-carriage to St. Paul's, and deposited in the Crypt.

Sept. 2nd. The Service for the Fire of London discontinued.

Sept. 26th. Alterations and enlargement of the Organ commanded. The week-day services during the time were held in the Morning Chapel: the Sunday Services in the Choir.

1860.

Feb. 8th. The Prince of Orange (late King of Holland) visited the Cathedral.

May 1st to May 5th. The daily services suspended, whilst taking down the Organ Screen.

July 2nd. The services in the Cathedral discontinued for alterations in the Choir. At this time the large Organ was erected over the porch in the South Transept, and the great arches, and parts of the roof of the Choir.

Dec. 2nd, Advent Sunday. The services partly resumed after the alteration in the Choir: viz. once on week-days and twice on Sundays. Until the present alterations the Minor Canons occupied seats below the Upper Stalls, in a line with the Vicars Choral. Raised desks had been fixed on the Decani and Cantoris sides for the Reader. The Litany also was chanted from the Lectern by two Minor Canons. [Since 1860 the Minor Canons have sat in the upper stalls, which were then just behind the singers towards the east. But after the second alteration (moving the organ, etc., between 1869 and 1872) they had stalls provided at the west end of the choir, viz. one on each side of the Reader, and four beyond the Residentiaries, as at present.]

1861.

Jan. 25th (Conversion of St. Paul). The great organ in the South Transept opened. The *Messiah* was rendered by an additional Choir. Sims Reeves took part. Dean Milman absent, very ill. (When the alterations in the chancel were finished, the choir-screen removed, and the whole of the stalls transferred to the edge of the dome, the new organ in the south transept was found to be unnecessary, and was sold.)

Jan. 28th. The usual daily services resumed in the Choir after the alterations.

March 16th. The Duchess of Kent died; the great bell was tolled.

April 21st. The London Rifle Brigade attended afternoon service under the Dome; Canon Dale preached as their Hon. Chaplain. (This was followed by a long series of parade services by different London regiments.)

August 16th. The King of Sweden visited the Cathedral; the Prince of Wales also the same day, who came privately.

Nov. 7th. The Grand Duke Constantine of Russia visited the Cathedral.

Dec. 14th. The Prince Consort died of fever after a short illness. Green and Cummings (another verger) were waiting at the Deanery anticipating his death. A special messenger arrived about midnight to announce it to Dean Milman, who ordered the great bell to be tolled from 12.15 a.m. to 2.15. On the Sunday following the death, a great crowd was at the Cathedral to hear funeral sermons. Dean Milman preached in the morning, and Canon Champneys in the afternoon. The Choir was draped with black with white edging.

1862.

May 1st. The great International Exhibition opened. A great number of visitors to the Cathedral during the summer.

318 MEMORIALS OF ST. PAUL'S CATHEDRAL

THE WELLINGTON FUNERAL CAR, WEST END OF CRYPT.

July 26th. The Prince of Saxony (afterwards King) visited the Cathedral.

August 18th. The Duchess of Cambridge and Princess Mary visited the Cathedral. To-day the Wellington Car at the West End of the Crypt was also opened to visitors.

Sept. 5th. Archbishop Sumner of Canterbury died: the great bell was tolled from 5 to 6 p.m.

1863.

March 7th. Great preparations in the Cathedral Yard, erections all along the south and east, on account of the Princess of Denmark and her daughter Princess Alexandra (to be married to the Prince of Wales on the 10th) passing through the City. The day was cold and showery: great crowds in the streets.

March 15th. Sunday evening (after the wedding), Dr. Magee preached: very crowded congregation: the National Anthem was sung in honour of the Prince and Princess of Wales.

April and May. The Ball and Cross were regilded by James Guthridge.

1864.

The first mosaic was fixed in the Dome. Subject, Isaiah. Artist, Stevens.

Sept. 23rd. Prince Humbert of Italy (afterwards King) visited the Cathedral.

Nov. 6th. The North East London Volunteers attended afternoon service. Prebendary William Rogers ("Hang Theology") preached as their Chaplain.

1865.

Sat., July 29th. Two Indian Princes, attended by Colonel Herbert, visited the Cathedral.

Sunday, July 30th. Queen Emma of the Sandwich Islands attended afternoon service, and was afterwards entertained by Archdeacon Hale at the Charterhouse (of which he was Master).

1866.

About this time new painted windows were placed in different parts of the Cathedral. (These were of Munich glass, and have since been greatly deplored.)

March 20th. Day of Humiliation for the Cattle-plague. Bishop of London preached in the afternoon: Cathedral very crowded.

May. The 2nd Mosaic (St. Matthew), by G. F. Watts, fixed in the Dome.

June 10th, Sunday. The Duchess of Mecklenburg (sister of the Duke of Cambridge) and suite came to the Cathedral, and were shown round after morning service.

1867.

March 14th. The great west window, the gift of Mr. Brown, bookseller, unveiled in the presence of Dean Milman, Archdeacon Hale, and several others. Mr. Brown himself was present, aged about 85.

April 24th. The Queen of Denmark visited the Cathedral.

Dec. 17th. The Cathedral closed to visitors in consequence of the Fenians attempting to blow up Clerkenwell prison: the Cathedral and other places threatened.

1868.

January. The excitement about the Fenians still continues. Visitors were not allowed to go to the upper part of the Cathedral till Friday, 24th; and then only to the Stone Gallery. On Tuesday, Feb. 11th, the Golden Gallery and Ball were opened again to visitors.

April 10th, Good Friday. A special service under the Dome in the evening, the first time. The Rev. H. P. Liddon preached an hour and twenty minutes.

May 26th. Execution of Barrett the Fenian for the

Clerkenwell explosion: the officials and sheriffs admitted to Newgate through Amen Court, as on several previous occasions, on account of the enormous crowds. [This was the last public execution: a great relief to most people living in the neighbourhood.]

Dec. 21st, Monday. Rev. R. Gregory installed as Canon Residentiary (important date for St. Paul's.—W. M. S.).

Christmas Day. Mr. Calvert (Minor Canon) had the Choir decorated, and for the first time a decoration was placed over the altar. This was followed by further decorations on Easter Day, 1869. The Epiphany Star of Christmas was replaced by a Cross.

November. The new iron staircase erected through the Dome to the Golden Gallery, in place of the wooden one.

1869.

Jan. 24th, Sunday evening. The great Organ failed: the Organ in the Choir used instead. During the time the great Organ was used (for the evening services under the dome), the Sunday Evening choir sat in the South Transept: a gallery was erected in front of the Organ (which was over the south porch), and Mr. Winn (Vicar Choral) conducted from a box, with the members of the Choir, men and women, in front of him.

Sunday, June 20th. King Theodore of Abyssinia's son (Prince Alamayou), attended by Captain Speedy, came to the morning service, and went into the Crypt afterwards. (Subsequently, Prince Alamayou died; and Theodore's conqueror, Lord Napier of Magdala, was buried in the crypt.—W. M. S.)

Nov. 28th, Advent Sunday. The hours of service altered on and from to-day. Sunday mornings at 10.30 instead of 9.45, Sunday afternoons at 3.15 as usual. On week-days, morning at 10.0 instead of 9.45, afternoon at 4.0 instead of 3.15. Also, on the above date and henceforth, the procession of Choristers and Clergy to be accompanied by a Voluntary on the Organ before and after each service.

1870.

Feb. 27th, Sunday. The Greek Archbishop at the service, when Canon Dale preached his farewell sermon on being appointed Dean of Rochester. The Rev. H. P. Liddon was nominated to the Canonry.

March 24th. Prince Christian and Col. Gordon visited the Cathedral.

April 22nd. The new music-room in the Belfry opened for the Choristers.

Easter Sunday. Flowers on the altar for the first time.

May 15th, Sunday afternoon. Canon Liddon preached from the Dome pulpit, as there was not room in the Choir, and continued to do so.

May 26th, Ascension Day. Special evening service under the Dome; the Bishop of London (Dr. Jackson) preached. The Cathedral was closed to-day except for services, as on Sundays; no parts open to visitors; and to be so in future by order of the Dean and Chapter.

May 30th to June 4th. The daily services suspended to prepare for the Charity Children's Annual Service in June. *Note.*—It was customary for many years to suspend the daily services for 4 weeks; but after Canon Gregory came, this was one of the things altered. The services on Sundays were held as usual, but under difficulties. (Huge wooden galleries, tier above tier, used to be erected round the dome for this service. At last the promoters were told that the children must occupy seats on the floor, like other congregations; and after this the service ceased.—W. M. S.)

May 30th, 8 a.m. A special Celebration in the Choir for the Lay Helpers' Association; about 118 communicants. (The Lay Helpers were for many years a useful and active body, gathered from the different parishes. Their place has now, to a large extent, been taken by the Readers'

Association and the Church of England Men's Society. By 1872 the number at this service was 320.—W. M. S.)

July. The Choir was open between 12 noon and 3 p.m. for private devotion, on application to the Verger in attendance by order of the Dean and Chapter.

July 13th. Meeting at the Mansion House for the decoration and completion of the Cathedral. Subscriptions received about £25,000; amount required £250,000.

August. The Dean or Canon gives the blessing after the sermon, at the Sunday evening service. (From February 22, 1891, the blessing was to be given from the altar.)

Nov. 27th, Advent Sunday. The Archdeacon of London (Hale) died and was buried in the Crypt on Sat., Dec. 3rd. (He was an able man of business, and the most active member of the Chapter before the arrival of Canon Gregory.—W. M. S.)

Nov. 30th, St. Andrew's Day. The First Consecration on record at St. Paul's: that of two Colonial Bishops, Dr. H. C. Huxtable for Mauritius and Dr. H. Cheetham for Sierra Leone. (Consecrations of Bishops used previously to take place at Lambeth Palace Chapel or the Chapel Royal, Whitehall.—W. M. S.)

Dec. 18th, Sunday. The Bishop of London's Ordination. The candidates joined in the procession into the Choir for the first time; to be continued in future.

1871.

Jan. 25th, Conversion of St. Paul. (The beginning of a special observance of the Dedication Festival of the Cathedral.) Communion at 8.0 a.m.: 50 communicants. The Dean (Dr. Mansel) preached in the afternoon. The Bishop of London (Jackson) and 17 Prebendaries attended the service, and afterwards dined at the Chapter House by invitation of the Dean and Chapter. The Minor Canons and Lay Officers were also invited; it was to be an annual Feast in future. (In 1873 began the custom of singing the oratorio *St. Paul* at evensong, with orchestra and large chorus.)

Feb. 8th, Wednesday. Canon Melville died. He was buried in the Crypt on Feb. 15th. (He was considered the greatest preacher of his day; Mr. Gladstone told me he never heard any who kept the attention of his hearers so closely. In his place, Mr. Gladstone appointed Dr. Lightfoot.—W. M. S.)

May 13th. (The beginning of the Saturday afternoon visits to the Cathedral.—W. M. S.) A large party of working men visited the Cathedral by invitation of Canon Gregory, who showed them the various places of interest; the number about 170. (Since then it has become the rule for the Canon-in-Residence to occupy his Saturday afternoons in this interesting way.—W. M. S.)

June 4th, Trinity Sunday. The Bishop of London (Jackson) wore the cope for the first time. (This was in consequence of a recent judgment of Lord Cairns: Bishop Wordsworth of Lincoln did the same.—W. M. S.)

June 30th. The Emperor and Empress of Brazil visited the Cathedral.

July 31. News came of the sudden death of Dean Mansel at Cosgrove. Great Bell tolled from noon till one o'clock, also on the day of the funeral.

Sept. 9th. The North entrance closed, the North porch (interior) being not yet completed. It has been in hand some three months; the Inscription to Wren (which formerly stood under the organ at the entrance to the choir) being placed there.

Nov. 7th, Tuesday evening. (The beginning of a long series of lectures for the young men of the City, which has culminated in the present St. Paul's Lecture Society.—W. M. S.) Canon Gregory's first Lecture to young men of the City, at 8.0 p.m. Females refused admission by order of the Canon, which caused a good deal of grumbling; the lectures to be continued every Tuesday evening this month; the number at the first about 1200.

1872.

Feb. 5th, Monday. Preparations began for the Thanksgiving Service on the recovery of the Prince of Wales after his serious illness; the Cathedral closed to visitors from the 7th; the services discontinued, except the 8.0 a.m. service in the N.W. Chapel; one service on week-days and two on Sundays at Christ Church, Newgate Street; the special Sunday evening services were suspended.

Feb. 27th, Tuesday. Thanksgiving Service. The Queen and most of the members of the Royal Family attended. A pew was erected just under the great arch towards the Nave. (The chancel was under repair at the time, and was not fully available.—W. M. S.) The Dean (Church) received Her Majesty. The day was fine but cold, the Cathedral crowded. (Archbishop Tait was the preacher. For this service the organist, Dr. Goss composed his grand *Te Deum* in D major, and the anthem, " The Lord is my strength."—W. M. S.)

February and March. During the erection of scaffolding for the Thanksgiving Service the monument of Sir William Jones (south) and Hallam (north) were lowered; Nelson and Cornwallis were removed from the entrance of the Choir to the South Transept (while Captain Cooke of the *Bellerophon* and Captain Duff of the *Mars* were removed from lofty panels in the chancel to the crypt, to which their scale is hardly suited.) This was done to make room for the organ when it was removed from the North Arch to its present position, and divided. (Up till 1858 it had stood on a screen across the chancel.) Many of the other monuments were lowered about the same time, and the iron railings round them removed. The organ was re-erected and improved by Willis.

April 3rd. The Fire Brigade left the Cathedral after the clearing away of materials from the Thanksgiving Service. (They had occupied it since February 11.)

April 30th. British and Foreign Bible Society's service under the Dome. (It became annual.—W. M. S.)

May 19th, Whit-sunday. Choral Celebration in the Choir for the first time.

June 19th. The Burmese Embassy visited the Cathedral.

July 3rd. At the S.P.G. Anniversary Service, when the sermon was preached by Bishop Temple of Exeter (afterwards Bishop of London and Primate), an alms-dish presented by the American Church was received by the Archbishop (Tait).

July 17th. A party of Belgian artisans visited the Cathedral. (This was about the time the Belgians used to come on their annual visit to Wimbledon for the shooting competitions.—W. M. S.)

Sept. 11th. The Japanese Embassy and suite visited the Cathedral, accompanied by the Lord Mayor and Canon Lightfoot.

Dec. 22nd, Sunday. Bishop of London's Ordination. Non-communicants allowed for the first time to remain during the Celebration; by order of the Dean and Canon Liddon.

1873.

Feb. 20th. The London Gregorian Association held their first annual service in the Cathedral; church very crowded.

March 8th and 25th. Large additions made to the number of choristers and assistant-vicars-choral: in future there are to be 6 men on each side of the choir on week-days, and 9 on Sundays.

April 6th, Sunday afternoon. The Bidding Prayer discontinued from to-day, except when the Corporation and Judges attend.

April 8th, Tuesday in Holy Week. Bach's *Passion-music* at 7 p.m. (for the first time); the Cathedral very crowded.

April 18th, Friday. Organ to be discontinued on this week-day.

June 15th, Sunday morning. The 1st Hospital Sunday; the Prince and Princess of Wales, the Duke of Edinburgh, and the Lord Mayor and Corporation attended the service. The Bishop of London (Jackson) preached; offertory about £480. The Cathedral was crowded, also a crowd outside.

June 22nd, Sunday. Some of the Shah's suite came to see the Cathedral. On Tuesday, July 1st, the Shah of Persia and suite visited the Cathedral. The notice from the Lord Chamberlain's office was for 1 p.m., but they did not arrive till 3.15.

Aug. 5th, Tuesday. The British Medical Association attended the morning service.

Sept. 4th, Thursday. The Prince of Baden and suite visited the Cathedral.

Oct. 11th, Saturday, 12 noon. The choral funeral of Sir Edwin Landseer. The body was brought in at the West Door after a hurried preparation, as the West Front was under repair (the re-arrangement of the steps, etc.). The body was lowered into the Crypt at the east end of the Choir near the altar, Bishop Claughton officiating as Canon-in-Residence (he had succeeded Archdeacon Hale, and was Archdeacon of London, Bishop-assistant of London, Canon of St. Paul's and Chaplain-General.—W. M. S.). Amongst the many floral wreaths was one from Her Majesty, to which were attached the following words: "A tribute of friendship and admiration for great talents from Queen Victoria."

Oct. 30th, Thursday. The London Church Choir Association held their 1st Annual Service in the Cathedral at 8 p.m. Very crowded. (This has been since one of the most popular events of the year.—W. M. S.)

Nov. 4th, 11.30 a.m. Special Service for the Dioceses of London, Winchester, and Rochester in connection with the proposed Mission in 1874: the Bishop of each Diocese gave an address. Service over at 1.30 p.m.

Nov. 10, Monday. The Prince Imperial (Napoleon) visited the Cathedral.

1874.

Jan. 8th, Thursday. The iron railings round the West Front (which Wren so bitterly deplored—W. M. S.) sold by auction, and began soon after to be removed.

Jan. 22nd, Thursday. The old colours of the 57th Regiment were brought to the Cathedral at 1 p.m. by Major Short, and several of the officers and non-commissioned officers. The Dean (Church) and Canon Gregory received them. A short ceremony took place, and the Dean addressed those assembled in a few touching words.

Jan. 26th, Monday. At 12 noon the corner-stone of the new Choir-school was laid by the Dean and Canons.

Feb. 6th, Friday. Devotional Day for the Clergy in connection with the London Mission; short addresses at 12.30, 2.0, 3.0, 5.0, and 6.0, by Rev. W. W. How (afterwards Bishop of Bedford and Wakefield), Hay Chapman, Body, Haslam and Benson. From 9th to 14th at 1.15 Litany and address by Dr. Barry; also a short service at 8 p.m., with address by Rev. W. Butler, Vicar of Wantage (afterwards Dean of Lincoln). 17th, Thanksgiving Service, with address by Rev. G. H. Wilkinson, Vicar of St. Peter's, Eaton Square (afterwards Bishop of Truro, Bishop of St. Andrew's and Primus of Scotland.—W. M. S.).

March. One Sunday morning preacher in each month to be a non-member of the Cathedral Body chosen by the Bishop; the first, Dr. Abbott, Headmaster of the City of London School.

April 5th, Easter Sunday. On and after to-day all

preachers, not being members of the Cathedral staff, to wear a surplice instead of a preaching-gown.

June 21st, Sunday evening. The Bishop of Manchester (Dr. Fraser) preached for the Society for the Prevention of Cruelty to Animals. The Baroness Burdett-Coutts and a large number of the delegates attended the service.

July. The floor of the Crypt round Nelson's tomb is bring lowered; also Collingwood's and Northesk's tombs removed into the recess on each side of Nelson. The floor is now much improved by the mosaic which is made by the prisoners at Woking.

Sept. 4th, Friday. The funeral of Mr. Foley, R.A., sculptor, 12 noon; plain service; Dr. Lightfoot officiated.

Sept. 13th, Sunday. The Syrian Patriarch and the Bishop of Jerusalem at the evening service. On Monday the 14th they visited the Cathedral.

Oct. 20th, Tuesday, 8 p.m. Special Service for the College of Organists.

Oct. 27th, Tuesday. Sermon for the Old Catholics (Anglo-Continental Society) at 4 p.m.

Nov. 5th, Thursday. Miss Maria Hackett died. She took particular interest in the Choristers of St. Paul's and other Cathedrals, and was a constant attendant at St. Paul's Cathedral for more than 50 years. Her age was 91; she was buried at Highgate cemetery, the Dean and many members of the Cathedral attending. A small tablet is placed in the Crypt by some of the old choristers to her memory.

Dec. 6th, Sunday. Copies of the Hymn and Anthem printed and distributed each Sunday afternoon; also in the evening (an admirable move.—W. M. S.).

Dec. 21st, Monday. The lowering of the monuments has continued; recently in the South Transept.

1875.

Jan. 6th. Mr. Martin (afterwards Sir George), came to the Choir School as "Master of Song" in place of Mr. Walker, resigned.

Feb. 2nd. Bishop Claughton's grandson baptized after morning service; the last baptism took place in the year 1713, a lapse of 162 years.

August 1st, Sunday. The Lord Mayor and Corporation, with the foreign Mayors and Provosts, and the English Provincial Mayors, Town-clerks, etc., attended the afternoon service. About 1200 seats reserved. Canon Liddon preached.

CHAPTER XXX

VERGER GREEN'S DIARY: THE LAST HALF OF THE NINETEENTH CENTURY.—PART II.: 1876-88

1876.

MAY 8th, Monday. The old colours of the 77th Regiment received in the Nave by the Dean and Canons. The Band, with several officers and men, was present, and played "Auld Lang Syne": very impressive.

May 22nd, Monday. The Crown Prince of Hanover (now Duke of Cumberland—W. M. S.) visited the Cathedral.

May 27th, Saturday afternoon. The "Dettingen Te Deum" sung in place of an anthem, accompanied by an orchestra, as a Thanksgiving Service for the safe return of the Prince of Wales from India: the "Old Hundredth" was sung at the end of the prayers.

June 10th, Saturday. The Duchess of Teck and the Princess of Hanover visited the Cathedral.

Nov. 30th. Archdeacon Johnson consecrated Bishop of Calcutta. (On May 1st, Dr. Mylne was consecrated Bishop of Bombay.)

1877.

Jan. 1st, Monday. Began daily celebrations in the N.W. Chapel at 8.0 a.m.

April 14th, Ash Wednesday. (Beginning of the Lent weekday services under the dome.—W. M. S.) Short Service, 1.15 p.m.; the address in the Nave, Hymn and Litany in the Chapel after; to be continued during Lent. The preachers are the Rev. G. H. Wilkinson (afterwards Bishop of Truro, etc.), the Rev. and Hon. A. Anson (afterwards Bishop of Qu'Appelle), the Rev. D. Elsdale (St. John's, Kennington), the Rev. H. M. Villiers (afterwards Prebendary), and the Rev. J. Ridgway. On Friday 16th, and always afterwards, the service was held in the Dome.

April 2nd, Easter Monday. On and from to-day, Morning Prayer to be said in the Crypt Chapel at 8.0 a.m. instead of the N.W. Chapel as heretofore.

April 25th, Wednesday, 11 a.m. Consecration of the first Bishop of Truro (Dr. Benson). Dr. Lightfoot preached. The service lasted till nearly 3.0 p.m.

July 21st, Thursday, 8.0 a.m. The Emperor of Brazil and suite visited the Cathedral.

August 9th, Thursday. The marriage of the Lady Mayoress (Miss L. White) took place to-day by special licence. The Archbishop of Canterbury, Dr. Liddon, and other clergy took part. The last marriage in the Cathedral was about the year 1760.

7.30 p.m. Special service for the Church of England Working Men's Society.

Sept. 14th, Friday. Early Celebration in N.W. Chapel for the Railway Guild, and a service in the evening for the same.

Sept. 29th, Saturday, 7.15 a.m. Special celebration in the Crypt on Bishop Steere leaving England for Africa. (There had been a similar one for the Bishop of Capetown on August 3, 1874.)

Nov. 24th, Saturday. The last of the new windows round the Dome finished, they having been in hand 20 years, and begun in 1857.

1878.

Feb. 2nd, Saturday. Dr. Bousfield consecrated Bishop of Pretoria.

Feb. 26th, Tuesday. Quiet Day for the Clergy of the Dioceses of London and Rochester.

April 15th, Monday in Holy Week. No organ from

to-day (except for Bach's *Passion-music*). Three hours' service on Good Friday for the first time (Preacher, Minor Canon Shuttleworth). In consequence of this service a disturbance was likely to take place by the Protestant League; the police were in attendance, but they were not required; everything passed off quietly.

April 20th, Saturday. The Wellington Monument (in the S.W. Chapel, or Consistory Court) opened to the public after being 20 years in hand. No ceremony at the opening. (Lord Leighton, P.R.A., afterwards had it removed to the place designed by the sculptor Stevens under one of the arches on the north side of the nave.— W. M. S.)

April 30th, Tuesday. The Princess of Wales and the two young Princes, the Crown Princess of Denmark (the present Queen) and suite visited the Cathedral; the Dean met them at the South door. The Princess and her sons went up to the Ball.

May 1st, Wednesday. Consecration of the Bishop of Newfoundland (Rev. L. Jones).

May 23rd, Thursday, 6.30 p.m. Service for the Guild of the Holy Standard (a religious society in the Army; since repeated annually).

May 28th, Tuesday, 3.30 p.m. Special Service for the School for Daughters of Officers. The Crown Prince and Princess of Germany (afterwards Emperor and Empress Frederic) attended the service; also the Lord Mayor and Sheriffs. Large congregation. The Bands of the Grenadiers, Coldstreams, Royal Artillery and Royal Engineers took part in the service.

June 24th, Monday, 11.30 a.m. Consecration of three Bishops: Maclagan for Lichfield, Roberts for Nassau and Stanton for North Queensland. The Rev. G. H. Wilkinson preached 53 minutes (on Aholibah and Aholibamah— W. M. S.); it was nearly half-past three before the service ended.

THE WELLINGTON MONUMENT: ALFRED STEVENS

July. The American and Colonial Bishops were appointed to preach in the Cathedral at the morning, afternoon and evening services: the Canons-in-Residence gave up their Sunday afternoons during July, August and September.

July 27th, Saturday. Closing service for the Lambeth Conference: sermon and Holy Communion. Bishop of Pennsylvania preached: a large gathering of Bishops, English, Colonial and American.

Aug. 15th. The first bell (No. 10) of the new peal arrived, brought in by the great West door. The others, including No. 12, the tenor, arrived the following week; and on Saturday, Sept. 21st, the peal was tried by the ringers without their clappers, to test their hanging, which appeared satisfactory. On Friday, Oct. 4th, a test peal was rung by the College Youths (so called from St. Michael's, College Hill, E.C., where they began in the seventeenth century—W. M. S.), at 6.0 p.m., for judges to give an opinion: Sir E. Beckett (afterwards Lord Grimthorpe) and others were present.

Nov. 1st, Friday, All Saints' Day. The new peal of bells dedicated this evening. Bishop of London, Dean, Canon Gregory and Bishop Claughton took part in the special service, which took place in the ringing room. A large congregation attended afternoon service, and waited outside to hear the bells.

Nov. 9th, Saturday, Lord Mayor's Day. The new bells were rung by the wish of the Corporation, and permission of the Dean and Chapter.

Nov. 29th, Friday. The remains of the late George Cruickshank (the celebrated caricaturist and teetotaller) were brought to the Cathedral from Kensal Green Cemetery at 5.30 p.m., and deposited in the Crypt: the Dean and Canon Gregory present.

Dec. 10th, Tuesday, 7 p.m. (Beginning of the Advent oratorio.—W. M. S.) Spohr's *Last Judgment* by our Choir and Organ only: no tickets.

Dec. 14th, Saturday. The Grand Duchess of Hesse (Princess Alice) died; the Great Bell was tolled from 5.15 to 6.15 p.m. (the last occasion for such a purpose had been for the infant son of the Prince and Princess of Wales, and the infant son of Prince and Princess Christian); and again on the day of the funeral from 2.0 to 3.0 p.m. At 7.0 p.m. a muffled peal was rung by the College Youths by order of the Dean and Chapter.

Dec. 31st, Tuesday. The bells were rung to-night at 11.45 p.m., to see the old year out, and the new year in; and again on Jan. 1st at 5.30 p.m.

1879.

Feb. 11th, Tuesday. Day of Devotion for the Clergy of London and Rochester. Celebration in the Choir at 8.0. Bishop of London, Dr. Currey (Master of the Charterhouse), Rev. W. Sinclair (afterwards Archdeacon of London), and Rev. H. C. Shuttleworth (Minor Canon).

Feb. 14th, Friday. The alterations in the Churchyard began; lowering the railings, and widening the south side for a pathway: St. Faith's and St. Gregory's burying-ground (the larger part of the Churchyard ground) to be planted and made ornamental. New entrance at the N.E. corner by Cheapside (very handsomely executed). These arrangements are being carried out by an arrangement between the Dean and Chapter and the Corporation, under Lord Mayor Whetham.

March 15th, Saturday. The Princess Frederick Charles of Prussia (mother of the Duchess of Connaught) and suite visited the Cathedral at 5.30 p.m.

March 26th, Wednesday. The King of the Belgians visited the Cathedral at 3.30 p.m. The Dean, Mr. Penrose (the Cathedral Surveyor) and Lord Elcho (the pioneer of the Volunteers, now Lord Wemyss—W. M. S.) received him.

April 29th, Tuesday, 3.30 p.m. Annual Service for Military School for Officers' Daughters. Duke of Cambridge, Duke and Duchess of Teck, and the Lord Mayor and Sheriffs attended.

May 9th, Friday. First Service of the Church of England Temperance Society, 7.30 p.m. Canon Ellison (the founder) preached.

Midsummer to Michaelmas. Three of the Minor Canons Houses completed. (This was part of a great scheme of building in Amen Court: a house for each Minor Canon, the Organist, and the Dean's Verger.)

June 26th, Thursday, 11.30 a.m. First Annual Service of the Girls' Friendly Society.

July 25th, Friday. Consecration of four bishops: Walsham How (Bedford, for East London), Barclay (Jerusalem), Speechley (Travancore), Ridley (Caledonia).

Oct. 21st, Tuesday, 7.30 p.m. First Annual Service of the Guild of St. Luke (medical).

Nov. 3rd, Monday. Prince Ferdinand of Glücksburg and Captain Shaw visited the Cathedral.

Nov. 18th, Tuesday, 2.30 p.m. Service in the Crypt for the Church and Stage Guild.

1880.

March 23rd, Tuesday in Holy Week, 7 p.m. The Princess of Wales and suite attended Bach's *Passion-music*.

May 1st, Saturday. Consecration of the Bishop of Newcastle, Australia.

May 10th, Monday. Sir John Goss, late Organist, died. The funeral took place on Sat. the 15th at Kensal Green: the first part in St. Paul's.

June 11th, Friday. Special Ordination for missionaries at 11.0 a.m.: 17 deacons and 5 priests.

June 28th, Monday. Centenary Service of the Sunday School Institute, 7 p.m. The Lord Mayor attended; Archbishop of York (Thompson) preached.

August 13th, Friday. Prebendary Wright (Secretary of

the Church Missionary Society) drowned whilst bathing in the Lake country.

Nov. 30th, St. Andrew. Choral Communion to-day, and on all Saints' Days henceforth.

Dec. 12th, Sunday afternoon. The Duke and Duchess of Edinburgh and Princess (Louise Marchioness of Lorne) attended service.

1881.

April 1st, Friday. Princess Louise and Princess Maud of Wales visited the Cathedral.

May 12th, Thursday, 7.30 p.m. First East London Mission Service.

May 18th, Wednesday, 3.30 p.m. Prince Leopold present at the Sons of the Clergy Festival.

May 29th, Sunday. The King of Sweden and Norway visited the Cathedral after morning service.

July 25th, Saturday. The Imperial Princesses of Germany visited the Cathedral.

Aug. 7th, Sunday afternoon. The Medical Congress attended the service: preacher, Dr. Liddon.

Sept. 1st, Thursday. The King of the Sandwich Islands visited the Cathedral. He also came to the morning service on Sunday, Sept. 4th.

Nov. 28th, Monday. Midday services begun in the N.W. Chapel, 1.15 p.m.; to be continued daily.

Dec. 10th, Saturday evening. The first scientific peal on the bells rung by the College Youths, which occupied them 4 hours 17 minutes, without leaving the ropes. R. R. Green locked them in the ringing chamber, so they had no communication with any one during that time.

1882.

April 4th, Tuesday in Holy Week. The Duke and Duchess of Edinburgh were present at Bach's *Passion-music*.

April 29th, Saturday, 5 p.m. The Queen of the Netherlands visited the Cathedral, and was received by Dr. Liddon.

May 22nd, Monday. The new bell, "Great Paul," arrived at the Cathedral this morning at 7.30; brought by road from Taylor's, Loughborough; dedicated June 3rd, at 5 p.m. A peal was rung on the occasion. The inscription on the Bell (suggested by Canon Liddon) is "VAE MIHI SI NON EVANGELIZAVERO": "Woe is me if I preach not the Gospel." (The translation given by Canon Liddon was: "May I be cracked if I don't call the people to church."—W. M. S.)

June 4th, Sunday. The new bell, "Great Paul," to be chimed 5 minutes before each service on Sundays and Saints' Days from this date.

June 18th, Sunday afternoon. Lord Mayor and Corporation with the Provincial Mayors attended service.

July 8th. The College Youths had permission to play the Handbells in the Whispering Gallery after the Cathedral was closed.

August 14th, Monday. Great Paul to be chimed on week-days at 1 p.m., on and from to-day.

Dec. 3rd, Advent Sunday. The Dean received a telegram at 9.0 this morning, stating that the death of the Archbishop of Canterbury (Tait) took place at 7.15 a.m. The old Great Bell (the State Bell, Edward of Westminster, given by William III.—W. M. S.) was tolled from 9.20 to 10.20 a.m.

Dec. 31st, Sunday. Bells at 11.30, and Great Paul at 11.55 p.m. Although so wet there was a large crowd at the west front of the Cathedral. (This was the origin of the multitude of Scotsmen and others who now assemble on that occasion.)

1883.

March 24th, Saturday afternoon, Easter Eve. A man named Campion rushed up the Choir during the Anthem,

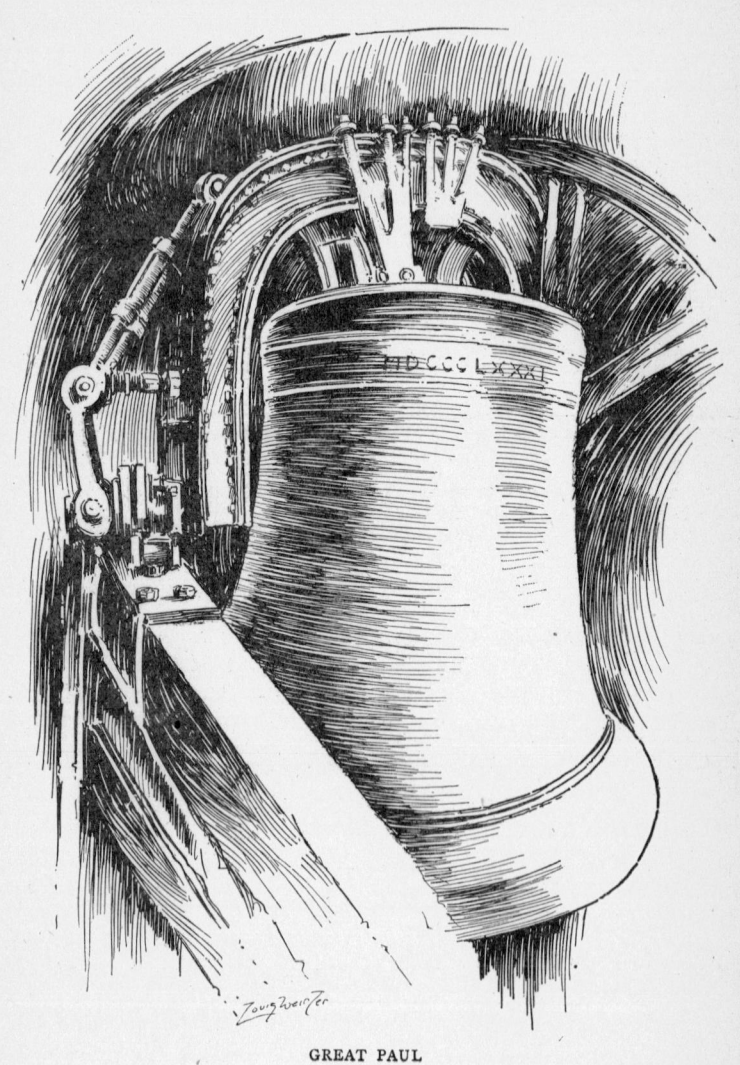

GREAT PAUL

jumped upon the altar, and threw the Cross, flowers and candlesticks on the floor, causing a great commotion and confusion. He was given into custody and locked up at the Police Station till Monday, when he was taken before the Magistrate (Sir Thomas Owden) and fined £5 or one month's imprisonment. The second charge, for damages, was not pressed by the Dean and Chapter; therefore he got off much too easily; the fine was paid by the Protestant Working Men's Association ... it was currently reported that he had cheques sent him afterwards for his courage and success.

March 28th, Wednesday. The Dean's daughter, Miss Church, married in the Cathedral to the Rev. F. Paget (son of Sir James Paget the physician, and afterwards Dean of Christ Church and Bishop of Oxford), by special licence at 11.30 a.m.

April 4th, Wednesday. The remains of the late Professor Palmer, Captain Gill and Lieutenant Charrington (murdered in Arabia when on service for the Government) were brought to the Cathedral early this morning (4.15 a.m.) from Portsmouth, and deposited in the Crypt. They were buried on Friday, April 6th, at 12 noon.

April 25th, Wednesday. Consecration of three Bishops, Truro (Wilkinson), Llandaff and Tasmania, 10 a.m. Canon Jayne (now Bishop of Chester) preached.

June 10th, Sunday morning. Dr. Philips Brooks preached the Hospital Sunday sermon.

Sept. 27th, Thursday, 11.30 a.m. Marriage of Miss Knight, the Lord Mayor's daughter, by the Archbishop of Canterbury.

Nov. 30th, Friday, 11.0 a.m. Consecration of the Bishop of Central Africa (Dr. Smythies).

1884.

March 28th, Friday. News received of the sudden death of the Duke of Albany. The State Bell (Edward of Westminster) was tolled from 8 to 9 p.m. The funeral took place at Windsor on Saturday, April 5th. Our bell was tolled from 11.30 to 12.30; and a muffled peal rung in the evening.

May 1st, Thursday. Consecration of the Bishop of Southwell and the Bishop of Riverina, 11.0 a.m.

June 5th, Thursday, 11.30 a.m. Burial of the late Sir Bartle Frere. The Bishop of London and Canon Gregory officiated; Duke of Cambridge present.

July 28th, Monday. The three daughters of the Crown Prince of Germany visited the Cathedral.

Sept. 14th, Sunday morning. Princess Christian present.

Nov. 14th, 11 a.m. Centenary service for Bishop Seabary, first bishop of the American Church. Archbishop Benson preached 53 minutes; the Bishop of London (Jackson) was celebrant, supported by the Bishops of Durham, St. Albans, Oxford, Chichester, Ely, Rochester, Lichfield, Truro, Colchester, Edinburgh, Aberdeen, Glasgow, Brechin, Argyll, Antigua, Nassau, Maritzburg, Sierra Leone, Travancore, Albany, Minnesota, Fond-du-Lac; also Bishops Tozer, Staley, Mitchinson and Titcomb.

Nov. 15th, Saturday, 12 noon. The Bishop of London held his first Confirmation in the Cathedral; the late Bishop Claughton used to hold them for him, or in his absence the Bishop of Bedford: 322 candidates.

1885.

Jan. 6th, Tuesday, Epiphany. The Bishop of London died suddenly, early this morning (he had preached in the Cathedral according to his custom on the first Sunday evening of the year, January 4, two days previously). The State Bell was tolled from 11.0 a.m. to 12 noon; the *Dead March* was played after evening service.

Jan. 8th, Thursday. The bells were rung this evening on the occasion of Prince Edward of Wales attaining his majority.

March 13th, Friday, 11.30 a.m. Service in memory of General Gordon and the officers and men who have fallen in the Soudan. The Bishop of Newcastle preached. The Archbishop of Canterbury, the Princess of Wales and suite, the Lord Mayor and Lady Mayoress, and many of the House of Lords were present: a very large congregation, quite orderly; service printed specially. The *Dead March* was played after the service. Great Paul was tolled 5 minutes before the service.

April 3rd, Good Friday, 8.0 a.m. Violent outrage by a man named Beere. During the Celebration in the N.W. Chapel, he rushed to the Credence Table and smashed the wine cruet with his umbrella; then rushed to the altar, and knocked over the Chalice and Paten, whilst the Dean was reading the Prayer for the Church Militant. He was taken into custody at once, and appeared before the Magistrate on Saturday; then remanded till Tuesday, for inquiries as to the state of his mind. The Alderman, Sir Thomas Owden, said the prisoner was perfectly aware of what he was doing, and sentenced him to a month's imprisonment.

April 11th, Saturday. The Lord Mayor (Nottage) died after a few days' illness. The State Bell was tolled from 11 to 12 to-day. The funeral took place on Saturday, April 18th, at 12 noon. The whole of the Cathedral was given up to the Corporation for tickets of admission. The grave was in the Crypt near that of Sir Bartle Frere; the Bishop of London and the Dean officiated.

April 25th, Saturday. Consecration of the Bishops of Lincoln (King) and Exeter (Bickersteth), 11 a.m. Dr. Liddon preached 63 minutes.

June 11th. Consecration of the Bishop of Brisbane (Thornhill-Webber); the Archbishop used his crozier for the first time, and the Bishop of London (Temple) his pastoral staff.

1886.

Jan. 6th, Wednesday, Epiphany. The Rev. C. A. Belli died (brother-in-law to Archbishop Howley). He was 67 years Precentor of the Cathedral; present officially at the Duke of Wellington's Funeral.

Jan. 13th, Wednesday. Opening of Convocation at St. Paul's: Latin sermon preached by Dr. Bradley, Dean of Westminster; Archdeacon Sumner elected Prolocutor.

Feb. 2nd, Tuesday. Consecration of the Bishops of Ely (Lord Alwyne Compton) and Japan.

May 6th, Thursday. The Duke and Duchess of Connaught and the Grand Duke and Duchess of Oldenburg visited the Cathedral.

June 5th, Saturday, 6 p.m. Duchess of Albany present at the Service of the Girls' Friendly Society.

June 20th, Trinity Sunday. The Lord Mayor and Corporation attended afternoon service to meet the Delegates for the Colonial Exhibition.

July and Aug. Choristers' holidays: first time all the boys were away at once; the services rendered by men's voices in the meantime.

Aug. 9th, Monday. Messers. Brindley and Farmer began to fix the Reredos.

1887.

Jan. 28th, Friday. The Glover Memorial unveiled in the Crypt this afternoon; Lord Wolseley and other General Officers present.

Feb. 27th, Sunday. The Socialists came to the Cathedral in great force this afternoon; the service very noisy in consequence, the congregation disorderly. A great number were unable to get in, so Canon Gregory, Prebendary Whittington, and Minor Canon Kelly, with four of the Choristers, went to the West Portico and held a short service to quiet the mob outside. The Archdeacon (Gifford) preached as Canon-in-Residence, and was frequently interrupted by hissing, hooting and cheering, much to the disgust of many who were present, myself included; and I hoped I should not see a repetition of such a service in our Cathedral. The Lord Mayor was present, and occupied his stall in the Choir; also a large body of police in the Crypt.

March 27th, Sunday. The Princess of Wales at the Morning Service, also on Monday 28th at the Afternoon; and on Tuesday 29th she came at 9.0 p.m. to hear Dr. Stainer at the organ.

April 3rd, Sunday. The Princess of Wales at Morning Service and Holy Communion.

April 12th, Easter Tuesday. Mr. and Mrs. Gladstone at the Afternoon Service.

May 1st, Sunday. The Princess of Wales at the Morning Service.

June 12th, Sunday morning. The Queen of the Sandwich Islands present.

June 23rd, Thursday, 4 p.m. Jubilee Service for the Queen. The Lord Mayor and Corporation and the different Companies attended; very large congregation.

July 21st, Thursday, 3 p.m. Monument to Sir Harry Parkes (Pioneer of Western Civilization in China—W.M.S.) unveiled in the Crypt.

Sept. 9th, Friday. Buffalo Bill's Red Indians at Morning Service; conducted afterwards round the Cathedral by Canon Holland.

1888.

Jan. 25th, Wednesday. Dedication of the Reredos at 10.0 a.m.

Feb. 24th, Friday. Consecration of two Suffragan Bishops: Archdeacon Earle (Marlborough), Archdeacon Sir Lovelace Stamer (Shrewsbury).

Feb. 26, Sunday; March 4, Sunday; March 18, Sunday. Princess of Wales present in the morning.

March 3rd, Saturday, 10.45 a.m. Unveiling of the monument to Sir Bartle Frere, in the Crypt by the Bishop of Salisbury.

March 6th, Tuesday. The new marble steps at the entrance to the Choir fixed to-day: given by Major Copeland, Treasurer of Bridewell Hospital.

June 3rd, Sunday. The Bishop of Japan preached this afternoon instead of the Canon-in-Residence. For the next three months the Bishops of the Lambeth Conference are appointed to occupy the pulpit, as they did 10 years back.

June 15th, Sunday, 10 a.m. Consecration of two Suffragan Bishops: Prebendary Billing (Bedford) and Archdeacon Thicknesse (Leicester). First Consecration on a Sunday.

July 27th, Friday. Unveiling of the Memorial to Sir Herbert Stewart in the Nave by Lord Wolseley.

July 28th, 11 a.m. Concluding service for the Bishops of the Lambeth Conference: Sermon and Holy Communion. Present, Archbishops of Canterbury, York, Dublin and Armagh, and many Bishops: in all about 130.

Oct. 21st, Sunday. The Princess of Wales present in the morning, Madame Patey (the famous Contralto) in the afternoon.

CHAPTER XXXI

VERGER GREEN'S DIARY: THE LAST HALF OF THE NINETEENTH CENTURY.—PART III.: 1889-1900

1889.

APRIL 6th, Saturday. The Duchess of Cambridge died at 12.30 to-day: the State Bell tolled from 6.0 to 7.0 p.m., and again on the day of the funeral, the 13th, from 12 noon to 1 p.m. (She was mother of the Duke of Cambridge, a Princess of Anhalt, aunt to the late Queen of Denmark; an excellent and kindly woman.—W. M. S.)

July 27th, Saturday. The Bells were rung in honour of the marriage of the Princess Louise of Wales to the Duke of Fife: 12. 0–1.15 p.m., and 6 to 7 p.m.

Royal Visits. (The royal visits became so numerous and regular that it is not necessary to quote them.—W. M. S.)

1890.

Jan. 21st, Tuesday, 12 noon. Funeral of the late Lord Napier of Magdala (the conqueror of Theodore of Abyssinia); the Prince of Wales and Prince George, the Duke of Cambridge and a large number of military officers present. The Sub-dean of the Chapel Royal (Edgar Sheppard) took part in the service; Canon Gregory read the lesson. All the Dome was reserved for tickets. The new opening under the Dome was used to lower the coffin into the Crypt, which was afterwards removed to the grave; so the service was finished without going into the Crypt, which had been the custom.

The same day the new Ambulance Station was opened under the West Steps of the Cathedral.

Feb. 28th, Friday, St. David's Eve, 7.30 p.m. The first Welsh Service held in the Cathedral; the Bishop of St. Asaph preached; all the service in the Welsh language; a large congregation. (The Welsh service has since been held every year at the same time, and has been greatly appreciated by the Welsh people in London.—W. M. S.)

March 7th, Friday. The Choristers returned after a fortnight's absence in consequence of Russian Influenza: (the beginning of that prolonged visitation which has since been with us).

May 24th, Saturday. The new Cross given by the Duke of Newcastle placed on the retable over the altar in the Choir this afternoon.

June 24th, Tuesday, 10 a.m. Consecration of four Bishops: St. Albans (Festing), Bangor (Lloyd), Sydney (Saumarez Smith), and Suffragan of Swansea (Lloyd): preacher, the Archdeacon of London (Sinclair).

July 13th, Sunday. Deputation of the Peace Conference attended afternoon service.

Sept. 9th, Tuesday. Received news of the death of Dr. Liddon at Weston-super-Mare. The funeral took place in the Cathedral on Tuesday the 16th at 12 noon. The new bell, "Great Paul," was tolled; used for the first time on such an occasion. The Dean (Church) read one prayer.

In November preparations were being made for the Mosaics in the roof of the Choir.

Nov. 29th, Sat. afternoon, Rev. W. C. E. Newbolt, Principal of Ely Theological College and Hon. Canon, installed as Canon Residentiary in place of Canon Liddon.

Dec. 9th, Tuesday, 11.30 a.m. Received a telegram to say the Dean died this morning at 8.0 a.m. The old State Bell was tolled from 1 to 2 p.m.

Dec. 15th, Monday. The first part of the funeral service for the late Dean Church was held in the Cathedral. The body had been brought into the N.W. Chapel on Sunday morning. The Archbishop of Canterbury and the Bishop of London were present. Canon Gregory read the Lesson, the Bishop read the Collects and gave the Benediction. After the Anthem, the procession moved to the West Door. The remains were then conveyed to Whatley, Somerset, to be buried according to his own wish, in the churchyard.

Dec. 20th, Saturday, 12 noon. Funeral of Sir Edgar Boehm, R.A., in the Crypt (in Artists' Corner).

1891.

Feb. 5th, Thursday. Installation of Canon Gregory as Dean of St. Paul's. During the Morning Service, the Lower House of Convocation, being in session, attended as a mark of honour.

Feb. 19th, Thursday afternoon. Rev. George Forrest Browne, Disney Professor at Cambridge, installed as Canon Residentiary in place of Canon Gregory.

May 9th, 1.30 p.m. Service for the Jews under the Dome; Prebendary Gordon Calthrop preached; repeated May 7th, 1892.

July 7th, 7 p.m. Tonic Sol-Fa Jubilee service in the Cathedral.

July 20th, Monday. Judgment given to-day in the House of Lords in the Reredos case, decided in favour of the Bishop and the Dean and Chapter on appeal from Lord Coleridge's decision. (The representation of the Crucifixion was held to be a group and not a crucifix.—W. M. S.)

August 2nd, Sunday morning. The Order of Foresters attended the service, about 1000 in number; Lord Mayor Savory and Sheriff Farmer present.

Sept. 29th, Tuesday, 10 a.m. Consecration of 5 Bishops, Truro, Lichfield, Southwark (Suffragan), Coventry (Suffragan), and Zululand.

Nov. 16th, Sunday morning. The crew of the ship *Benvenue*, about 27 in number, who were saved from the

THE REREDOS

wreck off Sandgate, attended service to return thanks for their safety.

Nov. 20th, Friday. The pastoral staff (promoted by the two Archdeacons) presented to the Bishop of London (Temple) at Sion College this afternoon.

Nov. 22nd, Sunday morning. Prayers said for Prince George of Wales; the Duke of Cambridge present.

1892.

Jan. 13th, Wednesday. Prayers said for the Duke of Clarence and Avondale. On Thursday the Dean received the news of his death, which took place at Sandringham this morning at 9.15. The old State Bell was tolled from 11 a.m. till noon. Wednesday, Jan. 20th, the day of the funeral, a Memorial Service was held in the Cathedral at 3 p.m.; the bell was tolled from 2.15 to 3.15 p.m. Lord Mayor Evans and Sheriffs, and several of the Companies attended the Service; a very large congregation present. On Sunday morning the 17th the Dean (Dr. Gregory) preached.

May 22nd, Sunday morning. Buffalo Bill's party attended the service; they represented a variety of countries: very orderly during the service.

June 17th, Friday. Mr. Harding began moving the Wellington Monument from the Consistory Court (or S.W. Chapel, where it could not be seen), to the central arch on the North side of the Nave (on the initiative of Lord Leighton, and where the sculptor, Stevens, wished it to be. Lord Leighton was responsible for the fund—£2000—for the removal, but gave £700 from his own pocket. —W. M. S.).

Sept. 25th, Sunday morning. The Lucknow Relief survivors, about 70, attended service.

Oct. 9th, Sunday afternoon. The *Dead March* in Saul was played for the late Lord Tennyson.

Dec. 21st, Wednesday. Consecration of Bishop Hornby as Assistant to Bishop Smythies in Central Africa.

Dec. 28th, Innocents' Day, 4 p.m. Children's Service; Canon Browne, preacher.

1893.

May 16th, Tuesday, 10.30 a.m. Special Service for Church Defence against the Welsh Suspensory Bill; Communion, no sermon. Very large gathering of Bishops, Clergy, and Churchwardens; also the two Houses of Convocation, Canterbury and York. The Prolocutor of the Southern Province (Bishop Sumner) sat in the Bishop's (Archbishop's) Stall on the South side of the Choir, and the Prolocutor of the Northern Province (Chancellor Espin) in the Lord Mayor's Stall opposite. (The number of communicants was so large that they knelt on the north and south steps as well as the east. The administrants in the usual place were the Archbishop of York, followed by the Bishop of Newcastle; the Bishop of Durham, followed by the Bishop of Exeter; and the Bishop of Gloucester and Bristol, followed by the Bishop of St. Albans. On the two platforms outside the Golden Gates the following administered: North—Archdeacon of London, followed by Prebendary Reynolds, and Canon Browne, followed by Minor Canon Milman. South—Dean of St. Paul's, followed by Prebendary Baker, and Canon Newbolt, followed by Minor Canon Sparrow Simpson.)

June. During this month two pilasters in the Choir were faced with marble.

June 26th, Sunday afternoon. The *Dead March* was played after the service, as a mark of sympathy with the disaster to H.M.S. *Victoria*.

June 29th, Thursday. Consecration of four Bishops: Rev. J. Sheepshanks (Norwich), Rev. Dr. Hill (Western Equatorial Africa), Rev. Dr. Olowole and Rev. D. Phillips as Assistant-Bishops to Dr. Hill. The two Assistants are natives of Africa. Bishop Wilkinson preached.

July 6th, Thursday. Wedding of the Duke and Duchess

VERGER GREEN'S DIARY.—PART III. 353

ALTAR IN THE JESUS CHAPEL (APSE)

A A

of York. Tickets were issued for seats outside the West Window to view the Royal Procession, on the way to Liverpool Street Station; the Corporation had seats erected in the S.W. part of the Churchyard, by permission of the Dean and Chapter; the South Portico was occupied by different members of the Cathedral body. The day was very hot; thermometer 84 in the shade. The Ambulance people were quite busy with cases of fainting.

During the months of July and August the new lower windows in the Apse are being fixed by Kemp (finished in September); also the recumbent figure of the late Dr. Liddon (Messrs. Bodley and Garner). The new Clock and Bells still in hand: the old hour bell is placed higher, also "Great Paul" and the quarter bells.

Sept. 22nd. During this week four marble slabs are being fixed in the panels by the Lord Mayor's Vestry with the names of the Deans of the Cathedral from 1066.

Dec. 21st, Thursday, St. Thomas. Dedication of the new Clock this morning; a service printed for the occasion, which was taken by the Dean and Canon Newbolt. The service was arranged to be over for the Clock to strike twelve.

The same day the Vergers, Clerk of the Works, and working staff of the Cathedral presented the Dean (Dr. Gregory) with a Reading-Lamp on the 25th anniversary of his connection with St. Paul's Cathedral.

1894.

During the months of February and March the different City Companies were invited by the Dean to come and view Sir William Richmond's Mosaics at the East End of the Choir before it was opened; also a number of members of the Press.

April 5th, Thursday. The Jesus Chapel dedicated this morning (formerly the sacrarium of the Cathedral; now called after a chapel in Old St. Paul's, in the old crypt, at the east end).

April 21st, Saturday. The new window in the Consistory Court (in memory of Archdeacon Hessey of Middlesex) unveiled this afternoon. Prayers were said by the Archdeacon (Sinclair) and the Dean gave a short address. (When the Consistory Court became the Chapel of the Order of St. Michael and St. George, the window was removed to the north wall of the west aisle of the north transept.—W. M. S.)

May 25th, Friday, 11.0 a.m. Communion for the South African Mission. Bishop of Derry (Alexander) preached.

May 28th, 4 p.m. The members of the Missionary Conference attended, and the Bishop of Durham preached. A large congregation.

June 5th, Tuesday, 7.30 p.m. Jubilee Service of the Young Men's Christian Association : the Bishop of Ripon (Boyd Carpenter) preached. (The prayers were printed in English, French, German, Swedish, etc., and all joined in.)

June 24th. The Cathedral bells were rung on the occasion of the birth of a Prince, son of the Duke and Duchess of York, in the direct line to the throne. The National Anthem was played in the afternoon by Dr. Martin.

June 30th, Saturday. The new large candlesticks placed in the sacrarium, copied from those belonging to the tomb of Prince Arthur, given by his brother Henry VIII., and sold by Oliver Cromwell to the Cathedral of Ghent.

July 13th, Friday, 5.30 p.m. Special Service for the parochial school-children of the different Wards (a revival of the old Charity Children's Service). The Archdeacon preached.

July 29th, Sunday morning. The Medical Congress. The members attended, with the Lord Mayor and Sheriffs.

Nov. 1st. Last of the statues in the Dome fixed.

1892. Nov. 24th, St. Chrysostom fixed
1893. Oct. 26th, St. Basil   ,,
1893. Nov. 21st, St. Augustine   ,,
1894. April 17th, St. Gregory   ,,
1894. May 18th, St. Jerome   ,,
1894. June 12th, St. Athanasius   ,,
1894. Oct. 19th, St. Gregory the Great fixed
1894. Nov. 1st, St. Ambrose   ,,

Nov. 1st, Thursday. Prayers were said this afternoon for the Emperor of Russia, and this evening the news of his death was received.

Nov. 4th, Sunday. The *Dead March* was played this afternoon most impressively by Dr. Martin for the late Emperor. His death was alluded to by the preachers: morning, Prebendary Barker; afternoon, Archdeacon of London; evening, the Dean.

Nov. 24th, Saturday, 5 p.m. The College Youths rang a peal of Kent Triple Bob Maxims, consisting of 5088 changes; the time occupied being 4 hours and 18 minutes. The peal was composed by the late Mr. John Cox; J. Pettit conductor.

Dec. 28th, Friday, 10 a.m. Consecration of the Bishops of Coventry and Colchester (Knox and Johnson). Preacher, Dr. Chavasse (afterwards Bishop of Liverpool).

1895.

April 21st, Sunday. Consecration of Canon Browne as Bishop-Suffragan of Stepney; the Bishop of London (Temple) took the service in the absence of the Archbishop; the sermon was preached by the Rev. A. F. Winnington-Ingram (Head of Oxford House, who succeeded Dr. Browne as Bishop of Stepney, and afterwards became Bishop of London). The Duke of Cambridge was present.

June 29th, Saturday. Consecration of five Bishops: Southampton (Suffragan, Hon. Arthur Lyttleton), New

Westminster, Riverina, Likoma and Zanzibar. Preacher, the Archdeacon of Middlesex (Dr. Thornton).

August 20th, Tuesday. Charles Macpherson (formerly chorister) appointed Sub-Organist in place of the late Mr. Hodge.

On Nov. 2nd, Saturday, King Khama of South Africa and two Chiefs visited the Cathedral. On Dec. 12th, Thursday, Duke and Duchess of Connaught, Princess Margaret, and the Duke of Oldenburgh and his daughter mounted the scaffolding with the Dean, and were shown the Mosaics.

1896.

Jan. 22nd, Wednesday. News received of the death of Prince Henry of Battenberg, at sea, after the Ashanti War: the *Dead March* was played at the afternoon service on Thursday, Jan. 23rd.

Feb. 3rd, Monday. Funeral of the late Lord Leighton, President of the Royal Academy, at 12 noon. The body was buried in the Crypt near the tomb of Wren.

Feb. 4th, Tuesday. Funeral Service in the Cathedral for the late Sir Joseph Barnby, at 12 noon. The body was buried at Norwood Cemetery.

Easter Eve. Unveiling of the Choir decorations.

June 26th, Hospital Sunday. The Fire Brigade and Ambulance Corps attended morning service.

July 5th, Sunday afternoon. The Delegates of the Evangelical Alliance present.

Aug. 8th, Saturday morning. Li-Chang, the Chinese Ambassador, visited the Cathedral at 9.15 a.m., and placed a wreath on Gordon's monument in the Nave: Canon Newbolt received him.

Aug. 20th, Thursday. Funeral of Sir John Millais, President of the Royal Academy, at 12 noon. The body was buried at the foot of that of his predecessor, Lord Leighton, in Artists' Corner.

Oct. 11th, Sunday. During the Afternoon Service a telegram was received from Hawarden, announcing the sudden death of the Archbishop of Canterbury (Dr. Benson), which took place in the Church during the Morning Service, when he was on a visit to Mr. Gladstone. After the sermon, the Bishop of Stepney made it known to the congregation in the Cathedral. The *Dead March* was played by Dr. Martin; the old State Bell was tolled from 5.30 to 6.30 p.m. The funeral took place at Canterbury Cathedral on Friday, Oct. 16th, at 12.30 p.m.; our Cathedral Bell was tolled from 12 to 1 p.m., and a muffled peal was rung by the College Youths in the evening, from 7 to 8.0 p.m.

Oct. 20th, Tuesday, 7.0 p.m. Special Service for the Church Lads' Brigade.

Oct. 26th, Monday. The Bishop of London (Dr. Temple) announced as the new Archbishop of Canterbury.

Dec. 23rd, Wednesday. The Bishop of London's Farewell Service (to the clergy and laity of the Diocese).

1897.

Jan. 5th, Tuesday. Election of the Bishop of London (Dr. Creighton) at the Chapter House.

Jan. 14th, Thursday, 1.30 p.m. Special Service for Headmasters: preacher, the Bishop of Stepney.

Jan. 30th, Saturday. Enthronement of the Bishop of London.

Feb. 24th, Wednesday. Consecration of the Bishops of Peterborough (Hon. E. C. Glyn) and Crediton (Suffragan, Canon Trefusis).

March 29th, Sunday. Dr. Sparrow Simpson (Minor Canon, Sub-dean, Librarian and formerly Succentor) died at 3 a.m. this morning after a short illness. The *Dead March* was played after the service. (He was a great loss; gentle, kindly, learned, devout. He published three antiquarian books about St. Paul's.—W. M. S.)

April 25th, Sunday. Collections for the Indian Famine Fund.

May 1st, 10 a.m. Consecration of the Bishop of St. Davids (Dr. John Owen).

May 27th, 10.30 a.m. Consecration of the Bishop of Sierra Leone.

June 5th, Saturday. Special service at 5 p.m. for the 1300th anniversary of the baptism of King Ethelbert by Augustine. A short address by the Bishop of Stepney.

June 20th, Sunday morning. The Queen's Accession, and 60th year of her reign. Special form of Thanksgiving: numbers of the Royal Family present: the Prince and Princess of Wales, Duke and Duchess of York, Princess Victoria of Wales, Prince and Princess Charles of Denmark (afterwards King and Queen of Norway), Grand Duke and Duchess of Mecklenburg, Duke of Cambridge, Prince and Princess Aribert of Anhalt, Prince and Princess of Schaumburg-Lippe, Prince Albert of Prussia and others with him, Duke and Duchess of Coburg, Grand Duke and Duchess of Hesse, Prince Alfred of Coburg, Grand Duke Cyril of Russia. The Bishop of London (Creighton) preached. In the afternoon the Lord Mayor, Corporation and Judges attended: Hospital Sunday.

June 22nd, Tuesday. The Queen's Diamond Jubilee, after sixty years' reign. Great preparations on the route of the Procession through the streets; decorations and illuminations. Special short service was held on the Western Steps of the Cathedral. Her Majesty arrived just before 12 noon (attended by the whole Royal Family, and a galaxy of Foreign and Indian Princes and potentates of every description). (Dr. Martin's magnificent *Te Deum* in A was sung with a military band and augmented choir; there were also a few prayers.) Great array of Clergy, Archbishops and Bishops, and most of those connected with the Cathedral. The Service did not exceed 20 minutes. A number of American, Foreign, and Colonial

Bishops were present, it being the year of the Lambeth Conference (which was held a year earlier, in order to coincide with the Diamond Jubilee). (It was a scene of unparalleled splendour and enthusiasm, bathed in the brilliancy of full sunshine; both the Prince of Wales and the Duke of York said afterwards that they had never seen anything equal to it.—W. M. S.)

June 23rd, Wednesday, 11 a.m. Annual Service of the S.P.G. Some 50 Bishops present.

Aug. 1st, Sunday evening. Service for the Board of Missions. Over 100 Bishops present; the Archbishop preached.

Aug. 2nd, Monday, 10 a.m. Concluding service of the Lambeth Conference: 149 Bishops present.

Aug. 3rd, Tuesday, 11 a.m. Service for the Deaf and Dumb in the N.W. Chapel.

The Bishop of Stepney (Browne) announced to be Bishop of Bristol.

Oct. 27th, Wednesday. The Duchess of Teck died unexpectedly; the State Bell was tolled from 5 m. past 1 to 5 m. past 2 p.m.

Nov. 3rd, Wednesday. Memorial Service for the late Duchess of Teck. The State Bell was tolled from 1 to 2 p.m. The Lord Mayor and Corporation attended.

Nov. 10th, Wednesday. Rev. A. F. Winnington-Ingram installed as Canon-Residentiary, in place of Dr. Browne.

Nov. 30th, Tuesday, 10 a.m. Consecration of Canon Winnington-Ingram as Bishop of Stepney.

Dec. 2nd, Thursday. Bi-centenary of the Cathedral (first opened in 1697 to celebrate the Peace of Ryswick) celebrated by the Freemasons. (The interest was so great that many could not get in.) Preacher, the Bishop of London (Creighton).

Dec. 14th, Tuesday. The old colours of the 1st London Fusiliers deposited in the Nave. Short Service by the Dean.

Dec. 15th, Wednesday. Unveiling of the Memorial in the Crypt to the late George Richmond, R.A. (the eminent portrait-painter, and father of Sir William Richmond, R.A., K.C.B.).

1898.

Sunday, Jan. 30th. Collections for St. Paul's Poor Benefices. (£100 is provided by the collections and the Cathedral, which is doubled by the Ecclesiastical Commissioners, and produces about £6 of additional income.—W. M. S.)

Wednesday, March 2nd. First Annual Service of the Queen Victoria Clergy Fund (London Branch). Archbishop of Canterbury preached.

Thursday, March 8th. The Bi-centenary Services of the S.P.C.K., 11.0 a.m. and 7.30 p.m. Archbishop of Canterbury preached.

May 26th, Saturday evening. Dumb Peal rung for Mr. Gladstone, funeral at Westminster Abbey. He died at Hawarden on May 19th.

June 11th, Saturday, 10 a.m. Consecration of the Bishops of Islington and Victoria: preacher, the Archdeacon of London.

June 18th, Saturday, 6 p.m. Special Foreign Mission Service for Children. Bishop of Stepney preached. About 200 children had to stand up for want of room.

Jnue 20th to June 24th. Lectures from the Dome pulpit (for the Diocesan Church Reading Union) by Dr. Robertson (now Bishop of Exeter), Professor Collins (now Bishop of Gibraltar), Rev. C. J. Ridgway (now Bishop of Chichester), Bishop of Bristol and Bishop Barry.

June 25th. South Transept Window unveiled in the presence of the Duke and Duchess of Westminster: the window was given by the Duke.

Sept. 26, Monday. Burial of Sir George Grey, the Prime Minister of New Zealand.

Nov. 5th, Saturday. Unveiling of the Mosaic in the North-east Quarter-Dome, given by the Merchant Taylors Company.

Nov. 7th, 7 p.m. Special Service for the United Friendly Societies: preacher, Bishop of London.

Nov. 30th, 10 a.m. Consecration of two Bishops: Calcutta (Welldon) and Southampton.

1899.

Feb. 7th, Tuesday, 6 p.m. The Bishop of Stepney began a Bible Class for the Workmen employed in the Cathedral; to be continued each week.

Feb. 9th. After the 4 p.m service, the Cathedral Clergy assembled at the Chapter House to present the Dean with his portrait, painted by Sir William Richmond, on the occasion of his 80th birthday. Canon H. S. Holland, as Senior, made the presentation. The Cathedral bells were rung in the evening on the occasion.

April 14th, Friday. Burial of the body of Lady Frere by that of her husband in the Crypt. The Dean and the Archdeacon of London took the service.

May 10th, Wednesday, 7 p.m. Centenary Service for the Bible Society: preacher, the Bishop of Ripon.

May 11th, Thursday, 6.30 p.m. Service for the Diocesan Training Colleges.

June 29th, Thursday. Consecration of the Bishops of Madagascar and Mombasa.

July 19th, Wednesday, 11.15 a.m. The Mosaics in the S.W. Quarter-Dome uncovered: present, the Dean and Archdeacon.

Oct. 10th, Tuesday, 10.30 a.m. The first Church Congress that was held in London: the opening Service took place in St. Paul's. Large attendance of clergy. The Archbishop (Temple) preached. The closing service was on Friday, Oct. 13th, at 7.30 p.m.

Oct. 29th, Sunday. Collections for the Widows and

VERGER GREEN'S DIARY.—PART III.

Children of Soldiers who had died so far in the South African War: £206.

Nov. 13th, Monday. At the Chapter meeting to-day, I resigned my office as Dean's Verger, having begun my 48th year of service in the Cathedral. (Robert R. Green, the writer of these notes.)

Dec. 19th, Tuesday, 3 p.m. Memorial Service for those who had fallen in the War this year. The Duke of Cambridge, Lord Lansdowne, the Lord Mayor and Sheriffs, attended. The band of the Coldstream Guards accompanied; many soldiers in uniform present.

Dec. 29th, Friday, 10.30 a.m. Solemn Service of Intercession for the War. Sermon and Holy Communion. Bishop of London (Creighton) preached.

1900.

Feb. 1st, Friday. I received from Her Majesty Queen Victoria a Silver Medal of the Victorian Order in consideration of my long service at St. Paul's Cathedral, from 1852 to Nov., 1899. (In 1897 he received a framed portrait from the Queen, with a letter from Sir Fleetwood Edwards.)

R. R. GREEN.

CHAPTER XXXII

ST. PAUL'S IN THE TWENTIETH CENTURY

1900.

NEARLY ten years have passed since, in Nov. 1899, our careful annalist, Robert Green, retired from the service of the Chapter. Many important events have happened since then. That winter was very gloomy from the want of success attending our arms at the opening of the Boer campaign, and the close investment of Kimberley, Ladysmith and Mafeking. The country was summoned to furnish fresh troops, and responded with enthusiasm. Lord Mayor Newton inaugurated the City Imperial Volunteers; two farewell services of the most impressive character were held for them in the Cathedral, the first in the week ending Jan. 13th, the second on Friday the 19th. At the first the farewell address was given by the Dean, at the second by Bishop Creighton: the latter was attended by the Duke of Connaught and other army chiefs. A special Service of Intercession for God's blessing on the British cause was held on the morning of Septuagesima Sunday. On Thursday evening, March 1st, the bells were rung for the news of the Relief of Ladysmith; thanksgiving was offered on the Sunday afternoon following. The Relief of Mafeking took place on May 17th: a special *Te Deum* was sung for it.

On Saturday, June 16th, was commemorated the bi-centenary of the Society for the Propagation of the Gospel: the sermon was preached by one of the most eloquent and beloved of the American Bishops, Dr. Doane of Albany.

THE CHOIR, LOOKING EAST

On Saturday, August 4th, a Memorial Service was held for the Duke of Saxe-Coburg; the choristers being absent on holiday their places were taken by the boys of St. Paul's, Knightsbridge.

A Thanksgiving Service for the return of the City Imperial Volunteers was held on Monday, Oct. 29th. Although the march from the railway-station through the streets was of a difficult character, owing to the uncontrollable and unrestrained enthusiasm of the crowd, the service was most orderly and impressive. Fifteen hundred of the regiment were present; many touching scenes of reunion took place at the conclusion.

On Nov. 27th, the remains of Sir Arthur Sullivan were buried in St. Paul's; the company of the Savoy Theatre sang "Yea, though I walk through the Valley of the Shadow of Death," from his oratorio, *The Light of the World*.

On Dec. 19th a service was held in memory of those who had fallen in the South African war during the year. It was repeated on Dec. 16th, at the end of 1901. Special services were held on Dec. 13th, 1900, and Jan. 1, 1901, for the close of the nineteenth century, and the opening of the twentieth.

1901.

The funeral of Bishop Creighton took place on Thursday, Jan. 17th, in the Cathedral. The body was received on Wednesday at 6.30, with a short office, and lay in the centre of the choir with the Duke of Wellington's candelabra round it, properly attended. The remains were buried east of those of Dean Milman, in front of the altar of the crypt.

Queen Victoria died on Tuesday, Jan. 22nd. On the day following, Wednesday, Jan. 23rd, a short form of supplication was used after morning prayer, and a long form in the afternoon. On the days following, until the funeral, the shorter form was said after evening prayer; and music of a penitential type was used throughout the services. St. Paul's Day happening to occur in the interval, the Dedication Festival was postponed to Friday, Feb. 8th, Jan. 25th being treated as a ferial day, with only the recitation of the collect to mark it. Every day the Cathedral was crowded by worshippers, all in mourning. On Saturday, the day of the Funeral Service at Windsor, matins were said after eight o'clock Celebration in the crypt, and the Cathedral closed till the solemn Memorial Service at 3 p.m., the hour of burial. On the Sunday morning after the Queen's death the police estimated that 30,000 were unable to obtain entrance to St. Paul's, as it was already full. Many of them went to the neighbouring churches.

At the end of February a Quiet Day was held in the Cathedral for the clergy of the diocese by Bishop Gott of Truro, and was attended by about three hundred.

On March 7th, the Bishop of Stepney, Canon and Treasurer of St. Paul's, was appointed Bishop of London, to the great pleasure of his colleagues in the Chapter. On March 17, a new Palestrina service ("Assumpta") was sung at Holy Communion. There are now four of these exquisite settings in use.

On Saturday, April 27th, the Rev. Cosmo Gordon Lang, Vicar of Portsea, was installed as Canon at evensong in place of the Bishop of London. On April 30th the Bishop of London was enthroned at 10 a.m., and received the oath of obedience from the Chapter in the S.W. Chapel. Canon Lang was consecrated Bishop of Stepney on May 1st.

On Thursday, June 11, at 3 p.m., 800 of the Royal Fusiliers attended a Thanksgiving Service: the Lord Mayor present.

During the week ending July 6th, the Moorish Embassy visited the Cathedral.

INTERIOR VIEW

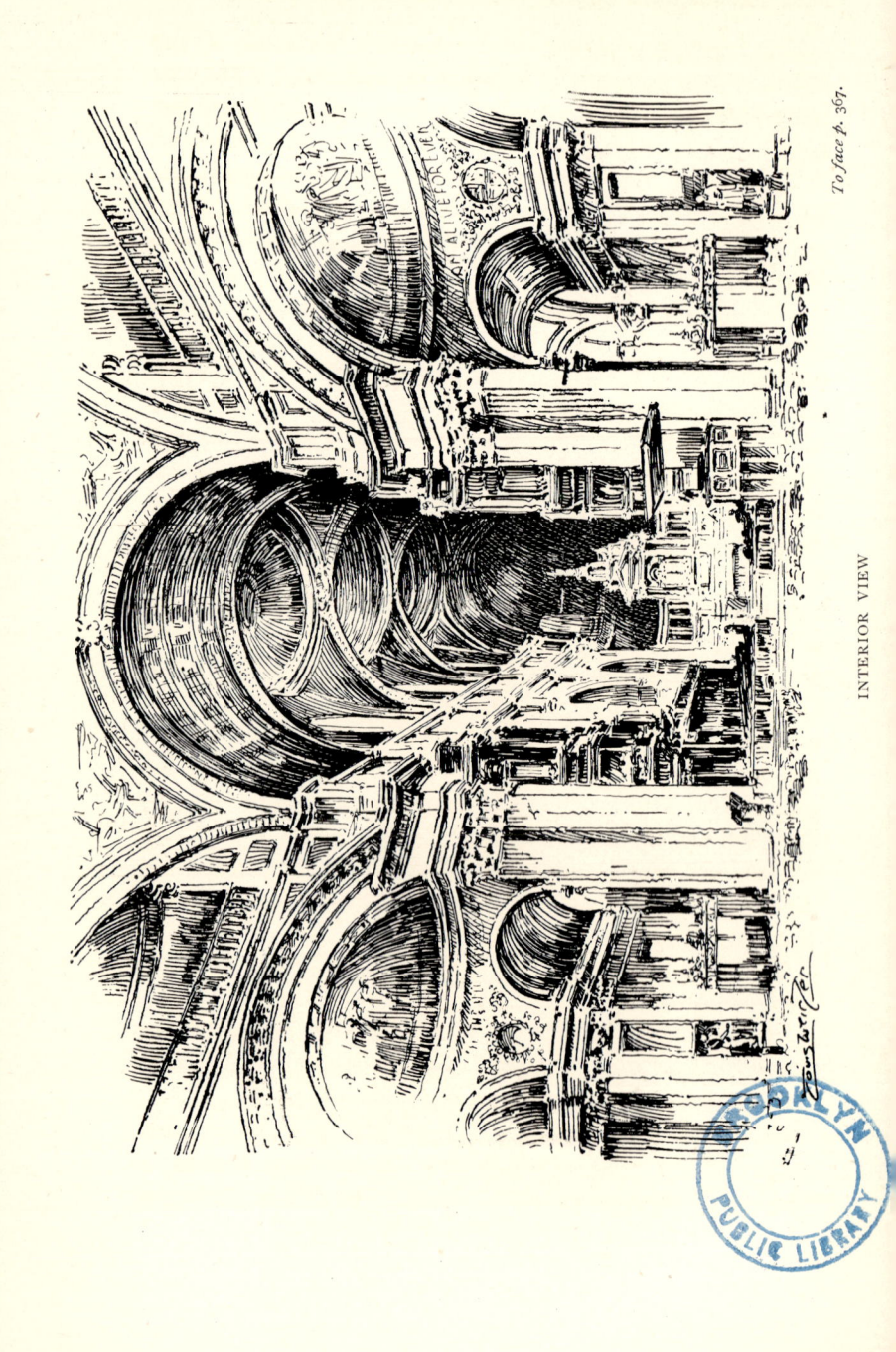

To face p. 367.

ST. PAUL'S IN THE TWENTIETH CENTURY

On Tuesday, August 6th, news was received of the death of the Emperor Frederick of Germany. The old State Bell was tolled, a special anthem was sung, and the *Dead March* in Saul played on the organ. On Tuesday, Aug. 13th, being the occasion of the Emperor's funeral, the bell was tolled from twelve to one o'clock; a special anthem was appointed for evensong, and the *Dead March* again played.

On Thursday evening, Nov. 7th, a great service of working-men was held, when the Bishop of London preached. Saturday, Nov. 9th, being Lord Mayor's Day, a vast crowd was present, and Handel's Coronation Anthem was sung. Prayers were offered for the first time for George, Prince of Wales, under that title. On Sunday morning, the 10th, the Duke and Duchess of Connaught, Prince Arthur and Princess Margaret were present at Holy Communion.

On Saturday, Nov. 23rd, it was agreed that the font might be removed from the S.W. Chapel to some other part, having not long been placed on that site, and also the Hessey window to another space, in order that the chapel may be given to the Order of St. Michael and St. George. But that requires a separate account. The font now looks exceedingly well in the west aisle of the south transept; the window in the west aisle of the north transept, whither also the Consistory Court has been moved, with the kind concurrence of the Chancellor of the Diocese, Dr. Tristram.

1902.

On Feb. 19th Sir E. J. Poynter, P.R.A., unveiled the beautiful Leighton Memorial (by Thomas Brock, R.A.); most of the Royal Academy were present.

During Holy Week (March 24–29) there were great congregations present at midday to hear the Bishop of London's addresses, especially during the Three Hours on

Good Friday. On Easter Eve, March 29th, the chancel was lighted for the first time by electricity; this, and the supply for the whole Cathedral, were the gift of Mr. Pierpont Morgan, the well-known American financier and Churchman, at a cost of £17,000.

On Thursday, April 10th, at 2.30 p.m., by special request was held a Memorial Service for the Right Hon. Cecil Rhodes, the South African statesman and patriot; there were present a representative of the King, several members of the Government, and a very large congregation.

On Wednesday, April 16th, at 5.30 p.m., was held a Farewell Service for the scholars of Christ's Hospital, now leaving London for their new buildings in Sussex. The sermon was preached by the Archbishop of Canterbury.

On Sunday, June 8th, at 10.30 a.m., there was a special thanksgiving for the restoration of peace after the South African war. The King and Queen, the Prince and Princess of Wales, many members of the Royal Family, and a congregation representative of all that was greatest in the nation. The Bishop of London preached.

On Thursday, June 26th, which was to have been the day of the coronation, was held, at 12 noon, a special service of humble supplication to Almighty God for the recovery of King Edward VII. from his sickness. It was attended by many members of the Royal Family, Indian Rajahs and Nawâbs, the High-Priest of the Sikhs, some Colonial troops, and a large number of American and Colonial guests. The same service was used on Sunday morning, the 29th; the afternoon and evening services were also thronged. During the week (June 30th—July 5th) "O God, save the King" was sung before the prayer for all sorts and conditions of men, followed by a prayer from the Visitation Service. On Tuesday the King was pronounced out of immediate danger, and the extra service of intercession was dropped; on Saturday he was pronounced out of danger altogether, and the extra collect was dropped. Large numbers came to the Cathedral all the week.

On Saturday, August 9th, the King and Queen were crowned at Westminster; the choir of St. Paul's took part in the service, and the Dean and Chapter occupied a gallery at the corner of the choir and north transept, close to the throne. On Sunday, August 10th, at 10.30 a.m., a Service of Thanksgiving was held in St. Paul's for the coronation; the sermon was preached by the Bishop of London.

The following special prayer was used both at this service and at that for the recovery—

"O Lord God of our fathers, Who in Thy goodness hast led this people hitherto by wondrous ways: Who makest the nations to praise Thee, and knittest them together in the bands of peace; we beseech Thee to pour Thine abundant blessing on the dominions over which Thou hast called Thy servant Edward to be King. Grant that one and all, of whatever race or colour or tongue, may draw together in heart and will beneath the shelter of the throne, united in the bond of brotherhood, in the ways of welfare and peace, and in the one fellowship of the Faith, so that we may be found a people acceptable unto Thee, through Jesus Christ our Lord. Amen.

On Wednesday, Sept. 24th, at 3 p.m., was held a Thanksgiving Service for the return of the 24th Imperial Yeomanry.

On Sunday, Oct. 26th, took place the Thanksgiving Service for the King's recovery, which was attended by their Majesties, the Prince of Wales, and most members of the Royal Family. The King, Queen and Royal Family were placed in the sacrarium, where they could hardly be seen; it would also have been better if, as in the Royal Thanksgiving of 1871, the whole space had been allotted

THRONES OF KING EDWARD VII. AND QUEEN ALEXANDRA ON NORTH SIDE OF SACRARIUM: MR. SOMERS CLARKE, ARCHT.

by ticket, in order to save disappointment both within and without, and to lighten the labours and responsibilities of the police. There was an immense throng, and the service was one of great beauty.

On Saturday, Dec. 27th, at 12 noon, a Memorial Service was held for the late Archbishop of Canterbury (Dr. Temple) at the hour of the funeral at Canterbury.

1903.

At the close of February a monument by Alfred Gilbert, R.A., was unveiled to Lord Lytton, late Governor-General of India. On Friday, March 20th, the monument of F.-M. Sir Sam. Browne, Commander-in-Chief in India, was unveiled by Lord Roberts.

In July, the plaster sketch, left by Alfred Stevens, of an equestrian statue of the Duke of Wellington was offered to view on the top of the Wellington monument. It was agreed that it was so crude as to be impossible, and the sculptor, Mr. Tweed, was authorized to prepare a finished model from the sketch, to be finally approved by the Chapter. It is not yet finished.

On Friday, Dec. 11th, a memorial bronze of Sir Walter Besant was unveiled in the crypt.

1904.

On Sunday morning, March 6th, was held a Centenary Service for the Bible Society, at 11 a.m., Holy Communion having been celebrated at 9.45 a.m., preceded by morning prayer and Litany. The King was unable to come, through a feverish cold : the Queen was present, with the Prince and Princess of Wales and the Princess Victoria.

On Wednesday, March 23rd, the remains of Mrs. Gregory, wife of the Dean, were buried in the crypt beside the grave of Dean Milman. She died on March 19th, after a very short illness.

On Thursday, May 5th, the 1300th Anniversary of Mellitus, the first Bishop of the Anglo-Saxons in London, and one of Pope Gregory's mission from Rome for their conversion, was observed at 8 p.m. by a service consisting of Litany, sermon and *Te Deum*, accompanied by an orchestra.

On Thursday, July 7th, a Memorial Service was held for the late G. F. Watts, R.A., at which all the members of the Royal Academy were present, and a great congregation of distinguished persons.

On Friday, July 15th, the Cathedral was visited by a large number of French workmen in the morning, and by the Atlantic Union in the afternoon.

On Friday, July 22nd, at 11 a.m., General Sir F. Stephenson unveiled a monument to the Coldstream Guards who fell in South Africa. Many distinguished officers were present, 400 of the men and the band, which played Sullivan's *In Memoriam* and the *Dead March*. The buglers gave the "Last Post" from the east end, with pathetic effect.

On July 25th, the Dean's son was consecrated Bishop of Mauritius.

1905.

March. This year, for the first time, the beautiful *Miserere* of Allégri (first taken down by Mozart, when a boy, from the singing at St. Peter's at Rome) was sung after evensong on Fridays in Lent; to be continued in future years. It has always been appreciated by a large congregation.

On Wednesday, May 24th, the Prince of Wales unveiled a beautiful memorial to 4200 Colonial volunteers who fell in the South African campaign. The sculpture was modelled by H.R.H. Princess Louise (Duchess of Argyll) and represents the Angel of Sympathy receiving the dead body of Christ on the Cross as the emblem of Self-sacrifice.

On Saturday, July 1st, was unveiled the monument of Bishop Creighton by the Archbishop of Canterbury, in the presence of the Bishop of London and a large congregation. It is an upright bronze figure, with cope and crozier, by Thornycroft, in the south aisle of the choir.

On Sunday, July 2nd, T.R.H. the Prince and Princess Gustavus Adolphus of Sweden, with the Duke and Duchess of Connaught, attended Holy Communion.

On Wednesday, July 5th, at 5 p.m., a Memorial Service for the late John Hay, American Secretary of State, was held at the request of the Americans, at which about 2000 of them were present, with the Lord Mayor and Sheriffs, and many members of both Houses of Parliament.[1]

On Sunday morning, July 23rd, the Royal Institute of National Health attended, and the Bishop of London preached.

On Tuesday, Nov. 14th, the funeral of Sir George Williams took place at 12 noon; a great citizen, who had received the freedom of the City and knighthood from Queen Victoria, in recognition of the fact that as founder and sixty-one years President of the Young Men's Christian Association, he was the greatest benefactor to young men of his day. At the time of his death the society had

[1] The following special collect was used—

"Almighty God, Who hast made of one blood all nations of men to dwell on all the face of the earth ; Who dost exalt every people that loveth righteousness, and hast blessed them that make for peace ; we humbly thank Thee for all the goodwill and kindliness that bind together those who, though of different dominions, are one in language, in faith, and in many gifts of Thy Providence. We praise Thee for all those who have worked for a common understanding, and for the increase of godly union and concord. And we beseech Thee that there may never be wanting among our peoples men of wisdom and power to guide our hearts, minds and counsels in the true way, for the good of men and for the increase of Thy Kingdom throughout the world : through Jesus Christ our Lord. Amen."

more than 500,000 members, in every civilized country. "Man that is born of a woman" was sung to Purcell's music; Purcell's trombone music was also played. The whole Cathedral was full of young men from every part of the country, and the singing of "The Saints of God" was magnificent. The service was taken by the Dean and the Archdeacon.

On Thursday, Nov. 30th, St. Andrew's Day, the Litany was sung in procession, in intercession for missions, the disturbed state of Russia, and the unemployed. The Bishop of London preached.

1906.

On June 12th, the Chapel of St. Michael and St. George was dedicated by the Prelate of the Order (Bishop Montgomerie) in the presence of the Sovereign of the Order (King Edward VII.), the Grand Master (The Prince of Wales), the Chancellor (the Duke of Argyll), and all the Grand Crosses, Knights and Companions who could attend, wearing robes (dark blue satin, lined with crimson satin, with white satin shoulder-knots and gold chains), uniforms and decorations. The dedicatory prayer was said in the chapel, and the rest of the service in the choir. A more beautiful and impressive scene has rarely been witnessed in St. Paul's. The fittings and decoration of the chapel were carried out under the direction of Mr. Somers Clarke, architect to the Cathedral. In future, on Saints' days, at morning and evening prayer, remembrance was to be made of the Order before the prayer for the King, in these words—*Priest:* O Lord, save the King. *Answer:* And the most distinguished Order of St. Michael and St. George.

On Tuesday, June 15th, a Memorial Service was held for the late Right Hon. John Seddon, Prime Minister of New Zealand.

On Tuesday, July 10th, at the request of Lord Strathcona,

Agent-General for Canada, a Memorial Service was held for the Canadians and Americans (some twenty-seven) who perished in the terrible railway disaster which befell the Plymouth boat train at Salisbury. The Agent-General and the American Ambassador were present, with the Lord Mayor and a very large congregation.

On Thursday, July 26th, a Memorial Service was held in the Chapel of St. Michael and St. George for the late Sir Walter Buller, K.C.M.G., a New Zealand notability, at the request of the Colonial Office and the Chancery of the Order.

On Thursday morning, Oct. 25th, the Duke of Connaught unveiled the monument in the crypt to F.-M. Sir Lintorn Simmons, Commander-in-Chief of the Royal Engineers.

On Friday, Nov. 16th, at 2 p.m., a Memorial Service was held for a famous schoolmistress, Miss Dorothea Beale, Head of the Ladies' College at Cheltenham, with a very large attendance.

On Wednesday, Nov. 22nd, the Company of Musicians attended evensong, it being their anniversary festival, St. Cecilia's Day. "Let the bright Seraphim" was sung; there was a large congregation, and a very impressive service.

1907.

On Saturday, March 9th, the Queen and the Empress Marie of Russia visited the Cathedral, and were shown round by the Archdeacon (Canon-in-Residence).

On Tuesday evening, July 2nd, was held the Jubilee Service of the London Diocesan Home Mission (which through the legacy of £120,000 made by Miss Fussell, has been able to create about 75 new parishes); the Bishop of Bristol, a former secretary, was preacher. The choir numbered 1000, the churchwardens over 80, the clergy over 60; the Bishop of London was present.

On Friday, July 11th, the Dean and his family returned

thanks for his recovery from his long illness. On the same day Prince Bernadotte of Sweden, and over 80 of the heads of the Y.M.C.A. in all parts of the world, laid a wreath on the grave of Sir George Williams. On Monday the Cathedral was visited by the new "Great Archimandrite," Dr. Posadis. On Tuesday the bust of Henley the poet was unveiled by Lord Plymouth, George Wyndham and Henry Cust. Letters were read from Rodin the sculptor and George Meredith.

On Thursday, Nov. 14th, the Cathedral was visited by the Infanta Isabel of Spain and suite.

On Monday, Dec. 2nd, the Musicians' Company attended afternoon service in connection with St. Cecilia's Day, to dedicate a window in the north transept, given by their Master, Mr. Crews.

1908.

On Sunday morning, Feb. 9th, the King and Queen, accompanied by the Prince and Princess of Wales and Princess Victoria, were present at a Memorial Service for the King of Portugal and his son the Crown Prince, assassinated at Lisbon on Feb. 1st. Their Majesties were received at the south door by the Chapter, and conducted to the choir, where the King occupied the stall usually allotted to the Archbishop of Canterbury, with the Queen and Princess Victoria on his right, the Prince and Princess of Wales on his left. The Portuguese Minister also occupied a stall on the same side. The service was attended by the Lord Mayor, Aldermen, Sheriffs and Common Council of London; by the mayors of the metropolitan boroughs, and by many members of the Government and their predecessors. The *Dead March* was played by the band of the Oxfordshire Light Infantry, of which the late King of Portugal was colonel, and by twelve drums drawn from the Brigade of Guards. The Blessing was given by the Archbishop of Canterbury.

On April 30th the Annual Service for the Order of St. Michael and St. George was held in the Chapel of the Order. The Prince of Wales was present, and the Prelate (Bishop Montgomerie) preached.

On Wednesday, July 1st, the Maharajah-Premier of Nepaul visited the Cathedral, ascended the dome, and was greatly interested by everything.

On August 6th, at ten o'clock, the Lambeth Conference of Bishops held their great Thanksgiving Service at the Cathedral. It was a celebration of Holy Communion, the six Archbishops officiating, and only the Bishops communicating. A very affecting address was given by the Archbishop of Canterbury. During the summer months, the Bishops preached on Sundays at morning and evening service, and special week-day services were held during the Pan-Anglican Congress.

On Friday, Nov. 6th, the monument of Sir George Williams (by Sir George Frampton, R.A.) was unveiled in the crypt in the presence of a very large congregation, chiefly young men.

1909.

On Feb. 20th the concurrence of the City authorities was received for the erection of the new Paul's Cross (for which the late Mr. H. C. Richards, M.P., left £5000) on the site of the Fountain in the Garden, the garden being under the superintendence of the City.

CHAPTER XXXIII

THE RICHMOND MOSAICS

WE have it on record by Sir Christopher Wren's son, in his *Parentalia*, or notes on his father's life and works, that when the structure of his great Cathedral of St. Paul was finished he sent for four artists from Italy to continue the completion of the design, by filling with mosaics the interior of the dome, and the spaces which he had left in the roofs of choir, nave, transepts and aisles, consisting of brick vaulting covered temporarily with plaster. But the Building Committee, which had been at work from first to last for more than thirty-seven years, and some of the older members of which had, of course, passed away, were tired of collecting money, and were not at all sure about the idea of mosaics. To the great architect's sorrow and disgust they refused to sanction the scheme, or to do anything more for St. Paul's, which Wren considered quite unfinished, and the Italian artists were countermanded.

There are many kinds of mosaics, but they may be roughly divided into two: the smooth work, where a polished surface is produced, and where the effect is intended to be pictorial, as in the modern Italian style, known chiefly in this country through the designs of Salviati; and the rough style, where the facets of the tessarae are placed for the most part at a slight angle to each other, and where the result aimed at is mainly jewel-like and decorative. These latter qualities are principally characteristic of the Byzantine period.

Sir William Richmond, K.C.B., R.A., was suggested to

the St. Paul's Decoration Committee in March 1891, as the best authority for the treatment of the roof of the Cathedral, by Messrs. Bodley and Garner. These architects had already done a great deal for the decoration of St. Paul's. Since the great impetus in that direction was given in connection with the thanksgiving service for the recovery of the Prince of Wales from his dangerous illness a quarter of a century ago, they had raised the level of the choir, removed the organ screen, placed the organ in two blocks on each side of the entrance to the choir near the dome, removed the choir-stalls from the far east end and brought them to the very edge of the dome, erected a new platform for the altar considerably to the west of the apse, built the new marble reredos at a cost of upwards of £17,000, and placed Tijou's exquisite ironwork gates in a new gilt-brass framework under the two great easternmost arches of the choir rendered vacant by the pushing of the stalls to the west. The question now arose, what was to be done to the walls, which were extremely dull and dirty, and to the roof. The advice of Mr. Richmond (as he then was) was in favour of mosaics, not only in the vacant spaces of the roof, but also in those of the upper walls; the vigorous cleaning and brightening of the walls and arches; and the touching of the stonework at salient points with gold and colour. Mr Richmond also offered to give up almost the whole of his time for three years, at a very moderate stipend, to the production of designs and the superintendence of the work.

This offer was gladly accepted by the Decoration Committee, of which the Dean and Chapter form the permanent basis. Mr. Richmond, who had for many years studied the art of mosaic in every part of Italy and Sicily, at Constantinople, and other places where the Byzantine influence reigned, and who had a studio at Hammersmith surrounded by a spacious garden, built a new *atelier* of enormous height, so as to give something of the effect of vast design seen at a considerable distance.

The manufacture of the glass materials (the tessarae are all squares of glass specially prepared) was entrusted to Messrs. James and Harry Powell, partners in the well-known firm at Whitefriars which has existed for over 200 years, as well as the engagement of the workmen, who were to be all British. Thus the designer, the manufacturers and the artificers were all of home birth. The treatment of the stone was handed over to Messrs. Mac-Millan and Houghton. The Cathedral was fortunate in having on its permanent staff a clerk of the works, Mr. E. J. Harding, whose skill and care in designing and erecting from time to time the firm and admirable scaffolding which gave access, in the most difficult positions, to the various portions of the roof and walls, was of integral importance to the whole scheme, and ensured the whole body engaged in the work from even a single accident. Great numbers of people visited the scaffolding in the choir during the progress of the decoration, and they always found the platforms as firm as a drawing-room floor. Among them H.R.H. the Princess of Wales and the Princesses Victoria and Maud climbed without difficulty to the very highest parts and placed some of the tessarae in their position in the cement.

Mr. Richmond first submitted small coloured designs to the Decoration Committee, which from time to time gave the general effect of the various portions. When these were approved he had them enlarged to the exact scale of the space which they would occupy, with every line strongly marked, and then coloured according to the tones of the design and of the tessarae. Most of the several designs so enlarged were exhibited in position in the Cathedral so that their effect might be judged. The enlargement and colouring having been completed, the design was then transferred in pieces of suitable sizes to tracing paper, and handed to the artificers for execution in the tessarae on the cement. The artificers pierced the pattern through the lines with a bradawl on a space of cement affixed to the brickwork of such a size as not to dry up and become hard before the day's work was finished. The cement was composed of putty, silica, pounded marble and various hard and durable substances.

Meantime the thick coloured glass had been prepared by Messrs. Powell for the tessarae. A large and convenient workshop was provided by the garret story of the aisles, above the vaulting of the roof, a wide and lofty space. Here all the materials were stored, and the tracings carried out. The glass appeared in flat cakes, about six or seven inches in length by four or five in breadth. These were separated into square inches, or whatever the required size of the tessarae might be, by boys manipulating a steel chopping machine. In 1894 about 150 tints were in use; at first the number was considerably larger. In 1896 those in general use were not more than about fifty. A considerable difference in tone was produced by some of the tessarae being produced in what is technically called "pot-metal," prepared in a different way from the ordinary glass, having a richer and whiter appearance, and looking as if it was mixed with what water-colour artists call "body-colour."

The actual number of artificers engaged in placing the tessarae was nineteen; they were chiefly young men, artists in the employment of Messrs. Powell, and for the most part trained to this special work in Mr. Richmond's studio.

The first design completed was that of the two warrior angels seated on the ramparts of the citadel of Heaven on the spandrils over the eastern end of the three arches on the north side of the choir. It will be noticed that the treatment here is rather lighter than it subsequently became. The next portion filled in was the easternmost of the three great "saucer-domes," as they are called, or vast concave circles, in the roof of the choir. This depicts the creation of the birds. There is a landscape, rising from the circular edge, of mountains, rivers, lakes, lawns and trees, among which are a great variety of birds in different attitudes of exultation; peacocks, pelicans, cranes, swans and the like; above them is a great circle of eagles, on a gold sky, approaching the central sun. The scale here was afterwards judged by Mr. Richmond to be somewhat delicate and minute. On a clear day, every leaf and every bird are visible from below; but the atmosphere of St. Paul's is not often clear, and Mr. Richmond felt impelled as the work progressed to strengthen his scale, outline and tone.

It is unnecessary to record the progress of the decorations in chronological order. That which forms the central point of the whole, and which is seen by all who approach the choir, is formed by the three converging panels of the roof of the apse, and presents the Lord seated on the Rainbow Throne after the description in the Revelation of St. John, surrounded by recording angels. The Saviour is robed in white, with a crimson and gold mantle falling back over His shoulders. His head wears a crown, magnificently rich, and His hand is lifted in the attitude of blessing. The face has a wonderful expression of mingled majesty and sweetness. It has been twice altered; firstly, to give greater strength, and secondly, to lessen the sternness induced by the access of depth of line. Behind is a great whirl of wings to imply eternity and infinity, and below are the sun and moon, darkened by the glory of the True Light. The northern side panel contains a group of recording angels who are beckoning to the righteous to approach. The southern group are in an attitude of repelling; all their heads glow with fire, and some are evidently weeping tears of sorrow.

It is impossible to mention all the minor details. The most prominent decorations near the roof of the apse are two large rectangular panels north and south, on a lower level, surmounting what may be called the transverse gangway of the apse, and under the great broad embossed arch which springs from north to south, and separates apse from choir. The same construction, an exceedingly broad embossed arch with rectangular panels on the wall-spaces which support it, springs again from wall to wall and separates choir from dome, dome from north and south transepts, and dome from nave. The construction of St. Paul's is splendidly simple, the dome in the centre, these four vast and broad arches crossing the interior spaces, and forming part of the roof, subtended by rectangular panels leading the way to choir, nave and two transepts; three great arches to the east, forming the choir; three great arches to the west, forming the nave; one corresponding arch forming the north, and another the south, transept; the broad embossed arch springs from north to south, forming part of the roof, and finishing the choir; the apse standing beyond the choir to the east, and the vast portico, or vestibule, with its great north and south chapels rising beyond the three arches of the nave to the west. The two great rectangular panels, then, north and south, over the transverse gangway of the apse, are filled with exquisite mosaic pictures, with rich and broad mosaic borders of flowers and fruit, corresponding to Wren's frequent wreaths of the same in stonework both within and without the Cathedral, and to Grinling Gibbons' employment of the same in the oak and limewood carvings of the choir-stalls and organ. The northern picture is Melchizedek blessing Abraham, with numerous attendant figures; the southern is Noah returning thanks after his departure from the Ark. Both are emblematically illustrative of the important subject of patriarchal religion. The broad, tying, embossed arches which spring from wall to wall, forming part of the roof, are, so far, treated alike; the flat surfaces are covered with gold, which has a delicate pattern traced on it in blue, hardly visibly from below, to prevent heaviness and monotony, and the huge bosses, which are formed of divers flowers or leaves, are relieved on their interior surfaces with white, and tipped externally with gold.

The next objects which strike the eye, after those which have been described, are the two remaining concave circles, or saucer-domes, in the roof of the choir. It has already been said that the third, or easternmost, represents the creation of the birds. The central circle has for its subject the creation of the fishes; the western the creation of the animals. In the one, eight whales divide the space, looking towards the spectator from the edge, and sending up silver sprays of water towards the centre. Blue and green waves, curling with foam, recede in perspective towards the golden central horizon; among them play dolphins and other brilliant fishes, all in the exultation of their newly created being. In the other, the compartments are provided by eight conventional palm-trees, in the spaces between which are groups of lions, tigers, elephants, camels, the rhinoceros, the hippopotamus and other notable beasts. The same circle of eagles floats round the golden central sun as in the creation of the birds. Each circle has a suitable Latin inscription: for the birds, "et volatile sub firmamento," "and fowl in the open firmament" (Genesis l. 20); for the fishes, "Creavit Deus cete grandia," "God created great whales" (Genesis l. 21); for the animals, "producat terra animam viventem," "let the earth bring forth the living creature" (Genesis l. 24).

Each of the circles is surrounded by a magnificent embossed wreath, treated in the same way as the broad embossed roof arches. Each wreath bears four boldly sculptured shields, north, south, east and west. The four shields of the western wreath bear the arms of England, Scotland, Ireland and the United Kingdom, the four of the central, short texts alluding emblematically to fishing subjects: "vado piscari," "I go a-fishing" (John xxi. 3); "mitte in dexteram," "cast the net on the right side" (John xxi. 6); "bonos in vasa," "the good into vessels" (Matt.

xiii. 48); "centum quinquaginta iii," "an hundred and fifty and three" (John xxi. 11); the four of the western, the arms of four of the great City Companies who have been large contributors to the Decoration Fund—the Fishmongers, Merchant Taylors, Goldsmiths and Mercers.

After the central circles of the roof, the eye rests on graceful sloping triangular spaces, four of which join each circle to the walls. These pendentives, as they are called, each contain an angel, with uplifted wings and outstretched arms, "the Sons of God shouting for joy," at the creation. Each figure is often the same design, a fine form, neither male nor female, or rather perhaps that of a radiant celestial youth, but differing in colour. Each pendentive has a Latin text. The four eastern give us "Populus qui ambulabat in tenebris videt lucem magnam," "the people who walked in darkness have seen a great light" (Isaiah ix. 2); "Puerculus enim natus est nobis, filius datus est nobis," "unto us a child is born, unto us a son is given" (v. 6); "Factus est principatus super humerum ejus," "The government shall be upon his shoulder" (v. 6); "Vocabitur nomen ejus Admirabilis," "His name shall be called Wonderful" (v. 6). The four central give us "Laudate Dominum omnes angeli ejus, laudate Eum sol et luna," "Praise Him all ye angels of His, praise Him sun and moon" (Psalm 148, vv. 2, 3); "Ignis, grando, nix, glacies, spiritus procellarum laudate," "Fire and hail, snow and vapours, wind and storm, praise Him" (v. 8); "Laudate Dominum de terra dracones et omnes abyssi," "Praise the Lord upon earth, ye dragons and all deeps" (v. 7); "Laudate Eum omnes stellae et lumen; laudent nomen Domini," "Praise Him all ye stars and light; let them praise the name of the Lord" (vv. 3, 5). The western pendentives give us sentences from the 104th Psalm: "Benedic anima mea Domino; Domine Deus meus magnificatus es," "Praise the Lord, O my soul: O Lord my God, Thou art become glorious" (v. 1); "Quam magnificata sunt opera tua

Domine : omnia in sapientia fecisti," " O Lord, how glorious are Thy works ; in wisdom has Thou made them all" (v. 24) ; " Hoc mare magnum et spatiosum manibus animalia pusilla cum magnis," " So is the great and wide sea ; both small and great beasts" (v. 25); " Qui facis angelos tuos spiritus, et ministros tuos ignem urentem," " Who makest Thine angels spirits, and Thy ministers a flaming fire" (v. 4).

Having thus surveyed the roof of the choir, we now begin to ask what are the splendid apparitions on the walls. On the north side we have six great pictures covering the spaces on each side of the attic or clerestory windows, representing prophetical subjects, both from the Old Testament and from the natural religion of the ancient world. We will begin as before, from the east, and we see the Delphic Sibyl, a noble form sealed in thought, with revelation brought to her by a human figure without wings. Next comes the Persian Sibyl, no less majestic, with a message brought by three winged figures after Persian sculptures. Beneath the window which connects the two are the words, " O Sapientia veni ad docendum nos, O oriens splendor veni et illumina nos," " O Wisdom come and teach us, O splendour of the East come to enlighten us," words from the old Latin offices connected with December 16 and 20.

The central clerestory window on the north side is flanked by pictures of great splendour, representing Alexander the Great and Cyrus : the one as bringing the eastern and western worlds together, the other as the Son of Prophecy, restoring the people of God to their ancient home after the Captivity. The inscription beneath the connecting window is also from the old Latin book of offices : " O rex gentium, et desideratus earum, veni, salva hominem," " O King of nations, earnestly longed for by them, come, save mankind."

The western window of this series is surrounded by two grand Biblical scenes : the three mysterious visitors appear-

ABRAHAM AND THE THREE ANGELS
(From Sir William Richmond's Mosaics)

[*To face p.* 386.

JOB AND HIS THREE FRIENDS
(*From Sir William Richmond's Mosaics*)

ing to Abraham (Genesis xviii.), representing the beginnings of Hebrew revelation, and Job and his three friends, representing the patriarchal religion outside the Hebrew family. The details of both scenes are interesting: Sarah, laughing behind the door of the tent: Job's wife imploring him to curse God. As these spaces are near the great arch connecting dome and chancel, and much in shadow, they are light and bright in colour. The sentence below the window is, " O Adonai qui Moysi apparuisti veni ad redimendum nos," " O Lord, who didst appear unto Moses, come to redeem us."

The corresponding spaces round the windows of the southern attic story, or clerestory of the choir, are all related to Temple-building.

In the eastern bay we see David on one side and Solomon on the other. David is an old man, in an attitude of sorrow, with his harp beside him, permitted to gather materials for the Temple, but forbidden to build it. Solomon is seated in all his glory, surveying the glorious shrine which he has been encouraged to erect. His face strongly recalls that of the late Canon Liddon. The inscription below the window is: " O Radix Jesse, veni ad liberandum nos: O Clavis David, veni et educ vinctum," " O Root of Jesse, come and release us: O Key of David, come and set the captive free."

The central window connects two gorgeous pictures, Aholiab and Bezaleel (Exodus xxxv. 34; xxxi. 2), the chief constructors of the Tabernacle; Aholiab has the seven-branched golden candlestick and some woven hangings; Bezaleel is engaged in metal work, and newly constructed pillars are seen in the background. Below the window are the words, " O Emmanuel, rex et lucifer noster, veni ad salvandum nos," " O Emmanuel, our king and morning star, come to save us."

The two panels of the western bay depict Moses receiving the Law, and Jacob's vision. Like those on the opposite side, they are bright and light in tone, in consequence of the darkness of their position. The face of Moses has a vigorous resemblance to that of William Booth, the famous General of the Salvation Army. He is surrounded by mysterious whorls of mist and light, and a golden hand out of a cloud writes on the Tables of the Law. Below the window you read the words, "O Adonai, et Dux domus Israel, veni ad redimendum nos," "O Lord, and Leader of the house of Israel, come to redeem us."

Beneath the attic windows on the north and south side of the choir is the classical architrave, a solid wall space, above the great cornice which rests on the piers and arches of the arcade. This space is divided in each bay into three panels. The three panels of each bay are exactly alike on each side, and relate to the subject of the concave circle above. Beneath the birds are gorgeous peacocks; beneath, the fishes, brilliant conventional dolphins in conventional blue waves of striking brightness; beneath, the animals, noble pairs of tigers and lions in a kind of heraldic attitude. There are corresponding panels under the broad embossed archway spanning the choir, and connecting choir and dome, on the walls of which the two portions of the organ are hung. These panels have exquisitely beautiful reclining figures of Adam and Eve in the glory of Paradise, naming the animals. Adam has a lion and lioness; Eve, crouching and affectionate tigers, besides peacocks and a splendid lyre bird.

It remains to describe the spandrils, or wall spaces filling up between the three arches of the two arcades north and south of the choir, and the flat line of the great cornice which surmounts them. Two of them, belonging to the eastern arch on the north side, have been mentioned already, because they were the first work which Mr. Richmond began. They were two warrior angels reclining on the citadel of Heaven. Opposite, on the south side, are two more of these sublime figures, somewhat stronger in tone and colour, with more emblems of the Passion. The spandrils on the central arch on the north gives a beautiful and very brilliant picture of the Annunciation ; the Angel on one side, the Virgin Mary at her cottage door on the other, with the landscape of Nazareth at the back, and a dove floating gently towards the Virgin. The spandrils over the arch nearest the dome on the north are exceedingly rich, and represent two glorious angels engaged in carrying out the mandates of creation, reducing order out of chaos, and starting vast spheres on their orbits, in the midst of whirling masses of blue and purple vapour, signifying infinity.

On the south side, the spandrils over the central arch are occupied with a delineation of the Temptation. On one side is a noble figure of Adam in the Garden; the sadness of the coming Fall seems already to have put a tinge of melancholy into his face. On the other side a dark, handsome, malevolent figure is whispering in the ear of Eve, who also has an expression of doubt and sadness. The spandrils of the western arch, nearest the dome, opposite the angels rolling the spheres, are used for the scene of the Fall; an angel with a sword of light on one side, on the other, Eve, bending in an attitude of bitterest and most crushing despair and remorse; Adam, still upright in figure, and with a protecting arm round Eve, but his fine, manly face stern with misery and dejection.

There are many other mottoes and texts, principally on the faces of the great ribs which divide the bays of the choir roof, all appropriate and suggestive, which cannot here be enumerated.

The extreme pillars of the north and south arcade, nearest the sacrarium, have been cased in very splendid white Pavonazzo marble, with veins of green and gold. The pilasters of the apse behind the reredos have likewise been cased in dark green verd antique. The other pillars have been cleansed and whitened, and their acanthus-leaved capitals touched with gold. Mr. Richmond has shown how he would treat the embossed interior surface of the archways through the Cathedral by what he has done in the case of the chancel arcades; the bosses are gold and white, the square spaces behind them blue, the surface of the stone gold, white and silver, and the carved patterns picked out with scarlet. All the colour work on the stone surfaces is in indelible and unfading tints of wax.

The choir is now complete, and stands rich with extraordinary beauty and splendour in comparison of the dingy appearance of the dull, yellow-washed surfaces which can be remembered. Sir William Richmond has completed the four great concave spaces under the lower arches which support the four corners of the dome. These contain the Crucifixion, the Entombment, the Resurrection and the Commission to St. Paul, all emblematically rather than realistically treated, after the custom of the primitive Church. Sir William has also fortunately been able to finish the aisles of the choir, with groups of emblematical figures and rich patterns.

The reason why further work (for example, the drum of the dome, which is so much needed) has not been attempted is to be found in the controversy that arose a few years ago about decorating part of the surface of the stonework near the mosaics with paint. The cost of the Richmond Mosaics is estimated at about £78,000. The debt of the Cathedral to Sir William's scholarly enthusiasm can never be sufficiently acknowledged.

CHAPTER XXXIV

THE ORDER OF ST. MICHAEL AND ST. GEORGE

A FEW words may be expected from me as to the history of the introduction of the Order of St. Michael and St. George into our south-west chapel.

Of the multitudes of interesting things that have occurred during the period of my service at St. Paul's Cathedral, few have given me greater pleasure than the installation of that Order, the Order of the Colonies and the Empire in St. Paul's Cathedral, the central church of the imperial City.

The Order of St. Michael existed originally for the Ionian Islands, that of St. George for Malta. The two were united in 1818, and extended in 1868, and again in 1877, to be an Order for the British Colonies in general; "for the natural-born subjects of the Crown of the United Kingdom, as may have held or shall hold high and confidential offices within Her Majesty's Colonial possessions, or in reward for services to the Crown in relation to the foreign affairs of the Empire." It consists of the Sovereign, the Grand Master (the Prince of Wales), the Prelate (always a Colonial Bishop), the Chancellor (the Duke of Argyll), several members of the Royal Family, 65 Grand Crosses, 200 Knights-commanders, 342 Companions, a Secretary, King of arms, Registrar and Officer of arms.

Some time before the year 1901 it occurred to me that, having a Prelate, it was a misfortune that the Order, so closely associated with imperial progress and unity, should have no religious centre; and if it should be found possible, St. Paul's, in the very middle of the religious life of the

CHAPEL OF THE ORDER OF ST. MICHAEL AND ST. GEORGE, FROM E.
(FORMERLY WELLINGTON CHAPEL AND CONSISTORY COURT)

nation, would furnish a fitting ecclesiastical home. The Dean and Chapter, after some reasonable scepticism and questioning, concurred. The Chancellor of the Order at that time was Sir Robert Herbert (a grandson of the first Earl of Carnarvon), who had been Premier of Queensland and Under-Secretary of State for the Colonies, and was a man of sincerely religious mind. Having had the pleasure of knowing him for about twenty years, I submitted the proposal to his friendly judgment, and it was most favourably received. The difficulty of finding a suitable part of the Cathedral was considerable. The Wellington Chapel, or Consistory Court, had recently been cleared of the great Duke's monument, through the energy and liberality of Lord Leighton—it could not be seen in the chapel, and was always intended for one of the arches of the nave—but the font had been moved in instead, and the chapel had become, for the time, the baptistery; but at last the Chapter agreed to move the font to a far more appropriate site, the west aisle of the south transept. The formal resolution was dated November 23, 1901.

Sir Robert had undertaken to speak on the subject to the Queen, the Grand Master (the Duke of Cambridge), the Prince of Wales (the present King) and others, and the suggestion was received with favour. I need not quote all his letters to me, which were numerous, but I make one or two extracts—

"*Nov.* 20, '01.

"I am very glad to hear from you again on the subject of the south-west chapel, and the Order of St. Michael and St. George; and also to hear that Lord Beauchamp has been seized of the same idea. . . .

"The time for taking action has arrived, or is approaching: if only we can surmount or get rid of the one obstacle which has caused warm supporters to draw back; I mean, of course, the font, but recently moved into the chapel, where it is incongruous in itself, and a grave impediment to such an adaptation as would meet the requirements of the Order. . . .

"We could make the S.-W. chapel a very beautiful shrine, lighted with electricity, and, with a translucent window, quite a glory of the Cathedral.

"Yours very truly,
"ROBERT G. W. HERBERT."

"*Nov.* 21, '01.

"I am greatly pleased and encouraged by your letter of to-day, and feel that the Dean and Chapter have shown great and very prompt consideration to the wishes of those who desire to see the south-west chapel adapted to the special uses of St. Michael and St. George.

"I must now rally my scattered forces, and organize a working committee of members of the Order, to get the subscriptions and general support of the members. . . .

"Yours very truly,
"ROBERT G. W. HERBERT."

"*Jan.* 8, 1902.

"I have written to-day to the Dean informing him that the King (as Sovereign) and the Duke of Cambridge (as Grand Master) of St. Michael and St. George, have heard with pleasure and approval that the south-west chapel has been placed at the disposal of the Order, and that the Duke has consented to be president of a Committee to consider the necessary financial and other arrangements.

"I did not fail to inform or remind them both that the Order is indebted to yourself, both for the original idea, and for valuable help in obtaining the concession.

"It is proposed that the Committee shall consist of the Officers of the Order, with a few others. I hope you will be willing to be a member of the Committee. . . .

"Yours very truly,
"ROBERT G. W. HERBERT."

"*Jan.* 16, 1902.

"The Duke of Cambridge (Grand Master) desires me to tell you that His Royal Highness will be obliged by your assisting him as a member of the Committee to consider the arrangements for installing the Order of St. Michael and St. George in the south-west chapel, and that the Committee will hold its first meeting at Gloucester House, at 5 p.m., on Tuesday next, the 21st inst., when I hope you will be able to attend.

"Could you meet me at the chapel at (say) 2.30 p.m. either on Saturday or Monday next, to consider what preliminary information we should lay before H.R.H. as to the potentialities of the chapel? . . .

"Yours very truly,
"ROBERT G. W. HERBERT."

I recommended the committee to ask Mr. Somers Clarke, as architect to the Cathedral, to be their architect for carrying into effect the fitting up and adornment of the chapel. His designs for the panels of the roof, rich in gold, with moulded shields of the arms of the King, the Prince of Wales and Sir Robert Herbert, were much admired. He also made as much use of the space available for stalls and seats as was possible. The chapel, the only proper place to be found in the Cathedral, is not large; on special occasions the great vestibule of the Cathedral, the vast space between the west doors and the actual nave is added; the chapel, separated from this only by one of Grinling Gibbons's exquisite screens, forms at such a time a kind of inner sanctuary. Mrs. Hessey very kindly agreed that the window in memory of her husband, the late Archdeacon of Middlesex, should be moved to the north transept; and with great promptitude Sir Walter Wilkin, K.C.M.G., a recent Lord Mayor, gave a very light window in memory of the Duke of Cambridge (who had in the meantime died). The design, combining in outline the emblems of St.

STALL OF THE SOVEREIGN OF THE ORDER OF ST. MICHAEL
AND ST. GEORGE

Michael and St. George, with cherubs, was by Mr. Somers Clarke. The stall of the Grand Master was given by the sons of the late Duke: Rear-Admiral Sir Adolphus Fitz-George, K.C.V.O., Colonel Sir Augustus FitzGeorge, K.C.V.O., and Colonel FitzGeorge. The reredos was provided by Lord Strathcona. There were many other gifts, and a rich memorial volume was initiated, recording the names of donors, to be kept in a coffer under the window. At length, on June 12, 1906, the inaugural service took place, as has been already described, in the presence of the Sovereign, the Grand Master and a great company of the Order. The following prayer, written for the occasion, reflects, I think, the solemn feelings of that most beautiful ceremony—

" O Lord God Almighty, Everlasting Father, Who didst make unto Thyself a chosen people of the family of Abraham, and didst lead them forth by Thy holy angels into the promised land; Who in these latter days, of Thine infinite mercy and all-seeing wisdom, and not for any merit or worthiness of ours, didst take of our fathers when they were yet few and feeble upon the earth, and didst make of them a great nation, even as the sands of the seashore for multitude; Who hast replenished us with all the gifts of earth and sky and sea, and hast given unto us the corn and the wine and the oil, the gold and the silver and the precious gems; Who hast made our sons to go forth from their country and their kindred and their father's house to bear the burden of government and dominion in many lands; And Who hast knit together peoples of many races and many regions into one great commonwealth of peace: For these Thy so great mercies and benefits we render unto Thee praise and thanks, and do magnify Thy glorious Name. And we beseech Thee to look in pity upon every failure of zeal and infirmity of purpose which have marred the task that Thou hast given us to do; Forgive the self-seeking and cupidity, the hardness and wickedness which have so often marred our opportunities and turned the gifts that Thou hast given us into dust and ashes; Make us to discern more clearly and to perform more faithfully what Thou wouldst have us to do; and as Thou hast been with our fathers before us, so Lord God of hosts, be with us yet. And grant, O Lord, that the course of this world may be so peaceably ordered by Thy governance, that Thy Church may joyfully serve Thee in all godly quietness; through Jesus Christ our Lord. *Amen.*"

The sermon was preached by the Prelate, Bishop Montgomerie.

Every year, on St. George's Day, April 23, the Order assembles in the chapel, and commemorates the members who have died during the year, their names being recited by the secretary. Several memorial tablets to departed members have already been placed. The members can have their children baptized in the Cathedral, and places are reserved for them at the special services which are so marked a feature of the life of St. Paul's.

As the multitudes of visitors and worshippers who throng the Cathedral every day pass in at the west door, their thoughts are at once arrested by the august recess of the chapel, hung with richly embroidered banners, and resplendent with carving and colour. As they learn that this is the shrine of the knightly brotherhood who have devoted their lives to the service of the empire in Colonial lands, their hearts are reminded that they too owe a duty, each in his own sphere, to their country. "These are the men," said the Prelate, at the Dedication, "who have built up and defended the empire; they deserve all their honours. From many a land dark faces look gratefully towards them, mindful of their unselfish work, of their kind and sympathetic rule." Something of this feeling touches the crowds who come in day by day; and so the great stream

THE SOUTH PORTICO

ORDER OF ST. MICHAEL AND ST. GEORGE

of true patriotism is deepened by the outflow from that honoured corner of St. Paul's.[1]

[1] It is interesting to note that the example of the Order of St. Michael and St. George has been followed by that of the Thistle, who have received the King's permission to provide themselves a chapel in Edinburgh. The late Lord Leven and Melville left £40,000 for the restoration of Holyrood Chapel. Nothing could have been easier, for no architecture could be simpler or more uniform than that of Holyrood. But adverse influences prevailed, the money was returned, and Holyrood is left exposed to the destructive blasts of the Forth. The present Lord Leven has given his share of the bequest (£23,000) for the purpose of providing a new Chapel for the Order of the Thistle.—April 1909.

THE STATUE OF ST. PAUL, WEST ENTRANCE

CHAPTER XXXV

THE ORGANISTS, ORGAN AND MUSIC OF ST. PAUL'S[1]

I. ORGANISTS.

THE list of organists at St. Paul's is but short, for in early days the duty now assigned to one musician was then distributed amongst many: the Master of the Children, or Master of Song, and such gentlemen of the choir as were players, taking the duty of presiding at the organ. At Durham a monk played at nocturns and matins, and the *Master of the Song School* at High Mass and vespers.[2] At Hereford, in the fifteenth century, the organist was styled *Clerk of the Organs*. At St. Paul's, the Almoner was an important official who generally had charge of the boys, and he was not always the organist.

John Redford	(about) 1530
Thomas Gyles	1549
Thomas Morley	1591
John Tomkins } Joint	{ 1622
Adrian Batten }	{ 1624
Albertus Bryne	1638
Isaac Blackwell	1687
Jeremiah Clark	1699
Richard Brind	1707
Maurice Greene	1718
John Jones	1756
Thomas Attwood	1796

[1] I am indebted in this chapter to Bumpus's *Organists and Composers of St. Paul's Cathedral*, 1891, and to Dr. Sparrow Simpson's *Gleanings from Old St. Paul's*, 1889.

[2] Walcott, *Sacred Archæology*: Organist.

John Goss	.	.	.	.	.	1838
John Stainer	.	.	.	.	1872
George Clement Martin	.	.	.	1888

One of the earliest names of an organist of the Cathedral is that of *John Redford*, Organist, Almoner and Master of the Choristers, between 1530 and 1540. His beautiful anthem, " Rejoice in the Lord alway," a good specimen of the writers of this sturdy period, is one of the examples in the First Volume of the Mottett Society. The name of Redford occurs in a contemporary poem by John Tusser (" The Five Hundred Points of Good Husbandrie,"), in which he mentions that, according to the custom of those days, he had been pressed to be a chorister at St. Paul's or the Chapel Royal. There is extant a warrant of Richard III. to that effect, addressed to one of the gentlemen of the Chapel Royal: and another of Queen Elizabeth's to Thomas Gyles, Redford's successor at St. Paul's, " to take up such apt and meet children as are most fit to be instructed and framed in the art and science of music and singing, as may be had and found out within any place of this our realm of England or Wales." John Tusser, in the poem, is giving his own experience, after his childhood at Wallingford—

> "Thence, for my voice, I must (no choice)
>   Away of force, like posting horse,
> For sundry men had placards then
>   Such child to take :
> The better breast, the lesser rest,
> To serve the quire, now there, now here ;
> For tyme so spent, I may repent,
>   And sorrow make.
>
> But mark the chance ! myself to 'vance,
> By friendship's lot to Paul's I got ;
> So found I grace a certain space
>   Still to remain
> With Redford there, the like nowhere
> For cunning such and virtue much,
> By whom some part of music art
>   So did I gain."

D D

Thomas Mulliner, Master of the Cathedral School in the middle of the sixteenth century, had some well-known pupils, amongst them (it is thought) Thomas Tallis, whose musical setting of the new English Prayer Book has helped the devotions of each generation to the present time. William Bird, a pupil of Tallis, born about 1538, was senior chorister at St. Paul's in 1554; he was an admirable Church composer, and to him is attributed the well-known grace, "Non Nobis Domine." In Queen Elizabeth's *Virginal Book* are nearly seventy of his compositions. He is said to have been the first Englishman who wrote a madrigal. He died in 1623. Mulliner was succeeded as almoner by Edward Pearce, one of whose most eminent pupils was Thomas Ravenscroft, who, in 1621, compiled *The Whole Book of Psalms*. No doubt many of those grand massive tunes were sung after sermon at Paul's Cross. Bishop Jewell, writing in 1560, to Peter Martyr, says: "You may now sometimes see at St. Paul's Cross, after the service, 6000 persons, old and young, of both sexes, all singing together, and praising God."

Thomas Morley, born towards the middle of the sixteenth century, educated, as it is believed, in the choir of St. Paul's, and certainly a pupil of Bird, was organist in 1591, and probably some years before. His fame rests on his madrigals, and his collection *The Triumphs of Oriana*, his *Plain and Easy Introduction to Practical Music* long held its ground as a text-book, and was translated into several languages.

John Tomkins, son of Thomas Tomkins (organist to the King, and of Worcester Cathedral, composer of many anthems and services), was organist about 1621 or 1622, and was buried in the crypt. Dr. Hullah, in his *Lectures on Musical History*, reminds us that with the seventeenth century begins in England, as elsewhere, the transition period of music, marked not only by increasing skill in musical performance, but especially by continually increasing attention to the conformity of notes with words, in fact, the diligent study of everything, which goes to perfect what is properly called *expression* in music.

Adrian Batten, who appears to have been joint-organist with Tomkins, was educated in the choir of Winchester Cathedral; became vicar-choral of Westminster Abbey; and organist and vicar-choral of St. Paul's in 1624. He also wrote a considerable amount of Church music, in the pure and solemn style of Tallis; and this is still in use at Westminster. He died in 1637.

Little is known of *Albertus Bryne*. He was a composer, and organist of St. Paul's about 1638; of Westminster Abbey and Dulwich College from 1671–77. In 1641 John Barnard, one of the Minor Canons of St. Paul's, published a "matchless and judicious collection of early Church music, called *The First Book of Selected Church Music*, consisting of such services and anthems as are now in use in the Cathedral and Collegiate Churches of the kingdom," and was dedicated to King Charles I. Another manual of this period was by another Minor Canon of St. Paul's, James Clifford: *A Collection of Divine Services and Anthems*.

Michael Wise, a well-known composer, was Almoner and Master of the Boys in 1686, and was followed by Dr. John Blow. At this time Wren's brother-in-law, the Rev. William Holder, D.D., one of the Residentiaries, was distinguished as a practical musician, and wrote a treatise on harmony. He was buried in St. Paul's in 1697.

Jeremiah Clark, educated in the Chapel Royal under Blow, became almoner in 1693, in succession to Blow, and organist and vicar-choral in 1699. He had previously been organist of Winchester Cathedral. Eight of his anthems are preserved: the best is considered to be " I will love Thee, O Lord," which abounds in deep pathos and dramatic force. " Praise the Lord, O Jerusalem," was written for the coronation of Queen Anne, and also performed on one of her state visits to St. Paul's. In a fit of melancholy he destroyed himself in 1707.

Dr. John Blow, Almoner and Master of the Choristers in succession to Wise, was born in 1648, at North Collingham, Notts. Brought up in the King's Chapel, he quitted it at the Rebellion, and received a captain's commission in 1642; and succeeded Pelham Humphrey as Master of the Children of the Chapel Royal in 1674. He was Purcell's second master. In 1699 he became composer to the Chapel Royal; a second composer, John Weldon, was appointed in 1715; and it was required of each that he should produce a new anthem on the first Sunday of his month in waiting.[1] He died in 1708, and was buried in Westminster Abbey, where he had been made organist at the age of twenty-one. His degree was conferred by Archbishop Sancroft. Boyce praised "his success in cultivating an uncommon talent for modulation." The following story is related by Hawkins: "In the reign of King James II. an anthem of some Italian composer had been introduced into the Chapel, which the King liking very much, asked Blow if he could make one as good. Blow answered he could, and engaged to do it by the next Sunday, when he produced the anthem, 'I beheld, and lo! a great multitude.' When the service was over the King sent Father Petre to acquaint Blow that he was much pleased with it. 'But,' added Petre, 'I myself think it too long.' 'That,' answered Blow, 'is but the opinion of one fool, and I heed it not.' The Jesuit was so nettled at this expression of contempt, that he meditated revenge, and wrought so with the King that Blow was put under a suspension; which, however, he was freed from by the Revolution, which took place very shortly after."[2]

Jeremiah Clark was succeeded as organist by *Richard Brind*, who had been educated in St. Paul's choir, was appointed in 1707, and died in 1718. His famous pupil,

---

[1] Dr. Burney, *Hist. Music*, iii. 445-453, 454.
[2] Hawkins, *History*, 742.

Maurice Greene, succeeded him. "Handel was very fond of St. Paul's organ, built by Father Smith, which was then almost a new instrument. Brind was at that time organist, and no very celebrated performer. The tone of the instrument delighted Handel (it is said also that he was attracted by the fact that it possessed a set of pedals, at this time quite a rarity in English organs), and a little entreaty was at any time sufficient to prevail upon him to touch it; but after he had ascended the organ-loft, it was with reluctance that he left it; and he has been known after evening service to play to an audience as great as ever filled the choir. After his performance was over, it was his practice to adjourn with the principal persons of the choir to the Queen's Arms Tavern, in St. Paul's Churchyard, where was a great room with a harpsichord in it: and often times an evening was spent there in music and musical conversation."[1] Handel continued his organ-playing at St. Paul's with Maurice Greene till he found that Greene was also worshipping at the shrine of his rival, Buononcini.

Charles King, chorister of St. Paul's in his seventh year, became Almoner and Master of the Boys on the death, in 1718, of Clark, whose sister he had married. He composed short popular services, two of which are still in use at St. Paul's, and was buried in the crypt, in 1748.

Maurice Greene, third son of the Rev. Thomas Greene, D.D., Vicar of St. Olave's, Jewry, was born in 1695, admitted chorister in 1706 under Clark, wearing his surplice for the first time at Queen Anne's Thanksgiving for Marlborough's victories in Brabant. He succeeded Brind as organist in 1718, and was a skilful player, inventing the fashion of playing with a solo-stop on the right hand, and soft stops on the left. In 1727 he succeeded Croft as organist and composer to the Chapel Royal, and in 1730 the University of Cambridge made him Professor of Music. In 1743 he published *Forty Select Anthems*. Rich in melody, these

[1] Hawkins, *History*, 767, 859.

have given him his permanent place in music. The transference of his remains from St. Olave's, Jewry, in 1888, to the crypt of St. Paul's, where they were laid in the grave of Dr. Boyce, has been already mentioned. A distinguished foreign conductor (Richter) thought some of his best work comparable to Handel, by whose mighty genius he was probably influenced.

John Jones, born about 1732, and organist of the Middle Temple in 1749, succeeded Greene in 1755 as organist and vicar-choral of St. Paul's. In 1785 he published *Sixty Chants, Single and Double* in the florid taste of his age. He is remembered by one of them, sung at the State Visit of George III. to St. Paul's, April 23, 1789, and at many of the Annual Services of the Charity Children. At that of 1791 Haydn heard it, and admired it so greatly that he said, "No music has for a long time affected me so much as this simple and reverential strain."[1] Anglican chants at this time were beginning to replace Gregorians, which had hitherto prevailed. Boyce, in his great collection of *Cathedral Music* (1760-78), inserted a few by different composers. It is stated that the first double chant was by the Rev. Luke Flintoft, Minor Canon of Westminster, who died 1727.

Jonathan Battishill, born in London, 1738, became a chorister of St. Paul's, 1747. After playing for Boyce at the Chapel Royal, he became conductor of the band at Covent Garden, but after the death of his wife devoted himself to religious composition, set music to Charles Wesley's hymns, and published Church music and glees. He was organist successively of St. Clement's, Eastcheap, and of Christ Church, Newgate Street. He died in 1801, and was buried in St. Paul's, near the grave of Dr. Boyce.

Thomas Attwood, the successor of Greene as organist of St. Paul's (1796), was born in 1767, and admitted chorister

[1] Grove, *Dict. of Music.*

at the Chapel Royal under Dr. Nares at the age of nine. The Prince of Wales (afterwards George IV.), noticing his musical ability, sent him at his own expense to Italy, where he studied two years at Naples; thence he went to Vienna, where he became a pupil of Mozart. Mozart said of him, " I have the sincerest affection for Attwood, and I feel much pleasure in telling you that he has imbibed more of my style than any scholar I ever had." The year he became organist of St. Paul's, he succeeded Dr. Dupuis as composer to the King. Thirty years later, on the death of Stafford Smith, he became organist to the Chapel Royal. He was one of the founders of the Philharmonic Society. He wrote seventeen operas, but it is his beautiful Church music that has survived. He "was a man of sincere piety, and when engaged in the composition of music for the Church, always felt that he was employing the genius given to him by God for the noblest purpose to which it could be devoted—His service: and his great aim and hope were, that he might be enabled to praise Him worthily." During Mendelssohn's first visit to England, in 1829, he was the guest of Attwood, at his house at Norwood; and in memory of his sojourn there dedicated to his host *Three Preludes and Fugues for the Organ*. In one of these he introduces the tone of Attwood's gate-bell.[1] He often accompanied his host to St. Paul's, and played on the organ after service. The main attraction to him was the C-pedal board, then the only one in London, and, therefore, the only one on which Bach's music could be rendered without destructive changes.

On the occasion of his second visit to England, in 1832, Mendelssohn gave an organ performance at St. Paul's, displaying " quite as transcendent a talent for that branch of executive skill as he had done at the Philharmonic on the pianoforte. Whether in working up one of Bach's mighty pedal fugues, or in extempore display of his own, he equally

[1] Barrett, *English Church Composers*, p. 154.

delighted and astonished many of the most eminent professors and critics of the metropolis."[1]

In the time of Attwood, Charles Greville describes the Cathedral service: "December 1, 1834.—Went to St. Paul's yesterday (Advent Sunday, St. Andrew's Day) to hear Sydney Smith preach. He is very good; manner impressive, voice sonorous and agreeable, *rather* familiar, but not offensively so, language simple and unadorned, sermon clever and illustrative. The service is exceedingly grand, performed with all the pomp of a cathedral, and chanted with beautiful voices; the lamps, scattered few and far between throughout the vast space under the dome, making darkness visible, and dimly revealing the immensity of the building, were exceedingly striking. The Cathedral service thus chanted and performed is my *beau idéal* of worship—simple, intelligible and grand; appealing at the same time to the reason and the imagination."[2]

The Princess Charlotte, a great friend and patroness of musical men, was exceedingly fond of Attwood's compositions, so much so indeed that she frequently carried them about with her. Being on a visit to Bishop Fisher of Salisbury, at his palace, on New Year's Day, 1816, she presented to Mr. A. T. Corfe, then organist of the cathedral, a very beautiful setting of the Sanctus and Kyrie, by Attwood.[3]

Nineteen anthems by Attwood are extant, including two for the coronation of George IV., one for that of William IV., and one for the Memorial Service at St. Paul's on the day of the funeral of Princess Charlotte. There was also a dirge in D minor for the funeral of Nelson. His best known composition is perhaps his exquisite setting of "Come, Holy Ghost, our souls inspire," for the Ordination

---

[1] Benedict, *Life and Works of Mendelssohn*, 20, 21.
[2] Hon. C. F. Greville, *Journals of the Reign of William IV.*
[3] J. S. Bumpus, *The Organists and Composers of St. Paul's Cathedral*, p. 128.

Service. He used to drive from his house at Norwood to service at St. Paul's, picking up on the way one of the choristers who lived near. On a beautiful spring morning, during this drive, he composed this gem; and the chorister sang it the same day. "What can there be more touching," asks Dr. Sparrow Simpson, "than this hymn? The scene, St. Paul's Cathedral: the Ordination. The Bishop has begged a brief interval for private prayer. The silence is almost oppressive. At length it is broken; a sweet, pure voice is heard floating away above the diapasons of the organ. Surely few strains can be so calm, so sweet, so exquisitely adapted to time and place." [1]

Attwood was taken ill soon after Christmas 1837, and neglecting the proper remedies in favour of some peculiar treatment, he died on March 28, 1838, at his house in Cheyne Walk, Chelsea, in his seventy-third year. He was buried "under his own organ" in the crypt of St. Paul's.

Sir John Goss, Attwood's pupil and successor, born 1800, came of a musical family; his father was organist of Fareham, his uncle a lay-vicar at Westminster, and deputy at St. Paul's and the Chapel Royal. Educated at the Chapel Royal under Stafford Smith, he studied under Attwood, and succeeded him in 1838, having been organist fourteen years at St. Luke's, Chelsea. One of his finest part-songs, "Ossian's Hymn to the Sun," was published in 1833; and in the same year his first important anthem, "Have mercy upon me, O God." In 1852, at the request of Dean Milman, he composed a noble dirge for the funeral of the Duke of Wellington. In 1854 he edited, with the Rev. W. Mercer of Sheffield, a pointed Psalter with a collection of chants and hymns, which for some years had an immense popularity. From 1852 onwards his rich and beautiful anthems came out year by year, and it is difficult to discriminate between them: 1854, for the Sons of the Clergy, "Praise the Lord, O my soul"; 1856, for the

[1] *Gleanings from Old St. Paul's*, p. 244.

enthronement of Bishop Tait, "O praise the Lord, laud ye the Name," sung in procession from west door to choir; 1857, "Behold, I bring you Glad Tidings" (Christmas) and "Christ our Passover" for Easter; 1859, "Almighty and merciful God"; 1860, for the public funeral of Lord Dundonald in Westminster Abbey, "O Lord God, Thou strength of my Health"; 1861, "The Wilderness" (written at the same time as Wesley's setting); 1862, "Blessed is the Man" (composed in 1842, at which time it is said that he proposed to set music to all the psalms), "These are they which follow the Lamb" and "I heard a voice from Heaven"; 1863, "Stand up and bless the Lord" (re-opening of Hereford Cathedral), "Lift up thine eyes" (Epiphany) and "O taste and see" (St. Paul's evening service); 1865, "Brother, thou art gone before us" (at the request of Dean Milman for the Sons of the Clergy); 1865 to 1868, a Burial Service, two Morning and Evening Services in A and C, and four anthems: "Come and let us return," "Hear, O Lord," "O give thanks" and "In Christ dwelleth"; 1869, *Te Deum* in F and "O Saviour of the World," which he delayed for some weeks in search of a right chord; 1869-71, "Fear not, O Land," "I will magnify Thee," "O praise the Lord of Heaven," "The Glory of the Lord": all "with music that lingers in the memory and refuses to be forgotten"; 1872, the *Te Deum* in D major and "The Lord is my Strength," both for the Thanksgiving Service for the recovery of the Prince of Wales. The accompanying *Benedictus* in D major, composed at a later date, came to a standstill for a fortnight from a difficulty like the one mentioned above: this time the cause being a fractious modulation. Soon after this he received knighthood, and retired, continuing to attend the Cathedral services. Four years later he received the honorary degree of Mus. Doc. from the University of Cambridge. He died in 1880, at his house on Brixton Rise, in his eightieth year. At the first part of his funeral, in St.

Paul's, was sung his anthem, "If we believe that Jesus died." "As a man, Goss commanded universal respect. The chief features of his character were humility, genuine religious feeling and a strong love of home and home ties. So deep-seated was his humility that it produced a sort of shyness in his manner which partially unsuited him for the rougher duties of public life. The discipline and efficiency of the Cathedral choir reached a very low standard in the latter portion of his career. But . . . he must not be solely blamed for this. The fact is, he had for a considerable period to deal with a Chapter which, taken as a body, had neither the power nor wish to face the unpleasant duty of becoming reformers. His hearty interest in all the improvements which he lived to witness in the reorganization of the choir staff by the later Dean and Chapter, and the sincere pleasure which the beautiful services gave him, prove that in better days Goss would have been second to none in his efforts to raise the musical credit of St. Paul's to its proper level."[1]

To *Sir John Stainer*, his successor, it is impossible to exaggerate the debt of St. Paul's. Born in 1840, he entered the choir in 1847 under William Bayley, Master of the Boys. Miss Hackett paid for organ-lessons for him from George Cooper, sub-organist of the Cathedral. While still in the choir, in 1855, he became organist of St. Benet's, Paul's Wharf. His friend Arthur Sullivan was at the same time chorister at the Chapel Royal; the two boys used to take holidays together on penny steamboats. In 1858 Stainer became organist of St. Michael's College, Tenbury, under Sir Frederic Gore Ouseley; in 1859 organist of Magdalen College, Oxford, in 1860 of the University Church. "From the time of his appointment to St. Paul's in 1872 until that of his resignation in 1888, Stainer continued to pour forth service after service, and anthem after anthem, in which beauty of melody,

[1] *Musical Times*, June 1880.

great individuality of form and harmony, scientific skill and expressive effect (tempered throughout with supreme devotional feeling) were blended in the happiest and most judicious manner. Where all is so fine it would be invidious to select, but it is impossible to resist pointing out the Morning Service in E flat, the Communion Service in A and D, the Evening Service in E major, and the anthems, 'I desired Wisdom,' the second part of 'And all the People saw the Thunderings,' beginning with 'When God of old came down,' and 'I saw the Lord' as among the highest flights of his genius." [1]

About ten complete services are enumerated, and upwards of fifty anthems. Besides these, he composed the oratorios of *Gideon* and *The Crucifixion*, and the cantatas *Jairus's Daughter* (Worcester Festival, 1878) and *St. Mary Magdalene* (Gloucester Festival, 1883).

At St. Paul's he threw himself with heart and soul into the work of the reforming Chapter. Discipline, rehearsals, oratorios, new choir-school, enlarged range of music, services rendered daily with the spirit of aim at the utmost perfection, the selection and encouragement of the ablest colleagues in the choir; all this was stamped with the individuality of Stainer. Sanguine, cheerful, straightforward, friendly, always seeking after the highest levels of his divine art, he had an influence over the choir and services that was unique and immense. He resigned office at St. Paul's in 1888, became Professor of Music at Oxford in 1889, and died full of honours in 1901.

Sir George Clement Martin, *Mus. Doc.*, *M.V.O.*, his successor, was born at Lambourn, in Berkshire, in 1844. The village church contained an unusually fine organ; the rector, Mr. Milman, afterwards Bishop of Calcutta, had unusually good services. In his sixteenth year, Martin devoted himself to music, and ere long became organist of Lambourn Church. One of his fine hymn tunes he

[1] Bumpus, *Organists and Composers of St. Paul's*, p. 176.

named after his native village. For more advanced study he went to Dr. Stainer at Magdalen, and took his degree of Bachelor of Music.

In 1871 he became organist to the Duke of Buccleuch, at Dalkeith, and St. John's, Edinburgh; in 1874 he was invited by the Dean and Chapter of St. Paul's to succeed Mr. Frederick Walker as Master of Song to the boys of the new choir-school; and in 1876 he followed George Cooper as sub-organist. When Stainer resigned in 1888, it was universally felt that no more fitting successor could be discovered than Martin. He had already shown his self-controlled command of the great instrument, his distinguished, elevated, refined and masterly skill in composition, his sympathetic fellowship with the choir and all its concerns, and his profound devotional feeling. In 1883 he received the high honour of the degree of Mus. Doc. (like Blow, Gauntlett, Oakeley, E. J. Hopkins, Warwick-Jordan and a few others) from the Archbishop of Canterbury. He has published seven or eight services of the highest calibre, including the unrivalled *Te Deum* for the Queen's Diamond Jubilee in 1897, and the accompanying Communion Service in A; and amongst his numerous anthems are "Behold now praise the Lord" (men's voices), "Ho, every one that thirsteth," "Holiest, breathe an Evening Blessing," "Holy Spirit come, O come," "As it began to dawn," "Magnify His Name," "O be joyful in the Lord," "O come before His Presence," "Rejoice in the Lord, O ye righteous," "The Great Day of the Lord," "Whoso dwelleth under the Defence," "Hail! Gladdening Light." The St. Paul's Evening Choir, the Special Service Choir and the Special Service Orchestra are incalculably indebted to him for sympathy, direction and inspiration.

The sub-organist, Mr. Charles Macpherson, an accomplished musician, composer, and trainer of boys, was himself educated at St. Paul's, and is full of its spirit.

II. THE ORGAN.

An early description of an organ is found in an epigram attributed to the Emperor Julian the Apostate, who died A.D. 363—

"I see reeds of a new species, the growth of another and a brazen soil; such as are not agitated by our winds, but by a blast that rushes from a leathern cavern beneath their roots; while a robust mortal, running with swift fingers over the concordant rules of wood, makes them, as they smoothly dance, emit melodious sounds."[1]

St. Ambrose is said to have used instruments of music in the public service of the Church of Milan.[2]

A description is given by the monk Wulstan of an organ erected by Bishop Elphege of Winchester about the close of the tenth century. It had six-and-twenty bellows. "These, by alternate blasts, supply an immense quantity of wind, and are worked by seventy strong men, labouring with their arms, covered with perspiration, each inciting his companions to drive the wind up with all his strength, that the full-bosomed box may speak with its four hundred pipes, which the hand of the organist governs. . . . Two brethren of concordant spirit sit at the instrument, and each manages his own alphabet. . . . They strike the seven differences of joyous sounds, adding the music of the lyric semi-tone. Like thunder the iron tones batter the ear, so that it may receive no sound but that alone. To such an amount does it reverberate, echoing in every direction, that every one stops with his hand his gaping ears, being in nowise able to draw near and hear the sound, which so many combinations produce. The music is heard throughout the town, and the flying thereof is gone out over the whole country."[3]

[1] Burney, ii. 65.
[2] Rimbault, *History of the Organ*, p. 17.
[3] *Ibid.*, pp. 16, 17.

"Up to the end of the sixteenth century, instrumental music holds so low a place in comparison with vocal, that it hardly claims serious consideration as a part of musical history."[1]

Not only organs, but other instruments also were used in cathedrals in the time of Elizabeth. Viols were employed at Exeter in 1631; the lyre and harp at Hereford; cornets and sackbuts in Worcester at the reception of Elizabeth in 1575. Ravenscroft wrote in 1621 for organs, lutes and harps.[2]

"In the days of which we are now treating, the organ in St. Paul's was placed over the north choir-stalls, at their eastern extremity. The great organ-case was of a handsome mediæval design, and harmonized admirably with the exquisite middle pointed architecture of the choir. It had folding-doors, to preserve the pipes from dust, which were closed when the instrument was not in use, and which were no doubt gorgeously illuminated with figures of saints and angels playing on various musical instruments. In some of the old engravings of the interior of the choir, these doors are depicted as standing open, thereby giving the organ the appearance of a triptich. Overhanging the richly carved stalls was a small choir-organ, forming, as at present, a screen for the performer."[3]

This organ escaped the iconoclastic zeal of the Puritans, remaining untouched during the Protectorate, and only falling a victim to the Great Fire of 1666.

The magnificent organ of the new Cathedral was completed in time for the opening ceremony. Bernhardt Schmidt, a German commonly called Father Smith, and who had been very generally employed in building cathedral organs to replace those destroyed during the

---

[1] Hullah, 30, 33.
[2] Walcott, *Customs and Traditions*, 138; Sparrow Simpson, *Gleanings*, 181.
[3] Bumpus, *Organists*, p. 35.

Civil War, was the builder. The cost—£2000—was a large sum of money in those days, but the result proved that it was well expended.

Sir Christopher Wren, with his usual great foresight, much wished to place the organ over the northern choir-stalls, as in the old Cathedral, in order that there might be an uninterrupted view from west to east, and also that the dome might be utilized for congregational purposes. In this design, however, he was over-ruled by the Building Commissioners, who wished to follow the traditions of all the other cathedrals, and to have an enclosed choir with return-stalls and a western organ-screen. Upon this screen Wren was compelled to place the instrument.

The contract for the organ was dated and signed December 19, 1694, and it was to consist of "Great and Chayre (choir) organs and echoes"; it was to be completed by Lady Day, 1696, and to receive the approval of several eminent musicians, "particularly Dr. John Blowe." When the time came for placing the pipes in position, Father Smith wished the case to be enlarged; but Wren gave a most decided negative, declaring that his building was already spoilt "by the confounded box of whistles."[1]

The following is an extract from the original specification discovered by Mr. W. H. Cummings—

Memd.: That in pursuance of the Order first above written it was then agreed by the Dean and Chapter of S. Paul's and ye Surveyor of the Workers of S. Paul's Cathedral for and in the behalfe of the Rt. Honable. ye Lords and others Coms. for rebuilding and adorning ye said Cathedral with Bernard Smith Organ-Maker, to make a large Organ containing 21 stops, part wood and part metall, and 6 halfe stops, according to Two Lists of ye said stops hereunder expressed as followeth—

[1] Bumpus, p. 57.

The First List.

Stops in the Great Organ.
Two Open Diapasons, Stop Diapason, Principal Great Twelfth, Ffifteenth, Cornet, Mixtures, Sesquialtera, Trumpet.

Stops in ye Chayre Organ.
Principall, Stop Diapason, Hol fleut, Voice Humane, Crum horne.

Echoes or halfe Stops.
Diapason, Principall, Cornet, Trumpet.

The Second List.

Stops in the Great Organ.
Hol fleut, Small Twelfths.

Stops in the Chayre Organ.
Quinta Dena Diapason, Great Twelfth, Ffifteenth, Cimball.

Echoes or halfe Stops.
Ffifteenth, Nason.[1]

For nearly one hundred years the instrument remained as originally designed. A swell organ was then added by a builder named Crang (or Cranz). In 1802, when Attwood was organist, the organ was taken to pieces and cleaned by Ohrmann, "an ingenious Swedish artist," and his partner and son-in-law, Nutt. Both these personages, we are informed by David Hughson, in his *History of London*, lost their lives through a severe cold contracted during the engagement.

In 1826, while Attwood was still organist, Bishop, a well-known organ-builder, added an octave of pedal-pipes which were, for many years, held in great estimation. He also first introduced the concussion valves, and thus secured what had never before been achieved—the steadiness of the wind. Previous to 1826, in order to preserve the mechanism

[1] Bumpus, p. 202.

of the organ from dust, etc., the front pipes of the Great
and Choir organ-cases were furnished with huge glass
window-sashes, which were shut down when the instrument
was not in use. In several old engravings of solemnities at
St. Paul's in the possession of Mr. Bumpus, these con-
trivances figure in a very prominent manner. Doubtless,
the idea was borrowed from the design of the organ-case
in the old Cathedral, where shutters, like those of a triptich,
concealed, at certain times, the pipes from view. Some
portions of the mechanism, for raising and letting down
these sashes, may be seen attached to the oak-work of the
present organ at this day.

Bishop again improved the organ in 1849, adding a very
beautiful swell extending in compass down to gamut G, *i. e.*
the lowest G of the bass stave. A new keyboard was at
the same time introduced, the colours of the keys having
previously been reversed, the long ones being black and the
short white. The same builder likewise increased the
compass and efficiency of the pedal organ, and placed in
the Great Organ, for the first time, the *clarabella* stop, his
own very beautiful invention.[1]

The organ remained in the above state until the year
1860, when the screen and return stalls were removed. It
was then rebuilt under the middle arch of the choir on the
north side. The manuals were placed in the stalls, but
this situation being attended with some inconvenience, they
were, in 1863, removed to the side of the organ in the
gallery. This portion of the work was entrusted to Mr.
Henry Willis.[2]

In 1871, much dissatisfaction being felt at this condition
of things, the organ was again removed, almost entirely
rebuilt and greatly enlarged by Henry Willis, from the
designs of Dr. (now Sir) John Stainer. It was, at the same
time, divided into two portions and erected at either side
of the entrance of the choir, the case being somewhat

[1] Bumpus, p. 204. [2] *Ibid.*, p. 205.

GAS ENGINE FOR THE ORGAN

To face p. 418.

remodelled to suit its new position. The stalls of the Greater Dignitaries, which were formerly returned under the screen, and which, since 1860, had been shamefully stowed away, were again brought to light, and arranged as we now see them.[1]

In 1897 certain portions of the mechanism had become worn and noisy. In order to rectify this, it was found necessary to take the instrument to pieces, and, in these circumstances, it was thought advisable not only to repair the worn parts, but also to bring the organ up to date, and really make it worthy of the position which St. Paul's Cathedral now holds in the hearts of the people of this country. Mr. H. Willis was again entrusted with this work, and the instrument, as it now stands, is one of the very finest church organs in the world. The specification was made by Sir George Martin.

"Two-thirds of the pedal-organ and three of the most powerful tubas are placed in the north-east quarter-dome, invisible except from the Whispering Gallery.

"The organist sits on the north side of the choir in that part of the instrument which juts out from the rest of the case; the connection with the opposite side is made by pneumatic tubes, which pass under the floor of the chancel.

"There are five rows of keys or manuals, as well as the pedals. The connection with the quarter-dome part is by means of electricity, and the weight imposed on the bellows for the most powerful stops is about three tons.

"There are 4822 speaking pipes in the instrument and 76 sounding stops, and, reckoning couplers, 102 stops in all."[2]

III. THE MUSIC.

The extant anthem music of the English Church seems naturally to divide itself into three periods—the first from

---

[1] Bumpus, p. 35.
[2] Sir George Martin, in Gilbertson's *Guide to St. Paul's Cathedral*.

E E 2

1500 to the beginning of the Great Civil War; the second period from the Restoration to the birth, let us say, of Handel in 1685; the third period may take to itself the title of the Modern School.

Or, *these* three periods may be preferred with their distinctive names—the *Motett* period, the *Verse* period, and the *Modern* period. The first of these extends from the time of the Reformation to the death of Henry Lawes—say, from 1550 to 1650; the second from 1670 to 1777, the time of the death of the elder Hayes; and the third from Thomas Attwood to the present time.[1]

Gounod has pronounced the choral Celebration at St. Paul's to be the finest eucharistic service in Europe.

Here is a tribute from Nathaniel Hawthorne—

"October 6, 1855. It rained heavily and being still showery when we got to Cheapside again, we stood under an archway (a usual resort for passengers through London streets) and then betook ourselves to sanctuary, taking refuge in St. Paul's Cathedral. The afternoon service was about to begin, so after looking at a few of the monuments, we sat down in the choir, the richest and most ornamented part of the Cathredral, with screens or partitions of oak cunningly carved. Small, white-robed choristers were flitting noiselessly about, making preparations for the service which by and by began. It is a beautiful idea that, several times in the course of the day, a man can slip out of the thickest throng and bustle of London into this religious atmosphere, and hear the organ, and the music of young pure voices."[2]

Lastly, here are some impressions of a visit paid to St. Paul's, during the days of Goss, by the eminent poet-bishop of Western New York, the Very Rev. Arthur Cleveland Coxe.

"Going to St. Paul's to morning service, on Sunday the

---

[1] Sparrow Simpson's *Gleanings*, p. 171.
[2] *Our Old Home* and *English Note Books*.

4th of May (1851), I entered the south transept, and, for the first time, beheld its interior. The effect of the immense vault of the dome as it first struck my sight, was overpowering; the more so because, at that moment, a single burst of the organ and the swell of an *Amen* from the choir, where service was already begun, filled the dome with reverberations that seemed to come upon me like thunder. I was so unprepared for anything impressive in St. Paul's, that I felt a sort of recoil, and the blood flushed to my temples. I said to a friend, who happened to be with me, 'After all, 'tis indeed sublime!' I now went forward with highly excited expectations, and the voice of the clergyman intoning the prayers within the choir increased my anxiety to be at once upon my knees. I glanced at the monument of Howard, and entered beneath the screen. The congregation seemed immense. A verger led us quite up to the altar; and so I was led about and put into a stall (inscribed 'Weldland,' with the legend, *Exaudi, Domine, justitiam*), where, kneeling down, I gave myself up to the solemn worship of God, and solemn worship it was! I never, before or since, heard any cathedral chanting, whether in England or on the Continent, that could be compared to it for effect. The two clergymen who intoned the Litany, knelt in the midst of the choir, looking towards the altar. Even now I seem to be hearing their full, rich voices, sonorously and articulately chanting the suffrage—*By Thy glorious Resurrection and Ascension*—to which organ and singers gave response—*Good Lord deliver us*—as with the voice of many waters. . . . Tears gushed from my eyes, and my heart swelled to my throat, as this overwhelming worship was continued."

CHAPTER XXXVI

THE LIBRARY, BELLS AND CLOCK OF ST. PAUL'S

I. The Library.

AMONG the catastrophes that have happened through fire to St. Paul's Cathedral, none is greater than the loss of its ancient library. It was, says Dr. Sparrow Simpson, the late learned and zealous librarian of the Cathedral, "marvellously rich—rich in early texts of Holy Scripture, illuminated in gold and colours; rich in early ritual books, glowing with the best specimens of the painter's art; rich in philosophy and history; rich in sermons and homilies. Many of the precious volumes were made still more precious by their sumptuous binding—velvet, gold, silver, rich gems lending their aid to enhance the labours of the scribe and of the painter. Others were more precious than even scribe and artist and well-skilled binder could make them; for they had been the cherished possessions of great men in the days gone by—scholars, bishops, saints. But all are swept away. The catalogues remain: the books themselves have vanished."

First there was the conflagration of 1561, which destroyed the spire, injured the roofs and wrecked part of the cloisters. Then, during the days of the Long Parliament, the Cathedral was turned into a cavalry barrack. Finally came the Great Fire of 1666, in which the whole Cathedral perished. Deeds and records were saved, but not the books. Only three books are extant which certainly belonged to the old library: (1) a MS. of Avicenna; (2) a MS. chronicle of the

THE LIBRARY, UNDER S.W. TOWER

illustrious Dean of St. Paul's, Ralph de Diceto, the historian, now in the library of Lambeth Palace; (3) a MS. account of the miracles of the Virgin Mary, now in the College library at Aberdeen.

The library in the new Cathedral occupies the space over the south-west chapel (formerly the Wellington Chapel, and now the Chapel of the Order of St. Michael and St. George). It is a fine and well-lighted hall, with a learned scent of oak, cedar and perfumed leather. A gallery is supported by brackets carved by Jonathan Maine, and the flooring is of 2300 pieces of oak, inlaid, and without pegs or nails. The library contains upwards of 10,500 books and 10,800 pamphlets.

The founder of the present collection of books was Henry Compton, who was the Bishop of London during the whole of the thirty-seven years of the rebuilding of the Cathedral. He bequeathed 1892 volumes to form the nucleus.

In 1783 a great addition was made, partly by purchase, partly by gift, in the acquisition of the collections of Dr. Thomas Mangey, Prebendary of Durham, and his son Thomas, Prebendary of St. Paul's.

The late Dr. Sparrow Simpson, Minor Canon of the Cathedral, was an enthusiastic custodian of the books. During his tenure of office he bought 10,000 pamphlets, including 6348 collected by Bishop Sumner, of Winchester; 1405 tracts gathered by Hale, Archdeacon of London, from 1842 to 1870; and an important collection presented by the widow of Prebendary Irons. The library was also greatly enriched by Dean Milman, Dean Mansel and Dean Church. Dr. Wace presented his *Dictionary of Christian Biography;* Dr. Freshfield his series on parochial history; Mr. Milman, Minor Canon and Librarian of Sion College, a complete set of the *Quarterly Review ;* and Dr. Hessey, late Archdeacon of Middlesex, a complete set of "Bampton Lectures."

The library is rich in Councils, patristic literature and

theology. It contains the publications of the following societies: the Surtees, the Camden, the Palæographical, the Henry Bradshaw, the Ecclesiastical History, the London and Middlesex Archæological, the St. Paul's Ecclesiological; the long series of Chronicles issued by the Master of the Rolls, the Calendars of the State Papers, and the Acta Sanctorum of the Bollandists.

Amongst the librarians was the brilliant author of the *Ingoldsby Legends*, Richard Harris Barham, a Minor Canon of St. Paul's and rector of a City church. He found the library in a sadly neglected condition, and did much to restore and rescue it.

But the passing visitor will be more interested in the glass case in the middle of the hall, containing objects of notable interest. Here is a modest volume containing promises of subscriptions for the rebuilding of the Cathedral. The first entry is in the hand of Charles II., undertaking to pay £1000 a year. Alas! it was not paid. Below is the handwriting of James, Duke of York, afterwards James II., promising £200 a year. This he paid. A large and beautifully written page open in another volume shows a specimen of the admirable manner in which Wren kept his accounts during the rebuilding, with his own exquisite signature below. Here is Luther's Bible and Laud's own annotated copy of his controversy with Fisher the Jesuit. Another book has the signatures of Laud, William Juxon (Bishop of London, and afterwards Archbishop of Canterbury, who attended Charles I. on the scaffold), Lord Clarendon the historian, and others. Another book belonged to Archbishop Cranmer, and has his signature. Here can be seen the autograph of Queen Victoria on her writ appointing Dr. Tait to be Bishop of London, and those of many other modern sovereigns.

Here, again, is a selection of casts taken from the seals of various Bishops of London, various Deans and Chapters, Archdeacons of London and other officials. Side by side with these are some fine medals, commemorative of Royal visits to the City, public thanksgivings and national events.

The librarian is almost always one of the Minor Canons; the present holder of the office is the Rev. W. P. Besley, in succession to the Rev. Lewis Gilbertson, who wrote the interesting and accurate *Authorized Guide to St. Paul's Cathedral.* The Dean and Chapter can only afford £100 a year for the purposes of the library. Still, the collection quietly grows, and increases in importance and interest. Housed in a beautiful hall, far above the roar of London, its silence only broken by the chimes of the neighbouring clock, or by the ringing of the bells, it is a type of the learning and tranquillity which should be characteristics of every cathedral body, and of that reasonable appeal to antiquity and to the lessons of the past which is a leading feature of the true spirit of the Church of England.

II. THE BELLS.

It was in the year 1882 that the bells of St. Paul's were finally completed by the erection of "Great Paul" in the south-west tower of the Cathedral.

It must be remembered that there are two great bells at St. Paul's: one, the old State bell, which is still tolled on the death of any member of the Royal Family, or of the Archbishop of Canterbury, the Bishop of London, the Dean of St. Paul's, or the Lord Mayor of London; the other is the huge monster of which I shall speak presently. Both hang in the south-west tower.

First, as to the old bell, now so greatly surpassed by the young giant of 1882. The old bell was originally cast in the reign of Edward I., and hung at the gate of Westminster Hall to notify the hour to the judges. It was first called "Edward of Westminster," afterwards "Westminster Tom." King William III. gave it to St. Paul's Cathedral, where it was brought on New Year's Day, 1699.

THE BELLS

It then weighed 8271 lbs., but it has since been twice recast with additional metal. It now weighs 11,474 lbs., and is 10 ft. in diameter. Its metal is 10 ins. thick. The hour is struck on the bell by a hammer weighing 145 lbs. The clapper weighs 180 lbs. The chimes are struck on two smaller bells below.

Before the Great Fire of 1666 a bell-tower stood at the angle of the east end of the churchyard of old St. Paul's, which, Dugdale tells us, "contained four very great bells, called 'Jesus Bells,' in regard that they specially belonged to Jesus Chapel, situate at the east end of the undercroft (crypt) of St. Paul's." He also narrates how these bells were in existence until the time of Henry VIII., when a certain Sir Miles Partridge, "having won them from the King at one cast of the dice, pulled them down." Sir Miles Partridge was put to death for high treason by Edward VI.

During the great revival of the activity of St. Paul's Cathedral, which was begun under Dean Milman, and reached a climax in the time of Dean Church, it was determined to have a new "ring" of twelve bells. They were rung for the first time on All Saints' Day, 1878. The Corporation of London unanimously agreed to take part in the cost, on a petition presented by Canon Lightfoot (afterwards the famous Bishop of Durham), the organist (Dr. Stainer), and Dr. Webber (the Sub-Dean, the head of the Minor Canons).

The following list contains exact information about this great addition to the Cathedral; namely, the donors of each bell, its musical note and precise weight, details which, I am sure, the reader will be glad to have.

	Note.	Cwt.	qrs.	lbs.	Donor.
No. 1.	F.	8	1	16	Drapers' Company.
„ 2.	E♭.	9	1	15	„ „
„ 3.	D.	10	0	3	Baroness Burdett-Coutts and the Turners' Company.

No.	Note.	Cwt.	qrs.	lbs.	Donor
„	4. C.	11	3	21	Baroness Burdett-Coutts and the Turners' Company.
„	5. B♭.	13	2	14	„ „
„	6. A.	14	0	4	„ „
„	7. G.	16	2	21	Salters' Company.
„	8. F.	22	1	18	Merchant Taylors' Company.
„	9. E♭.	28	0	7	Fishmongers' Company.
„	10. D.	30	0	22	Clothworkers' Company.
„	11. C.	44	2	0	Grocers' Company.
„	12. B♭.	62	0	0	Corporation of the City of London (Lord Mayor Cotton).

The bells were cast by Messrs. John Taylor & Co. of Loughborough, and were pronounced by Lord Grimthorpe (then Sir Edmund Beckett) to be "on the whole unquestionably the grandest ringing peal in England, and therefore in the world."

The bells are rung by the Guild of College Youths (so called from a society founded in the reign of Charles I. in connection with a church on College Hill, E.C.) on Sunday mornings, the great festivals and days of national rejoicing. The guild also practises from time to time, after six o'clock, when houses of business are closed and very few are left in the City. There are several records of change-ringing on this new and glorious peal. One of the most notable was on December 10, 1881, when 5,014 changes of Stedman's Cinques were rung in 4 hrs. 17 mins., the St. Paul's bells being the heaviest set of twelve bells in the United Kingdom. Amongst other sets of twelve, the highest place is usually given to those of St. Peter Mancroft, in the city of Norwich.

To come now to the great bell of all—the young giant, as I have called it (giantess, perhaps, it should be, for bells are treated as feminine in the craft)—"Great Paul." It was founded by Messrs. Taylor & Co., and was placed in

THE CLOCK

[*To face p.* 429.

the south-west tower in 1882. It weighs 16 tons 14 cwt. 2 qrs. 19 lbs. The height is 8 ft. 10 ins. The diameter at the base is 9 ft. 6½ ins.; the height inside the crown is 6 ft. 11¼ ins.; and the thickness where the clapper strikes is 18¾ ins. The clapper is 7 ft. 9 ins. in length, and weighs 4 cwt. 20 lbs. The note is E flat. The motto chosen by the witty and devout Canon Liddon has already been recorded in the notes of Verger Green.

The pilgrimage of "Great Paul" from Loughborough to London attracted great attention. It was by road, and the machinery consisted of two traction-engines and a trolley. The trolley weighed 2 tons, so that the weight on the roadway was nearly 19 tons. The journey took about a week. The lifting of the bell took about fifteen hours. The work was done very expeditiously and quietly. The appliances for raising the bell answered their purpose admirably. No hitch whatever occurred. "Great Paul" is now heard every day at 1 p.m. tolling with solemn and melodious tones for the midday meeting for prayer in the midst of the vast and bustling emporium of business.

"Great Paul" has not superseded "Edward of Westminster" as the State bell of St. Paul's Cathedral. "Edward of Westminster" still tolls for the national deaths before enumerated. But "Great Paul," in being by far the largest bell in the United Kingdom, has added dignity to the Cathedral of the imperial City. And his twelve companions in the opposite (north-west) tower give voice to the various emotions which pass through the building and City, as the haunts and homes of living men and women, with all their daily tale of hopes and fears, joys and sorrows, aspirations and experiences. The Cathedral has become the centre of religious life in London, and its bells, great and small, new and old, contribute to the outward expression of that life. May the Christianity of London ever grow deeper, broader and truer, like the strong note which booms forth daily from our chief House of Prayer!

III. The Clock.

The old clock was not the best of its kind, and was so difficult to wind that it was said to have shortened the lives of several Cathedral workmen.

It had two faces, one looking to the west, the other to the south; each of them 57 ft. in circumference, or nearly 20 ft. in diameter. The minute-hand in each was 9 ft. 8 ins. long, and weighed 75 lbs.; the hour-hand 5 ft. 9 ins. long, and weighed 44 lbs. The pendulum was 16 ft. in length; the weight at the bottom was 108 lbs., yet it was suspended by a spring no thicker than a shilling. It beat 30 times in a minute, or once in 2 seconds.

The new clock will always be connected with the name of Dean Gregory. It was completed in 1893, two years after he had been appointed Dean, and it was his own idea. He was driving home one evening with Lord Grimthorpe from some engagement, and knowing him to be the first authority on clocks, he told him how cumbersome the old clock was, and how desirable it would be to have a new one. Lord Grimthorpe threw himself into the idea with enthusiasm, and the scheme was soon matured. Lord Grimthorpe sketched out the specifications, and the order was entrusted to Messrs. John Smith & Sons, of the Midland Clock Works, Queen Street, Derby. Besides being clockmakers to the Dean and Chapter of St. Paul's, they are also in that relation to His Majesty's Government, the Duke of Devonshire, the Midland, Great Northern, South Indian and other railway companies, the corporations of Leicester, Manchester, Salford, Wolverhampton, Salisbury, Derby, Burton-on-Trent, Sheffield and Chesterfield, and the London School Board. So the Chapter was likely to get a good clock.

The two faces were not altered, but a third was added, looking east. The new works are greatly larger than the old: and though the dials are surpassed in size by others,

LIBRARY, BELLS AND CLOCK

the works are thought to be the largest in the kingdom. The frame is 19 ft. long, and the pendulum weighs 7 cwts. The two main girders are 28 ft. long.

The Chapter much wished to have more musical chimes, such as those at Oxford, Cambridge, Westminster and many other places: but as the space in the clock tower was taken up by the two great bells, "Edward of Westminster" (the old State bell) and "Great Paul" (the gigantic new bell of the Cathedral) and the two small bells for the old ding-dong chime, and as the ring of twelve bells was in the other tower (the north-west), it was found difficult to alter the chime, and any attempt to do it would have been far too costly.[1]

The following are some of the principal chimes in use at other cathedrals and churches. The first set is the copyright of Messrs. John Smith & Sons. It is called the "Tennyson Chimes"; the music was composed by Sir John Stainer, and it was first fixed at Freshwater Church, Isle of Wight.

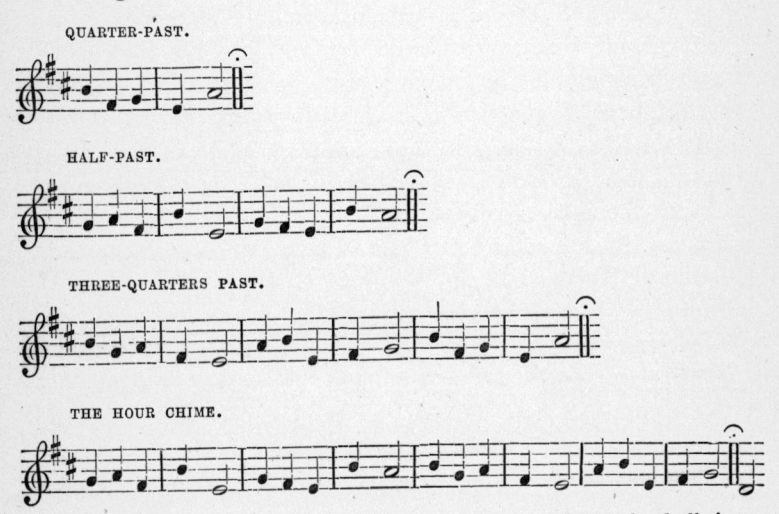

QUARTER-PAST.

HALF-PAST.

THREE-QUARTERS PAST.

THE HOUR CHIME.

[1] A Carillon might be easily added at any time to the twelve bells in the N.W. Tower to play *after* the striking of the hour at certain intervals.

432 MEMORIALS OF ST. PAUL'S CATHEDRAL

"Derby" Chimes (Ten Bells).

FIRST QUARTER.

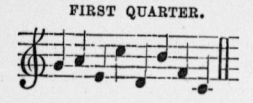

SECOND QUARTER.

THIRD QUARTER.

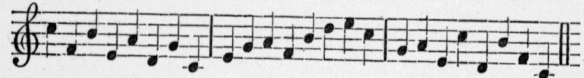

FOURTH QUARTER, BEFORE STRIKING.

"Chard" Chimes (Eight Bells).

FIRST QUARTER.

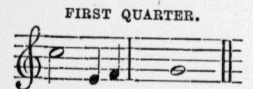

SECOND QUARTER.

THIRD QUARTER.

FOURTH QUARTER, BEFORE STRIKING.

Cambridge Chimes.

FIRST QUARTER.

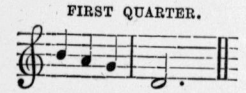

LIBRARY, BELLS AND CLOCK

SECOND QUARTER.

THIRD QUARTER.

FOURTH QUARTER, BEFORE STRIKING.

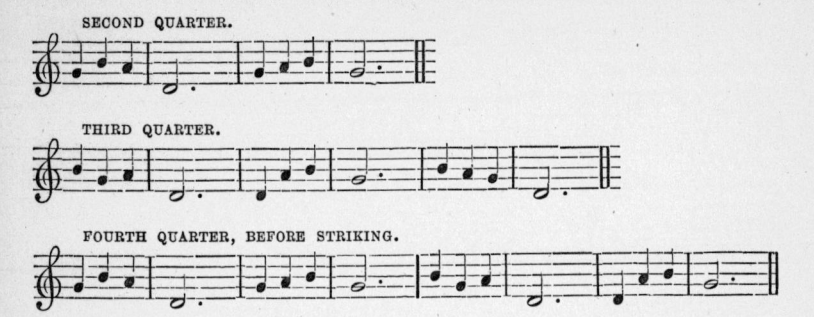

The Dean was anxious that the clock should be illuminated at night: but this was found a matter of difficulty and great cost, especially as the open space of the dial is comparatively small; the figures are on a vast circular band of flat stone, which is part of the architecture of the tower. Finally, the architects said that the centre of the clock must be dark.

An important piece of knowledge on the subject is that it is generally most convenient for the bells to be placed in the highest room of the tower, and for the surrounding walls to be pierced with openings as large as possible, so that the sound may get away freely. The "louvres" (frames of strips of wood or metal) that one sees in the windows of church towers, block in the sound, and are not much use in keeping out the wet. The wet does not much affect bells or bell-fittings. The floor of the belfry should be leaded, or made weather-proof in some other way.

For ease in working of the clock, the weights (say Messrs. Smith & Sons) should have as much fall as can be obtained down one of the angles of the tower, with a free fall to the ground floor if possible, so that in the event of a rope breaking little damage need be done. For this reason the exquisitely beautiful domed roof over the Geometrical Staircase in the clock-tower of St. Paul's Cathedral had to be pierced, to admit the proper length of descent for the clock-weights.

F F

"Smith of Derby," wrote Lord Grimthorpe to a friend, "will clock you in the best way, and as near eternity as possible." That is high praise. The new clock at St. Paul's has certainly gone with admirable accuracy since its completion in 1893. There is a legend that the old clock once saved the life of a foot-guardsman at Windsor Castle by striking thirteen instead of twelve. He was accused of being asleep on sentry-go. It was in the reign of William III., on a clear and frosty night. The soldier's name was John Hatfield, who died in 1770, at the age of 102. He declared that he was not guilty of the charge, because he had heard the clock of St. Paul's strike in that singular and extraordinary manner. The matter was investigated, and it was found that the clock had struck on that particular night in that abnormal way.

The chimes of St. Paul's have sung their ding-dong over London since they were erected in the days of Queen Anne, some two hundred years ago. They will continue their solemn note over the immeasurable bustle of the City long after the bodies of all of us have returned dust to dust. The thoughts that come into our minds on the passing of time, and the warning voice of its watchman, are expressed as none else could give them, by Shakespeare. He thinks of all the changes that are brought about by time, while the great tower stands motionless, steadfastly gazing into heaven, with the persistent warnings of its clear, melancholy voice—

"Time's glory is to calm contending kings;
  To unmask falsehood, and bring truth to light;
 To stamp the seal of time on aged things;
  To wake the morn, to sentinel the night;
 To wrong the wronger, till he render right;
 To make the child a man, the man a child;
 To mock the subtle, in themselves beguiled;
 To cheer the ploughman with increaseful crops;
 And waste huge stones with little water-drops."

CHAPTER XXXVII

PAUL'S CROSS

IT seems to have been the custom in early days to erect a tall cross in every churchyard. The Emperor Justinian made a law that "none shall presume to erect a church until the Bishop shall come and consecrate the place to God by prayer, and erect the symbol of our salvation, the venerable and truly precious rood." An Irish canon of the eighth century indicates that such a cross used to mark the limit as well as the sanctity of the place. In 1299, William of Blois, Bishop of Winchester, ordered that a handsome cross should be erected in every churchyard, to which the procession shall be made on Palm Sunday. These crosses were constantly used for preaching; when standing by themselves, not in a churchyard, they often received the name of St. Martin, who was regarded as the greatest preacher of the early centuries. There were also market and town crosses, which gave the sanction of the Church to the meetings of the people.

Paul's Cross, standing in the north-east part of St. Paul's Churchyard, in the angle between the choir and the north transept, served both for preaching and for citizens' meetings. Stowe says that the antiquity of the folk-mote which used to assemble there went beyond the written annals. The earliest record of any occurrence at the Cross was the delivery of a seditious address by William FitzOsbert in 1191; from that time until towards 1643, when the pulpit and Cross were pulled down by order of the Long Parliament, many stirring events took place on this site. Its probable position was discovered in 1888 by the Cathedral surveyor, Mr. Penrose. Stones forming an octagon of considerable size were laid bare; it was known that an elm-tree was planted on the demolition of the old preaching-station; that elm was blown down in 1879, and was close by this spot. The notices of the sermons and events are exceedingly numerous, and only some of them need be given.

Chronology.[1]

Richard I.

1191. FitzOsbert's harangue.

Henry III.

1257. Feb. 2. Visit of John Maunsel (King's Justice), the Earl of Gloucester, Henry de Bath and others to levy tallage on the City.

Nov. 6. Henry III., with the Lords of the Council, took leave of the citizens on going to France to conclude the Treaty of Abbeville with Louis IX.

1259. Henry III. and his brother Richard, King of Almayne, present at a folk-mote.

1260. Feb. 14. Henry III., Richard, King of Almayne, the Archbishop of Canterbury (Boniface of Savoy), with Justice Maunsel, received the fealty of William Fitz-Richard, Mayor of London, and others.

1261. Lent. Bull read from Pope Urban IV., absolving Henry III. from the oath he made to the Parliament of Oxford to observe " the Provisions " for better government.

June 29. Henry III. took leave of the citizens on passing into France.

1269. Nine Bishops present at the reading of the Bull of the Pope, confirming the Charters and Liberties of England. (If the date is right, the Pope was Clement IV.)

[1] From *St. Paul's Cross*, by John B. Marsh. Raithby, Lawrence and Co., 1892.

Edward I.

1285. The churchyard walled round: the Cross first used for ecclesiastical purposes: sermons preached regularly.

1299. Dean Ralph de Baldock cursed those who had searched for gold in St. Martin's-le-Grand.

Edward II.

1311. July 22. Edward II. received homage from the earls who supported him.

Richard II.

1382. The Cross and pulpit damaged by a "tempest of lightning."

1397–8. The Statutes and Ordinances of the Parliament begun at Westminster and ended at Shrewsbury confirmed by Pope Benedict XIII., and proclaimed at Paul's Cross.

Henry VI.

1429. The second day of Advent. Two heretics abjured, and a third was carried to prison.

1440. Aug. 28. Proclamation of the submission of Palæologus, Emperor of Constantinople, to the Roman faith.

1441. July 25. Roger Boltyngbroke, the necromancer, exposed, with all his instruments, during sermon; he then abjured. He was afterwards hanged, drawn and quartered at Tyburn.

1449. Thomas Kemp, Bishop of London, rebuilt the pulpit and Cross in a more splendid style.

1457. Abjuration of alleged errors by Bishop Pecocke of Chichester (as in the text).

1465. The controversy between the Friars and the Secular Priests reached Paul's Cross. Harry Parker, a White Friar, preached that priests ought to live on alms; he was answered another Sunday by Edward Storry; then came another Friar. Lord Chancellor Kirkham committed Parker to prison; then Parker abjured. The Provincial of the White Friars went to Rome to consult the Pope, where he was imprisoned two years in the castle of St. Angelo, and narrowly escaped burning.

1469. Bull read from Pope Paul II. cursing all shoemakers who made peaks to shoes of more than two inches; all those who worked or attended fairs on Sunday.

Richard III.

1483. May. Dr. Shaw's sermon advocating the claims of Richard to the throne.

May. Penance of Jane Shore, mistress of Edward IV.

Henry VII.

1502. Feb. Proclamation of marriage contract between James IV. of Scotland and Margaret, daughter of Henry VII.

Lent. Sir Edmund de la Pole, Earl of Suffolk, denounced for treason.

Henry VIII.

1520. July 2. Henry Standish (afterwards Bishop of St. Asaph) preached furiously against Erasmus and the translators of the New Testament.

1521. May 12. Cardinal Wolsey, Archbishop of York and Lord Chancellor, with the Archbishop of Canterbury and most of the Bishops of the realm, as well as the Ambassadors of the Pope and the Emperor (four Doctors of Divinity held a canopy of cloth of gold over the Cardinal's head during the time), listened to a sermon by John Fisher, Bishop of Rochester, against Martin Luther, preached by command of Pope Leo X. Many of Luther's books burned during the service.[1]

[1] A striking picture of this scene was exhibited lately by J. Seymour Lucas, R.A.

1528. March. John Hig abjured certain Lutheran doctrines. On Palm Sunday he had to bear a faggot at the head of the procession.

1530. Cardinal Wolsey again present in great pomp; burning of three copies of Tyndale's translation of the New Testament. Fisher, Bishop of Rochester, again preached.

1531. First Sunday in Advent. Stokesley, Bishop of London, prohibited the reading of thirty books in English. Amongst them were the *New Testament*, the *Psalter*, several books of the *Old Testament*, the *Supplication of the Beggars*, the *Burying of the Mass*, the *Books of Moses*, the *Matrimony* of Tyndale, the "*A.B.C.*" *against the Clergy*, a book *Against St. Thomas of Canterbury*, a *Disputation of Purgatory*, and the *Practice of Prelates*.

1532. James Baynham, Barrister of the Middle Temple, stood at the Cross with a lighted taper in his hand, and a bundle of faggots on his shoulder, in token of recantation of Protestant errors. He afterwards professed Protestantism at St. Augustine's Church, was imprisoned, scourged and burnt at Smithfield, April 30.

1533. Henry VIII., through his council, ordered that all who preached at Paul's Cross should deny the supremacy of the Pope.

1534. Remembrances sent by Thomas Crumwell for the Council to the Bishop of London to order the preachers not to pray for the Pope at Paul's Cross: also to the Lord Mayor and nobles that they should commonly assert that the Pope is only Bishop of Rome.

1534. Penance of Elizabeth Barton (the Maid of Kent) and her associates before execution at Tyburn for pretended revelations against the King's divorce.

1538. March 10. Sermon by Hugh Latimer, Bishop of Worcester.

1538. John Hilsey, Bishop of Rochester, after a sermon, exposed the machinery in the Rood of Grace from Boxley Abbey, Kent; it was thereupon broken to pieces.

1540. Lent. Gardiner, Bishop of Winchester, preached in favour of the Six Articles (a reactionary statute enacted in 1539 and repealed in 1547).

1540. The following Sunday Barnes replied to Gardiner. He subsequently held a dispute with him in a London church, and was ultimately burnt.

Edward VI.

1547. Ridley, Bishop of Rochester, preached on the Lord's Supper. From this time for some years, Paul's Cross was frequently occupied by preachers who took a prominent part in the religious controversies of the time: Ridley, Latimer, Gardiner, Bonner and Miles Coverdale often occur.

1548. Jan. 1, 8, 15, 18. Latimer's four famous sermons on "The Ploughers."

Feb. 6. Sermon by Gardiner, Bishop of Winchester, before Lord Chancellor Wriothesley, Lord Mayor Sir H. Amcotes, the Aldermen, Livery and many Judges.

1549. The Parson of St. Katherine Cree preached against the old Maypole at St. Andrew Undershaft (the second name of the church came from the pole). It had rested thirty-two years on the hooks, but was now taken down and sawn in pieces.

1531. Miles Coverdale, Bishop of Exeter, in a sermon, told the story of his share in the translation of the Bible. When the King was asking the Bishops their judgment on its merit, he inquired if it had any faults. They replied there were many. "Any heresies?" They had found none. Then said the King: "In God's name let it go abroad amongst my people." Coverdale's Bible was ordered to be publicly placed in the choir of every parish church; for security it was chained to a pillar.

1552. Nov. 1. Ridley, Bishop of London, expounded the value of the new Book of Common Prayer, used for the first time, before Lord Mayor Sir George Barnes, the Aldermen and Liverymen.

Queen Mary.

1553. Dr. Harding, Chaplain to the Duke of Suffolk, urged the people not to revolt from their allegiance to Queen Mary.

1553. July 16. Bishop Ridley, for a sermon at Paul's Cross, committed to the Tower, where he lay till April 10, 1554.

1553. Aug. 13. Dr. Bourne, Chaplain to Bishop Bonner, attacked Bishop Ridley, on which there was a great uproar. (Compare the text.)

1553. Aug. 20. Dr. Watson preached, urging the people "to come home and rebuild the old temple." One hundred and twenty or more halberdiers of the Guard stood round the Cross. Lord Mayor Sir Thomas White, the Aldermen and Liverymen present: the Marquis of Winchester, the Earl of Bedford, the Earl of Pembroke, Lord Wentworth, Lord Rich and Bishop Bonner.

1553. Sept. 24. Dr. Feckenham preached the Sunday before the coronation.

1554. June 10. Dr. Pendleton, while preaching, exhibited a cat, made to resemble a priest with a wafer, taken from a gallows in Cheapside. As he denounced the outrage a gun was fired at him.

1554. July 29. Nicholas Harpsfield, champion of the Papacy, preached.

1554. Sept. 30. Gardiner preached on the Queen's marriage (which took place on July 25 at Winchester).

1554. Nov. 4. Harpsfield preached, and five persons did penance in sheets; and lighted tapers in one hand, a rod in the other. The preacher, in the course of his sermon, struck the penitents with a rod.

1554. Dec. 9. Dr. Bourne, Bishop of Bath, prayed for Pope Julius III., and for all souls in Purgatory.

1556. March 8. During the sermon a man did penance for transgressing Lent, having the carcasses of two pigs ready dressed, the one on his head, the other in his hand.

1557. Aug. 15. Procession of all the clergy in London with the Lord Mayor and others, round the Cross, singing "Hail, Festal Day!" for the Battle of St. Quentin. The preacher, Harpsfield, Archdeacon of London, declared the numbers taken prisoners.

Queen Elizabeth.

1558. Nov. 20. Dr. Bill, Chaplain to Queen Elizabeth, preached on the Reformation in Religion.

1558. Proclamation against unlicensed preachers.

1559. April 2. The pulpit of the Cross opened after long silence (see text).

1559. April 2. Grindal preached. Present, Duke of Norfolk, Lords Arundel, Northampton, Sussex, Westmoreland, Rutland, Russell, the Lord Mayor and Aldermen. All dined with the Lord Mayor.

1559. April 9. Dr. Bill preached on the Rejection of Papal Authority.

1559. Sept. 17. After sermon "began the new Morning Prayer, German fashion; men and women all do sing, and boys" (Machyn).

1560. March 30. Bishop Jewell of Salisbury's famous sermon, challenging the Romanists to prove their special views of the Eucharist from any authoritative Doctor of the first six centuries.

1564. Jan. 26. Archdeacon Cole of Essex preached, before Lord Mayor Sir Richard Malorie and the rest, against Romanism, which rested, he said, on four false pillars: Images, Purgatory, Sacrifice of the Mass and Transubstantiation.

1576. Dec. 9. Thomas White, Professor of Divinity, preached on the disregard of Sunday: "all manner of games and plays, banquetings and surfeitings are very rife."

1577. April 30. Edwyn Sandys, late Bishop of London, appointed Archbishop of York, preached a farewell sermon.

1577. Aug. 24. John Stockwood preached against plays, and compared the crowded attendance at theatres with the scanty attendance at sermons.

1579. April 29. Mr. Spark preached against theatres, calling them "the nest of the devil, and the sink of all sin."

1585. Richard Hooker, Master of the Temple, preached.

1588. Sept. 8. Queen Elizabeth, in state, was present at a Thanksgiving Sermon for the defeat of the Spanish Armada, preached by Dr. Piers, Bishop of Salisbury.

1589. Nov. 17. Thomas White, Professor of Divinity, preached in commemoration of the thirty-second year of Elizabeth's reign.

1596. During sermon, Thomas Skinner, Lord Mayor of London, with his Aldermen and Livery, received a message from Queen Elizabeth to raise 1000 men for service abroad to aid the French in the defence of Calais. The command was executed before 8 o'clock that evening; the men were accoutred and armed in the night, and set out next morning for Dover. Before they reached Calais, it had been captured by the Spaniards, so they returned home at once.

1599. Aug. 23. The Lord General and principal Officers of State came to sermon in great bravery on Sunday morning week, and afterwards dined with Lord Mayor Sir N. Morley.

1601. Feb. 1. Ordered that the preacher at Paul's Cross should decry the Earl of Essex as a hypocrite, Papist and confederate with the Pope and King of Spain, to make him King and bring in idolatry.

1602. Oct. 24. Sermon by Dr. John King (afterwards Bishop of London) against Romanism and worldliness;

thanksgiving for the forty-fourth year of Her Majesty's happy government, and especially for God's mercy to the nation, in prosperity of trade, avoidance of foreign attempts, and appeasing of inbred treasons and dissensions.

1602. Nov. 17. Queen's Accession Day. Preacher, Dr. Thornborough, Bishop of Limerick: "a dull sermon."

James I.

1603. April 14. Sermons by Mr. Hemmings, of Trinity College, Cambridge: very severe on women.

1605. April 30. A cuckoo flew over the pulpit of Paul's Cross, and cried out.

1609. August. Many books (probably against Royal government) burnt at Paul's Cross.

1613. Nov. 25. Some books of Suarez the Jesuit, derogatory to princes, burnt.

1617. March 29. Dr. Donne did Queen Elizabeth "great right in a sermon at the Cross, before Archbishop Abbot of Canterbury and certain other great Lords."

1617. Nov. Lady Markham, wife of Sir Griffin Markham, stood at the Cross in a white sheet, and was also amerced in a fine of £1000 for marrying one of her servants, her husband being still alive.

1619. April 4 or 10. Public thanksgiving at the Cross for the King's recovery from illness. Sermon by John King, Bishop of London. Present, Lord Mayor Cokayne, the Aldermen, City Companies, and most of the nobility.

1620. March 26. The King present at a sermon by Bishop King. He had come to the Cathedral in state in order to encourage the repairs of the Cathedral, then ruinous.

1622. July 1. Mountaigne, Bishop of London, preached on the benevolence asked by the King, and urged the repairing of the Cathedral.

1622. Sept. 25. John Donne, Dean of St. Paul's, preached on the King's orders concerning preachers and preaching, His Majesty's constancy in religion being suspected.

1623. Feb. 23. All the Lords of the Council in London went to the Cross to service; and afterwards dined with Lord Mayor Sir Martin Lumley, when a health was drunk to the prosperity of the journey of Charles, Prince of Wales, to Spain, and his safe return.

1625. Sir Robert Howard publicly excommunicated at Paul's Cross, for contempt in refusing to answer certain questions.

Charles I.

1629. Sunday before Whit-sunday. Two papers found tied round at Paul's Cross, expostulating with the King.

1630. May 30. Charles I., attended by Officers of State, Lord Mayor Sir Robert Ducie (a man of great wealth, who afterwards gave large sums to the King in his troubles, receiving in return a portrait-ring, still in the possession of the Earl of Ducie), the Aldermen and Livery.

1631. April. Laud, Bishop of London, preached.

1633. The preaching at the Cross ceased; Paul's Cross sermons were afterwards delivered in the Cathedral.

1643. Paul's Cross was taken down by order of the Long Parliament. This was in the time of Lord Mayor Pennington. At the time of its decay and destruction it was not beautiful, being little more than a kind of octagonal booth or summer-house, of debased architecture. The beautiful cross of Bishop Kemp must have disappeared long before. The cross which the Chapter propose to erect near the site, with the legacy (£4500 net) left by the late Mr. H. C. Richards, M.P., will be a true cross in the Italian renaissance style, to suit the architecture of the present Cathedral: a pillar, surmounted by a statue of St. Paul, rising from an ambo, or octagonal pulpit platform, with memorial carvings, bronzes and adornments.

CHAPTER XXXVIII

THE INTERMENTS AND MONUMENTS IN OLD ST. PAUL'S

A GENERAL view of the monuments of St. Paul's was given in the chapter describing a walk within its historical aisles. The old Cathedral was exceedingly rich in these relics of past ages, and no account of it could be complete without fuller details of those whose records were obliterated by the Great Fire.

ROYAL PERSONS.

Sebbe, King of the East Saxons, son of Sigebert I., converted by St. Erkenwald, Bishop of London (son of Anna, seventh king of the East Saxons). Sebbe became a monk. Died 677.

King Ethelred the Unready. Died 1017.

Eadward the Atheling, otherwise the Outlaw, son of King Edmund Ironsides, and father of Edgar Atheling; exiled to Sweden. Died 1057.

John of Gaunt, Duke of Lancaster. Died 1399.

Constance of Castile and Leon, his second wife.

Anne of Burgundy, wife of John Plantagenet, Duke of Bedford, the famous Regent of France, third son of King Henry IV.

MEN OF THE STATE.

Chancellors of England—
　Henry de Wengham, Bishop of London, 1262.
　John de Chishull, Bishop of London, 1280.
　Ralph de Baldock, Bishop of London, 1313.
　Robert de Braybrooke, Bishop of London, 1404.
　Sir Christopher Hatton, K.G., 1591.

INTERMENTS AND MONUMENTS 447

Lord Treasurers—
  Sir John Northbury, 1399.
  Canon Laurence Allerthorpe, 1406.
  Eustace de Fauconberg, Bishop of London, 1436.
  A Canon of St. Paul's, Treasurer to King Richard, 1490.
  (Robert Hare, Treasurer of the Exchequer), 1611.

Lord Keeper—
  Sir Nicholas Bacon, 1579.

Secretary of State—
  Sir Francis Walsingham, P.C., 1590.

Soldiers.

Henry de Lacy, Earl of Lincoln, 1312. Commanded a division in the Welsh War, 1276; Joint-Lieutenant of England in Edward I.'s absence, 1279; with Edward I. in Gascony, 1296–9; commanded the army in France, 1296–8; with Edward I. in Scotland, and present at his death, 1307; one of the lords-ordainers in Edward II.'s absence, 1310.

Sir John Beauchamp, Standard-bearer at Crécy, one of the original Knights of the Garter, Lord Beauchamp of Warwick, 1360.

William Herbert, Earl of Pembroke, K.G., 1569, and Ann Parr, his wife, sister of Queen Katherine Parr.

Knights, Nobles, Courtiers.

Alice de Bethun, wife of William Earl of Pembroke, Earl Marshal (second of that line), 1230.

Sir Simon Burley, Banneret, K.G., c. 1388.

Margaret Talbot, daughter of Richard Beauchamp, Earl of Warwick, wife of John, Earl of Shrewsbury, 1469.

John Nevill, Lord Latimer, of the Lords Latimer, descended from Joan, Countess of Westmoreland, sister of King Henry IV., 1542 or 1577.

Elizabeth Bruges, widow of John, Lord Chandos of Sudeley, 1559.

Sir Thomas Heneage, P.C., 1594, and *Anna Poins*, his wife, 1592.

Sir John Wolley, P.C., Chancellor of the Garter, 1595.

Peter Gilderstiern, Lord of Bistrup, 1636.

Sir Alan Boxhull, K.G.

BISHOPS OF LONDON (other than those who held high office in the State).

St. Erkenwald, son of Anna, King of the East Angles. (Some make him son of Offa, King of the East Saxons, but Offa did not come to the throne till 701, and Erkenwald died in 693.) Among his sisters were Etheldreda, Abbess of Ely; Sexburga, wife of Erkombert, King of Kent, and afterwards Abbess of Ely, and Ethelburga, Abbess of Barking; 693.

Ecgwulf, 745.
Theodred the Good, 953.
William, 1075.
St. Roger Niger, 1241.
Fulk Basset, 1258.
Henry de Sandwith, 1273.
Richard de Gravesend, 1303.
Gilbert de Segrave, 1317.
Richard de Newport, 1318.
Stephen de Gravesend, 1338.
Michael de Northborough, 1361.
Richard Clifford, 1421.
Robert FitzHugh, 1436.
Thomas Kemp, 1489.
Richard Hill, 1496.
Richard FitzJames, 1522.
John Stokesley, 1539.
John Aylmer, 1594.
Richard Vaughan, 1607.
Thomas Ravis, 1609.
John King, 1621.

INTERMENTS AND MONUMENTS

Lord Mayors of London.

Hamond Chikwell (formerly), c. 1330.
Sir John Poultney (four times), 1380.
Sir John Ward (formerly), 1501.
Sir Thomas Martin, Lord Mayor in 1518.
Sir Henry Barton, Lord Mayor in 1519.
Sir William Cockayne (formerly), 1626.

Deans of St. Paul's.

Hervey Borham, 1275.
Roger de la Leye, 1285.
John Everdon, 1336.
Gilbert Brewer, 1353.
Thomas Eure, D.D., 1400.
William Say, D.D., 1468.
Thomas Winterbourne, LL.D., 1478.
William Worsley, LL.D., 1499.
John Colet, D.D., 1519.
William May, twice Dean of St. Paul's, Archbishop of York Elect, 1560.
John Barwick, D.D., 1564.
Alexander Nowel, D.D., 1601.
Valentine Carey, Bishop of Exeter, 1626.
John Donne, D.D., 1631.

Ecclesiastics.

Fulk Lovell, Archdeacon of Colchester, Bishop Elect of London, 1297.
William Melford, Canon, Archdeacon of Colchester, 1334.
Richard Piriton, Canon, Archdeacon of Colchester, 1387.
John Newcourt, Canon, Doctor of Decrees, 1485.
Richard Lichfield, LL.D., Canon Residentiary, Archdeacon of London, 1496.
Richard Morton, Bishop of Worcester, 1497.

John Mullins, Archdeacon of London, 1591.
John Howson, Bishop of Durham, 1632.
Brian Walton, Prebendary, Bishop of Chester, 1661.

DOCTORS.

Thomas Lynacre, Priest, Physician to Henry VIII., 1524.
John Smith, Canon Residentiary, Doctor of Physic, 1539.
William Baronsdale, M.D., St. John's College, Cambridge, Linacre Lecturer on Medicine, President of the College of Physicians, 1589-1600. 1608.
Sir Simon Baskerville, Fellow of Exeter College, Oxford, M.B., 1611; M.D., F.C.P., 1615; Physician successively to James I. and Charles I.; knighted 1636. 1641.

ARTISTS.

Roger Waltham, Canon, Decorator of St. Paul's, 1326.
Sir Anthony Van Dyck, 1641.

MUSICIAN.

John Tomkins (1586-1638) (brother of Thomas Tomkins, organist of Worcester Cathedral and of the Chapel Royal), organist of King's College, Cambridge, 1606; organist of St. Paul's Cathedral, 1619; epistler and gospeller (musical reciter), Chapel Royal, London; composer of anthems; the "Thomalin" of three of Phineas Fletcher's Eclogues. 1638.

CHAPTER XXXIX

MEMORIALS AND BURIALS IN THE NEW CATHEDRAL

I. Naval—II. Military—III. Statesmen—IV. Ecclesiastical—V. Men of Letters—VI. Painters, Sculptors, Architects, Engineer : (i) Painters ; (ii) Sculptors ; (iii) Architects ; (iv) Engineer—VII. Musicians—VIII. Philanthropists—IX. Doctors—X. Explorers.

I. NAVAL.

1. *Admiral Lord Rodney* (1719–92), Harrow. Famous for naval victories in the West Indies : Martinique, St. Lucia, Grenada, St. Vincent, Dominica ; received the thanks of Parliament.   1792, Rossi.

2. *Captain Robert Faulknor* (1763–95). Hero of many fights in the West Indies : Grenada, 1779 ; capture of Fort Royal alone, 1794 ; foremost at capture of St. Lucia, Guadeloupe and Fort Fleur d'Épée, 1794 ; killed on board the *Blanche* while trying to lash the bowsprit of the French frigate *Pique* to his capstan.   1795, Rossi.

3. *Admiral Earl Howe* (1726–99). After a brilliant career became Lord of the Admiralty, Treasurer of the Navy and Commander-in-Chief on the American station ; Commander in the Channel ; relieved Gibraltar against superior forces in 1782 ; First Lord of the Admiralty ; with Channel Fleet won the great victory of the 1st June, 1794, capturing six French ships ; after retirement, pacified mutineers at Portsmouth. The signalling code was perfected and refined by him.   1799, Flaxman.

4. *Captain Rundell Burgess.* Fell gloriously in the victory of Camperdown, when trying to force his ship, *Ardent*, through the enemy's lines.   1797, Banks.

THE RODNEY MONUMENT.

MEMORIALS AND BURIALS

5. *Captain Westcott, R.N.* (1743–98). Killed in command of the *Majestic* at the Nile. Banks.

6. *Captain Ralph Willett Miller, R.N.* (1762–99). Served under Rodney; Flag-captain to Nelson, 1796; Cape St. Vincent, 1797; the Nile, 1798; served under Sir Sidney Smith off Egypt and Syria; killed during defence of St. Jean d'Acre by accidental explosion.

7 and 8. *Captains Mosse and Riou.* Distinguished in the Detached Squadron against Copenhagen (1801), where they were killed. 1801, Rossi, R.A.

9. *Admiral Viscount Duncan* (1731–1804). Defeated the Dutch admiral De Winter off Camperdown, 1797.
1804, Westmacott.

10. *Lord Nelson.* 1805, Flaxman.

11. *Captain George N. Hardinge, R.N.* (1781–1808). Cut out Dutch *Atalante* in Vlie Roads, Texel, 1804; took part in capture of the Cape; killed at capture of French cruiser off Ceylon; public money voted for the monument; brother of F.M. First Viscount Hardinge.

Manning.

12. *Admiral Lord Collingwood* (Cuthbert Collingwood, 1750–1810). Served in West Indies; served in Nelson's ship, 1778; commanded ship in battle of 1st of June, 1794; good service at Cape St. Vincent, 1797; blockaded Cadiz, 1797–8; blockaded Brest, 1795–1805; took command on Nelson's death at Trafalgar, 1805, but lost many of the prizes through neglecting Nelson's last order; culpably missed a chance of destroying the Toulon fleet, 1808; died at sea, 1810. Westmacott.

13. *Admiral of the Fleet Earl St. Vincent* (Sir John Jervis, 1735–1823). One of the greatest of naval commanders and administrators. His chief victory was the defeat of the Spanish Fleet off Cape St. Vincent, 14th February, 1797. Baily.

14. *Admiral the Earl of Northesk* (William Carnegie, seventh earl, 1758–1831). Imprisoned by the Nore

THE NELSON MONUMENT

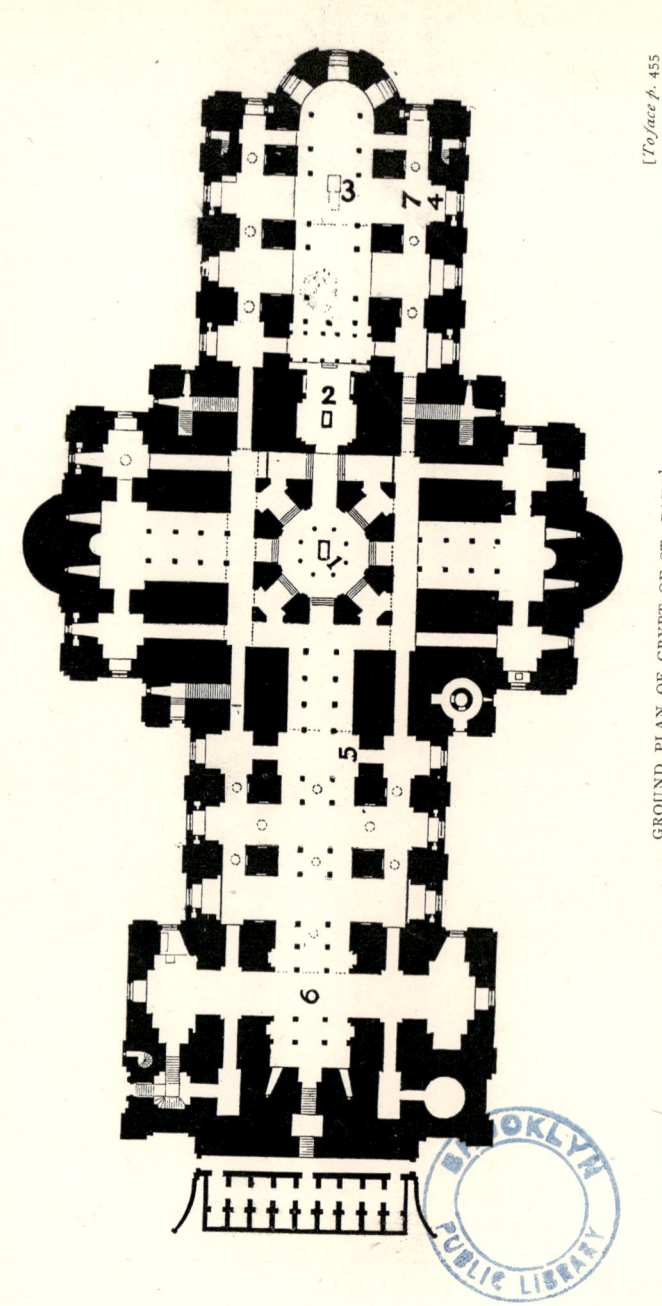

GROUND PLAN OF CRYPT OF ST. PAUL'S

1 Admiral Lord Nelson's Tomb.   2. The Tomb of the Duke of Wellington.   3. Dean Milman.   4. Sir Christopher Wren.   5. Cruickshank.
6. Wellington's Funeral Car.   7. The Artists' Corner.

[*To face p.* 455

MEMORIALS AND BURIALS

mutineers; fought at Trafalgar; Commander-in-Chief at Plymouth; buried in the crypt.

15. *Captain Sir Wm. Hoste, K.C.B.*, first baronet (1780–1828). Served under Nelson at Toulon, St. Vincent, Santa Cruz; took or destroyed 200 French or Venetian vessels in Adriatic (1808–9); destroyed forty-six sail in 1810; defeated greatly superior squadron at Lissa, and took many prizes, 1811; other exploits in 1813–14.
Campbell.

16. *Admiral Sir Pulteney Malcolm, K.C.B.* (1768–1838). Distinguished in the West Indies, East Indies, China and under Nelson in the Mediterranean; Commander-in-Chief at St. Helena and in the Mediterranean. Baily.

17. *Admiral Sir Edward Codrington, K.C.B.* (1770–1851). Commanded ship at Trafalgar; Commander-in-Chief in Mediterranean; joined French and Russian squadrons in the Battle of Navarino.

18. *Captain Granville Gower Loch* (1813–53). Distinguished in China, Nicaragua and second Burmese war; shot while attacking Donabew, 1853. Marochetti.

19. *Captain Edward Mowbray Lyons.* Killed in attack on the batteries of Sevastopol in H.M.S. *Miranda,* June 23, 1855, made under his father's orders, after brilliant successes in the Sea of Azov. Son of Admiral Sir Edmund Lyons, Commander of the Black Sea Squadron. His death made a deep impression. Queen Victoria mourned his loss as one who was a bright ornament to the Navy. Aged 36. Monument erected in deepest grief by officers and men of H.M.S. *Miranda.* Noble.

20. *Admiral Lord Lyons* (1790–1858). Active service in Dardanelles, East Indies and Mediterranean; Minister in Athens, Switzerland and Stockholm; Commander-in-Chief 1855–8, Black Sea, Crimean War. 1858, Noble.

21. *Admiral Sir Charles Napier, K.C.B.* (1786–1860). Commander of the fleet of Donna Maria, Queen of Portugal, against Don Miguel; and in the Mediterranean with Sir

Robert Stopford, especially at Beyrout; his unauthorized convention the basis of negotiations; decorated by the European Powers; Commander of the Channel Fleet, 1846; Commander in the Baltic, 1854.   1860, Adams.

22. *Officers and Men of H.M.S. "Captain,"* which foundered on its first voyage in the Bay of Biscay, 1870.

23. *Admiral Sir James Scott, K.C.B.* (1790–1872). Flag-captain to Sir George Cockburn; distinguished in the West Indies, the Pacific and the China Station.

II. MILITARY.

1. *General Lord Heathfield* (George Augustus Eliott, 1717–90). Adjutant at Dettingen in 1743 and Fontenoy 1745; *aide-de-camp* to George II.; second-in-command of the Cuban expedition; governor of Gibraltar, 1755; defended Gibraltar against D'Arzon and the Spaniards, 1779–83.   1790, Rossi.

2. *General Sir Ralph Abercromby* (1734–1801), Rugby. Active service in Germany, Flanders, West Indies; reduced St. Lucia and Trinidad; Commander-in-Chief in Ireland and Scotland; capture of Dutch Fleet; command in Mediterranean, defeated French at Alexandria, and died of wounds.   Westmacott.

3. *Charles, First Marquis Cornwallis* (1738–1805). Governor-General of India; Eton; active service in Germany, North America, subdued N. Jersey, occupied Philadelphia, invaded Virginia; took command at Calcutta and reformed abuses in India; defeated Tippoo Sahib at Seringapatam; Viceroy and Commander-in-Chief in Ireland; sent to India again to make lasting peace with native powers; took command at Calcutta; died of fever at Ghazipore.   1805, Rossi.

4. *General Sir John Moore* (1761–1809). Active service in Corsica, West Indies, Holland, Mediterranean, Egypt, Portugal, Spain. Famous retreat from Madrid to Corunna;

MEMORIALS AND BURIALS

mortally wounded at embarkation; lived to hear of defeat of French; buried at midnight. Bacon.

5 and 6. *Major-General Mackenzie and Brig.-General Langwerth.* Fell gloriously at the victory of Talavera, 1809.
Manning.

7. *Lieut.-Colonel Sir William Myers, Bart.* (1784–1811). Fell gloriously at the head of the Fusilier Brigade at the victory of Albuera, aged 27. Kendrick.

8. *Major-General Daniel Hoghton* (1770–1811). Distinguished in Jamaica, India and the Peninsula; fell gloriously at the victory of Albuera. Chantrey.

9. *General Sir Isaac Brock*, K.C.B. (1769–1812). Distinguished in wars in West Indies, Baltic, Canada and United States; received surrender of General Hull's forces at Detroit; fell gloriously in engagement with General van Rennselaar at Queenstown. Westmacott.

10 and 11. *Major-Generals Crauford and Mackinnon.* Robert Crauford (1764–1812), distinguished in India, Ireland, Buenos Ayres and Peninsula. Fell gloriously at Ciudad Rodrigo, with Henry Mackinnon, in command of the Highlanders. Bacon, jun.

12. *Major-General B. E. Bowes.* Fell gloriously in the victory of Salamanca, when leading the storming party. Chantrey.

13. *Major-General John Gaspard Le Marchant*, famous in Peninsula (1766–1812). Intimate friend of George III.; devised new system of cavalry sword exercise; projected schools of instruction for officers, issuing in Sandhurst; Lieut.-Governor of the schools; Major-General in the Peninsula; mortally wounded at Salamanca, 1812.

14. *Colonel Hon. Henry Cadogan* (Peninsula hero), son of first Earl Cadogan (1780–1813). Eton; *aide-de-camp* to Wellesley in the Peninsula, 1808–10; commanded 71st Highlanders, 1810–11; commanded brigade, 1811–13; killed at Vittoria.

15. *Major-General Andrew Hay* (1762–1814). Com-

manded a brigade at Walcheren and in the Peninsula; mortally wounded before Bayonne. Hopper.

16 and 17. *Major-Generals Gore and Skerrett.* Two major-generals killed at Bergen-op-Zoom, March 10, 1814. Chantrey.

18. *General Robert Ross* (hero in American War, 1766–1814). Greatly helped to defeat the French at Maida; with Sir John Moore at Corunna; Walcheren; *aide-de-camp* to George III.; commanded expeditionary force against United States in 1814 in co-operation with Admiral Sir A. Cochrane; won Battle of Bladensburg and took Washington, August 24, 1814; died from wound received at Baltimore. Widow and descendants to be called "of Bladensburg."

19. *General Sir Robert Gillespie, K.C.B.* (1766–1814). As Adjutant-General in San Domingo, 1766, was attacked by eight assassins, and killed six; did heroic deeds in India, Java and Sumatra; killed in attack on Kalunga, Nepaul. Chantrey.

20. *Major-General the Hon. Sir William Ponsonby, K.C.B.* (1772–1815). Waterloo hero; son of first Lord Ponsonby; served in the Peninsula; led his brigade at Vittoria; led the famous charge of the Union Brigade on d'Erlon's shattered corps at Waterloo, and was killed by French Lancers. Theed and Baily.

21 and 22. *General Edward Pakenham, G.C.B., and General Sir Samuel Gibbs, K.C.B.* Both mortally wounded in the assault on New Orleans. Pakenham (1778–1815) commanded the 64th at the capture of St. Lucia; joined Wellington in the Peninsula after Talavera; led the decisive movement of the 3rd Division at Salamanca, earning remarkable eulogy from Wellington. Gibbs commanded the 11th in the West Indies, and the 39th at the Cape and Travancore; distinguished in the Java expedition. 1815, Westmacott.

23. *General Sir Thomas Picton, G.C.B.* (1758–1815).

GENERAL GORDON'S MONUMENT

[*To face p.* 459.

MEMORIALS AND BURIALS

Distinguished in the West Indies and the Peninsula; thanked by the House of Commons seven times; commanded the 5th division at Quatre-Bras (wounded) and Waterloo, where he fell gloriously; buried in St. Paul's.

1815, Gahagan.

24. *Major-General Sir John Jones, R.E., K.C.B.*, first baronet (1783–1843). *Aide-de-camp* to General Leith with Spanish Army, 1808; Chief of Engineers in Walcheren expedition, 1809; completed lines at Torres Vedras, 1810; sole inspector of the defences of the Netherlands; *aide-de-camp* to George IV., 1825; drew up plans for defence of United Kingdom and Gibraltar, 1840; works of contemporary military history. Behnes.

25. *The Duke of Wellington* (1769–1852). For a long time this great monument was in the S.W. Chapel, where it could not be seen. Lord Leighton obtained its removal to the site under one of the arches of the nave, where the sculptor intended it to be. His design is at length being completed by an equestrian figure. 1852, Alfred Stevens.

26. *General Sir Charles Napier, G.C.B.* (1782–1853). The conqueror of Scinde. 1853, Adams.

27. *Officers and Men of the Cavalry and the 57th and 77th Foot* (now 1st and 2nd Battalions of the Middlesex Regiment) *who died in the Crimea*, with the Crimean colours of the Middlesex Regiment. 1854, 1856, Noble.

28. *The Coldstream Guards.* Inkerman, 1854, Marochetti. South Africa, 1899–1902, Goscombe John.

29. *Major-General Sir Arthur Wellesley Torrens, K.C.B.* (1779–1828). Distinguished in the West Indies, Portugal, Netherlands; military secretary to Wellington in the Peninsula; Adjutant-General of the Forces.

1855, Marochetti.

30. *Brigadier-General Sir Henry Lawrence, K.C.B.* (1806–57), Bengal Artillery. Cabul Expedition, 1842; Resident of Nepaul, 1843; agent for foreign relations and affairs of the Punjab and N.W. Frontier; Resident at

Lahore, 1847; Chief Commissioner in Oudh, 1856; on breaking out of Mutiny, Brigadier-General over all the troops in Oudh; killed while holding Lucknow successfully against the mutineers, 1857.   Lough.

31. *General Sir William Napier*, K.C.B. (1785–1860). The historian of the Peninsular War, Conquest of Scinde, etc., and himself distinguished in the Peninsula; brother of the conqueror of Scinde.   Adams.

32. *Major-General Sir John Inglis*, K.C.B. (1814–62). Succeeded Sir Henry Lawrence in command at Lucknow during the Mutiny: gallant defence.

33. *Officers and Men killed in New Zealand* (1861–66).

34. *Field-Marshal Lord Strathnairn* (Sir Hugh Rose, 1801–85), G.C.S.I., G.C.B. After distinguished service (the Crimea and India) was Commander-in-Chief in India (1860) and Commander-in-Chief in Ireland (1865–70), where he suppressed a rebellion.

35. *Officers and Men of the Royal Fusiliers (7th Foot) who died in the Afghan Campaign*, 1879–80.   Forsyth.

36. *Officers killed in the Afghan War* (1878–80).

37. *Officers and Men killed in the First Boer Campaign* (1880–81).

38. *Major-General Charles George Gordon*, C.B. (1833–85). "Chinese Gordon," the hero of the suppression of the Taeping Rebellion in China; Governor-General of the Soudan under Ismail Pasha; died at Khartûm, after a siege of 317 days, in the attempt to rescue the European garrisons from the Mahdi.   Boehm.

39. *Major-General Sir Herbert Stewart*, K.C.B. (1843–85). Distinguished in the Zulu War, 1879, the Egyptian War, 1882, and the Suakim Campaign, 1884; killed at Abu-Klea in Lord Wolseley's Gordon Relief Expedition.
   Boehm.

40. *Colonel Sir Duncan Macdougall* (1787–1886). Distinguished at the Cape of Good Hope, the Peninsula and the American War of 1814–15; charged with organization

MEMORIALS AND BURIALS

of Colonial Militia in Nova Scotia, 1825; Second-in-command of British Legion in Spain, 1835; prominent figure in Volunteer Movement.

41. *Major-General Sir Charles Metcalfe Macgregor, K.C.B.* (1840–87). Distinguished in Indian Mutiny, China, Abyssinia and Afghanistan; Quarter-Master-General of India and Commander of Punjab Frontier Force; wrote on Afghanistan.

42. *Field-Marshal Lord Napier of Magdala, G.C.S.I., G.C.B.* (1810–90). After an illustrious career in India was conqueror of Theodore of Abyssinia.

43. *Field-Marshal Sir Patrick Grant, G.C.B., G.C.M.G.* (1804–95). Distinguished in Gwalior; first and second Sikh Wars; Commander-in-Chief of Army of Madras; Governor of Malta. 1895.

44. *Field-Marshal Sir Donald Stewart, Bart., G.C.B., G.C.S.I.* (1824–1900). Famous for the march to Cabul, 1880; Commander-in-Chief in India. 1900.

45. *Officers and Men of the Duke of Cambridge's Own (Imperial Yeomanry) who died in South African War,* 1900–02. 1902.

46. *Officers and Men of the Middlesex Yeomanry.* South African War (1900–02). 1902.

47. *Field-Marshal Sir Samuel Browne, G.C.B., V.C.,* etc. Victorious in Afghanistan and Commander-in-Chief in India.

48. *Colonial Troops* (4200) *who died in South Africa.*
H.R.H. Princess Louise, 1905.

49. *Field-Marshal Sir Henry Norman, G.C.B., G.C.M.G.,* distinguished in Punjaub campaign, the Mutiny, and Oude; A.D.C. to the Queen; member of Council of India; Colonial Governor; declined the Viceroyalty of India.

50. *Field-Marshal Sir Lintorn Simmons, G.C.B., G.C.M.G.,* distinguished in Crimea; Inspector-General of Fortifications; Military Adviser at Berlin Conference; Governor

and Commander-in-Chief at Malta; Commander-in-Chief of the Royal Engineers.

III. STATESMEN.

1 and 2. *William and Frederick, second and third Viscounts Melbourne* (1779–1848 and 1782–1853); Eton. William was first Prime Minister and adviser to the young Queen Victoria. Frederick, G.C.B., Ambassador, was created Lord Beauvale and was Minister-Plenipotentiary to Bavaria and Spain, and Ambassador at Lisbon and Vienna.
Marochetti.

3. *Hon. Mountstuart Elphinstone, D.C.L.* (1779–1859). Son of the eleventh Lord Elphinstone; Governor of Madras and afterwards of Bombay; offered the Governor-Generalship of India; wrote on the history of India, and was one of the ablest of Indian statesmen. Noble.

4. *Earl of Mayo* (Richard Southwell Bourke, sixth). Viceroy of India (1822–72). Assassinated by a fanatic[1] at Port Blair.

5. *Rt.-Hon. Sir H. Bartle Frere, Bart., K.C.B., G.C.S.I., D.C.L., LL.D.* (1815–84). Thanked by Parliament for conduct in Indian Mutiny; Governor of Bombay; Governor of Zanzibar for suppression of Slave Trade; conducted Edward VII. as Prince of Wales round India; Governor

---

[1] Shere Ali was an Afridi, and enlisted in the Punjab. Attractive to everybody, he was made orderly to the Lieut.-Governor at Peshawur, and attended his children in their walks. Solemnly summoned by his tribe to avenge a murder, he applied for leave, was refused, and absented himself. Unfortunately the avenging of the murder took place just inside British territory. Convicted by circumstantial evidence, he was condemned to penal servitude for life in the Andaman Islands. In vain he petitioned Supreme Court and Governor-General. Unable to understand British justice, and brooding over what he thought a wrong, he seized the opportunity of the visit of Lord Mayo, and stabbed him as he was stepping from the pier to regain his ship; asked if he had any accomplices, he answered, "Only God and I knew of it." I had these details from Col. Sir Edward Henry, K.C.V.O., C.S.I.

of Cape and High Commissioner of South Africa; made war on Cetewayo; predicted whole course of events in South Africa.

6. *Sir Harry Parkes*, G.C.M.G. (1828–85), diplomatist. Served many years in China; arrested while negotiating close of third Chinese War, 1860, kept in heavy chains in Peking eleven days, constantly threatened with death, closely confined for three weeks; Minister to Japan, where he was associated with every forward movement, in spite of many attempts at assassination; Minister to China, and concluded treaty with Corea, opening it to British trade.

7. *Sir John Hawley Glover*, G.C.M.G. (1829–85). Colonial Governor; Administrator of Lagos; commanded Houssas in Ashanti War, 1873; Governor of Newfoundland and Governor of the Leeward Islands.

8. *Sir Robert Montgomery*, K.C.B., G.C.S.I. (1809–87). Indian Administrator. Distinguished for activity and prudence in the Indian Mutiny; Lieutenant-Governor of the Punjab; Member of the Indian Council.

9. *The Rt.-Hon. William Bede Dalley* (1831–88). Leading statesman in New South Wales; memorable for the fact of sending voluntary Colonial troops to aid the Imperial forces (Soudan).

10. *The Rt.-Hon. Sir John A. Macdonald*, G.C.B. (1815–91). The organizer of the Dominion of Canada; of Scots origin, born at Kingston, Canada; Prime Minister of Canada, 1857; first Prime Minister of the Dominion, 1867; Premier and Minister of the Interior, 1878–91; his widow was created a peeress.

11. *Earl of Lytton* (Edward Robert Bulwer (first)), Governor-General of India (1831–91). Statesman and poet; proclaimed Queen Victoria Empress of India at Delhi, 1877; Ambassador at Paris. Alfred Gilbert, R.A.

12. *The Rt.-Hon. Sir George Grey*, K.C.B., D.C.L., LL.D. (1812–98). Colonial Governor; Governor successively of South Australia, New Zealand and Cape Colony; again

Governor of New Zealand; Prime Minister of New Zealand, 1877-9; successfully advocated adult franchize, triennial parliaments, taxation of land values, leasing Crown lands and compulsory repurchase of private estates; buried publicly in St. Paul's.

13. *Sir Charles Pritchard.* Able Indian administrator and financier.

IV. ECCLESIASTICAL.

1. *John Donne*, Dean of St. Paul's (1573-1631). His biography has been given in the text. The effigy is a relic of the old Cathedral.   1631, Nicholas Stone.

2. *Thomas Newton* (1704-82). Dean of St. Paul's and Bishop of Bristol. An account of him is given in the text; buried in the crypt.

3. *Thomas Fanshaw Middleton*, D.D., F.R.S. (1769-1822). Christ's Hospital and Pembroke College, Cambridge. Calcutta was the first English Bishopric created in India (1813), and Middleton the first Bishop. He was sent out by the Society for Promoting Christian Knowledge and the Society for the Propagation of the Gospel; promoted education and established Bishop's College, Calcutta; died there.

4. *Reginald Heber* (1783-1826). Bishop of Calcutta, 1822-6; Prizeman at Oxford for English Essay, Latin Poem and English Verse ("Palestine"); Bampton Lecturer; Fellow of All Souls; poet and hymn-writer; travelled in all parts of India; died of apoplexy at Trichinopoli.

Chantrey, R.A.

5. *Rev. William Nelson, D.D., First Earl Nelson* (1757-1835). Created an earl on the death of his younger brother, the great admiral, Horatio Viscount Nelson; buried in the crypt.

6. *Charles James Blomfield*, D.D. (1786-1857). Bishop of London from 1828 to 1856. The notice of him is in the text.   George Richmond, R.A.

MEMORIALS AND BURIALS 465

7. *Henry Milman, D.D.*, Dean of St. Paul's (1791–1868), to whom this book is greatly indebted. A biography of him is given in the text; his grave is in front of the sacrarium in the crypt. 1868, Williamson.

8. *Henry Melvill* (1798–1871). Canon of St. Paul's; the most eloquent preacher of his day; buried in the crypt.

9. *Prebendary Henry Venn* (1796–1873). Son of John Venn, Rector of Clapham, a founder of the Church Missionary Society (son of Henry Venn, 1775–79, Evangelical Divine); Hon. Secretary of the Church Missionary Society.

10. *Bishop Piers Calverley Claughton, D.D.* (1814–84). Bishop of St. Helena; Bishop of Colombo; Archdeacon of London and Assistant Bishop of London; Chaplain-General.

11. *John Jackson* (1811–85). Bishop of London, 1869–85. The notice of him is in the text. Woolner, R.A.

12. *Robert Claudius Billing, Bishop of Bedford*. A hard-working suffragan in East London under Bishop Temple.

13. *Henry Parry Liddon* (1829–90). Canon and Chancellor of St. Paul's; D.D. and D.C.L.; student of Christ Church, Oxford; Ireland Professor of Exegesis; his sermons at St. Paul's for twenty years a central fact of London life; biographer of Pusey. Kempe.

14. *Mandell Creighton* (1843–1901). Bishop of London, 1896–1901. His biography is in the text.

Thornycroft, R.A.

15. *Frederic Temple*. Archbishop of Canterbury; Bishop of London from 1885 to 1896. A biography of him is given in the text. Pomeroy.

16. *Miss M. Fussell*. Bequeathed £120,000 to the London Diocesan Home Mission, and thereby founded between seventy and eighty new parishes.

H H

V. MEN OF LETTERS.

1. *Dr. Samuel Johnson* (1709–84). The famous lexicographer, essayist, moralist, scholar and critic; buried in Westminster Abbey. The monument in consequence of essential connection with Fleet Street and the City.

Bacon.

2. *Sir William Jones* (1746–94). Celebrated orientalist and jurist; Harrow; University College, Oxford; tutor to second Lord Spencer; member of Johnson's Club; intimate with Burke and Gibbon; Judge of High Court at Calcutta; published six volumes of Commentaries on Asiatic poetry; translated sacred books of Hindus. Bacon.

3. *Rev. Richard Harris Barham* (1788–1845). Author of *Ingoldsby Legends;* Minor Canon of St. Paul's and Vicar of St. Faith's, E.C.

4. *Henry Hallam* (1779–1859). The historian; Eton and Christ Church, Oxford; *Europe in the Middle Ages, Constitutional History of England, Literature of Europe.*

Theed.

5. *Charles Reade* (1814–84). Popular novelist and dramatist: *Masks and Faces, Foul Play, The Cloister and the Hearth, Hard Cash, Never too late to Mend;* employed fiction to expose social abuses.

6. *War Correspondents of Lord Wolseley's two Egyptian Campaigns*, including Frank Power (of the *Times*), who was with Gordon at Khartûm; was sent home by him with Colonel Stewart in a small steamer to carry dispatches, which ran aground at Berber. They were tempted ashore by the Arabs and murdered.

7. *Sir Walter Besant.* Popular novelist; *All Sorts and Conditions of Men* was the cause of the People's Palace in East London.

8. *Archibald Forbes* (1838–1900). War Correspondent, *Morning Advertiser, Daily News* (Franco-Prussian War, Russo-Turkish War, Afghanistan, Zulu).

[To face p. 46.

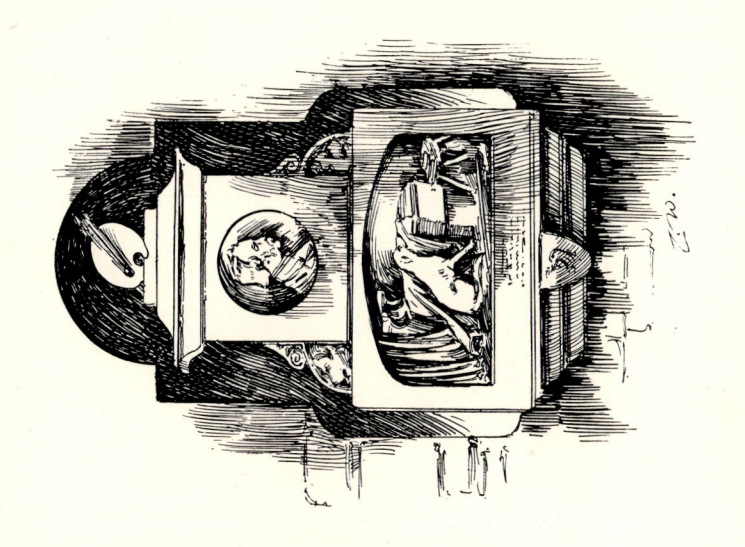

9. *The War Correspondents of the South African Campaign.*

10. *W. E. Henley.* Poet and essayist. Bust by Rodin.

11. *Sir William Henry Russell.* The War Correspondent of the Crimea and other campaigns.

Herbert Mackennal, A.R.A.

VI. Painters, Sculptors, Architects, Engineer.

(i) *Painters.*[1]

1. *Sir Joshua Reynolds, P.R.A.* (1723–92). Founder and first President of the Royal Academy ; buried in the crypt.

1792, Flaxman.

---

[1] The Council of the Royal Academy has promised a monument of Vandyke, who was buried and commemorated in the Old Cathedral.

2. *James Barry, R.A.* (1741–1806). Historical painter; buried in Artists' Corner in the crypt. Bust.

3. *John Opie, R.A.* (1761–1807). Portrait and historical painter; son of a Cornish carpenter; buried in Artists' Corner in the crypt.

4. *Benjamin West, second P.R.A.* (1738–1820). An original R.A.; born in Pennsylvania; historical and scriptural painter; buried in Artists' Corner in the crypt.

5. *Henry Fuseli, R.A.* (1741–1825). Native of Zurich; painted scenes from Shakespeare and Milton, and other subjects; buried in Artists' Corner in the crypt.

6. *George Dawe, R.A.* (1781–1829). Portrait-painter; painted a series for the Emperor Alexander, and many Court portraits; buried in Artists' Corner in the crypt.

7. *Sir Thomas Lawrence, third P.R.A.* (1769–1830). The famous portrait-painter; buried in Artists' Corner in the crypt.

8. *J. M. W. Turner* (1775–1851). The greatest of landscape-painters; buried in the crypt.

1851, Macdowell.

9. *Sir Edwin Landseer, R.A.* (1802–73). The animal-painter; declined the Presidency of the R.A.; finished the lions for Nelson's monument in Trafalgar Square; buried in Artists' Corner in the crypt, with a monument near.

10. *George Cruikshank* (1792–1878). Caricaturist and illustrator; illustrated for Charles Dickens, Harrison Ainsworth and many others; an ardent teetotaler; buried in the crypt.

11. *Randolph Caldecott* (1846–86). Artist; made his mark as a book-illustrator, 1875; designed in colour for children's books, 1878–85. Monument in Artists' Corner.

Alfred Gilbert, R.A.

12. *Frank Holl, R.A.* (1845–88). Son and grandson of engravers; painted 198 portraits, including Duke of Cambridge, Sir William Jenner, Sir Henry Rawlinson,

John Bright, Lord Roberts and two of King Edward VII. while Prince of Wales. Monument in Artists' Corner.

Alfred Gilbert, R.A.

13. *Lord Leighton, P.R.A.* (1830–96). Buried in the crypt. 1896, Brock.

14. *Sir John Everett Millais, Bart., P.R.A.* (1829–96). Buried in Artists' Corner in the crypt.

15. *George Richmond, R.A.* (1809–96). Son of Thomas Richmond, miniature-painter, and father of Sir William Richmond, K.C.B., R.A., the eminent painter and decorator of St. Paul's Cathedral. World-wide fame by portrait in water-colour of William Wilberforce; painted portraits of eminent persons in crayons and oils for over forty years; monument in Artists' Corner.

(ii) *Sculptors.*

1. *John H. Foley, R.A.* (1818–74). Sculptor: equestrian statues of Sir James Outram, Lord Canning and Lord Hardinge at Calcutta; statues of O'Connell, Goldsmith and Burke in Dublin; Lord Clyde at Glasgow and Lord Clive at Shrewsbury; the group of Asia in the Prince Consort's Monument, Hyde Park; John Stuart Mill on the Thames Embankment, and Sir Charles Barry in the House of Commons. Buried in Artists' Corner in the crypt.

2. *Sir J. Edgar Boehm, R.A., Bart.* (1834–90). Sculptor; born at Vienna; Sculptor-in-Ordinary to Queen Victoria; buried in Artists' Corner in the crypt.

(iii) *Architects.*

1. *Sir Christopher Wren* (1632–1723). A chapter is devoted to him; buried in Artists' Corner in the crypt.

2. *Robert Mylne, F.R.S.* (1734–1811). Architect, engineer and surveyor to St. Paul's Cathedral. (Blackfriars Bridge, the Gloucester and Berkeley Canal, etc.) Buried in crypt.

THE LEIGHTON MONUMENT

MEMORIALS AND BURIALS

3. *George Dance, R.A.* (1741–1825). Architect. (Newgate, St. Luke's Hospital and the front of Guildhall.) Buried in Artists' Corner in the crypt. (Son of the Architect Dance who designed the Mansion House.)

4. *Charles Robert Cockerell* (1788–1863). Architect; R.A., D.C.L.; Oxford; Surveyor to St. Paul's Cathedral; designed the Taylorian Building, Oxford, and finished the Fitzwilliam Museum at Cambridge, and St. George's Hall, Liverpool.   F. P. Cockerell.

5. *F. C. Penrose.* Architect; Surveyor of St. Paul's Cathedral; Principal of the British School at Athens; son of Elizabeth Penrose, authoress of *Mrs. Markham's History of England*, in which he figured as "Mary."

(iv) *Engineer.*

John Rennie, F.R.S. (1761–1821). Engineer; designed Waterloo Bridge, London Bridge, Southwark Bridge and Plymouth Breakwater; buried in crypt.

VII. MUSICIANS.

1. *Maurice Greene*, Mus. Doc. (1696–1755). Organist of St. Paul's; remains transferred to the crypt, and placed in Boyce's grave.

2. *William Boyce*, Mus. Doc. (1710–79). Chorister at St. Paul's; organist and composer to the Chapel Royal; a great Church composer; buried in the crypt.

3. *Philip Hayes*, Mus. Doc. (1738–97). Professor of Music at Oxford; organist of Magdalen and St. John's; composed concertos, anthems, songs, glees, an oratorio and odes; buried in the crypt.

4. *Thomas Attwood*, Mus. Doc. (1765–1838). Organist of St. Paul's; buried in the crypt.

5. *Sir John Goss* (1800–80). Musical composer and organist of St. Paul's; chorister at Chapel Royal; pupil of Attwood; a wonderfully fertile author of the best class of Church music; monument.

6. *Sir John Stainer.* Notice of him is given amongst the organists of St. Paul's; bas-relief. 1901, Pegram.

7. *Sir Arthur Sullivan* (1842–1900). The greatest English composer since Purcell; buried in the crypt.
1900, Goscombe John.

VIII. Philanthropists.

1. *John Howard* (the hero of Prison Reform, 1726–90). Member of the Society of Friends; imprisoned in France, 1756; inspected prisons of England, Scotland, Ireland, France, Belgium, Holland, Germany, Switzerland, Denmark, Sweden, Russia, Spain, Portugal; visited lazarettos in France, Italy and Turkey; died of camp-fever while with the Russian Army at Khersen. First monument in the Cathedral. Bacon.

2. *Edward Vansittart Neale* (1810–92). Christian Socialist and Co-operator; pioneer of co-operative production and profit-sharing.

3. *Sir George Williams* (1821–95). Founder of the Young Men's Christian Association and the Young Women's Christian Association; merchant in St. Paul's Churchyard. When he died the Y.M.C.A. had more than 500,000 members, in every civilized country. Buried in the crypt; monument by Sir George Frampton, R.A.

IX. Doctors.

1. *William Babington* (1756–1833). Physician and mineralogist; physician to Guy's Hospital; M.D., Aberdeen; Hon. M.D., Dublin; one of the founders of the Geological Society and president; geological and chemical works. 1833, Behnes.

2. *Sir Astley Cooper, Bart.* (1768–1841). Eminent surgeon; great practice; lecturer to St. Thomas's, Guy's and the Royal College of Surgeons; published surgical and anatomical treatises. Baily.

MEMORIALS AND BURIALS

X. EXPLORERS.

1. *Professor E. H. Palmer, Captain William John Gill and Lieut. Harold Charrington.* Murdered by being thrown over a cliff while on a secret service mission to the Arabs of the Sinaitic Peninsula for the purchase of mules, at the outbreak of the Egyptian War of 1882. The remains were discovered and brought back eighteen months later by Sir Charles Warren. (*Life of E. H. Palmer*, by Walter Besant.)

2. *Lieut.-Colonel James Augustus Grant* (1827–92). African traveller; journeyed in Central Africa with Captain Speke in 1861–3, and discovered the sources of the Nile in the Mountains of the Moon.

It will be noticed that by Rossi there are 6 monuments, by Chantrey 5, by Westmacott 5, by Bacon 4, by Noble 4, by Adams 3, by Flaxman 3, by Gilbert 3, by Marochetti 3, by Baily 3, by Banks 2, by Behnes 2, by Forsyth 2, by Manning 2, by Boehm 2; and one each by Bacon, jun., Brock, Cockerell, Frampton, Gahagan, Goscombe John, Hopper, Kempe, Lough, Macdowell, Pegram, Pomeroy, Stevens, Theed, Thornycroft, Williamson and Woolner.

CHAPTER XL

STRUCTURAL NOTES

I HAVE been supplied by Mr. Harding, for many years the invaluable foreman of the works at St. Paul's, with some facts and dates as to modern changes, which are not unimportant.

In 1871 the morning, or north-west, chapel (now known as St. Dunstan's) was arranged for Holy Communion. The marble floor and steps were put in their present position, and the oak-seating rearranged.

In 1872 the whole of the marble monuments were considerably lowered, and the western area, in front of the western portico, was opened to the public after the removal of the railings.

In 1873, as an extra precaution against fire in the dome, in the section used by the public in going up to the Golden Gallery from the Stone Gallery, and the oak timbers and floors were coated two inches thick with a fireproof composition; iron staircases were put in, and fireproof partitions erected. This part is therefore quite secure.

In 1875 the Wellington Monument was completed, without the equestrian figure, and fixed in the south-west chapel (now that of St. Michael and St. George). It was moved to its present position in 1894.

In 1876 the oak lobbies were added at the two entrances on either side of the great west door, to keep out draughts, as the public use this way since the removal of the railings. At the same time the present oak desks for the officiating Minor Canons were erected, and seats and desks for the choir.

1877. The east end of the crypt was made into a chapel, by the addition of the mosaic floor, the marble steps, altar and other fittings. This year also saw the removal of the matting which used to cover the whole of the marble floor under the dome. The seating arrangements were also changed, as now, with wide gangways. These have been grand improvements, as now the beautiful design of the marble floor can be seen.

1878. The present white marble floor was laid in the choir; the new peal of bells was hung, and the Wellington car, which up to this date stood where is now the grave of Sir George Williams, was removed to its present position at the west end. This was the means of opening out the whole of the west end of the crypt. The iron railings were also added at the sides, to protect the workmen at the employments. Until this change took place, the space west of the former site of the car was a dark and dirty hole for lumber. In the same year the very fine bronze standards were placed under the arches of the nave for improved gas-lighting. They are now adapted to electricity.

1879. The remains of Old St. Paul's (Chapter-house and south transept) were first discovered, as seen in the south-west churchyard.

1883. Paintings were executed by Sir Frederick Leighton and Sir E. J. Poynter as cartoons for the decoration of the dome, and were placed in position over Sir James Thornhill's pictures. It was thought, however, that the scheme would be too costly, and they were not used. They now hang in the corridor over the south aisle of the nave outside the library.

1886 and 1887. The new reredos was erected, from designs from Messrs. Bodley (R.A.) and Garner, at a cost of £17,000. In 1892 the pilasters of the apse were covered with green marble, and in 1893 those near the sacrarium with white.

The discussion about the security of St. Paul's arose in consequence of representations made by the Chapter to the London County Council in reference to the proposed line of their new great sewer through the City, the line of which would come about forty feet from the corner of the south-west tower. The question had arisen in previous years from time to time; Dean Milman, Mr. Cockerell and Mr. J. B. Lee had successfully opposed some such proposal forty years before; Dean Gregory, Mr. Penrose and Mr. J. H. Lee had prevented a tube-railway from being made under Carter Lane, a short distance south of the Cathedral, a few years ago. In the pressure of the affairs of a vast metropolis such facts are liable to be forgotten, and the danger has from time to time to be met afresh as if it were new. It was the late County Council that passed the scheme, and the present that listened favourably to the representations of the Dean and Chapter, and diverted the course of the sewer. The danger lies in the loose nature of the soil on which St. Paul's is built. Ludgate Hill is composed chiefly of pot- or brick-earth over sand, and the London clay lies many yards below. The consistency of the pot-earth is preserved by the water which circulates in its layers; if this is drained away it is liable to shrink, and then of course a building of incalculable weight, resting on a shrinking substratum, must necessarily crack. Sir Christopher Wren built as far as he could for eternity, and laid the concrete foundations with all the care of a consummate engineer, distributing the weight of the dome over as wide an area as possible with marvellous ability, but he could not foresee the era of tube-railways and gigantic sewers. Such structures at first check the gentle flow of subterranean waters, and then create a stream

[To face p. 476.

PROCESSIONAL CROSS GIVEN BY MRS. BARRY.

on their external surface; and wherever a stream flows other water joins it, and it tends to drain the neighbouring soil. Even as far down the hill as Blackfriars Station it has been necessary for years to employ a great pumping-engine. This probably represents only the natural outflow; but the same result higher up the hill, and so much nearer the Cathedral, brought real elements of danger in its train.

In order to make a convincing representation to the London County Council, the Chapter obtained the services of three of the most eminent architects of the day, who submitted the Cathedral to the most searching examination, following cracks which were known to exist in some of the buttresses of the dome as far as they could be traced, and making the most careful diagrams of these and any other imperfections, such as those in the front of the south transept, in one of the windows of the south aisle of the nave, and in the west front. For so vast a structure, now more than two hundred years old, these cracks were comparatively slight, and after being watched for some months gave not the smallest sign of movement. It is believed indeed that the cracks in some of the buttresses of the dome date from the time when Wren tried the experiment of making the sixteen great internal columns of the dome monoliths, when they all cracked and had to be replaced by pillars constructed of sections of the hardest stone that could be found; or, at any rate, to the early history of the dome. Still it was obviously necessary that these cracks, however comparatively slight, must be filled up and the stones once more solidly and indissolubly connected; and this was done at a cost of £4000. The same process was carried out in the south wall of the transepts, and wherever any dislocation could be discovered. At the west end the two great towers lean ever so slightly apart; and this has caused the stones of the great flattened arch under the gable of the upper portico slightly to gape.

This arch has consequently been rebuilt, and the whole west front, on the united opinion of Mr. Macartney, the architect to the Cathedral, and Mr. Caroë, the architect to H.M.'s Ecclesiastical Commissioners, has been more securely united to the main body of the building by great rods of metal. These works have not been carried out without great expense; and the Ecclesiastical Commissioners have felt that, as they draw such vast sums from the former estates of the Bishopric and the Cathedral, they might reasonably contribute half of the cost. The Chapter were grateful to their late architect, Mr. Somers Clarke, for the way in which he summoned public opinion to their aid in so serious a matter, and to their present architect, Mr. Macartney, for the skill and ability with which he assisted the survey, and carried out the resultant repairs. The Press showed deep interest in the matter; the *Daily Mail*, for instance, made it almost its own concern, and supplied a machine for some months for measuring the rise and fall (if any) of the water in the soil at a great depth below the surface. St. Paul's may now be pronounced to be in as sound a condition as ever it was since its first construction: the vital point is that no fresh sewer or tube should penetrate and disturb the calm tranquillity of the depths of its sacred hill.

EPILOGUE

THE story of St. Paul's has been traced with reverent loyalty and earnest aim, though with imperfect achievement. It is long and varied, sometimes needing only outline, often ampler detail. It is necessarily closely dependent on the character of the men, more or less noble or the reverse, who were responsible for its guidance—Bishops, Deans, Primates, Kings, Preachers. The thoughts of those who in the stately procession of generations successively filled its aisles, must be gathered chiefly from what was said and done by the leaders within, and from the contemporary condition of civilization and feeling. It is clear that from early days men looked to St. Paul's and Paul's Cross for inspiration and suggestion, and that in large measure they were not disappointed. At St. Paul's was discussed the idea of Magna Carta; here patriotic voices were raised against the yoke of the Legates; here were promulgated Constitutions which became the ecclesiastical law of England; the clergy of St. Paul's petitioned for the canonization of the enlightened Hugh Grossetête; here Bishop Pecock and Dean Colet prelude the Reformation; preachers deny the Papal supremacy; the leaders of the Reformation publish the simpler faith; Mary's preachers obtain reluctant hearing; those of Elizabeth are welcomed; the English liturgy is first used; the national gratitude for the restoration of the Church of England after the Puritan supremacy is embodied in the grand and united achievement of building the present Cathedral. And though it is too early to speak of the modern influence of St. Paul's, the central Church of the Imperial City has certainly long come to be considered the most fitting place for the expression of the religious emotions of the nation. On the Sunday morning, for example, after the death of the late Queen Victoria, the police estimated that the number of those who wished to enter the Cathedral, and could not because it was full, was not less than 30,000. And the vast congregations that assemble do not come for mere sensation: they are in a special degree reverent and devout. During the time that elapsed between Queen Victoria's death and burial, every afternoon at four o'clock the Cathedral was filled from end to end with sincere worshippers, in fitting mourning dress, who came without invitation to show the genuineness of their sorrow. These and innumerable other indications show that by the blessing of God St. Paul's is not unworthy of its place in the national esteem.

It would be a high responsibility to be the mother church of London itself. For several centuries every British subject in foreign parts was regarded in law as sailing from the Parish of Stepney, and every child born on the high seas was registered in that parish. This invested the Bishop of London with a jurisdiction over every member of the Church of England throughout the world, until the modern creation of bishoprics beyond the United Kingdom. Formerly the Church in Canada and the United States was administered by the Bishop, who also had jurisdiction over the congregations of British subjects throughout the whole of Europe. In the Porteus Library at Fulham there are rows of volumes bound in vellum recording the transactions of the Bishops of London in America; when resident-chaplain to Bishop Jackson, I had charge of the "Log of the *Mayflower*," subsequently handed by Bishop Creighton to the President of the United States. In 1842 the Bishopric of Gibraltar was founded for South Europe. Northern and Central Europe continue for British purposes under the jurisdiction of the Bishop of London, and for this purpose he has a special suffragan. The diocese itself is vast. In 1832 it consisted not only of the City of London and the county of Middlesex, but also of the Archdeaconries of Essex, Colchester and St. Albans, including the county of Essex, a considerable part of Herts, and four parishes in Bucks, as well as a large territory in Surrey, on the south of the Thames, extending from Mortlake to Kingston. At present it is exactly conterminous with the county of Middlesex, with a population, according to the last census, of 3,558,000.

But besides being the mother church for this enormous mass of people, St. Paul's is the official sanctuary of the empire in a way that belongs to no other cathedral. Canterbury is the See of the Primate, but it is too far off to fulfil such duties as must fall to the chief church of the capital City. The Primate himself is a trustee of St. Paul's, and as such has a stall opposite his fellow-trustee the Lord Mayor. Westminster Abbey is a Royal chapel, the august scene of the coronations, as formerly also of the Royal burials, and is endowed with a rich accumulation of historical and religious associations. But it will be realized from these pages, especially from those chapters about the old Cathedral where I followed mainly the light and guidance of Milman, one of the most independent and competent of ecclesiastical historians, how St. Paul's has had a share in the religious life of the nation that is quite unique. It is partly from its official character, partly from its prolonged series of stately and impressive solemnities, partly from momentous events, partly as the ancient place of Convocation and still its meeting-place, but, above all, by the living voice which it sends forth from generation to generation of faith, hope, love and courage to men and the nation, that it has filled this lofty position. And as the dome rears its huge and peaceful mass above the teeming turmoil of the City below, so the message of the Christian temple rises above the varying eddies of the controversies of the day. It is a witness to the simple faith, the time-honoured creeds, the quiet, unostentatious ways of primitive times. Ecclesiastical fashions and customs vary, but the central Cathedral of the English people can be blamed by none for its faithful, undeviating adherence to a form of worship which has stood the test of centuries, which has satisfied the cravings of millions of hearts that sought a message from God, and which changes not but for an ever greater perfection.

> "Open your gates, ye everlasting Piles!
> Types of the spiritual Church which God hath reared;
> Not loth we quit some hallowed village sward,
> Or humble altar, 'mid your stately aisles
> To kneel, or thrid your intricate defiles,
> Or down the nave to pace with motion slow;
> Watching, with upward eye, the great dome grow,
> And mount, at every step, with living wiles
> Instinct—to rouse the heart and lead the will
> By a bright ladder to the world above.
> Open your gates, ye Monuments of Love Divine!"[1]

---

[1] Slightly altered from Wordsworth's *Ecclesiastical Sonnets*, xlii.

APPENDIX I

A YEAR'S SPECIAL AND DIOCESAN SERVICES AT ST. PAUL'S: OCTOBER 1906—OCTOBER 1907

1906.
Oct. 2. Christian Social Union, 8.30 a.m.
„ 3. Guild of St. Paul (old choir-boys), 7.30 p.m.
„ 5. St. Paul's Lecture Society, 7.15 a.m., and Oct. 5, 12, 16, 19, 26; Nov. 2, 5, 9, 12, 16, 19, 23, 26, evening.
„ 7. Ordination, 10 a.m.
„ 8. London Diocesan Church Lads' Brigade, Annual Service, 8.30 p.m.
„ 9. Admission of Lay Readers by the Bishop of London, 5.15 p.m.
„ 10. Unveiling by Lord Roberts of the memorial to the Middlesex Yeomanry, crypt, 3 p.m.
Seafarers' Annual Service, 6 p.m.
„ 11. Service for Cathedral staff, in the crypt (and on the 2nd and 4th Thursdays in the month).
„ 15. Lay Helpers' Service, 6.30 p.m.
„ 17. Guild of St. Luke, Annual Festival, 7.30 p.m.
„ 21. } Retreat for Laymen.
„ 22. }
„ 25. Church of England Men's Society, 8 a.m.
Unveiling by H.R.H. the Duke of Connaught of the memorial to the late Field Marshal Sir J. Lintorn Simons, 3 p.m.
„ 29. Girls' Friendly Society, Annual Service, 8 p.m.
Nov. 10. Confirmation, 11.30 a.m.
„ 15. London Church Choir Association, Annual Service, 7.30 p.m.
Memorial Service for the late Miss Dorothea Beale, 2 p.m.

Nov.	19.	Lay Helpers' Service, 6.30 p.m.
,,	20.	Federation of Working Men's Clubs, Annual Service, 8.30 p.m.
,,	27.	Ordination Candidates, 8.45 a.m.
,,	30	Litany sung in procession: Intercession for Foreign Missions, 10 a.m.
Dec.	4.	Special Advent Service (Brahm's *Requiem*), 7 p.m.
,,	8.	Post Office Guild, Quiet Day.
,,	10.	Lay Helpers' Service, 6.30 p.m.
,,	15.	Confirmation, 11.30 a.m.
,,	17.	Post Office Guild, Special Service.
,,	19.	Guild of St. Paul.
,,	23.	Ordination, 10 a.m.
,,	24.	Preparation Service for Christmas.
1907. Jan.	11.	Guild of the Epiphany, 8.45 a.m. and 11 a.m. St. Paul's Lecture Society; also Jan. 18; Feb. 8, 15, 19, 22, 26 and March 1, 5, 8, 15, 22, evening.
,,	21.	Lay Helpers' Service, 6.30 p.m.; also Feb. 18, March 11 and 23, April 22 and June 13.
,,	25.	Dedication Services. Oratorio, *St. Paul*, etc. (with orchestra).
,,	29.	Ordination Candidates' Service, 8.45 a.m.
Feb.	6.	Queen Victoria Clergy Fund, Annual Service, 4 p.m.
,,	8.	Admission of Lay Readers, 5 p.m.
,,	9. 10.	} Laymen's Retreat.
,,	11.	Quiet Day for West London clergy. Service for West London Church Workers, 8 a.m.
,,	14.	Lecture to Business Women; also on Feb. 21, 27, March 7, 14, 21.
,,	16.	Confirmation, 11.30 a.m.
,,	17.	Amen Court Guild.
,,	24.	Ordination, 10 a.m.
,,	28.	Annual Welsh Service, 7 p.m.
March	2. 3.	} Laymen's Retreat.
,,	15.	Short Memorial Service for the late Prebendary Kempe.
,,	16.	Post Office Guild, 2.30 p.m. to 5 p.m.

APPENDIX I

March 18. Confirmation (St. Paul's Girls' School), 2.30 p.m.
,, 19. Guild of St. Paul, 7.30 p.m.
,, 20. Confirmation (St. Paul's Boys' School), 2.30 p.m.
,, 23. Lay Helpers' Quiet Day.
,, 26. Bach's *Passion Music*, 7 p.m.
,, 27. Confirmation of Cathedral choristers, 2.30 p.m.
April 10. St. Paul's Lecture Society.
,, 23. Service for the Order of St. Michael and St. George, 11 a.m.
,, 24. Qu'Appelle Mission Service, 8.45 a.m.
Annual Service of the S.P.G., 11 a.m.
,, 27. Church Missionary Children's Service, 5.30 p.m.
,, 29. Sons of the Clergy Annual Festival, 3.30 a.m.
,, 30. Ordination Candidates' Service, 8.45 a.m.
Bible Society's Annual Service, 4 p.m.
May 6. Sunday School Institute, Annual Service, 7.30 p.m.
,, 7. Mothers' Union Service, 11.15 a.m.
Waifs and Strays Society, 8.30 a.m.
,, 11. Confirmation, 11.30 a.m.
,, 13. Women's Help Society, Annual Service, 8 p.m.
,, 16. Universities' Mission, 8.30 a.m.
,, 23. Post Office Guild, 7.45 a.m.
,, 26. Ordination, 10 a.m.
June 3. East London Nurses' Service, 5 p.m.
,, 5. Unveiling by Lord Roberts of the memorial to the late Sir Henry Norman, 3 p.m.
,, 6. Parochial Mission Women's Annual Service, 11.15 a.m.
,, 11. Diocesan Women's Association, 10 a.m.
,, 13. East London Church Festival, 8 p.m.
,, 25. Guild of St. Alban, 7 a.m.
Confirmation, 11.30 a.m.
S.P.G. Children's Service, 6 p.m.
,, 20. Girls' Friendly Society, Annual Service, 11.15 a.m.
,, 22. Guild of the Epiphany, 8.30 a.m.
,, 29. Guild of the Good Shepherd, 5.30 p.m.
July 2. London Diocesan Home Mission, Jubilee Service, 8 p.m.
,, 3. Guild of St. Paul, 7.15 a.m.
,, 4. Girls' Friendly Society, Annual Service, 7 p.m.

July	11.	Unveiling by Lord Plymouth of the memorial to the late W. E. Henley, 3 p.m.
,,	20.	Confirmation, 11.30 a.m.
,,	29.	Service for boys going to Bisley.
Sept.	3.	Ordination Candidates, 8.45 a.m.
,,	17.	Guild of St. Paul, 7.30 p.m.
,,	24.	St. Paul's Lecture Society, 6.15 and 7.15 p.m.
,,	28.	Christian Social Union, 8.30 a.m.

ONE OF THE CAMPANILES AT THE WEST ENTRANCE

APPENDIX II

BISHOPS OF LONDON

(FROM THE MEMORIAL LIST OF BISHOPS IN THE CATHEDRAL)

(Those whose names are marked with an asterisk were buried in Old St. Paul's.)

A.D.		A.D.	
314	Restitutus	926	*Theodred
		953	Byrhthelm
		959	St. Dunstan
604	Mellitus	961	Ælfstan
		996	Wulfstan
		1004	Ælfhun
654	Cedd	1014	Ælfwig
666	Wine	1035	Ælfward
675	*St. Erkonwald	1044	Robert
693	Waldhere	1051	*William
706	Ingwald	1075	Hugh of Orval
745	*Ecgwulf	1086	Maurice
772	Sighaeh	1108	Richard de Belmeis I.
774	Eadberht	1128	Gilbert (Universalis)
789	Eadgar	1141	Robert (de Sigillo)
791	Coenwalh	1152	Richard de Belmeis II
794	Eadbald		
794	Heathoberht	1163	*Gilbert Foliot
802	Osmund	1189	Richard FitzNeal
811	Æthilnoth	1199	William of Ste Mere l'Eglise
824	Ceolberht		
860	Deorwulf		
	Swithwulf	1221	*Eustace Fauconberg
		1229	*Roger (Niger)
898	Heahstan	1244	*Fulk Basset
898	Wulfsige		

487

488 MEMORIALS OF ST. PAUL'S CATHEDRAL

A.D.		A.D.	
1260	*Henry Wengham	1577	*John Aylmer
1263	Henry Sandwich	1595	*Richard Fletcher
1274	*John Chishull	1597	Richard Bancroft
1280	*Richard Gravesend	1604	*Richard Vaughan
1306	*Ralph Baldock	1607	*Thomas Ravis
1313	*Gilbert Segrave	1610	George Abbot
1317	*Richard Newport	1611	*John King
1319	Stephen Gravesend	1621	George Mountain
1338	Richard Bintworth	1628	William Laud
1340	*Ralph Stratford	1633	William Juxon
1355	*Michael Northburgh	1660	Gilbert Sheldon
1362	Simon Sudbury	1663	Humfrey Henchman
1375	William Courtenay	1675	Henry Compton
1382	*Robert Braybrook	1714	John Robinson
1405	Roger Walden	1723	Edmund Gibson
1406	Nicholas Bubwith	1748	Thomas Sherlock
1407	*Richard Clifford	1761	Thomas Hayter
1421	John Kemp	1762	Richard Osbaldeston
1426	William Gray	1764	Richard Terrick
1431	*Robert FitzHugh	1777	Robert Lowth
1436	Robert Gilbert	1787	Beilby Porteus
1450	*Thomas Kemp	1809	John Randolph
1489	*Richard Hill	1813	William Howley
1496	Thomas Savage	1828	Charles James Blomfield
1502	William Warham		
1504	William Barons	1856	Archibald Campbell Tait
1506	*Richard FitzJames		
1522	Cuthbert Tunstall	1869	John Jackson
1530	*John Stokesley	1885	Frederick Temple
1540	Edmund Bonner	1897	Mandell Creighton
1550	Nicholas Ridley	1901	ARTHUR FOLEY WINNINGTON-INGRAM
1553	Edmund Bonner		
1559	Edmund Grindal		
1570	Edwin Sandys		

APPENDIX III

DEANS OF ST. PAUL'S

(The early spelling varies, and some of the early dates mean that the Dean was known to be in office at the time.)

A.D.		A.D.	
	Wulstan	1285	William de Montford
1111	William	1294	Ralph de Baldock
1142	Ralph de Langford	1306	Raymond de la Goth
	Taurin de Stamford	1307	Arnold de Cantilupe
1160–1181	Hugo de Marny	1311	John de Sandale
1181	Ralph de Diceto	1314	Richard de Newport
	Alardus de Burnham	1323	Vitalis de Testa
	Gervase de Hobrugg	1323	John de Everden
1212	William of Basing	1336	Gilbert de Bruera
1218	Robert de Watford	1353	Richard de Kilmyngton
1228	Martin de Pateshull		
	Walter Langford	1362	Walter de Alderbury
	Richard Wethershed	1363	Thomas Trilleck
1231	Geoffry de Lucy	1364	John de Appleby
1241	William de Sancta Maria	1376	Robert Brewer
		1389	Thomas de Evere
1243	Henry de Cornhill	1400	Thomas Stow
1254	Walter of London	1406	Thomas Moor
1256	Robert de Barton	1421	Reginald Kentwoode
	Peter de Newport	1441	Thomas Lisieux
1262	Richard Talbot	1456	Laurence Booth
1263	Geoffry de Feringes	1457	William Say
1268–1273	John de Chishull	1468	Roger Radclyff
		1471	Thomas Wynterbourne
1273	Hervey de Borham		
1276	Thomas de Inglethorp	1478	William Worseley
		1499	Robert Sherbon
1283	Roger de la Leye	1505	John Colet

A.D.		A.D.	
1519	Richard Pace	1726	Francis Hare
1536	Richard Sampson	1740	Joseph Butler
1540	John Innocent	1750	Thomas Secker
1545	William May	1758	John Hume
1553	John Howman de Feckenham	1766	Frederick Cornwallis
		1768	Thomas Newton
1556	Henry Cole	1782	Thomas Thurlow
1559	William May	1787	George Pretyman-Tomline
1560	Alexander Nowell		
1602	John Overall	1820	William Van Mildert
1614	Valentine Carey	1826	Charles Richard Sumner
1621	John Donne		
1651	Thomas Winniff	1827	Edward Copleston
1660	Matthew Nicolas	1849	Henry Hart Milman
1661	John Barwick	1868	Henry Longueville Mansel
1664	William Sancroft		
1677	Edward Stillingfleet	1871	Richard William Church
1689	John Tillotson		
1691	William Sherlock	1891	ROBERT GREGORY
1707	Henry Godolphin		

APPENDIX IV

GIFTS TO ST. PAUL'S

H. F. Vernon.—Window at end of South Aisle of Nave: St. Peter.
Rev. J. W. Vivian, D.D.—Window at end of North Aisle of Nave: St. Paul.
Thos. Brown.—The West Window: Conversion of St. Paul.
Drapers' Company.—Window in South Transept: The Crucifixion.
Goldsmiths' Company.—Window in South Transept: The Agony.
Corporation of London, with the Companies of Grocers, Merchant Taylors, Goldsmiths, Mercers, Fishmongers} Gilding of Choir, and the arches near Dome.
Friends of Captain Fitzgerald.—Marble Pulpit.
Friends of Bishop Blomfield.—Window and Marbles near Monuments.
Friends of W. Cotton.—Window in South Aisle of Choir: St. Stephen.
Friends of Archdeacon Hale.—Mosaic in St. Dunstan's Chapel: The Maries at the Sepulchre.
Friends of Dean Mansel.—Window in St. Dunstan's Chapel: St. Thomas.
Friends of Canon Liddon.—Decoration of the Jesus Chapel with Windows and Marbles, and the new Holy Table in the Choir (ebony and brass).
Friends of Archdeacon Hessey.—Window in West Aisle of North Transept: Christ and the Doctors.
Friends of the Rt.-Hon. W. H. Smith.—Mosaics in eight spandrils of the Choir.
Henry Lindo.—Mosaic in one spandril of the Choir.

Richard Benyon.—Mosaic in east part of North Aisle of Choir.

Friends of Henry, 4th Earl of Carnarvon.—Window in North Aisle of Choir: St. Paul at Athens.

Hugh, Duke of Westminster.—Large windows in North and South Transepts. He also gave £500 a year to the Mosaics.

Fishmongers' Company.—Mosaic in Chancel roof: Creation of Fishes.

The Freemasons.—Mosaics in a section of the South Aisle of the Choir.

The Mercers' Company.—Mosaic under the Quarter-Domes.

The Merchant Taylors' Company.—Mosaic under the Quarter-Domes.

The Goldsmiths' Company.—Mosaic under the Quarter-Domes.

The Grocers' Company.—Mosaic under the Quarter-Domes.

Duke of Newcastle.—Cross on the retable in the Chancel.

Rt.-Hon. H. Cavendish Bentinck.—Brass Candlesticks on the retable in the Chancel.

Mr. D. Murray (in memory of his father, Prebendary Murray).—Great Bronze Candelabrum at the West End. The others were added by the Decoration Fund.

Mrs. Barry.—Processional Cross.

Canon H. S. Holland.—A complete Gold Service for Holy Communion.

Canon Liddon.—Carved Stone Fragment of Nehemiah's Temple; Carved Marble Fragment of Herod the Great's Temple; Roman Pavement from Jerusalem.

G. F. Watts, R.A.—His great picture, "Life, Death and Judgment."

Mrs. G. F. Watts.—Picture by G. F. Watts, R.A.: "Charity."

The Rt.-Hon. Charles Booth.—Holman Hunt's famous picture, "The Light of the World" (large edition).

Alderman Sir Reginald Hanson, Bart.—A set of large Morocco Service-books in memory of the Jubilee of 1897.

A. O. Miles, C.B.—A set of Morocco Hymn-books in memory of the Jubilee of 1897.

J. Pierpont Morgan.—Electric lighting, £17,000.

H. C. Richards, M.P.—The new Paul's Cross, £5000; or £4500 net.

APPENDIX IV

Alderman Sir Walter Wilkin, K.C.M.G.—Memorial Window to H.R.H. the Duke of Cambridge in Chapel of St. Michael and St. George.

Family of the late Duke of Cambridge.—Stalls of Sovereign and Grand Master in the Chapel of St. Michael and St. George.

Lord Strathcona and Mount Royal, G.C.M.G.—Reredos in Chapel of St. Michael and St. George.

Several other members of the Order have made handsome gifts.—Brass Rail, Communion Plate, Marbles for the Sacrarium.

Somers Clarke, F.S.A.—Brass Railings round nearly the whole interior of the Cathedral, on the cornice.

The American Bishops.—Great Alms-dish, embossed with the Conversion of St. Paul.

C. T. D. Crews, J.P., D.L., F.S.A.—The St. Cecilia Window, for the Musicians' Company.

BIBLIOGRAPHY

Annals of St. Paul's Cathedral. Henry Hart Milman, D.D. London: John Murray, 1st ed. 1868, 2nd 1869.

The Three Cathedrals dedicated to St. Paul in London. William Longman. London, 1873.

History of St. Paul's Cathedral. Sir William Dugdale, continued by Henry Ellis. London: Longmans, 1818.

Stow's *Survey of London.* Edited by C. L. Kingsford. 2 Vols. Oxford, 1908.

Evelyn's *Diary.*

Pepys's *Memoirs and Diary.* Edited by Lord Braybroke. London, Warne & Co.

Diary of Henry Machyn (A.D. 1550-1563). Edited by J. G. Nichols. Camden Society, 1848.

Tombs in Old St. Paul's. By Payne Fisher, 1684. Edited by G. B. Morgan, 1885.

Stow's *Summarie of the Chronicles of England.* London: John Harison, 1604.

Organists and Composers of St. Paul's Cathedral. By John S. Bumpus. London: Bowden, Hudson & Co., 1891 (privately printed).

St. Paul's Cross. By John B. Marsh. London: Raithby, Lawrence & Co., 1892.

Handbook to St. Paul's Cathedral. Abridgment of Dean Milman's Annals. London: John Murray, 1879.

St. Paul's Cathedral and See. By the Rev. Arthur Dimock. London: George Bell & Sons, 1900.

St. Paul's Cathedral: the Authorized Guide. By the Rev. Lewis Gilbertson. London: R. E. Thomas & Co., 1907.

St. Paul's Cathedral, London. By George Clinch. London: Methuen & Co., 1906.

Old St. Paul's Cathedral. By Canon Benham. London: Seeley & Co., 1902.

Dictionary of National Biography, Index and Epitome. Edited by Sidney Lee. London: Smith, Elder & Co., 1906.

Registrum Statutorum et Consuetudinum Ecclesiae Cathedralis Sancti Pauli Londinensis. Edited by Dr. Sparrow Simpson. London: Nichols & Sons, 1873.

Supplement to Registrum, etc. Dr. Sparrow Simpson, 1897.

Chapters in the History of Old St. Paul's. By Dr. Sparrow Simpson. London: Elliot Stock, 1881.

BIBLIOGRAPHY

Gleanings from Old St. Paul's. By Dr. Sparrow Simpson. London: Elliot Stock, 1889.

St. Paul's Cathedral and Old City Life. By Dr. Sparrow Simpson. London: Elliot Stock, 1894.

Catalogue of St. Paul's Cathedral Library. By Dr. Sparrow Simpson. London: Elliot Stock, 1893.

Wren's *Parentalia.* London, 1750.

Memoirs of the Life and Works of Sir Christopher Wren. By James Elmes. London, 1823.

The Works of Sir Christopher Wren. By John Clayton. London, 1848-9.

Sir Christopher Wren and his Times. By James Elmes. London, 1852.

Life of Sir Christopher Wren. By Lena Milman. London, 1908.

Historia de Episcopis et Decanis Londinensibus. By Henry Wharton. London, 1695.

Strype's *Annals.*

Wilkins' *Concilia.*

Milman's *History of Latin Christianity.*

Hume's *History of England.*

Froude's *History of England.*

Macaulay's *History of England.*

Giles's *Patres Ecclesiae Anglicanae* (1837-1843).

Newcourt's *Repertorium, a History of the Diocese of London.* 2 Vols. London, 1708.

Life of Pecock. By Lewis.

Works of Pecock. Rolls Commission.

Malcolm's *Londinium Redivivum* (1802-7).

Sir Henry Ellis's *Original Letters Illustrative of English History* (1824-1846).

History and Survey of London. By William Maitland, F.R.S. 2 Vols. London, 1756.

Seebohm's *Oxford Reformers.*

Domesday of St. Paul's. By Archdeacon Hale. London: Camden Society, 1858.

The Grey Friars Chronicle. Edited by J. G. Nichols. London: Camden Society, 1852.

Calendar of State Papers from Venice. Edited by Rawdon Brown (A.D. 1202-1558).

J. S. Brewer's *Calendar of State Papers of Henry VIII.*

Hayward's *Annals of Queen Elizabeth.* Camden Society.

Bishop Earle's *Microcosmographie.* Bliss's Edition, 1811.

Daniel Neal's *History of the Puritans* (1732-1738).

Thomas Fuller's *History of the Church of Britain* (1655).

INDEX

ABBOT, George, Bishop of London, 183
Abercromby, General Sir Ralph, 456
Abuses in episcopal appointments, 70
Adams, sculptor, 473
Afghan War, 460
Agincourt, Battle of, *Te Deum* for, 67
Aidan, St., 8
Alamayou, Prince of Abyssinia, 321
Albany, Leopold, Duke of, death of, 341
Alexandra, Queen, 368, 369, 371, 375, 376
Alice, Princess, 314; her death, 335
Allectus, rebel emperor, 3
Allégri, *Miserere* of, 372
Allerthorpe, Laurence, Lord Treasurer, 447
Alphege, St., buried in St. Paul's, 11
Ambrose, St. (instrumental music), 414
Americans and Canadians killed in Salisbury railway disaster, Memorial Service, 375
Ammianus Marcellinus, 3
Anne Askew, burning of, 135
—— Boleyn's Procession, 129
—— of Brittany, Queen of France, obsequies of, 100
—— of Burgundy, 446
——, Queen, her numerous thanksgivings at St. Paul's, 277
——, Queen, wife of Richard II., obsequies of, 100
Anselm, Abbot of St. Edmund's, 20
Archdeacon of London, Rule of St. Chrodegang, and position in St. Paul's, 108
Archdeaconries in St. Paul's, 109
Arles, Council of, 4
Asclepiodotus, 3
Atlantic Union, 372

Attwood, Thomas, 406–409, 471
Aubrey, William, tomb of, 99
Augustine, St., Archbishop of Canterbury, 4
Aylmer, John, Bishop of London, 172, 173

Babington, William, M.D., 472
Bach's *Passion-music* begun, 326
Bacon, sculptor, 473
——, Sir Nicholas, tomb of, 97
Baden, Prince of, 327
Baily, sculptor, 473
Bancroft, Richard, Bishop of London, 174
Banks, sculptor, 473
Barham, Rev. R. H., 425
Barkham, Sir Edward, Lord Mayor, 13
Barnby, Sir Joseph, 357
Barnes, William, Bishop of London, 83
Baronsdale, William, M.D., 450
Barry, James, R.A., 468
Barton, Elizabeth, 439
——, Sir Henry, Lord Mayor, 449
Barwick, John, Dean of St. Paul's, 202
Baskerville, Sir Simon, M.D., 450
Basset, Fulk, Bishop of London, 38
Batten, Adrian, 403
Battishill, Jonathan, 406
Baynham, James, burnt, 439
Beale, Miss Dorothea, 375
Beauchamp, Sir John de, K.G., tomb of, 91
Becket, Archbishop of Canterbury, 31
Behnes, sculptor, 473
Belgian artisans, 326
Belgians, King of the, 336
Bells, new peal of, 334, 426–429
Benedict XIII., Pope, 437
Ben Jonson on Paul's Walk, 169

INDEX

Benson appointed surveyor in place of Wren, 262
Benson, Archbishop, 358
Benvenue, shipwrecked crew of, 351
Besant, Sir Walter, 371
Bill, Dr., preacher for Elizabeth at Paul's Cross, 156
Billing, Bishop, 465
Bird's Font, Conversion on pediment, and Queen Anne, 257
Bishop, organ-builder, 417
Bishops of London and St. Paul's, 108
Bishop's Stortford, Castle of, given to Bishopric of London by William I., 14
Bistrop, Lord of, 448
Blanche, Duchess of Lancaster, tomb of, 95
Blomfield, Charles James, Bishop of London, 294
Blow, Dr. John, 404
Boadicea, Queen, 3
Bocher, Joan, burning of, 141
Boehm, Sir Edgar, R.A., burial of, 349, 469
Boer War, First, 460
Boltyngbroke, Roger, necromancer, 437
Bonifice of Savoy, Archbishop of Canterbury, 39
Bonner upholds Royal Supremacy, 130; Bishop of London, 133, 135; changes at St. Paul's, 142; sent to the Tower, 143; released, 148; tyranny of, 151; deposed, 160; imprisonment and death, *ib.*
Bouchier, Archbishop of Canterbury, 77
Bowes, Major-General, 457
Bowine, Dr., 147
Boxley, Rood of, 439
Boyce, Dr., 471
Braybroke, Robert de, Bishop of London, 62; his reforms, 63; venerated by the City, 65; tomb, 97
Brewer, the, at St. Paul's, 113
Brind, Richard, 404
British Church, 4
—— Medical Association, 327
Brock, General Sir Isaac, 457
Browne, Professor George Forrest (afterwards Bishop of Bristol), 349, 356, 360, 361
—— Field-Marshal Sir Samuel, 371, 461
Brut, 2

Bryne, Albertus, 403
Bubwith, Nicholas, Bishop of London, 66
Buller, Sir Walter, K.C.M.G., 375
Burdett-Coutts, Baroness, 313, 329
Burgess, Captain, R.N., 451
—— Cornelius, Lecturer of St. Paul's, instead of Dean and Chapter, 195-198
Burley, Sir Simon, K.G., tomb of, 94
Burmese Embassy, 326
Burnings, 66, 131, 135, 141, 150, 151, 152, 153, 183
Butler, Joseph (Bishop of Bristol and afterwards Bishop of Durham), Dean of St. Paul's, 285

Cadogan, Colonel Hon. Henry, 457
Caldecott, Randolph, 468
Cambridge, Augusta, Duchess of, 315; death, 347
Canons of St. Paul's, 110
Cantilupe, Walter de, Bishop of Worcester, 35, 41
Captain, H.M.S., 456
Cardinals, 112
Carey, Valentine, Dean of St. Paul's, 184
Cathedrals, area of seventeen great, 237
Catherine of Aragon, marriage of, to Prince Arthur, 115
Cattle-plague, Day of Humiliation for, 320
Cedd, Bishop of London, 8
Chancellor of St. Paul's, 110
Chandos, Elizabeth, Lady, 447
Chantrey, sculptor, 473
Chantries in St. Paul's, 101
Chantry priests, 113
Chapter House, the former, 92; clerical riot at, under Bishop Stokesley, 127
Charles I., his vow at St. Paul's, 193
—— II.'s commission, 206; his subscription to St. Paul's, 226
—— V., Emperor, obsequies of, 100; visits St. Paul's, 121
—— VIII., King of France, obsequies of, 100
Charnock, Principal of St. Mary's Hall, Oxford, 85
Charrington, Lt. Harold, 473
Chicheley, Archbishop of Canterbury, 67
Chikwell, Hamond, Lord Mayor of London, 449

INDEX

Chimes, 431–433
Chishull, John de, Bishop of London, 44, 94
Choir-school, corner-stone laid, 328
Christ's Hospital, 113, 368
Chrodegang, St., Rule of, and the Archdeacon, 108
Church, Richard William, Dean of St. Paul's, 306 ; death of, 348
Cibber's Phœnix, 257
City Imperial Volunteers, 364, 365
—— of London pay Coal Dues to the Building Fund, 227 ; Wren's noble plans for the rearrangement of, 232
Clarence, Duke of, death and memorial service, 351
Clark, Jeremiah, 403
Claudius, Emperor, 1
Claughton, Bishop Piers, Archdeacon of London, 465
Clement IV., Pope, 436
Clifford, Robert, Bishop of London, represents England at Council of Constance, A.D. 1416, 67
Clock, the new, 430–434
Cobham, Eleanor, Duchess of Gloucester, penance of, 76
Cockerell, C. R., 471
Codrington, Admiral Sir Edward, 455
Cokayn, Sir William, Lord Mayor, monument of, 97 ; receives James I., 180, 444
Coldstream Guards, 459
—— Guards, Crimean monument, 314 ; S. African monument, 372
Colet, John, Dean of St. Paul's, 83
College Youths, 356
Collingwood, Admiral Lord, 453
Colonial Exhibition Delegates, 344
—— Troops (S. Africa), 461
Common Council, Act of, against traffic in St. Paul's, 168
Compton, Henry, Bishop of London, 273–275 ; crowns William and Mary, 275 ; visits Holland with King and Council, 276
Consecration of Bishops, 183, 323, 331, 332 ; *ib.*, 333 ; *ib.*, 337, 341 ; *ib.*, 342, 343 ; *ib.*, 344, 345, 346, 348, 349, 351, 352, 356 ; *ib.*, 358 ; *ib.*, 359 ; *ib.*, 361, 362 ; *ib.*, 366, 372
Consort, the Prince, 315 ; mourning for the death of, 317
Constance, daughter of King Pedro the Cruel, wife of John of Gaunt, tomb of, 95

Constance of Castile, 446
Constantius, Emperor, 3
Convocation and St. Paul's, 122
—— under Mary Tudor, 148 ; Elizabeth's first Reformed, 170
Cooper, Sir Astley, M.D., 472
Coplestone, Edward, Dean of St. Paul's and Bishop of Llandaff, 303
Cornhill, Henry de, Dean of St. Paul's, 40
Cornwallis, Charles, 1st Marquis, 456
——, Frederick, Dean of St. Paul's and Bishop of Lichfield, 288
Council at Westminster, A.D. 1457, 72
—— of Constance, A.D. 1416, 67
—— of London, A.D. 1075, 14 ; 1309, 47
Courtenay, William de, Bishop of London, 58
Coverdale, Miles, Bishop of Exeter, 440
Coxe, Bishop Cleveland, 420
Cranmer, Archbishop, 133, 135
Crauford, Major-General, 457
Creighton, Mandell, Bishop of London, 300, 358, 365, 373
Cruickshank, George, buried in the Crypt, 335, 468
Crumwell, Thomas, 439

Daily Celebrations begun, 331
Dalley, Rt.-Hon. W. B., 463
Dance, George, R.A., 471
Dangers averted from St. Paul's : a deep sewer in Dean Milman's time, 231 ; a new tube-railway, *ib.* ; the L.C.C. sewer, *ib.*
Daughters of Officers, service for, 333
Dawe, George, R.A., 468
Denmark, Louisa, Queen of, 320
Diana, image of, 2
Dickens, Charles, 314
Dome, construction of, 255
Donne, Dean, monument of, 97 ; account of, 184–186, 444
Dowgate, 1
Ducie, Lord Mayor Sir Robert, 445
Duncan, Admiral Lord, 453
Dunstan, St., Bishop of London, 10

Earle, Bishop, *Microcosmographie*, and St. Paul's, 169
Ecclesiastical Commission, 295
Edinburgh, Duke and Duchess of, 338 ; Duke of Saxe-Coburg, Memorial Service for, 365

K K 2

INDEX

Edward Atheling, 446
—— I. and the clergy, 45
—— II. at Paul's Cross, 437
—— IV., homage to, at St. Paul's, 79
—— VI., 137–145
—— VII., King, 368, 369, 374, 376
—— of Westminster, State Bell, 426
—— the Confessor, King, 12
Elizabeth, Queen, 156–177; proclamation against profanation of St. Paul's, 168
Elizabethan bishops, difficulties of, 161
Elphinstone, Hon. Mountstuart, 462
Emma, Queen of the Sandwich Islands, 319
Erasmus, 85
Erkonwald, St., Bishop of London, 9
Essex, 2
Ethelbert, King, 5, 359; altar to, 95
Ethelred the Unready, King, 95, 446
Eucharist, Sermons on, 140; debate on, 148; great debate at Westminster Abbey, 161
Eustace de Fauconberge, Bishop of London, 31, 93
Evelyn, John, on the Commission for restoring St. Paul's, 207; account of the Great Fire, 210; account of Grinling Gibbons, 249–253
Evere, Dean, tomb of, 93

Falcodi, Cardinal Ugo, Legate, 43; becomes Pope (Clement IV.) and excommunicates Bishop Henry de Sandwith, 43
Farley, Henry, stirs for eight years for restoration of St. Paul's under James I., and at last succeeds, 180
Faulknor, Captain, 451
Feckenham, Dean of St. Paul's, 147, 441
Fenians, precautions against, 320
Ferdinand, Emperor, obsequies of, 100
——, King of Aragon, obsequies of, 100
Ferrar, Bishop of St. David's, reforming sermon at Paul's Cross, 141

Finan, Bishop of Lindisfarne, 7
Fisher, Bishop of Rochester, preaches at burning of Tyndale's Bibles, 127
FitzGeorge family, 397
FitzHugh, Robert, Bishop of London, 68, 93
FitzJames, Richard, Bishop of London, 83
FitzNeal, Richard, Bishop of London, 26
FitzOsbert, William, popular leader, 28, 436
FitzThomas, Lord Mayor, joins Simon de Montfort, 43
Flaxman, sculptor, 473
Fleet River, 3
Fletcher, Richard, Bishop of London, 173
Foley, John Henry, R.A. (sculptor), buried in the Crypt, 329, 469
Foliot, Gilbert, Bishop of London, 21; excommunicated by Becket, 22; desires London to be an Archbishopric, 24
Forbes, Archibald, 466
Foresters, Order of, 349
Forsyth, sculptor, 473
Frampton, Sir George, R.A., 472
Francis I., King of France, obsequies of, 100
Frederick, Emperor of Germany, 367
Freemasons, the, celebrate Bicentenary of opening of Cathedral, 360
French workmen, 372
Frere, Sir Bartle, burial of, in the Crypt, 342, 462
Fulham, 20
Fuseli, Henry, R.A., 468
Fussell, Miss, 375, 465

Gardiner, Bishop of Winchester, upholder of Royal Supremacy, 130; preaches at Paul's Cross for Philip, 149, 440, 441
Gascoigne, Thomas, author of *Dictionary of Theology*, moderate reformer, 70
Gaunt, John of, 60; tomb of, 95
Geoffrey of Monmouth, 2
Geometrical staircase, 255
George I., procession to St. P ul', 289
—— III.'s Thanksgiving for Recovery, 289; Thanksgiving for Naval Victories (June 1, Camperdown, etc.), 290

INDEX

George IV., 407
Germany, Crown Prince of, 333
Gibbon or Gibbons, Grinling, account of him by Evelyn, 249-253
Gibbs, General Sir William, 458
Gibson, Edmund, Bishop of London, 284; *Codex Juris Ecclesiastici Anglicani*, and *Preservative from Popery*, 285
Gilbert de Segrave, Bishop of London, 47
——, Robert, Bishop of London, 68
——, sculptor, 473
—— the Universal, Bishop of London, 19
Gilbertson, Rev. Lewis, 426
Gill, Captain W. J., 473
Gillespie, General Sir R., 458
Gloucester, Richard Duke of, at St. Paul's, 80
——, Mary, Duchess of, 315
Glover, Sir J. H., 463
Godolphin, Henry, Dean of St. Paul's, 285
Goldsmiths' Hall, 3
Gordon, General, Memorial Service for, 343, 460
Gore, Major-General, 458
Goss, Sir John, 409-411, 471
Gounod, 420
Grant, Field-Marshal Sir Patrick, 461
——, Lieut.-Colonel J. A., 473
Gray, William, Bishop of London, appointed by Pope Martin V., 68
——, Right Hon. Sir George, 463
Green, Robert, Verger at St. Paul's, his notes, 312-363
Greene, Maurice, 405
Gregory the Great, Pope, 4
——, St., Church of, removed from west of St. Paul's, 189
——, Robert, Dean of St. Paul's, previously Canon, 308; his reforms, 309; inaugurates working-men's parties, 324; and lectures, *ib.*; eightieth birthday, 362; thanks for recovery, 375
Grey, Sir George, 361
Grimthorpe, Lord, 430
Grindal, Edmund, at Paul's Cross, 136; Bishop of London, 160; account of, 161; Archbishop of York, 170
Grocyn at Oxford, 85
Guilt, Joseph, his architectural account of St. Paul's, 239
Gyles, Thomas, 400

Hackett, Maria, 329
Hale, Archdeacon, his plan for warming the Cathedral, 312; death, 323
Hallam, Henry, 466
——, Bishop, moderate reformer, present at Council of Constance, 69
Handel, 405
Hanover, Crown Prince of (Duke of Cumberland), 331
Harding, Mr. E. J., 474
Hardinge, Captain, R.N., 453
Hare, Francis, Dean of St. Paul's, 285
Harvest Festival, the first at St. Paul's, 313
Hatton, Sir Christopher, Lord Chancellor, tomb of, 99
Hawthorne, Nathaniel, 420
Hay, Major-General Andrew, 457
——, Senator John, 373
Hayes, Dr. Philip, 471
Hayter, Thomas, Bishop of London, 287
Heathfield, General Lord, 456
Heber, Bishop, 464
Henchman, Henry, Bishop of London, 201
Heneage, Sir Thomas, tomb of, 99
Hengest, 3
Henley, W. E., 467
Henry of Battenberg, Prince, 357
—— de Bolingbroke (afterwards Henry IV.), 63
—— of Blois, Bishop of Winchester, 20
—— II., King of France, obsequies of, 100, 159
—— III., King, 31, 436
—— V., funeral of, 67
—— VI., reconciliation of with Richard Duke of York, 77; body lies in State at St. Paul's, 79
—— VII., lies in State at St. Paul's, 116
Herbert, the Hon. Sir Robert, 393
Hessey, Archdeacon, 355
——, Mrs., 395
Hill, Thomas, Bishop of London, 83
Hoghton, Major-General, 457
Holl, Frank, R.A., 468
Homilies, First Book of, Cranmer and Bonner join in, 135
Honorius III., Pope, 31
Horne, Dr., at Paul's Cross, 157
Horsey, Dr., 87
Hospital Sunday, the first (1873), 327
Hoste, Captain Sir W., R.N., 455
Howard, John, 472

INDEX

Howe, Admiral Lord, 451
Howley, William, Bishop of London, 294
Hugh de Orivalle, Bishop of London, 15
Hume, John, Dean of St. Paul's and Bishop of Oxford, 288

Imperial Yeomanry (South African War), 461
Indian Mutiny, Day of Humiliation for, 315
Indulgences, 24, 37, 52, 105
Inglis, General Sir John, 460
Innocent IV., Pope, demands of, 38
Isobel, Empress, obsequies of, 100
Italy, Humbert, Crown Prince of, 319

Jackson, John, Bishop of London, 300; sudden death, 342
James, Duke of York (James II.), President of the Building Committee, 224 n., 404
—— I., Procession to St. Paul's to encourage restoration, 180
Jaruman, Bishop of Mercia, 9
Jerusalem, Jacobite, Bishop of, 329
Jewel, John, at Paul's Cross, 158; challenge on eucharistic doctrine of first six centuries, 160
Jews, services for, under the Dome, 349
Joan, Empress, obsequies of, 100
John, Goscombe, A.R.A., 473
——, King, 29
——, King of Portugal, obsequies of, 100
——, King of France, at St. Paul's, 104
Johnson, Dr., 466
Jones, Inigo, and James I.'s restoration of St. Paul's, 181, 188, 189
——, John, 406
——, Major-General Sir John, 459
——, Sir William, 466
Julian the Apostate (organ), 414
Juxon, William, Bishop of London, 192; Lord High Treasurer, 193; retires to Fulham, ib.; with Charles I. at his execution, ib.; protected by Parliament, 198; restored, 201; Archbishop of Canterbury, 201

Kemp, John, Bishop of London, appointed by Pope Martin V., 67

Kemp, Thomas, Bishop of London, by provisor of Pope Nicolas V., 75, 437
Kempe, his windows, 354
Kent, 2
——, Duchess of, 317
Khama, King, 357
King, Charles, 405
——, John, Bishop of London, 180

Lacy, Henry de, Earl of Lincoln, tomb of, 93
Lady Mayoress, marriage of, 332
Lambeth Conference, 333, 346, 360, 377
Landseer, Sir Edwin, funeral of, 327, 468
Lanfranc, Archbishop of Canterbury, 14
Lang, Cosmo Gordon, Bp. of Stepney and Abp. of York, 366
Langton, Simon, Archbishop of Canterbury, 30
Langwerth, General, 457
Latimer, Hugh, Bishop of Worcester, Convocation Sermon, 131
——, John Nevill, Lord, 447
Laud, William, Bishop of London, 187; efforts for the restoration of St. Paul's, 188; promotes Jeremy Taylor, 191; Archbishop of Canterbury, ib.; threats against, ib.; execution, 193
Lawrence, Brigadier-General Sir Henry, 459
——, Sir Thomas, P.R.A., 468
Lay Helpers' Association, 322
Lea, River, 3
Lectern, Jacob Sutton's, 257
Leggatt, Bartholomew, last victim of the stake in England, 183
Leighton, Lord, 357, 367, 469, 475
Le Marchant, Major-General, 457
Lent week-day services under the Dome, 331
Leo X., Pope, sends presents to Henry VIII., 116; sentence against Martin Luther, 120, 438
Library, 422–426
Li-Chang, Chinese Ambassador, 357
Liddon, Canon, his sermons at St. Paul's, 310; first afternoon sermon under the Dome, 322; death and burial, 348, 465
Linacre, Thomas, 85; tomb of, 99
Lincoln, Henry de Lacy, Earl of, 447
Lindisfarne, 7
Loch, Captain, R.N., 455

INDEX

London, Ancient, 1–11
—— Church Choir Association, 327
—— Church Congress, 362
—— Diocesan Home Mission, Jubilee of, 375
—— Gregorian Association, 326
—— House, French Ambassador at, 157; Pope Pius V.'s Bull of Excommunication against Elizabeth nailed to gate of, 170; Great Fire of, 209, and foll.
Louis (afterwards VIII.), son of Philip II., King of France, 31
—— XII., King of France, obsequies of, 100
Louise, Princess (Duchess of Argyll), 372; sculpture by, 461
Lowth, Robert, Bishop of London, 287
Lucius, King, 4
Lucknow Relief Survivors, 351
Ludgate, 1
—— Hill, 2
Lumley, Lord Mayor Sir Martin, 445
Lyons, Captain, R.N., 455
——, Admiral Lord, 455
Lytton, 2nd Lord, 371, 463

Macdougall, Colonel Sir D., 460
Macgregor, General Sir Charles, 461
Mackenzie, General, 457
Mackinnon, Major-General, 457
Macpherson, Charles, 357, 413
Malcolm, Admiral Sir Pultney, 455
Mansel, Henry Longueville, Dean of St. Paul's, 305
Margaret of Anjou, Queen, 77–79
—— daughter of Henry VII., marriage of, to James IV. of Scotland, 116
Marlborough, victories of, commemorated at St. Paul's, 277–280
Marochetti, Baron, sculptor, 473
Martin V., Pope, appoints John Kemp Bishop of London, 67; and William Gray, 68
——, Bishop of St. David's, tomb of, 92
——, Sir George, 329, 412, 413, 419
—— Marprelate attacks Whitgift and Aylmer, 173
——, Sir Thomas, Lord Mayor, 449
Mary Tudor, Queen, 146, etc.
Mason, Sir John, tomb of, 99
Masses for the Dead, 101
Mass-priests, 103

Maurice, Bishop of London, 16; crowns Henry I., 17
Maximilian, Emperor, obsequies of, 100
May, Dean of St. Paul's, 138; nominated for Archbishopric of York, and death of, 162
Mayo, Earl of, 462
Mecklenburg-Strelitz, Grand Duchess of (Princess Augusta), 320
Melbourne, 1st and 2nd Viscounts, 462
Mellitus, Bishop of London, 5–7, 372
Melvill, Canon, 324
Mendelssohn, 407
Messiah sung at opening of Great Organ in S. Transept, 317
Michael, St., and St. George, Order of, assigned chapel in Cathedral, 367; dedication of chapel, 374, 391–398
Middlesex, 2
—— Regiment, 459
—— Yeomanry, 461
Middleton, Bishop, 464
Millais, Sir John, 357, 469
Miller, Captain, R.N., 453
Milman, Dean, on the geology of Ludgate Hill, 231; Dean of St. Paul's, 303
Minor canons, 112
Montacute, Sir John, tomb of, 90
Montgomerie, Bishop (St. Michael and St. George), 398
——, Sir Robert, 463
Moore, General Sir John, 456
Moorish Embassy, 366
More, Sir Thomas, 85, 129
Morgan, J. Pierpont, lights St. Paul's with electricity at cost of £17,000, 368
Morley, Lord Mayor Sir N., 443
——, Thomas, 402
Morton, Archbishop of Canterbury, 83
Mosse, Captain, R.N., 453
Mulliner, Thomas, 402
Musicians, Company of, 375, 376
Myers, Colonel Sir W., 457
Mylne, Robert, F.R.S., 469

Napier, Admiral Sir Charles, 455
——, General Sir Charles, 459
——, General Sir William, 460
—— of Magdala, Lord, burial of, 347
Neale, E. Vansittart, 470
Nelson, funeral of, 301
——, second Lord, 464

Nepaul, Maharajah-, Premier of, 377
Netherlands, Queen of, 338
Newbolt, Canon, 348
New Foundation, cathedrals of, 107
Newton, Lord Mayor, 364
——, Thomas, Dean of St. Paul's, Bishop of Bristol, 288
New Zealand War, 460
Nicholas, Cardinal Legate, 31
——, William, Dean of St. Paul's, 202
Noble, sculptor, 473
Norman, F.-M., Sir Henry, 461
Northbury, Sir John, Lord Treasurer, 447
Northesk, Admiral Lord, 453
Nottage, Lord Mayor, funeral of, 343
Nowell, Alexander, Dean of St. Paul's, 163, 174; brushes with Queen Elizabeth, 175, 176; tomb of, 99
Nun of Kent, exposure of, 130

Oblations in St. Paul's, 104
Old Catholics, 329
Old Foundation, cathedrals of, 107
Opie, John, R.A., 468
Orange, Prince of (late King of Holland), 316
Organ, the, 414–419
Organists of St. Paul's, 400–413
Osbaldiston, Richard, Bishop of London, 287
Otho, Cardinal Legate, 33; Synod at St. Paul's, 34; adventure at Oxford, 36
Ottobuoni, Legate, 44
Overall, John, Dean of St. Paul's, 184

Paul's, St.: First Cathedral built by Ethelbert, 5; burnt and rebuilt 962 A.D., 11; privileges bestowed by William the Conqueror, 13; Lanfranc's Council, 14; Bishop Maurice's Norman Cathedral, 16; St. Erkonwald's building, *ib.*; fire of 1136 A.D., 20; building of, supported by Indulgences and Masses for the Dead, 24, 37, 52, 105; arraignment of William de Longchamp, Bishop of Ely and Chancellor, 28; Pope's Interdict read by Bishop William de Santa Maria, 29; Louis of France at, 31; Langton's Council, 32;

Paul's, St. (*continued*)
Cardinal Otho, the Legate, synod of, 34; Cardinal Ottobuoni's synod, 44; completion of Old St. Paul's, 50–57; wall and gates, 53; Pardon-churchyard, 54; Sherrington Chapel, 55; Chapel of the Holy Ghost, *ib.*; Jesus Chapel, *ib.*; Church of St. Faith, *ib.*; Church of St. Gregory, 56; dimensions of Old St. Paul's, 57; Wycliffe before Bishop Courtenay, 60; reforms of Bishop de Braybrooke, 63–65; Convocations of Archbishop Arundel, 66; Archbishop Chicheley's Convocations, 67; *Te Deum* for Agincourt, *ib.*; magnificent funeral of Henry V., *ib.*; Bishop Pecock at St. Paul's, 69 ff.; Richard Duke of York's oath to Henry VI., 1452, 76; his reconciliation to Henry VI., 77; ratification of successor to Duke of York, 78; homage to Edward IV., 1461, 79; bodies of Salisbury, Warwick and Montagu on view, 1471, *ib.*; Henry VI.'s body lies in state, 1471, *ib.*; Richard Duke of Gloucester at, 80; Archbishop Morton's Convocation, 81; Colet's sermons and lectures at, 86; Convocation on the Lollards, *ib.*; Whitsunday Pigeon in, 91; Twelve Scribes, *ib.*; the former Chapter House, 92; chapels of St. Paul, St. Catherine, Holy Trinity and St. John the Evangelist, *ib.*; the great North Crucifix, *ib.*; chapels of St. James, St. Thomas, the Holy Ghost, St. John Baptist and St. Margaret, 93; St. Wilgefort's Image, *ib.*; St. Dunstan's Chapel, *ib.*; St. George's Chapel, 95; Choir of the old Cathedral, *ib.*; altars to St. Paul, St. Ethelbert and St. Mellitus, *ib.*; shrine of St. Erkonwald, 96; Lady Chapel, *ib.*; chapels of St. John Baptist, St. Anne and St. Radegund, 97; Guilds of the Holy Ghost, St. Catherine, the Annunciation and All Saints, *ib.*; revenue before the Reformation, 100–106; obsequies of Queen Anne, wife of Richard II., the Earl of St. Paul, Emperor Maximilian, Emperor Charles V., Isabel and Joan his wives, Emperor

INDEX

Paul's, St. (*continued*)
Ferdinand, King Charles VIII. of France, Anne Queen of France, King Louis XII., King Francis I., King Henry II. of France, King Philip of Castile, King Ferdinand of Aragon, King John of Portugal, 100 ; chantries, 101 ; mass-priests, 103 ; oblations, 104 ; relics, *ib.* ; personal staff in the Middle Ages, 107–113 ; connection of Bishop with, 108 ; Rule of St. Chrodegang and the Archdeacon, *ib.* ; the Dean, *ib.* ; Archdeaconries in, 109 ; Treasurer and Sacrist, *ib.* ; Precentor, Succentor and Master of Song, 110 ; Chancellor, *ib.* ; Canons, *ib.* ; Residentiaries, 111 ; Vicars-choral, 112 ; Minor Canons, *ib.* ; Cardinals, *ib.* ; Chantry priests, 113 ; Sub-dean, *ib.*; brewer and baker, *ib.*; sermons at Paul's Cross, *temp.* Henry VIII., 114; marriage of Catherine to Prince Arthur, 115 ; marriage of Margaret, Henry VII.'s daughter to James IV. of Scotland, 116 ; Henry VII.'s lying-in-state, *ib.* ; ceremony of delivering presents from Pope Leo X. to Henry VIII., 1514, *ib.*; Thanksgiving for the Peace of 1515, 119 ; proclamation of Emperor Charles V., 120 ; publication of Pope Leo X.'s sentence against Luther, *ib.* ; visit of Emperor Charles V., 121 ; Convocation and St. Paul's 122 ; Thanksgiving for victory of Pavia, *ib.* ; Thanksgiving for Sack of Rome, *ib.* ; Wolsey and the destruction of Tyndale's Bibles, 126 ; Clerical riot at the Chapter House, 127; Anne Boleyn's procession, 129; exposure of the Nun of Kent, 130 ; preachers at Paul's Cross ordered to uphold denial of Papal supremacy, *ib.* ; Bishop Latimer preaches Convocation sermon, 131; exposure of the Rood of Boxley, *ib.* ; Thanksgiving for the Peace of 1546, 135 ; Reformation sermons at Paul's Cross, 137 ; Edward VI.'s procession, *ib.* ; Commissioners to remove the images, 138 ; Sir Miles Partridge wins the Jesus Bells from Henry VIII., *ib.* ; spoils of St. Paul's at Valencia and Saragossa, 139 ; petition of Dean and Chapter

Paul's, St. (*continued*)
to Edward VI.'s Council for necessary articles, *ib.* ; Holy Communion in, 140; changes, 141 ; Bonner's sermon, 143 ; altar replaced by Holy Table, 144 ; general demolition of altars and chapels, *ib.* ; Thanksgiving for Mary's accession, *ib.* ; inauguration of Second Prayer-book, All Hallows' Day 1552, *ib.* ; last sweep of the treasures, 145 ; re-action under Mary, 146–155 ; tumult at Paul's Cross against Dr. Bourne, 147 ; mass, etc., revived at the Cathedral, *ib.* ; processions and sermons, *ib.*, 148 ; re-erection of Rood, 149 ; Thanksgiving for suppression of Wyatt's rebellion, *ib.* ; visit of Philip of Spain, *ib.* ; services in expectation of birth of a child to Mary, 150 ; Bishop Ridley and Canon Rogers burned, 151 ; obsequies of the Queen of Spain, 153 ; Procession of the Buck, *ib.* ; Thanksgiving for victory at St. Quentin, 154; sermons at Paul's Cross for Elizabeth, 155–158 ; visitation by Elizabeth's Commissioners, 158 ; all traces of the Marian re-action obliterated, *ib.* ; obsequies of Henry II. of France, 159 ; Jewel's challenge at Paul's Cross on eucharistic doctrine of first six centuries, 160 ; St. Paul's nearly destroyed by fire in 1561, 163 ; Elizabeth's restoration of St. Paul's, 167 ; spire never re-erected, 168 ; attempts to check profanation, Bishop Pilkington, Common Council, Queen Elizabeth, Bishop Earle, *ib.*, 169 ; Elizabeth's first reformed Convocation at, 170 ; Puritanism at Paul's Cross, 172 ; Alexander Nowell, Dean of, 174 ; Elizabeth returns thanks for victory over the Armada, 176 ; four Gunpowder Plot conspirators executed at West End, 179 ; procession of James I., A.D. 1620, to encourage restoration, 180 ; James's Royal Commission for restoring, 181 ; consecration of three Scottish Bishops at London House, *Errata*, vi.; Laud's zeal, 188 ; Inigo Jones's work, 189; liberality of Sir Paul Pindar, *ib.* sums contributed, 190 ; checked by

Paul's, St. (*continued*)
Civil War, *ib.*; Cross demolished by order of Long Parliament, *ib.*; property of the Dean and Chapter seized, 191; Charles I.'s vow, 193; Puritan's contempt for, 194; orders for destruction of copes and monuments of superstition, *ib.*; silver to be sold, 195; sequestration, *ib.*; Cornelius Burgess appointed lecturer, and placed in charge, *ib.*; portico let for shops, 199; Cathedral turned into cavalry barracks, *ib.*; revival of services at the Restoration, 205; Charles II.'s Commission, 206; new subscription-book, *ib.*; Wren on the Commission, 207; destroyed by the Great Fire, 210; portion of ruins fitted up by Wren for service, 217; Sancroft's sermon before Charles II. in the ruins, 218; Dean Sancroft tries patching up in opposition to Wren, 220; gives way, 221; King's warrant for demolition of Choir, *ib.*; Wren's various plans, 223; letters-patent for a totally new Cathedral, A.D. 1673, 224; subscription-lists, 226; Order in Council on Bishops' expenses, *ib.*; removing the ruins, 228; the foundations and the deep shaft, 230; the first stone laid, May 14, 1675, 232; progress, 233, 234; James II.'s Commission, 234; opened for Thanksgiving for Peace of Ryswick Dec. 2, 1697, *ib.*, 276, 277; Morning Chapel opened Feb. 1, 1698, 235; the final stone laid by Wren's son, with Wren and a company of Freemasons, 1710, *ib.*; dimensions of, 237; size compared with that of other cathedrals, *ib.*; Guilt's architectural account of, 239; Wren, Father Smith and the Organ, 248; Grinling Gibbons's work at St. Paul's, 249-253; Tijou's ironwork, 253; baldacchino proposed, *ib.*; Geometrical Staircase, 255; Whispering Gallery, *ib.*; construction of the Dome, *ib.*; Sir James Thornhill's paintings, 256; Jacob Sutton's Lectern, 257; Bird's Font, Conversion on the pediment, and statue of Queen Anne, *ib.*; Cib-

Paul's, St. (*continued*)
ber's Phœnix, *ib.*; windows left plain, *ib.*; Wren and the Commissioners, 259-264; George I.'s Commission, 261; a balustrade imposed, *ib.*; Wren dismissed, 1718, 262; Benson appointed surveyor, *ib.*; Queen Anne's eight thanksgivings at St. Paul's, 277; offer of Sir Joshua Reynolds and the Royal Academy to paint pictures for St. Paul's, 288; George I.'s procession, 289; George III.'s thanksgiving for Recovery, *ib.*; George III.'s thanksgiving for Naval Victories (1st June, Camperdown, etc.), 290; funeral of Sir Joshua Reynolds, 291; great robbery at St. Paul's, Dec. 23, 1810, 292; Bishop Tait's movement for evening services under the Dome, and its consequences, 296-300; list of special preachers at the evening services, 299; funeral of Nelson, 301; funeral of Wellington, 304; installation of Canon Gregory, 308; his reforming address to the choir, 309; commutation of the estates, *ib.*; Stainer's reforms in the music, 310; first Harvest Festival at St. Paul's, 313; Thanksgiving for the capture of Sebastopol, *ib.*; Day of Humiliation for the Indian Mutiny, 315; Bishop Tait's First Visitation Charge (4 h. 20 m.), *ib.*; Thanksgiving for suppression of Indian Mutiny, 316; funeral of General Sir Thomas Picton, *ib.*; erection of Great Organ in South Transept, *ib.*; alterations in the Choir, *ib.*; the *Messiah*, and Sims Reeves, 317; mourning for the death of the Prince Consort, *ib.*; Watt's mosaics, 320; precautions against Fenians, *ib.*; alteration of hours of service, 321; first afternoon service under the Dome (for Dr. Liddon), 322; Charity Children's annual service gradually discontinued, *ib.*; Mansion House meeting for decoration, 323; first consecration of Bishops on record at St. Paul's, *ib.*; observance of Dedication Festival begun, *ib.*; working-men's parties begun by Canon Gregory, 324; lectures, *ib.*; Thanksgiving for recovery of

INDEX

Paul's, St. (*continued*)
Prince of Wales, 325 ; moving and lowering of monuments, *ib.* ; large increase to staff of choir, 326 ; Bach's *Passion-music* begun, *ib.* ; non-communicants allowed to remain during celebrations, *ib.* ; burial of Sir Edwin Landseer, 327 ; London Church Choir Association, first service, *ib.* ; Devotional Day for Clergy (London Mission), 328 ; black gown discontinued, *ib.* ; burial of Foley the sculptor, 329 ; Thanksgiving for Prince of Wales' safe return from India ("Dettingen Te Deum"), 331 ; first Lent week-day services under the Dome, *ib.* ; Daily Celebrations begun (N.W. Chapel), *ib.* ; Three Hours' Service first held, 333 ; sermons and closing service of Lambeth Conference (1878), 334, 335 ; new peal of bells, 334 ; burial of George Cruickshank, 335 ; Spohr's *Last Judgment* first given, *ib.* ; alterations in the Churchyard, 336 ; new houses in Amen Court, 337 ; arrival of "Great Paul," 339 ; burial of Professor Palmer, Captain Gill and Lieut. Charrington in the Crypt, 341 ; death of Duke of Albany, *ib.* ; burial of Sir Bartle Frere, 342 ; Centenary of Bishop Seabury, *ib.* ; burial of Lord Mayor Nottage, 343 ; reredos dedicated, 345 ; sermons and closing service of Lambeth Conference of 1888, 346 ; burial of Lord Napier of Magdala, 347 ; first annual Welsh Service, 348 ; burial of Sir Edgar Boehm, R.A. ; services for the Jews under the Dome, 349 ; House of Lords on Reredos, *ib.* ; Memorial Service for Duke of Clarence, 351 ; service for Defence of Welsh Church, 352 ; dedication of new clock, 354 ; dedication of Jesus Chapel, *ib.* ; Jubilee Service of Y.M.C.A., 355 ; eight statues in the Dome, *ib.* ; burial of Lord Leighton, 357 ; funeral of Sir Joseph. Barnby, *ib.* ; burial of Sir John Millais, *ib.* ; Bishop Temple's farewell on leaving for Canterbury, 358 ; 1300th anniversary of baptism of King Ethelbert, 359 ; Thanks-

Paul's, St. (*continued*)
giving for Queen Victoria's 60th Accession-Day, *ib.* ; celebration of Diamond Jubilee at West Steps, *ib.* ; concluding service of Lambeth Conference, 360 ; Memorial Service for Duchess of Teck, *ib.* ; Bi-centenary of opening of Cathedral celebrated by Freemasons, *ib.* ; first Annual Service of Q.V.C.F., 361 ; Bi-centenary of S.P.C.K., *ib.* ; burial of Sir George Grey, N.Z., *ib.* ; first Church Congress in London, 362 ; Memorial Service for victims of first year of South African War, 363 ; services for C.I.Vs., Ladysmith, Mafeking, 364 ; Bi-centenary of S.P.G., *ib.* ; Memorial Service for Duke of Saxe-Coburg, 365 ; Thanksgiving for return of C.I.Vs., *ib.* ; burial of Sir Arthur Sullivan, *ib.* ; War victims of 1900, *ib.* ; services for Old and New Century, *ib.* ; burial of Bishop Creighton, *ib.* ; Mourning Services for Queen Victoria, *ib.* ; mourning for Emperor Frederick, 367 ; S.W. Chapel assigned to Order of St. Michael and St. George, *ib.* ; electric lighting given by J. Pierpont Morgan, 368 ; Memorial Service for Cecil Rhodes, *ib.* ; Farewell Service for Christ's Hospital, *ib.* ; Thanksgiving for Peace, *ib.* ; Intercession for recovery of King Edward VII. on Coronation Day, *ib.* ; Thanksgiving for recovery, 369 ; Memorial Service for Archbishop Temple, 371 ; 1300th Anniversary of Mellitus, 372 ; Memorial Service for G. F. Watts, R.A., *ib.* ; Allégri's *Miserere*, *ib.* ; Prince of Wales unveils Princess Louise's Monument to 4200 Colonial Volunteers, *ib.* ; Memorial Service for John Hay, 373 ; burial of Sir George Williams, *ib.* ; dedication of Chapel of St. Michael and St. George, King Edward present, 374 ; Memorial Service for Seddon, Premier N.Z., *ib.* ; Memorial Service for American and Canadian victims of Salisbury Railway disaster, *ib.* ; Company of Musicians resume their service on

INDEX

Paul's, St. (*continued*)
St. Cecilia's Day, 375; Memorial Service for King and Crown Prince of Portugal, 376; Farewell Service for Lambeth Conference of 1908, *ib.*; memorial to Sir George Williams, 377; new Paul's Cross, *ib.*; the Richmond Mosaics, 378–390; Fishmongers, Merchant Taylors, Goldsmiths and Mercers, 385; the Order of St. Michael and St. George, 391–398; its history, 391; idea of installing in St. Paul's conveyed to Sir Robert Herbert, 393; his warm co-operation, *ib.*; his letters, 393–395; committee and architect, 395; Sir Walter Wilkin's window, 396; dedication by the King and Prelate, 397; Organists, 400–413; John Redford, 400; Thomas Morley, *ib.*; John Tompkins, *ib.*; Adrian Batten, 403; Albertus Bryne, *ib.*; Jeremiah Clarke, *ib.*; John Blow, Almoner, 404; Richard Brind, *ib.*; Maurice Greene, 405; John Jones, 406; Thomas Attwood, 406–409; Sir John Goss, 409–411; Sir John Stainer, 411, 412; Sir George Martin, 412, 413; the Organ, 414–419; the Music, 419–421; the Library, 422–426; the Bells, 426–429; the Clock, 430–434; Paul's Cross, 435–445. Interments and Monuments in Old St. Paul's (446–450)—Royal Persons, 446; Men of the State, 446, 447; Soldiers, 447; Knights, Nobles, Courtiers, *ib.*, 448; Bishops of London, 448, 449; Deans of St. Paul's, 449; Ecclesiastics, 449, 450; Doctors, 450; Artists, *ib.* Memorials and Burials in the New Cathedral (451–473)—Naval, 451–456; Military, 456–462; Statesmen, 462–464; Ecclesiastical, 464–465; Men of Letters, 466, 467; Painters, Sculptors, Architects, etc., 467–471; Musicians, 471, 472; Philanthropists, 472; Doctors, *ib.*; Explorers, 473. Structural Notes, 474–478; a year's Special and Diocesan Services, 483–486

Pace, Richard, Dean of St. Paul's, 121, 123–125; Shakespeare on Wolsey and Pace, 124

Paddington, estate of, granted by Elizabeth to Bishopric of London, 162

Pakenham, General, 458
Palæologus, Emperor, 437
Palestrina, 366
Palmer, Professor E. H., 473
Parker, Archbishop, consecration of, 160
Parkes, Sir Harry, 463
Parkinson, Joseph, paper on St. Paul's in *All the Year Round*, 307
Partridge, Sir Miles, wins the Jesus Bells from Henry VIII., 138
Paul, Great, arrival of, 339, 428
—— II., Pope, 438
Paul's Cross, 435–445
Pavia, thanksgiving for, 122
Peal by College Youths, the first, 338
Peckham, Archbishop of Canterbury, 44
Pecock, Reginald, Bishop of St. Asaph, at St. Paul's, 69–74
Pegram, H., sculptor, 473
Pembroke, Alice, Countess of, 447
——, William Herbert, Earl of, tomb of, 99
Pepys, Samuel, account of the Fire, 209
Peter of Blois, Archdeacon of London, 29
Philip, King of Castile, obsequies of, 100
——, King of Spain, visit of, to St. Paul's, 149
Picton, General Sir Thomas, buried in Crypt, 316, 458
Pindar, Sir Paul, liberality of, 189
Pius V., Pope, excommunicates Elizabeth, 171
Pole, Cardinal, received at St. Paul's, 149; death of, 155
Pomeroy, F. W., A.R.A., 473
Ponsonby, Major-General Hon. Sir W., 458
Porteus, Beilby, Bishop of London, 287
Portugal, King of, and Crown Prince of, 376
Poultney, Sir John, four times Lord Mayor, 449
Poynter, Sir E. J., P.R.A., 367, 475
Prebendaries of St. Paul's, 110
Precentor of St. Paul's, 110
Pretyman-Tomline, Sir George, Dean of St. Paul's and Bishop of Lincoln, 289
Prichard, Sir Charles, 464

INDEX

Prince Imperial (Napoleon), 328
Profanation of St. Paul's: Bishop Pilkington, the Common Council, Queen Elizabeth, Shakespeare, Dekker, Ben Jonson, Bishop Earle, 168, 169
Prussia, Princess Frederick Charles of, 336
Puritanism, rise of, 171, 172
Purvey, John, eminent Wycliffite, recants, 66

Radulph de Diceto, Dean of St. Paul's, 26
Ralph de Baldock, Bishop of London, 47
Randolph, John, Bishop of London, 294
Ravis, Thomas, Bishop of London, 179
Reade, Charles, 466
Redford, John, 400
Reeves, Sims, 317
Reforms of Bishop de Braybrooke, 63
—— of Canon Gregory, 308
—— in the music, by Stainer, 310
Relics, 104
Rennie, James, F.R.S., 471
Reredos, Judgment on, 349
Residentiaries, 111
Restitutus, Bishop of London, 4
Reynolds, Sir Joshua, his offer and that of the Royal Academy to paint pictures for St. Paul's, 288; funeral at St. Paul's, 291, 467
Rich, Edmund, Archbishop of Canterbury, 33
Richard de Belmeis, Bishop of London, 18; benefactor to St. Paul's, *ib.*; desires London to be an Archbishopric, *ib.*
—— de Ely, Bishop of London, 27. *See* FitzNeal, Richard
—— de Gravesend, Bishop of London, 45; his will, 46
—— de Newport, Bishop of London, 47
Richards, H. C., M.P., 377
Richmond, George, R.A., 361, 469
——, Sir William, 361
Ridley, Nicolas, Reformation Preacher at Paul's Cross, 137, 440; Bishop of London, 143; supports Lady Jane Grey, 146, 441; burned, 151
Ringing the old year out, 336
Riou, Captain, R.N., 453

Robert, Abbot of Jumièges, Bishop of London, 12
—— de Belmeis, Bishop of London, 21
—— de Sigillo, Bishop of London, 20; carried off by Geoffry de Mandeville, Earl of Essex, *ib.*
Robinson, John, Bishop of London, 284
Rodney, Admiral Lord, 451
Roger Niger, Bishop of London, 32; urges completion of St. Paul's, 37; canonized, 38; tomb, 94
Rogers, Proto-martyr of the Reformed Church, 151
Rome, Sack of, Thanksgiving for, 122
Rood of Boxley, exposure of, 132
Ross, Major-General, 458
Rossi, sculptor, 473
Rovezzano, Benedetto de, sculptor of Wolsey's monument used for Nelson, 302
Royal, Princess, 314
—— Fusiliers (Afghan War), 460
Russell, Sir W. H., 467
Russia, Grand Duke Constantine of, 317; Emperor of, 355
Rustand, Legate, 41
Ryswick, Peace of, Thanksgiving for, first public service at new St. Paul's, December 2, 1697, 234

Sacraments, Debate on, A.D. 1539, 133
Sacrist of St. Paul's, 109
St. Albans, Battle of, 77
St. Michael and St. George, Order of, 391–398
St. Paul, Earl of, obsequies of, 100
St. Quentin, Battle of, 442
St. Vincent, Admiral Lord, 453
Sancroft, William, Dean of St. Paul's, 216; Archbishop of Canterbury, 282
Sandwich Islands, King of, 338
Sandwith, Henry de, Bishop of London, 42
Sandys, Edwin, at Paul's Cross, 158 Bishop of Worcester, 160; Bishop of London, 170, 443
Saragossa, spoils of St. Paul's at, 139
Sautree, William, Wycliffite priest, degraded and executed, 66
Savage, Thomas, Bishop of London, 83
Saxony, Crown Prince of, 319
Schmidt, Bernhardt (Father Smith), 415

INDEX

Seabury, Bishop, Centenary of, 342
Sebba, King, tomb of, 93, 446
Sebert, King of East Saxons, 5
Secker, Thomas, Dean of St. Paul's and Bishop of Oxford, 288
Seddon, Right Hon. John, Premier of New Zealand, 374
Sequestration of St. Paul's by the Puritans, 195
Sermon at St. Paul's Cross, *temp.* Henry VIII., 114
Seventy-seventh Regiment, Colours of, 331
Shah of Persia, 327
Shakespeare on Paul's Walk, 169
Shaw, Dr., preaches for Richard III., 80
Sheldon, Gilbert, Bishop of London, 201
Sherlock, Thomas, Bishop of London, 286
——, William, Dean of St. Paul's, Macaulay on his appointment, 283
Shore, Jane, 81
Shrewsbury, Margaret Countess of, tomb of, 97
Sigebert the Good, King of the East Saxons, 7
Simmons, Field-Marshal Sir Lintorn, 375, 461
Simon of Sudbury, Bishop of London, accused of lenity to Wycliffites, 49; beheaded by rabble, *ib.*
Simpson, Dr. Sparrow, 358, 424
Sinclair, Sir George, 295
Six Articles, the, 133
Skerrett, Major-General, 458
Smith, Father, his organ, 248
Socialists at St. Paul's, 345
Society for Prevention of Cruelty to Animals, 328
—— for Promoting Christian Knowledge, 361
—— for the Propagation of the Gospel, 364
Somerset, Protector, violence of, 141
South African War, 363-365
Spain, Infanta Isabel of, 375
Special Services, a Year's, 483
Sperafocus, Abbot of Abingdon, 12
Spohr's *Last Judgment* first given, 335
Spoliation of St. Paul's by the Puritans, 195
Spotswood consecrated Archbishop of Glasgow, with two other Scottish bishops, at London House, *Errata*, vi.

Stainer, Sir John, 411, 412, 472
Standish, Henry, furious sermon at Paul's Cross, 438
Stapleton, Walter, Bishop of Exeter, Lord High Treasurer, murdered near Cheapside, 48
Stephen de Gravesend, Bishop o London, 47; claims independence of Canterbury, *ib.*; disapproves deposition of Edward II., 48; accused of asserting his survival and imprisoned, *ib.*
Stevens, Alfred, 371
Stewart, General Sir Herbert, monument, 346, 460
——, Field-Marshal Sir Donald, 461
Stillingfleet, Edward, Dean of St. Paul's, 282; Bishop of Worcester, *ib.*
Stokesley, John, Bishop of London, 114, 128; upholder of Royal Supremacy, 130, 133
Strathnairn, Field-Marshal Lord, 460
Strong, Thomas and Edward, Masters of Masons, 235
Succentor of St. Paul's, 110
Suetonius, 1, 3
Suicides, 1856, 1869, 1878, 1890, 313
Sullivan, Sir Arthur, 365, 472
Sumner, Charles Read, Bishop of Llandaff and Dean of St. Paul's, 303
Sunday School Institute, Centenary of, 337
Surrey, 2
Sweden, Prince Oscar of, 314; King of, 317
Syrian Patriarch, 329

Tacitus, 1
Tait, Archibald Campbell, Bishop of London, 295; enthronement, 315; First Visitation Charge, 315; moves for Sunday evening services, 296; preaches at first evening service under Dome, 315; death of, 339
Taswall, Dr., account of Great Fire, witnessed as Westminster boy, 214
Taylor, Jeremy, promoted by Laud, 191
Taynton, quarries of, 235
Teck, Duchess of (Princess Mary), 315, 360
Temple, Frederick, Bishop of London, 300; his farewell, 358; death, 371

INDEX

Tennyson, Lord, death of, 351
Terrick, R., Bishop of London, 287
Tertullian, 4
Thanksgiving for George III.'s recovery, 289; for George III.'s naval victories, 290; for capture of Sebastopol, 313; for Peace with Russia, 314; for suppression of Indian Mutiny, 316; for recovery of Prince of Wales, 325; for his safe return from India, 331
Thanksgiving for the Peace of 1514, 119
—— for the Peace of 1546, 135
Thanksgivings for Queen Anne's victories, 277
Theodore, Archbishop of Canterbury, 9
Thornhill, Sir James, paints the Dome, 256
Thornycroft, Hamo, R.A., 473
Thurlow, Thomas, Dean of St. Paul's and Bishop of Lincoln, 289
Tijou, the French metal-worker, his work at St. Paul's, 253
Tilbury, 8
Tillingham, Manor of, granted to St. Paul's, 5
Tillotson, Dean of St. Paul's, 276; Archbishop of Canterbury, 282
Tomkins, John, 402
Tonic Sol-fa Jubilee Service, 349
Torrens, Major-General Sir A., 459
Treasurer of St. Paul's, 109
Tubes and drains, 476
Tunstal, Cuthbert, Bishop of London, 83
Turner, J. M. W., R.A., 468
Tusser, John, 401
Tyndale's Bibles burnt by Wolsey at St. Paul's, 126

Urban IV., Pope, 436
—— VI., Pope, promotes Robert de Braybrooke to Bishopric of London, 62

Valencia, spoils of St. Paul's at, 139
Vandyke, Sir Anthony, tomb of, 99
Van Mildert, Dean of St. Paul's and Bishop of Llandaff, 303
Vaughan, Richard, Bishop of London, 179
Venn, Prebendary Henry, 465
Vicars-choral, 112
Victoria, Queen: returns thanks for Prince of Wales' recovery, 325; Jubilee of 1887, 345; 60th Accession-Day, 359; commemoration of Diamond Jubilee, *ib.*; death, 365
Victoria, H.M.S., loss of, 352
Visitation of St. Paul's by Elizabeth's Commissioners, 158

Walden, Roger de, Bishop of London, 65
Wales, Albert Edward, Prince of, thanksgiving for recovery, 325
—— Alexandra, Princess of, commemoration of her wedding, 319
——, Anne (widow of Edward, Prince of), 80
——, George, Prince of, 351, 359, 360, 367, 369, 371, 372, 374, 376
——, Mary, Princess of, 353, 355, 359, 368, 371, 376
——, Prince and Princess of, attend first Hospital Sunday, 327
—— Prince of, safe return from India, "Dettingen Te Deum," 331
——, Princess of (Joan, Fair Maid of Kent), 61
Walsingham, Sir Francis, 447
War Correspondents: Lord Wolseley's two Egyptian campaigns, 466; Archibald Forbes, *ib.*; South African campaign, 467; Sir W. H. Russell, *ib.*
Ward, Sir John, Lord Mayor, 449
Warham, William, Bishop of London, 83
Warwick, Richard Nevill, Earl of, 77, 79
Watling Street, 3
Wat Tyler's Rebellion, 49, 62
Watts, G. F., and the Mosaics in the Dome, 320, 372
Wellington, Funeral of, 304; monument moved, 351
Welsh Service, First Annual, 348
—— Church, Service for Defence of, 352
West, Benjamin, P.R.A., 468
Westcott, Captain, R.N., 453
Westmacott, sculptor, 473
Westminster Abbey, Great Debate between Reformers and Romanists, 161; Bishop Tait's move for Sunday evening services, 296
—— Hugh, First Duke of, 361
Whispering Gallery, 255
Whitby, Council of, 8
White Friars and Secular Priests, controversy between, 437

INDEX

Wilfrid, St., 9
Wilkin, Alderman Sir Walter, K.C.M.G., gives window, 395
William III., accession and coronation of, 275; gives thanks for Peace of Ryswick, 276
—— Bishop of London, 12
—— de Santa Maria, Bishop of London, 29
William of Malmesbury describes Bishop Maurice's Cathedral, 17
—— the Conqueror, benefactor to St. Paul's, 14, 17
Williams, Sir George, 373, 376, 377, 472
Willis, Henry, 418
Winchelsey, Archbishop of Canterbury, 45
Windows, why left plain, 257
Wine, Bishop of London, 9
Wingham, Henry de, Bishop of London, 42, 93
Winnington-Ingram, Arthur Foley, Bishop of London, 301, 360, 366
Wise, Michael, 403
Wolly, Sir John, K.G., tomb of, 99
Wolsey, Cardinal, 119, 120, 122, 124, 125, 126, 127, 438, 439
Wren, Sir Christopher, on Commission for repairs of St. Paul's, 207; his report, *ib.*; principal architect for rebuilding the whole City, 217; various plans for St. Paul's, 223; noble scheme for rearrangement of the City, 232; a Freemason, 234; present when his son lays the last stone on the cupola, 235; troubles with the Commissioners, 259-264; Greek *v.* Latin Cross, 259; screen imposed, *ib.*; Thornhill's paintings, *ib.*; complaints of delay and salary attached, 260; the high disfiguring fence, *ib.*; appeals to Queen Anne, the Primate and the Bishop of London, *ib.*; successfully petitions the House of Commons, *ib.*; malignant pamphlets, 261; George I.'s Commission, *ib.*; a balustrade imposed, *ib.*; Wren dismissed through German intrigue, 262; retires to house near Hampton Court, 263; sketched as "Nestor" by Steele in the *Tatler*, *ib.*; life of him, 265-272; family and education, 265; professorships in London and Oxford, 266; introduced to Charles II., *ib.*; foundation of Royal Society, *ib.*; Assistant-Surveyor-General, 267; Surveyor of St. Paul's, *ib.*; visits Paris, *ib.*; buildings at Oxford and Cambridge, *ib.*; marriages and children, 268; Greenwich Observatory, Kilmainham Hospital, Chelsea Hospital, Winchester Palace, *ib.*; domestic architecture, 269; churches, 269-271; death and burial, 271; tomb in St. Paul's, 290
Wulfhere, King of Mercia, 9
Wulstan (organs), 414
Wyatt's rebellion, thanksgiving for suppression of, 149
Wycliffe, 58 ff.

York, Richard, Duke of, 76
——, Duke and Duchess of, wedding, 352
Young Men's Christian Association, 355
Ythancester, 8

Richard Clay & Sons, Limited, London and Bungay.

283-S616

BROOKLYN PUBLIC LIBRARY.

This Book may be kept FOURTEEN days from the last date stamped below.

A fine of 2 CENTS will be charged for each day the Book is kept beyond that time.

2 F'10 N		
25 F.'10 S		
26 Fe'10 C		

Form No. Ds. Nf. 1-09 85M. M &C.